# CliffsNotes

# AP®

# Psychology

# CRAM PLAN™

by *Joseph M. Swope, Ph.D.*

Contributor: *Joy Mondragon-Gilmore, Ph.D.*

Houghton Mifflin Harcourt
Boston • New York

*About the Author*

**Joseph M. Swope, Ph.D.,** is a Nationally Board-Certified teacher who holds a doctorate in psychology. He has taught Advanced Placement Psychology since 2002 and has been a recipient of the American Psychological Association's Excellence in Teaching Award. His video instruction series can be viewed at www.swopepsych.com.



*Acknowledgments*

I'd like to thank two students, Molly Skinker and Noah Garvey, for their help. This book would not have been possible without the many outstanding teachers who have guided me, especially Scott Reed, whose leadership and guidance have benefitted thousands of teachers. This book would not be possible without the expertise of Joy Gilmore and the outstanding editorial staff at Houghton Mifflin Harcourt, especially senior editor, Christina Stambaugh.


*Dedication*

I would like to dedicate this book to my wife, Heather, who, with our two girls, Arden and Madeline, has given me unconditional support and encouragement.


*Editorial*

**Executive Editor:** Greg Tubach
**Senior Editor:** Christina Stambaugh
**Production Editor:** Jennifer Freilach
**Copy Editor:** Lynn Northrup
**Technical Editor:** R. Scott Reed
**Proofreader:** Susan Moritz

**CliffsNotes® AP® Psychology Cram Plan®**





Library of Congress Control Number: 2020933942
ISBN: 978-0-358-12183-1 (pbk)

Printed in the United States of America
DOC 10 9 8 7 6 5 4 3 2 1

# Table of Contents

# Introduction to the AP Psychology Exam

Congratulations, you've made the decision to take charge of the AP Psychology course. *CliffsNotes AP Psychology Cram Plan* takes the guesswork out of how to approach exam questions. This easy-to-follow study guide provides the maximum benefit in a reasonable amount of time. You can use it as a quick reference guide, an in-depth resource, a source for practice, or a refresher of one or more topics in psychology.

This guide contains nine unit reviews that can supplement your textbook and your teacher's lectures. It is not meant to substitute for a formal high school AP Psychology class, but teachers and students alike will find this preparation guide to be a valuable course supplement to refresh your understanding of the topics outlined in the *AP Psychology Exam Course and Exam Description.*

As you begin your preparation, know that while the AP Psychology exam is challenging, it is manageable. The exam focuses on your ability to think logically to define a variety of concepts, explain reasons for behavior, and apply theories and perspectives of important research contributors. The skills and concepts defined in this book will not only help you pass the AP PSYCH exam, but will also provide you with exam-oriented approaches and practice material. If you study this book regularly, you will deepen your understanding of psychology, which will strengthen your performance on the exam.

## Navigating This Book

*CliffsNotes AP Psychology Cram Plan* is organized as follows:

- **Introduction to the AP Psychology Exam** A general description of the AP PSYCH exam, exam format, scoring, question types, units, frequently asked questions, and test-taking strategies.
- **Chapter 1 — Two-Month Cram Plan** A study calendar that provides a detailed suggested plan of action for preparing for the AP PSYCH exam 2 months before the exam.
- **Chapter 2 — One-Month Cram Plan** A study calendar that provides a detailed suggested plan of action for preparing for the AP PSYCH exam 1 month before the exam.
- **Chapter 3 — Diagnostic Test** A shortened version of the AP PSYCH practice exam in Chapter 13, the diagnostic test evaluates your areas of strength and weakness and provides you with a baseline starting point.
- **Chapter 4 — Unit 1: Scientific Foundations of Psychology**
- **Chapter 5 — Unit 2: Biological Bases of Behavior**
- **Chapter 6 — Unit 3: Sensation and Perception**
- **Chapter 7 — Unit 4: Learning**
- **Chapter 8 — Unit 5: Cognitive Psychology**
- **Chapter 9 — Unit 6: Developmental Psychology**
- **Chapter 10 — Unit 7: Motivation, Emotion, and Personality**
- **Chapter 11 — Unit 8: Clinical Psychology**
- **Chapter 12 — Unit 9: Social Psychology**

- **Chapter 13 — Full-Length Practice Exam** Includes answers and in-depth explanations for multiple-choice questions, and sample responses for the free-response essay questions.

# How to Use This Book

You're in charge here. You get to decide how to use this book. You can decide to read it from cover to cover or just refer to it when you need specific information. Most people find it useful to start by learning *general* psychology themes before memorizing *specific* facts, concepts, and contributors.

Here are a few of the recommended ways to use this book.

- Create a customized study "action plan." Be time-wise because your study plan depends on the total amount of time until your exam date. Preview the cram plan calendars in chapters 1 and 2 to organize your study time.
- Read (and then reread) the Introduction to become familiar with the exam format, question types, and test-taking strategies.
- Take the diagnostic test (Chapter 3) to assess your strengths and weaknesses.
- Get a glimpse of what you'll gain from a chapter by reading through the AP PSYCH course curriculum framework referenced at the beginning of each chapter.
- In Chapters 4–12, take detailed notes on the pages of this book to highlight important facts and topics related to the AP PSYCH course curriculum framework.
- Pay attention to the intermingled callout features in chapters 4–12 that focus on what you need to study to pass the AP PSYCH exam.
  - **Did You Know?** — Covers interesting information about people, theories, and concepts related to topics to aid in your overall understanding of psychology.
  - **Heads Up: What You Need to Know** — Summarizes details about specific content that may be on the actual AP PSYCH exam.
  - **Test Tip** — Offers quick strategies and tips for approaching exam questions.
- Use the "Chapter Review Practice Questions" to gauge your grasp of questions on the AP PSYCH exam. Although it is tempting to look ahead at the answer explanations, try to simulate testing conditions by answering the questions and writing your free-response question (FRQ) responses before reviewing the explanations. Initially, it may be difficult, but this strategy will reinforce your learning, particularly for writing FRQ responses.
- Test your knowledge more completely in the full-length practice exam in Chapter 13.

If you have moments of self-doubt, keep reminding yourself that even though the material is challenging, it is manageable. Take a deep breath, and know that you can do this by using the content, tips, and practice questions offered in this study guide.

Finally, the lessons and strategies you are learning in this book will help you throughout your high school and college learning experiences. If you make the commitment to review the unit chapters and study regularly, you will not only statistically increase your odds for passing the AP PSYCH exam, but you will also learn skills that can help you manage future college coursework!

# Exam Format

The AP PSYCH exam is divided into two sections: Section I consists of 100 multiple-choice questions, and Section II consists of two free-response questions. The chart below summarizes the format of the exam.

Note: Format and scoring are subject to change. Visit the College Board website for updates: https://apcentral.collegeboard.com.

| Section | Question Type | Time | Number of Questions | Approximate Percent of Total Score |
|---|---|---|---|---|
| **Section I**<br>**Multiple-Choice Questions** | Multiple choice | 70 minutes | 100 questions | 66.7% |
| **Section II**<br>**Free-Response Questions** | Concept application<br>Research design | 25 minutes (suggested time)<br>25 minutes (suggested time) | 1 question<br>1 question | 33.3% |
| **TOTALS** | | **2 hours** | **100 multiple choice**<br>**2 free response** | **100%** |

# Scoring

Your score on the AP PSYCH exam will be based on the number of questions you answer correctly for the two separate sections.

> Section I: Multiple-choice questions are approximately 67 percent of your overall score.
>
> Section II: Free-response questions are approximately 33 percent of your overall score.

Based on the combination of the two sections, the scores are converted into a grading scale of 1 to 5. A score of 5 is the best possible score. Most colleges consider a score of 3 or better a passing score. If you receive a passing score, the AP PSYCH exam can be applied as a college course equivalent—two-semester units will apply toward your college bachelor's degree as an introductory psychology course.

As a reference, approximately 50 percent of the students who take the AP PSYCH exam score at least a 3 on the exam.

| AP Score | Score Translation | College Course Grade Equivalent |
|---|---|---|
| 5 | Extremely well qualified | A+ or A |
| 4 | Well qualified | A-, B+, or B |
| 3 | Qualified | B-, C+, or C |
| 2 | Possibly qualified | n/a |
| 1 | No recommendation | n/a |

The AP PSYCH exam is graded on a curve, particularly the multiple-choice questions. Oftentimes, students panic when they see their score on their first practice exam. "A 65 percent on the multiple choice? I'm failing!" In reality, a 65 percent on the multiple-choice questions can be good enough for a 4 or even a 5 on the entire exam, depending on your score on Section II. Note: For multiple-choice questions, no points are deducted for incorrect answers. If you don't know the answer, take an educated guess because there is no penalty for guessing.

## Question Types

Knowing what information is covered on the exam provides a significant advantage to students preparing for test day, but equally as important is the ability to anticipate the approach to questioning. Knowing how the exam is structured and having a working familiarity with the types of questions goes a long way toward alleviating testing anxiety.

As you approach each of the questions, consider the following points to receive your best possible score.

- What are the main psychology topics of each unit?
- What are the broader theories, concepts, behaviors, and perspectives within each unit?
- What are the important supporting examples and evidence of the psychology theories—key contributors, research methods, limitations, and conclusions?
- What connections can you make between the main psychology topics and real-life scenarios?

### Multiple-Choice Questions

Section I consists of multiple-choice questions that require you to draw reasonable conclusions based on your knowledge of psychology.

**Key points about the multiple-choice questions:**

- The exam contains 100 multiple-choice questions—approximately 66.7 percent of your overall score.
- Select one answer from among five choices in each question.
- Questions are drawn from the unit content framework and ask you to define, analyze, compare, or apply course concepts to real-life scenarios.
- Some questions show data, graphs, charts, or tables.
- No points are deducted for incorrect answers; therefore, there is no penalty for guessing.

### Free-Response Questions

Section II consists of two free-response questions that focus on knowledge from psychology. If you answer all parts of each question and write a response that addresses *all* points in the scoring criteria as described by the College Board, you can increase your score. Throughout the chapters of this book you will find many opportunities to answer and review a variety of free-response questions similar to those you will encounter on the exam.

**Key points about the free-response questions:**

- The two free-response questions comprise approximately 33.3 percent of your overall score.
- The exam contains one free-response question about concept application and one free-response question about research design that connects topics to real-life scenarios.
- Write a response that considers the relationship among the topic question and supporting evidence for all parts of the question.
- Each point is earned independently. For example, in a research design question, you can earn a point for identifying a concept in the study, but fail to earn a point for not explaining another concept of the research study.
- Essay responses are considered first drafts and may contain some errors.
- Essay responses should use definitions of concepts that enhance the application of the concepts; definitions alone are not acceptable.
- Write a response that addresses all points in the scoring criteria as described by the College Board (see the chart that follows).

| Scoring Rubric for Free-Response Questions | | |
|---|---|---|
| **Question Type** | **Scoring Criteria** | **Possible Points** |
| **Concept Application** | The concept application question will require that you explain and respond to *seven* of the learning targets outlined in the course framework.<br>❏ Describe and apply characteristics, attributes, traits, and elements of concepts.<br>❏ Explain behavior in a particular concept in authentic context.<br>❏ Apply theories and perspectives in context. | 7 points |
| **Research Design** | The research design question will require that you analyze, interpret, and respond to *seven* of the psychological research study learning targets outlined in the course framework.<br>❏ Analyze the quantitative data results of a research study.<br>❏ Connect the results of a research study to a psychological principle, process, concept, theory, or perspective.<br>❏ Identify the research method or design used.<br>❏ Explain why the conclusion is or is not appropriate based on the design method.<br>❏ Describe implications or limitations of the research. | 7 points |

# Units

The AP PSYCH exam will expect you to understand the essential key topics and concepts outlined in the *AP Psychology Course Framework*. The good news is that the College Board has identified nine separate units that give you the framework for understanding the major learning targets.

| Unit | Chapter | Learning Target | Multiple-Choice Exam Weight |
|---|---|---|---|
| Unit 1 | Chapter 4 | Scientific Foundations of Psychology | 10–15% |
| Unit 2 | Chapter 5 | Biological Bases of Behavior | 8–10% |
| Unit 3 | Chapter 6 | Sensation and Perception | 6–8% |
| Unit 4 | Chapter 7 | Learning | 7–9% |
| Unit 5 | Chapter 8 | Cognitive Psychology | 13–17% |
| Unit 6 | Chapter 9 | Developmental Psychology | 7–9% |
| Unit 7 | Chapter 10 | Motivation, Emotion, and Personality | 11–15% |
| Unit 8 | Chapter 11 | Clinical Psychology | 12–16% |
| Unit 9 | Chapter 12 | Social Psychology | 8–10% |

# Frequently Asked Questions (FAQs)

**Q: Who administers the AP Psychology exam?**

**A:** The College Board prepares and scores the AP PSYCH exam. For further information regarding test administration, contact Advanced Placement Program (AP), P.O. Box 6671, Princeton, NJ 08541-6671, (888) 225-5427 or (212) 632-1780, e-mail: apstudents@info.collegeboard.org, website: https://apcentral.collegeboard.com.

**Q: Can I take the AP PSYCH exam more than once?**

**A:** Yes, but you may not retake the exam within the same year. If you take the exam again, both scores will be reported unless you cancel one score.

**Q: What do I bring to the exam?**

**A:** Bring several no. 2 pencils with erasers for the multiple-choice questions, and bring several pens with black or dark-blue ink for the free-response questions. Bring your 6-digit school code. Bring a watch that does not have Internet access, does not beep, and does not have an alarm. If you do not attend the school where you are taking the exam, bring identification (school-issued photo ID or government-issued ID).

**Q: What items am I NOT allowed to bring to the exam?**

**A:** You cannot bring electronic equipment (cell phone, smartphone, listening devices, cameras, or any other electronic devices). You cannot bring books, scratch paper, highlighters, notes, food, or drinks. Note: You can take notes in the margins of your exam booklet.

**Q: Can I cancel, withhold, or change my report recipient score?**

**A:** Yes, you can request to cancel your scores at any time before the deadline. Contact AP Services for deadlines and policies.

**Q: How long does it take to receive my score?**

**A:** Once you sign up for a College Board account at www.collegeboard.org/register, you will receive your scores online sometime in July. You will get an e-mail reminding you how to access your scores. You must enter your AP number (the 8-digit number on the labels inside your AP Student Pack) or your student identifier to access your scores.

**Q: Should I guess on the AP PSYCH exam?**

**A:** Yes. Your score is based on the number of questions you answer correctly. If possible, use the elimination strategy (see p. xv) for multiple-choice questions to increase your chances of guessing the correct answer. Don't leave any questions unanswered.

# Test-Taking Strategies

To be successful on the AP PSYCH exam, you must spend time learning about the exam and how best to approach it, study to increase your knowledge, and practice answering simulated questions. This section covers test-taking strategies, information, and approaches to tackle the questions.

Memorization is good for solidifying key terms, concepts, theories, and contributors in your long-term memory, but the exam will ask you to analyze questions based on real-world scenarios. Therefore, if you start to use these strategies before you even take the exam, you are way ahead of the curve.

Instructions for multiple-choice questions will appear in your exam booklet, but here are specific strategies to help you work through the multiple-choice questions quickly, accurately, and efficiently.

## Multiple-Choice Test-Taking Strategies

Consider the following guidelines as a road map to taking the test:

- Stick to the unit learning targets.
- Know psychology terms and concepts.
- Budget your time wisely.
- Use the elimination strategy.
- Mark the answer sheet correctly.
- Read each question and source carefully.
- Watch for "attractive distractors."
- Be on alert for EXCEPT and NOT questions.
- Make an educated guess if necessary.
- Practice, practice, practice.

### Stick to the Unit Learning Targets

The AP PSYCH course content can seem overwhelming because it has so many psychological concepts, theories, and perspectives—it is a lot to follow! Take the guesswork out of what to expect on the exam and follow the guidelines in the course framework. Take a deep breath and understand that the College Board has provided learning targets for each unit in the *AP Psychology Exam Course and Exam Description* (https://secure-media.collegeboard.org/apc/ap-psychology-course-description.pdf) that can help you focus on what is testable.

As you go through the unit reviews in chapters 4–12, focus on important theories as well as significant contributors to the field of psychology. Who did what and why? How can their research be connected to other theories? Who would have opposed these theorists and why? How can these theorists be linked to the broader context of other contemporary theoretical perspectives? These types of questions will help you connect, organize, and remember the narrative of the course framework.

## Know Psychology Terms and Concepts

The AP Readers of free-response essays are looking for effective, appropriate psychology vocabulary that conveys a clear meaning of concepts, theories, and behavior terms. Refer to the "Important Terms and Concepts Checklist" at the beginning of each review chapter for key terms.

## Budget Your Time Wisely

You have 70 minutes to answer 100 multiple-choice questions. You might calculate that you have less than a minute per question, but this does not include the time it takes to read questions. Some questions may take more time, while others may take less time. Students who spend too much time dwelling on a single question don't get the score they deserve because they leave insufficient time to answer other questions. With sufficient practice, you will almost automatically know when a question is taking too much time and when to make an educated guess and move on to the next question. There is no penalty for guessing, so make sure you answer every question.

## Use the Elimination Strategy

Take advantage of being allowed to mark in your exam booklet. Eliminate one or more answer choices to narrow down your choices to statistically improve your odds of selecting the correct answer.

Keep this marking system very simple and mark your answers in your exam booklet (no need to erase the markings in your booklet because you are allowed to write in your exam booklet). Practice this strategy as you take the diagnostic test and the full-length practice exam in this study guide.

Use a question mark (?) to signify a possible answer, use a diagonal line (/) to cross out an answer choice that is incorrect, and leave the choice blank if you are uncertain. This strategy will help you avoid reconsidering those choices you've already eliminated. Notice that in the example below, you've just narrowed your chances of answering correctly to 60 percent.

? **A.**
~~**B.**~~
**C.**
~~**D.**~~
? **E.**

## Mark the Answer Sheet Correctly

Make sure that your marked responses on the bubble answer sheet match your intended responses. When answering questions quickly, it is common to select the wrong answer choice by mistake. Students who skip questions might make the mistake of continuing to mark their answers in sequence and forget to leave a blank space for the unanswered questions. To avoid this mistake, mark your answers (and any other notes) in the exam booklet before you fill in the answer sheet. If necessary, you will be able to double-check your answers.

## Read Each Question Carefully

Don't work so quickly that you make careless errors. Read actively and take notes as you read each multiple-choice question. Do not make a hasty assumption that you know the correct answer without reading the whole question and all of the answer choices. The hurried test-taker commonly selects an incorrect answer when jumping to a conclusion after reading only one or two of the answer choices in the easy questions.

## Watch for "Attractive Distractors"

Watch out for *attractive distractors*—answer choices that look good but are not the *best* answer choice. Attractive distractors are usually the most commonly selected incorrect answers and are often true statements, but not the best choice. Be aware that facts and concepts presented in answer choices may often contain subtle variations that make it difficult for test-takers to narrow down correct answers.

## Be on Alert for EXCEPT and NOT Questions

Another common mistake is misreading a question that includes the word *except* or *not.* A negative question reverses the meaning of the question and asks for the opposite to be true in order to select the correct answer. Negative questions can initially be confusing and challenge your thinking. It is helpful to write down brief notes to avoid misreading a question (and therefore answering it incorrectly). To help answer a negative question, treat the answer choices as true or false statements, searching for the answer choice that is false.

## Make an Educated Guess If Necessary

Remember, there is no penalty for guessing. If you get stuck on a question, reread it. The answer may become apparent when you take a second look. If not, make an educated guess by eliminating some of the answer choices to increase your odds of choosing the right answer. You have nothing to lose, and quite possibly, something to gain. If you have time, you can always go back to rethink a marked question and change the answer.

If you do not have time to finish the exam, save 1 minute of your exam time to mark the answers for all of your remaining unanswered questions. There is no penalty for guessing, so pick your favorite letter—A, B, C, D, or E—and fill in all of the unanswered questions with this letter.

## Practice, Practice, Practice

The College Board recommends consistent practice to attain a high score. This is why we have included practice questions throughout this study guide: Chapter 3 (diagnostic test), chapters 4–12 (review chapters), and Chapter 13 (full-length practice exam). These practice questions include answers and thorough explanations. Be sure to practice in the exam format as often as possible. To benefit from further practice, you can view instructional resources on the AP College Board website. Register at "My AP" for more practice and access to a customized AP question bank.

# Free-Response Test-Taking Strategies

The AP PSYCH exam contains two free-response questions that ask students to do what psychologists do—analyze and interpret concepts and research studies. You must be able to construct and support a clear explanation using the provided scenario, concept, or data and demonstrate that you can support your response with specific knowledge.

## Essay-Writing Tips

To write effective free-response essays, stay focused on the AP essay-scoring rubric, follow the free-response essay-writing strategies, and practice writing essays.

Use the following checklist when you complete each of the practice free-response essay questions for the AP PSYCH exam.

- Did I memorize the differences between the two types of free-response questions?
- Did I stay focused on *all* parts of the question?
- Did I use prewriting techniques to organize my response?
- Did I provide supporting evidence and/or examples?

**Note: Sample essays are available at the end of the diagnostic test (Chapter 3), the unit review chapters (chapters 4–12), the full-length practice exam (Chapter 13), and on the College Board website found on the AP Psychology Course Homepage.**

## Know the Free-Response Question Types

The two types of free-response questions are:

- Concept application (1 question)
- Research design (1 question)

Let's review the question setup for free-response questions. Free-response questions will ask you to construct a graph, define a term, describe information, draw conclusions, explain your reasoning, or identify specific psychology topics.

The AP PSYCH exam uses the following task verbs in free-response questions.

| Free-Response Essay Questions | | |
|---|---|---|
| **Task Verb** | **Description** | **Strategy** |
| **Construct/Draw** | Draw a graph | Read, analyze, and interpret statistical or numerical data presented to create a graph or chart that illustrates the relationships of the phenomena. Note: Labels may not be required. |
| **Define** | Define words and concepts | Provide a specific meaning for a word or concept. |
| **Describe** | Describe important characteristics | Provide essential details of a particular concept, theory, or term related to the specified topic. |
| **Draw a conclusion** | Analyze information to arrive at an outcome | Focus on evidence from the information, scenario, or data provided to formulate a conclusion about the psychological content. |
| **Explain** | Provide reasons to support your claims | Focus on the evidence provided to develop reasons for a relationship, process, pattern, position, situation, or outcome (e.g., how or why a relationship exists). |
| **Identify/State** | Identify psychological topics | Provide a specific answer about a specified psychological topic, concept, theory, or term. |

## Stay Focused on the Question

One of the most important strategies is to keep your essay focused on the question and to address all parts of the question prompt. On the AP PSYCH exam, many students lose valuable points because they do not focus on the question or answer all parts of the question. To help you stay focused, underline or circle key words in the question prompt before you start writing. For example, if the research design question prompt reads "Describe one ethical flaw in this study and provide a resolution to correct the problem," you must respond to *both* parts of the question—(1) describe the ethical flaw and (2) provide an appropriate solution to rectify the error.

## Prewrite to Organize Your Essay

Think before you write by brainstorming, planning, and prewriting to organize your thoughts. The technique of brainstorming means that you should write down all ideas and examples that come to mind. After you brainstorm, organize those ideas in a logical sequence of events in your response. These ideas should emphasize important points, offer evidence, and provide the psychology context related to the question prompt.

## Provide Supporting Psychological Evidence and/or Examples

To receive the highest score possible, you need to be able to explain psychological concepts related to the question with specific supporting evidence, details, and reasoning. Remember, you are not imposing your own biased opinions, thoughts, or feelings. Think about describing specific psychology facts related to the question prompt—and remember that when asked to *describe* your evidence, it must include at least one sentence, not just a definition. As you provide this evidence and knowledge, it must support the claims.

Chapter 1

# Two-Month Cram Plan

The calendar below details a two-month action plan for the AP PSYCH exam. The first step is to determine how much time you have to prepare and then pick the plan that fits your schedule: two-month plan or one-month plan (see pp. 4–6 for a one-month plan). Ask yourself, "How many hours a week can I realistically devote to preparing for the exam?" Be specific. For example, you may be able to study on Tuesdays, Thursdays, and Fridays from 4 to 6 p.m., or you may only have time on Saturdays and Sundays from 8 to 11 a.m. It doesn't matter what plan you pick; what matters is that you stick to the schedule to get your best possible results.

Note: If you are using Internet sources for your additional reading, use at least two trustworthy sources to compare information.

| Two-Month Cram Plan | |
|---|---|
| **8 weeks before the exam** | **Study Time:** 2 hours<br>❑ Chapter 3: Take the diagnostic test and review the answer explanations, comparing your responses with topics covered in chapters 4–12.<br>❑ Browse the AP PSYCH official website: https://apstudents.collegeboard.org/courses/ap-psychology.<br>❑ Read the Introduction.<br>    ❑ Study the AP PSYCH exam format (p. x).<br>    ❑ Take notes as you study the test-taking strategies (pp. xiv–xviii). |
| **7 weeks before the exam** | **Study Time:** 3 hours at least three times a week (or as often as your schedule permits)<br>❑ Chapter 4: Read and take notes on Unit 1, "Scientific Foundations of Psychology."<br>    ❑ Use additional resources to read more about general and specific topics discussed in Chapter 4.<br>    ❑ Reread the AP Psychology Course Framework table (p. 18) for Unit 1.<br>    ❑ Answer the multiple-choice practice questions and compare your answers to the explanations provided. If you miss a question, be sure to note the logic behind the correct answer.<br>    ❑ Answer the free-response practice question. Compare your response to the sample response.<br>❑ Chapter 5: Read and take notes on Unit 2, "Biological Bases of Behavior."<br>    ❑ Use additional resources to read more about general and specific topics discussed in Chapter 5.<br>    ❑ Reread the AP Psychology Course Framework table (p. 50) for Unit 2.<br>    ❑ Answer the multiple-choice practice questions and compare your answers to the explanations provided. If you miss a question, be sure to note the logic behind the correct answer.<br>    ❑ Answer the free-response practice question. Compare your response to the sample response. |

*Continued*

| | |
|---|---|
| **6 weeks before the exam** | **Study Time:** 3 hours at least three times a week (or as often as your schedule permits)<br>❑ Chapter 6: Read and take notes on Unit 3, "Sensation and Perception."<br>❑ Use additional resources to read more about general and specific topics discussed in Chapter 6.<br>❑ Reread the AP Psychology Course Framework table (pp. 87–88) Unit 3.<br>❑ Answer the multiple-choice practice questions and compare your answers to the explanations provided. If you miss a question, be sure to note the logic behind the correct answer.<br>❑ Answer the free-response practice question. Compare your response to the sample response.<br>❑ Chapter 7: Read and take notes on Unit 4, "Learning."<br>❑ Use additional resources to read more about general and specific topics discussed in Chapter 7.<br>❑ Reread the AP Psychology Course Framework table (pp. 114–115) for Unit 4.<br>❑ Answer the multiple-choice practice questions and compare your answers to the explanations provided. If you miss a question, be sure to note the logic behind the correct answer.<br>❑ Answer the free-response practice question. Compare your response to the sample response. |
| **5 weeks before the exam** | **Study Time:** 3 hours at least three times a week (or as often as your schedule permits)<br>❑ Chapter 8: Read and take notes on Unit 5, "Cognitive Psychology."<br>❑ Use additional resources to read more about general and specific topics discussed in Chapter 8.<br>❑ Reread the AP Psychology Course Framework table (pp. 134–135) for Unit 5.<br>❑ Answer the multiple-choice practice questions and compare your answers to the explanations provided. If you miss a question, be sure to note the logic behind the correct answer.<br>❑ Answer the free-response practice question. Compare your response to the sample response.<br>❑ Chapter 9: Read and take notes on Unit 6, "Developmental Psychology."<br>❑ Use additional resources to read more about general and specific topics discussed in Chapter 9.<br>❑ Reread the "AP Psychology Course Framework table (p. 167) for Unit 6.<br>❑ Answer the multiple-choice practice questions and compare your answers to the explanations provided. If you miss a question, be sure to note the logic behind the correct answer.<br>❑ Answer the free-response practice question. Compare your response to the sample response. |
| **4 weeks before the exam** | **Study Time:** 3 hours at least three times a week (or as often as your schedule permits)<br>❑ Chapter 10: Read and take notes on Unit 7, "Motivation, Emotion, and Personality."<br>❑ Use additional resources to read more about general and specific topics discussed in Chapter 10.<br>❑ Reread the "AP Psychology Course Framework table (pp. 196–197) for Unit 7.<br>❑ Answer the multiple-choice practice questions and compare your answers to the explanations provided. If you miss a question, be sure to note the logic behind the correct answer.<br>❑ Answer the free-response practice question. Compare your response to the sample response.<br>❑ Chapter 11: Read and take notes on Unit 8, "Clinical Psychology."<br>❑ Use additional resources to read more about general and specific topics discussed in Chapter 11.<br>❑ Reread the AP Psychology Course Framework table (p. 226) for Unit 8.<br>❑ Answer the multiple-choice practice questions and compare your answers to the explanations provided. If you miss a question, be sure to note the logic behind the correct answer.<br>❑ Answer the free-response practice question. Compare your response to the sample response. |
| **3 weeks before the exam** | **Study Time:** 1½ hours at least two times a week (or as often as your schedule permits)<br>❑ Chapter 12: Read and take notes on Unit 9, "Social Psychology."<br>❑ Use additional resources to read more about general and specific topics discussed in Chapter 12.<br>❑ Reread the AP Psychology Course Framework table (p. 263) for Unit 9.<br>❑ Answer the multiple-choice practice questions and compare your answers to the explanations provided. If you miss a question, be sure to note the logic behind the correct answer.<br>❑ Answer the free-response practice question. Compare your response to the sample response. |

| | |
|---|---|
| **2 weeks before the exam** | **Study Time:** 4 hours<br>❑ Chapter 13: Take the full-length practice exam and review your answers and the explanations and sample responses.<br>  ❑ Based on your performance, identify topics and their corresponding chapters that require further review.<br>  ❑ Use additional resources to read more about general and specific topics discussed in the practice exam.<br><br>**Study Time:** 2 hours<br>❑ Based on your review, target general and specific topics.<br>❑ Reread the "Test-Taking Strategies" in the Introduction (pp. xiv–xviii). |
| **7 days before the exam** | **Study Time:** 2 hours<br>❑ Review the AP Psychology Course Framework table for Unit 1 (p. 18) and Unit 2 (p. 50).<br>❑ Study and target specific topics as needed. |
| **6 days before the exam** | **Study Time:** 2 hours<br>❑ Review the AP Psychology Course Framework table for Unit 3 (pp. 87–88) and Unit 4 (pp. 114–115).<br>❑ Study and target specific topics as needed. |
| **5 days before the exam** | **Study Time:** 2 hours<br>❑ Review the AP Psychology Course Framework table for Unit 5 (pp. 134–135) and Unit 6 (p. 167).<br>❑ Study and target specific topics as needed. |
| **4 days before the exam** | **Study Time:** 1 hour<br>❑ Review the AP Psychology Course Framework table for Unit 7 (pp. 196–197).<br>❑ Study and target specific topics as needed. |
| **3 days before the exam** | **Study Time:** 1 hour<br>❑ Review the AP Psychology Course Framework table for Unit 8 (p. 226).<br>❑ Study and target specific topics as needed. |
| **2 days before the exam** | **Study Time:** 1–2 hours<br>❑ Review the AP Psychology Course Framework table for Unit 9 (p. 263).<br>❑ Study and target specific topics as needed.<br>❑ Reread any material you feel is necessary. |
| **1 day before the exam** | ❑ Relax. You have covered all of the material necessary to score well on the exam.<br>❑ Get plenty of sleep the night before the exam. |
| **Morning of the exam** | ❑ Eat a balanced, nutritious breakfast with protein.<br>❑ Keep your usual habits. Don't try something new today.<br>❑ Bring your photo ID, your ticket for admission, a watch (that does not have Internet and does not beep), your 6-digit school code, several sharpened no. 2 pencils with erasers, and a few pens with black or dark-blue ink. Note: Cell phones, scratch paper, books, smartwatches, and food/drinks are not allowed at the testing center. |

Chapter 2

# One-Month Cram Plan

The calendar below details a one-month action plan for the AP PSYCH exam. The first step is to determine how much time you have to prepare and then pick the plan that fits your schedule: two-month plan or one-month (see pp. 1–3 for a two-month plan). Ask yourself, "How many hours a week can I realistically devote to preparing for the exam?" Be specific. For example, you may be able to study on Tuesdays, Thursdays, and Fridays from 4 to 6 p.m., or you may only have time on Saturdays and Sundays from 8 to 11 a.m. It doesn't matter what plan you pick; what matters is that you stick to the schedule to get your best possible results.

Note: If you are using Internet sources for your additional reading, use at least two trustworthy sources to compare information.

| One-Month Cram Plan | |
|---|---|
| **4 weeks before the exam** | **Study Time:** 2 hours<br>❑ Chapter 3: Take the diagnostic test and review the answer explanations, comparing your responses with topics covered in chapters 4–12.<br>❑ Browse the AP PSYCH official website: https://apstudents.collegeboard.org/courses/ap-psychology.<br>❑ Read the Introduction.<br>    ❑ Study the AP PSYCH exam format (p. x).<br>    ❑ Take notes as you study the test-taking strategies (pp. xiv–xviii).<br><br>**Study Time:** 3 hours at least three times a week (or as often as your schedule permits)<br>❑ Chapter 4: Read and take notes on Unit 1, "Scientific Foundations of Psychology."<br>    ❑ Reread the AP Psychology Course Framework table (p. 18) for Unit 1.<br>    ❑ Answer the multiple-choice practice questions. If you answer a question incorrectly, make sure you understand the logic behind the correct answer.<br>    ❑ Answer the free-response practice question. Compare your response to the sample response.<br>❑ Chapter 5: Read and take notes on Unit 2, "Biological Bases of Behavior."<br>    ❑ Reread the AP Psychology Course Framework table (p. 50) for Unit 2.<br>    ❑ Answer the multiple-choice practice questions. If you answer a question incorrectly, make sure you understand the logic behind the correct answer.<br>    ❑ Answer the free-response practice question. Compare your response to the sample response.<br>❑ Chapter 6: Read and take notes on Unit 3, "Sensation and Perception."<br>    ❑ Reread the AP Psychology Course Framework table (pp. 87–88) for Unit 3.<br>    ❑ Answer the multiple-choice practice questions. If you answer a question incorrectly, make sure you understand the logic behind the correct answer.<br>    ❑ Answer the free-response practice question. Compare your response to the sample response. |

<table>
<tr><td>3 weeks before the exam</td><td>Study Time: 3 hours at least three times a week (or as often as your schedule permits)<br>❑ Chapter 7: Read and take notes on Unit 4, "Learning."<br>❑ Reread the AP Psychology Course Framework table (pp. 114–115) for Unit 4.<br>❑ Answer the multiple-choice practice questions. If you answer a question incorrectly, make sure you understand the logic behind the correct answer.<br>❑ Answer the free-response practice question. Compare your response to the sample response.<br>❑ Chapter 8: Read and take notes on Unit 5, "Cognitive Psychology."<br>❑ Reread the AP Psychology Course Framework table (pp. 134–135) for Unit 5.<br>❑ Answer the multiple-choice practice questions. If you answer a question incorrectly, make sure you understand the logic behind the correct answer.<br>❑ Answer the free-response practice question. Compare your response to the sample response.<br>❑ Chapter 9: Read and take notes on Unit 6, "Developmental Psychology."<br>❑ Reread the AP Psychology Course Framework table (p. 167) for Unit 6.<br>❑ Answer the multiple-choice practice questions. If you answer a question incorrectly, make sure you understand the logic behind the correct answer.<br>❑ Answer the free-response practice question. Compare your response to the sample response.</td></tr>
<tr><td>2 weeks before the exam</td><td>Study Time: 3 hours at least three times a week (or as often as your schedule permits)<br>❑ Chapter 10: Read and take notes on Unit 7, "Motivation, Emotion, and Personality."<br>❑ Reread the AP Psychology Course Framework table (pp. 196–197) for Unit 7.<br>❑ Answer the multiple-choice practice questions. If you answer a question incorrectly, make sure you understand the logic behind the correct answer.<br>❑ Answer the free-response practice question. Compare your response to the sample response.<br>❑ Chapter 11: Read and take notes on Unit 8, "Clinical Psychology."<br>❑ Reread the AP Psychology Course Framework table (p. 226) for Unit 8.<br>❑ Answer the multiple-choice practice questions. If you answer a question incorrectly, make sure you understand the logic behind the correct answer.<br>❑ Answer the free-response practice question. Compare your response to the sample response.<br>❑ Chapter 12: Read and take notes on Unit 9, "Social Psychology."<br>❑ Reread the AP Psychology Course Framework table (p. 263) for Unit 9.<br>❑ Answer the multiple-choice practice questions. If you answer a question incorrectly, make sure you understand the logic behind the correct answer.<br>❑ Answer the free-response practice question. Compare your response to the sample response.</td></tr>
<tr><td>7 days before the exam</td><td>Study Time: 4 hours<br>❑ Chapter 13: Take the full-length practice exam and review your answers and the explanations and sample responses.<br>❑ Based on your performance, identify topics and their corresponding chapters that require further review.<br>❑ Use additional sources to read more about general and specific topics discussed in the practice exam.<br><br>Study Time: 2 hours<br>❑ Based on your review, target general and specific topics.<br>❑ Reread "Test-Taking Strategies" in the Introduction (pp. xiv–xviii).</td></tr>
</table>

*Continued*

| | |
|---|---|
| **6 days before the exam** | **Study Time:** 2 hours<br>❏ Review the AP Psychology Course Framework table for Unit 1 (p. 18) and Unit 2 (p. 50).<br>❏ Study and target specific topics as needed. |
| **5 days before the exam** | **Study Time:** 2 hours<br>❏ Review the AP Psychology Course Framework table for Unit 3 (pp. 87–88) and Unit 4 (pp. 114–115).<br>❏ Study and target specific topics as needed. |
| **4 days before the exam** | **Study Time:** 2 hours<br>❏ Review the AP Psychology Course Framework table for Unit 5 (pp. 134–135) and Unit 6 (p. 167).<br>❏ Study and target specific topics as needed. |
| **3 days before the exam** | **Study Time:** 2 hours<br>❏ Review the AP Psychology Course Framework table for Unit 7 (pp. 196–197) and Unit 8 (p. 226).<br>❏ Study and target specific topics as needed. |
| **2 days before the exam** | **Study Time:** 1–2 hours<br>❏ Review the AP Psychology Course Framework table for Unit 9 (p. 263).<br>❏ Study and target specific topics as needed.<br>❏ Reread any material you feel is necessary. |
| **1 day before the exam** | ❏ Relax. You have covered all of the material necessary to score well on the exam.<br>❏ Get plenty of sleep the night before the exam. |
| **Morning of the exam** | ❏ Eat a balanced, nutritious breakfast with protein.<br>❏ Keep your usual habits. Don't try something new today.<br>❏ Bring your photo ID, your ticket for admission, a watch (that does not have Internet and does not beep), your 6-digit school code, several sharpened no. 2 pencils with erasers, and a few pens with black or dark-blue ink. Note: Cell phones, scratch paper, books, smartwatches, and food/drinks are not allowed at the testing center. |

# Chapter 3

# Diagnostic Test

This chapter contains a diagnostic test that will give you valuable insight into the types of questions that may appear on the AP PSYCH exam. It is for assessment purposes only and is NOT a full-length practice exam. Additional practice questions are included at the end of each unit review chapter (chapters 4–12) and a full-length practice exam is included in Chapter 13.

As you take this diagnostic test, try to simulate testing conditions and time.

The questions and explanations that follow focus on essential knowledge, course skills, and course content.

**Directions:** Choose the best answer for each question.

**20 minutes**
**25 questions**

1. Four-year-old Anabel insists on playing a make-believe game. According to Erikson's theory, Anabel is most likely at which of the following stages of psychosocial development?

**A.** Intimacy vs. isolation
**B.** Concrete operations
**C.** Initiative vs. guilt
**D.** Autonomy vs. shame
**E.** Trust vs. mistrust

2. Which of the following concepts of creativity best describes generating multiple solutions to find the answer to a problem?

**A.** Convergent thinking
**B.** Divergent thinking
**C.** Top-down thinking
**D.** Bottom-up thinking
**E.** Metacognition

3. Which of the following brain structures is most likely damaged if a person can draw a circle with his left hand and a square with his right hand simultaneously?

**A.** Cerebellum
**B.** Corpus callosum
**C.** Hippocampus
**D.** Thalamus
**E.** Amygdala

4. According to Carl Rogers, which of the following best describes the most important aspect of effective counseling when the therapist uses unconditional positive regard?

**A.** The number of times the client and therapist meet
**B.** The relationship between the client and therapist
**C.** The cognitive-behavioral techniques used in therapy
**D.** The psychodynamic techniques used in therapy
**E.** The age and gender of the therapist

5. Based on Pavlov's theory of classical conditioning, which of the following best describes when learning is attained?

**A.** When the unconditioned stimulus produces an unconditioned response
**B.** When the positive punishment eliminates the unwanted behavior
**C.** When the negative punishment eliminates the unwanted behavior
**D.** When the conditioned stimulus produces a conditioned response
**E.** When the neutral stimulus produces an unconditioned response

6. Lakeesha is writing an advertisement for the high school Facebook account to convince her fellow students to donate at a school blood drive. She creates a short video clip that shows hospitalized children with sad songs in the background. Lakeesha is using which of the following persuasive techniques to communicate her message?

   **A.** Central route to persuasion
   **B.** Foot-in-the-door technique
   **C.** Door-in-the-face technique
   **D.** Elaboration likelihood technique
   **E.** Peripheral route to persuasion

7. Andrew has very strong political opinions. Every day, he scans news articles on multiple websites to corroborate his views, but some of the websites are untrustworthy. Which of the following best describes Andrew's mental reasoning process?

   **A.** Deductive thinking
   **B.** Confirmation bias
   **C.** Algorithm
   **D.** Availability heuristic
   **E.** Formal reasoning

8. According to Jean Piaget's cognitive theory, which of the following best describes the stage of development when problem solving occurs?

   **A.** Sensorimotor
   **B.** Concrete operations
   **C.** Formal operations
   **D.** Preoperational
   **E.** Assimilation

9. Dr. Garvey designed an experiment to measure whether caffeine causes students to pay more attention in class. Dr. Garvey gave 15 students 1 cup of decaffeinated coffee and 15 students 1 cup of regular caffeinated coffee to drink in the morning before class. In this experiment, which of the following research design concepts describes the measured results of the amount of attention that the students showed?

   **A.** Confounding variable
   **B.** Independent variable
   **C.** Dependent variable
   **D.** Null hypothesis
   **E.** Testing effect

10. After evaluating the results, Dr. Ball believed that his experiment had a positive result, but a colleague pointed out that the difference between the control group and the experimental group had a *p*-value of 0.08. Which of the following explains the false results?

    **A.** Type I error
    **B.** Type II error
    **C.** Confounding variable
    **D.** Using causation instead of correlation
    **E.** The *p*-value is less than the correlation coefficient

11. Which of the following concepts best explains the idea that dreams are random firings of neurons as we sleep?

    **A.** Activation synthesis
    **B.** Manifest content
    **C.** Latent content
    **D.** K-complex
    **E.** Sleep spindles

12. Madeline was not listening when her mother asked her to do chores. Exasperated, her mother said, "Madeline, did you hear me?" Even though Madeline was not listening, she was able to repeat her mother's last sentence. Which of the following concepts most accurately describes Madeline's recall ability?

    **A.** Elaborative rehearsal
    **B.** Effortful encoding
    **C.** Echoic memory
    **D.** Iconic memory
    **E.** Short-term memory

13. When countries compete for economic dominance at the expense of natural resources it is called

    **A.** social trap
    **B.** social loafing
    **C.** social facilitation
    **D.** altruism
    **E.** just-world hypothesis

14. Which of the following brain structures is most active when remembering a frightening event?

    **A.** Hypothalamus
    **B.** Cerebellum
    **C.** Amygdala
    **D.** Pons
    **E.** Corpus callosum

15. Arden is studying physics homework, but is stumped by the concept of electromagnetic waves. After hours of feeling confused, she suddenly grasps the concept. Which of the following best explains Arden's learning experience?

    **A.** Fixed-ratio reinforcement
    **B.** Fixed-interval reinforcement
    **C.** Observational learning
    **D.** Latent learning
    **E.** Insight learning

16. William James published the first scientific psychology textbook, *The Principles of Psychology,* in 1890. Which of the following models of psychology was first developed by James?

    **A.** Structuralism
    **B.** Functionalism
    **C.** Dualism
    **D.** Determinism
    **E.** Behaviorism

17. Maya can sense the change in light when a flashlight is turned on in a dark room. To sense the change in light in a brightly lit room, four flashlights must be turned on. Which of the following best describes this phenomenon?

    **A.** Fechner's law
    **B.** Weber's law
    **C.** Absolute threshold
    **D.** Retinal disparity
    **E.** Auditory disparity

18. Extrinsic motivation is closely aligned with which of the following social motivation concepts?

    **A.** Arousal theory
    **B.** Fixed action pattern
    **C.** Maslow's lowest hierarchy of needs level
    **D.** Self-actualization
    **E.** Self-serving bias

19. Jamal has an IQ score of 130. How many standard deviations is Jamal away from the mean?

    **A.** 2
    **B.** 1
    **C.** −1
    **D.** −2
    **E.** 0.05

20. Which of the following diagnoses is classified in the DSM-5 as a chronic major depressive disorder?

    **A.** Hoarding
    **B.** Tourette Syndrome
    **C.** Agoraphobia
    **D.** Adjustment disorder
    **E.** Selective mutism

21. Anika is overly nervous about giving an oral presentation in her psychology class. As she approaches the front of the classroom to give her presentation, she forgets a part of her speech and her mind goes blank. Which of the following theories of emotions and stress best describes this scenario?

    **A.** Cannon-Bard theory
    **B.** James-Lange theory
    **C.** Yerkes-Dodson law
    **D.** Schachter-Singer theory
    **E.** Drive reduction theory

22. Which of the following Freudian defense mechanisms best explains the phenomenon of unconsciously placing blame onto others and attributing thoughts, feelings, and desires onto others?

    **A.** Regression
    **B.** Sublimation
    **C.** Rationalization
    **D.** Projection
    **E.** Displacement

23. Madeline has a test in her psychology class tomorrow, but she just started studying for the test. Her plan is to make connections between what she already knows and the ideas she needs to memorize. Which of the following provides the best explanation for this method of memorization?

    **A.** Effortful processing
    **B.** Distributed practice
    **C.** Attention
    **D.** Maintenance rehearsal
    **E.** Sensory register

24. As defined by the American Psychiatric Association (APA) Ethics Code, which of the following set an important precedent that it is unethical for professionals to diagnose a person whom they have not examined in person because it does not follow proper diagnostic procedures?

    **A.** Stanford Prison Experiment
    **B.** Rosenhan study
    **C.** Milgram obedience experiments
    **D.** Asch line experiments
    **E.** Robbers Cave Study

25. Which of the following inner-ear structures is where vibrations are transduced into sound?

    **A.** Tympanic membrane
    **B.** Stirrup
    **C.** Semicircular canals
    **D.** Pinna
    **E.** Cochlea

## Answer Key

| | | | | |
|---|---|---|---|---|
| 1. C | 6. E | 11. A | 16. B | 21. C |
| 2. B | 7. B | 12. C | 17. B | 22. D |
| 3. B | 8. B | 13. A | 18. C | 23. A |
| 4. B | 9. C | 14. C | 19. A | 24. B |
| 5. D | 10. A | 15. E | 20. B | 25. E |

## Answer Explanations

1. **C.** Choice C, *initiative vs. guilt,* is a stage of development whereby children (ages 3–6 years) learn to play and initiate behavior that leads toward their goal. Developmental psychologists agree that play, especially imaginary play like Anabel is exhibiting, is extremely beneficial during early childhood to strengthen cognitive development. *Intimacy vs. isolation* (choice A) is a stage of development whereby an adult (ages 20–40 years) is unconsciously driven to find an intimate partner. *Concrete operations* (choice B) is a stage in Jean Piaget's theory of cognitive development when children (ages 7–11 years) are able to solve problems by thinking about multiple perspectives. *Autonomy vs. shame* (choice D) is a stage of development when a toddler (ages 1½–3 years) learns to be independent from primary caregivers and learns personal control over his physical skills like potty-training, testing limits, and saying "no." *Trust vs. mistrust* (choice E) is the first stage of development when an infant (birth–1½ years) acquires secure attachment by feeling that his needs will be met. *(Chapter 9)*
2. **B.** *Divergent thinking* is a type of creativity whereby the person views an existing problem and creates multiple new solutions, choice B. *Convergent thinking* (choice A) is a type of creativity whereby a person views an existing problem and narrows the answer to one most efficient, practical solution. *Top-down thinking* (choice C) is a deductive reasoning process that begins with higher-level thinking and works down to the senses. *Bottom-up thinking* (choice D) is an inductive reasoning process that begins with gut feelings and works up to the brain. *Metacognition* (choice E) is the ability to think about thinking. *(Chapter 8)*
3. **B.** The *corpus callosum* is the part of the brain that links the two hemispheres. If the corpus callosum is damaged, the two hemispheres can operate independently from each other; therefore, choice B is correct. The *cerebellum* (choice A) has been called the "little brain" and allows a person to do simple or well-practiced tasks without paying attention to them. The *hippocampus* (choice C) is the memory organizer of the brain (not the memory warehouse); it categorizes new memories when something is learned and retrieves them when the memories need to be recalled. The *thalamus* (choice D) is the router for the information that flows to and from the forebrain (vision, learning, taste, and touch). If the thalamus is damaged, it can cause the person to be in a vegetative state. The *amygdala* (choice E) stores emotional experiences (e.g., fear, trauma, aggression). *(Chapter 5)*
4. **B.** Humanistic psychologist Carl Rogers provided one of the most effective theoretical approaches to counseling psychology. Rogers' person-centered psychotherapy focuses on the client's subjective view of the world, and in order for a therapeutic alliance to form, the therapist must be congruent, extend empathic understanding, and offer unconditional positive regard. Rogers believed that these conditions help to build a therapeutic *relationship between the client and the therapist,* choice B. The number of

times the client and therapist meet (choice A) and the age and gender of the therapist (choice E) can be factors in a client selecting a therapist, but neither is the most important factor in effective counseling. *Cognitive-behavioral techniques used in therapy* (choice C) and *psychodynamic techniques used in therapy* (choice D) are not humanistic (unconditional positive regard) approaches to counseling psychology. *(Chapter 11)*

5. **D.** Learning, according to classical conditioning, is demonstrated only when a previously valueless *conditioned stimulus* (sound, sight, or other stimulus) produces a reaction (a *conditioned response*), choice D. An *unconditioned stimulus* (e.g., loud noise) will produce an unconditioned response (e.g., flinching) without anything being learned, so choice A is incorrect. *Positive punishment* (choice B) and *negative punishment* (choice C) fall under the category of operant conditioning, not classical conditioning. A *neutral stimulus* does not produce a response (choice E). *(Chapter 7)*
6. **E.** *Peripheral route to persuasion* uses emotion to convince someone to make a quick decision, choice E. *Central route to persuasion* (choice A) uses facts and logic to motivate someone to focus on the strengths of the argument. The *foot-in-the-door technique* (choice B) is when a person who is trying to persuade someone else asks for a small favor. Once the small favor is granted, the persuader makes increasingly greater demands until the persuader meets his original goal. The *door-in-the-face technique* (choice C) is when the persuader asks someone for a very large favor. When the offer is refused, the persuader asks for what they originally wanted so the demand seems more reasonable. The *elaboration likelihood technique* (choice D) is a dual theory model (central and peripheral routes) that explains how attitudes are changed by arguments. *(Chapter 12)*
7. **B.** *Confirmation bias* is the tendency of people to look for facts or opinions that support their existing beliefs, making choice B correct. *Deductive thinking* (choice A) is a type of formal reasoning in which a person gathers information and then forms a conclusion. *Algorithm* (choice C) is a step-by-step formula used to solve a problem. *Availability heuristic* (choice D) is the tendency to think of a solution that most easily comes to mind, and *formal reasoning* (choice E) is similar to deductive thinking because a person starts with general information and then looks for evidence to form a specific conclusion. *(Chapter 8)*
8. **B.** *Concrete operations* is the third stage in Piaget's theory of cognitive development. In this stage, a child (ages 7–11 years) is successful at problem solving and can think rather complexly, but only about things that exist in the material world, choice B. *Sensorimotor* (choice A) is the first stage of development when a baby (birth–2 years) experiences the world through senses and movements. *Formal operations* (choice C) is the fourth stage of development when a person (12 years to adulthood) can not only problem solve, but can also think abstractly and think about things that do not exist concretely (e.g., love, justice, and beauty). *Preoperational* (choice D) is the second stage of development when the child (ages 2–7 years) can use words to represent objects symbolically. *Assimilation* (choice E) is not one of Piaget's stages of cognitive development. *(Chapter 9)*
9. **C.** The measured result (outcome) in an experiment is called the *dependent variable,* choice C. To help you understand this concept, think of the *dependent* variable as the result that *depends* on what the researcher does. In this case, how much the students paid attention depended on how much caffeinated coffee they drank, choice C. A *confounding variable* (choice A) is anything that the experimenter did not account for that might affect the results. In this case, a confounding variable could have been that all of the students stayed up late the night before for a school party. The *independent variable* (choice

B) is anything the experimenter manipulates to see if it might change the dependent variable. In this case, the independent variable is the amount of caffeinated coffee the students drank. The *null hypothesis* (choice D) is a prediction that there will not be a significant result due to the independent variable. The *testing effect* (choice E) is a confounding variable where improvement on a test is not necessarily due to capabilities, but rather because the subject has become good at the test due to retained knowledge. *(Chapter 4)*

10. **A.** *Type I errors,* choice A, can be thought of as false alarms. This means the researcher thought that there was a significant change in the dependent variable, but it was untrue. To reach the level of significance, the *p*-value must be below 0.05. Think of *p* as randomness, chance, or accident. It is good to have a small number that represents such things. A *type II error* (choice B) is when there is a significant result, but the researcher did not identify it. A *confounding variable* (choice C) is something that can negatively impact the study, so a researcher wouldn't use, or would avoid, the variable. A researcher would not use *causation* or *correlation* (choice D) as a research technique. In most cases, the *p*-value (representing randomness or chance in a study) doesn't have much to do with the *correlation coefficient* (representing the strength of relationship between variables), so choice E is incorrect. *(Chapter 4)*

11. **A.** *Activation synthesis* is the idea that dreams are the mind's attempt to make sense of the random byproducts of the brain's activity during sleep, choice A. *Manifest content* (choice B) is what a person remembers during a dream—seeing, hearing, experiencing. *Latent content* (choice C) is a hidden part of a dream that is represented by the manifest content. For example, the manifest content might be a pink elephant and the latent content is what the pink elephant symbolically represents. *K-complex* (choice D) is neurological activity that is a response to a stimulus in the environment. *Sleep spindles* (choice E) are bursts of neurological activity during sleep. *(Chapter 5)*

12. **C.** *Echoic memory* is the ability to re-hear sounds that happened up to 2 seconds before. Think of the word *echo* to remember this term. While the daughter wasn't processing the meaning of her mother's words, she had a 2-second "recording device" in her mind that allowed her to replay the words her mother spoke, choice C. *Elaborative rehearsal* (choice A) is the process of going into detail to help you encode and retain memories in your long-term memory. *Effortful encoding* (choice B) is hopefully what you are doing right now as you read this explanation. Effortful encoding is consciously making an effort to remember, rather than passively reading or skimming this explanation. *Iconic memory* (choice D) is the fleeting ability to "re-see" something that happened less than 1 second ago. Football referees might use their iconic memory when they decide if a play requires a penalty or not. *Short-term memory* (choice E), also called working memory, is a temporary storage unit that has a limited capacity. *(Chapter 8)*

13. **A.** *Social trap,* choice A, is the result of short-sighted competitiveness, such as the example of countries competing for economic dominance at the expense of natural resources. Imagine athletes on a team competing for individual records to catch a scout's attention. The team may have more losses and ironically attract fewer recruiting scouts. *Social loafing* (choice B) occurs when members of a group do not put forth their best effort because they assume the project will get done by others in the group. *Social facilitation* (choice C) is the tendency for a person to demonstrate a stronger performance in the presence of others. *Altruism* (choice D) is doing something charitable without expecting repayment. *Just-world hypothesis* (choice E) is the idea that the world is fair and that people who suffer misfortune somehow deserve the bad luck. *(Chapter 12)*

14. **C.** The *amygdala* (the brain has two, one in each hemisphere) processes and stores reactions to fearful and traumatic events in the forebrain, choice C. It helps people remember when something bad has happened so the person can avoid that situation again. *Hypothalamus* (choice A) is the part of the forebrain that is most involved in biological urges, such as the desires to eat and to mate. *Cerebellum* (choice B) is the part of the hindbrain that plays a vital role in coordination, balance, and physical performances that do not need concentration. The *pons* (choice D) is in the hindbrain and helps with life functions such as breathing and heartbeat. The *corpus callosum* (choice E) links the brain's two hemispheres and allows them to communicate with each other. *(Chapter 5)*

15. **E.** *Insight learning* is a cognitive function that is explained by the sudden understanding of a solution when applying all of your knowledge to the problem, choice E. Choices A and B are learning reinforcement schedules of operant conditioning. Reinforcing behavior occurs when something positive or negative is introduced to change behavior. *Fixed-ratio reinforcement* (choice A) is a preset number of reinforcers that occurs after a definite number of behaviors. For example, after buying five cups of coffee you will receive the positive reinforcement of one free cup of coffee. *Fixed-interval* (choice B) is reinforcement after a period of time (e.g., every hour). *Observational learning* (choice C) results when watching the behavior of others. *Latent learning* (choice D) may have been a possible choice if Arden did not experience an "aha" moment. Latent learning is sometimes thought of as "hidden, subconscious learning." People and animals subconsciously retain information, but do not demonstrate the knowledge until the right conditions are met. *(Chapter 7)*

16. **B.** *Functionalism* is William James' study of the mind to determine the most important functions of it, choice B. Wilhelm Wundt's study of *structuralism* (choice A) attempted to examine the basic cognitive structures of the mind by discovering what cognitive structures make up the consciousness. *Dualism* (choice C, known as Cartesian dualism) is based on the philosophical contributions of Rene Descartes that state the mind and body are divided, but connected, entities. *Determinism* (choice D) is a theory that asserts that all events are inevitable consequences determined by previously existing conditions, and not by free will. For example, biological and environmental factors determine who a person is psychologically. *Behaviorism* (choice E) is a theory in psychology that suggests human behavior can be explained by conditioning, not by feelings and thoughts. *(Chapter 4)*

17. **B.** *Weber's law* is the idea that if the original stimulus is dim, faint, quiet, or bland, it will only take a little bit of stimulation to notice a difference. If the original stimulus is bright, intense, loud, or vibrant, it will take a great deal of new stimulation to be able to notice a difference, choice B. *Fechner's law* (choice A) is the idea that sensation and perception are not related by a linear relationship. For example, if a person wants to perceive music twice as loud, the person must do more than double the amplitude. The relationship is *logarithmic* (representing values that are an equal distance apart), so that twice as salty might require four times as many salt grains on the tongue. *Absolute threshold* (choice C) is the minimum amount of stimulation a person will notice. *Retinal disparity* (choice D) is one of the many depth cues humans use; it is the difference in images between the two retinas. If the difference is massive, the brain knows that that object is close. *Auditory disparity* (choice E) is the difference between the signals the ear sends to the brain. If the left ear senses the sound first, the brain knows the source of the sound is to the left. *(Chapter 6)*

18. **C.** *Maslow's lowest hierarchy of needs level,* choice C, relates to survival needs such as food, water, and shelter. Because these needs come from outside of the body, they are considered extrinsic motivators. The *arousal theory* (choice A) suggests that people are motivated to engage in certain activities for the purpose of reaching an optimal level of arousal to meet psychological or physiological needs. *Fixed*

*action pattern* (choice B) is an instinctual behavior that causes animals to carry out something in a fixed (unchangeable) pattern. *Self-actualization* (choice D) is the highest point of Abraham Maslow's hierarchy of needs. Maslow suggested that once a person has met the four lower levels of motivation, the person will desire to continue growing, improving, and developing because all people, at some level, want to improve. *Self-serving bias* (choice E) is a cognitive process that suggests people have a tendency to make decisions based on what allows them to feel good about themselves, and ignore any threatening facts. *(Chapter 10)*

19. **A.** Jamal's IQ (intelligence quotient) is superior. Using a normal distribution on standardized tests, you can calculate the standard deviation by determining how far the score deviates from the mean. The mean of intelligence scores is 100 and the standard deviation is 15. Thus, an IQ score of 130 is $2 \times 15 = 30$, or two standard deviations above the mean of 100, choice A. One standard deviation above the mean (choice B) is $100 + 15 = 115$ IQ. One standard deviation below the mean (choice C) is $100 - 15 = 85$ IQ. Two standard deviations below the mean (choice D) is $100 - 30 = 70$ IQ. One half of a standard deviation above the mean (choice E) would be $100 + 7.5 = 107.5$ IQ. *(Chapter 8)*

20. **B.** *Tourette Syndrome,* choice B, is a neurological condition that causes involuntary muscle movements and vocal sounds known as *tics. Hoarding* (choice A) is the inability to throw away possessions. *Agoraphobia* (choice C) is an intense fear of open spaces, crowds, or anywhere that is not one's comfort zone (e.g., home). *Adjustment disorder* (choice D) is a short-term emotional condition characterized by emotional or behavioral problems in reaction to an "identifiable" stressor. *Selective mutism* (choice E) is a childhood disorder that explains when a person is unable to speak in certain situations. For example, a child may speak at home, but be unable to speak to the teacher in a classroom setting even though the child may want to speak. *(Chapter 11)*

21. **C.** The *Yerkes-Dodson law* suggests that when people are emotionally aroused (sympathetic nervous system) (e.g., scared or embarrassed), thinking and concentrating become inhibited, choice C. The *Cannon-Bard theory* (choice A) suggests that the physical response to a stimulus happens at the same time as the emotional feeling. The *James-Lange theory* (choice B) is one of the earliest theories of emotions and has since been refuted. The theory suggests that emotions come from bodily responses. For example, the physical response of flinching, crying, or laughing comes before the emotional feeling of fear or sadness. The *Schachter-Singer theory* (choice D, known as the two-factor theory of emotion) suggests that the emotions are determined by cognitive and physiological factors. For example, a person must cognitively appraise the stimuli that cause a physical reaction. *Drive reduction theory* (choice E) suggests that people are driven to learn. A person feels the need to achieve a certain goal (eat, sleep, etc.) in order to reduce the drive and restore a balanced state. If the goal of the drive is achieved, the drive is reduced and a balanced state is restored. *(Chapter 8)*

22. **D.** *Projection* is a Freudian defense mechanism that is activated when a person unconsciously blames others, choice D. For example, if the parent of a high school student irrationally blames the teen for something, it might be because the parent has difficulty facing his or her own issues related to a similar issue. *Regression* (choice A) is when a person unconsciously regresses to an earlier stage of development in childhood. *Sublimation* (choice B) is when objectionable urges such as aggression are converted into socially acceptable behavior (e.g., joining a martial arts class). *Rationalization* (choice C) is when a person unconsciously justifies reasons for objectionable behavior. *Displacement* (choice E) is a Freudian defense mechanism when one part of the mind deals with unconscious issues by placing those issues on another person or object. For example, a student who is angry with her teacher might angrily say mean things to her little sister. *(Chapter 10)*

23. **A.** *Effortful processing* is a type of encoding in which one is consciously making an effort to remember things, choice A. This can be done by thinking about or making connections, or taking notes to encode the information in your memory. (Note: We hope you will do this as you read this book.) *Distributed practice* (choice B) is when a person encodes and practices over time rather than cramming the night before. *Attention* (choice C) is what is necessary to get something from one's sensory memory to one's working memory. *Maintenance rehearsal* (choice D) is repeating something out loud or mentally to store information in the short-term memory. *Sensory register* (choice E) is another term for *sensory memory* and is a temporary storage location for sounds and images. *(Chapter 8)*

24. **B.** The *Rosenhan study* in 1973, choice B, was an experiment to determine the validity of psychiatric diagnoses in hospitals. Volunteers pretended to have severe symptoms of schizophrenia in order to fool the staff of a psychiatric hospital. Not only did they fool the staff to be admitted, once the volunteers stopped pretending to have symptoms, the staff continued to believe the volunteers were mentally ill. The Stanford Prison Experiment (choice A) was an experiment to determine if "average" people would conform to the identified roles of prison guard or prisoner when placed in a make-believe prison. The *Milgram obedience experiments* (choice C) were a series of social psychology experiments that concluded that most people would harm a stranger when instructed to do so by an authority figure. The *Asch line experiments* (choice D) was a study to show how individuals yielded (conformed) to a group's majority. The *Robbers Cave Study* (choice E) was an unethical study in which 12-year-old boys at a summer camp were used to study group conflict. *(Chapter 11)*

25. **E.** The *cochlea* is a pea-sized, snail-shaped organ inside the ear that transduces the vibrations of sloshing fluid inside the cochlea into neural signals that the brain perceives as sound, choice E. The *tympanic membrane* (choice A) is another term for *eardrum,* where vibrating air molecules are turned into vibrations within the middle ear. The *stirrup* (choice B) is a tiny bone that knocks against the oval window in the cochlea and makes the fluid inside the cochlea slosh around. The *semicircular canals* (choice C) are fluid-filled, U-shaped structures that tell the brain when the head is moving. The *pinna* (choice D) is the visible part of the ear. *(Chapter 6)*

Chapter 4

# Unit 1: Scientific Foundations of Psychology

AP Psychology Unit 1 covers the history of psychology, historical and contemporary theories of psychology, and how research in psychology is conducted.

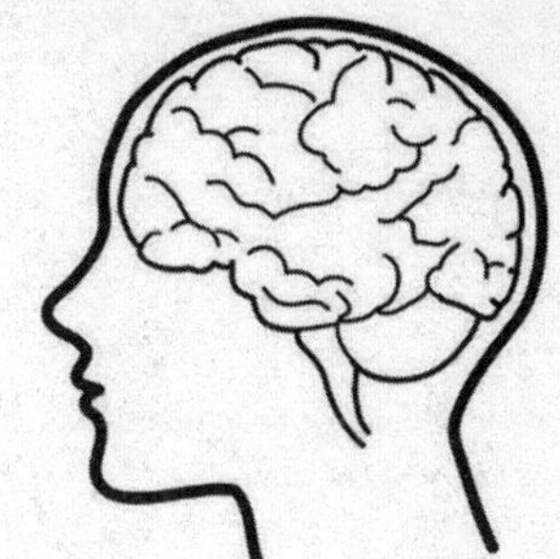

- The Origins of Psychology
- Key Contributors to Psychology
- Theoretical Approaches in Psychology
- Professions in Psychology
- Research Methods
- Statistics in Research
- Ethics in Research

## Overview of AP Psychology Unit 1

The key concepts for this chapter focus on the history of psychology, important theoretical contributions to psychology, understanding research methods in psychology, and ethical standards in psychology. **The topics discussed in this unit will count toward 10–14 percent of your multiple-choice score.**

### AP Psychology Framework

Success on the exam depends on your ability to make connections to the major concepts described in the content topics of the *Course Framework for AP Psychology.* Remember that these concepts highlight the fundamental ideas that every student should take with them into the AP PSYCH exam and beyond.

Use the table below to guide you through what is covered in this unit. The information contained in this table is an abridged version of the content outlines with topic examples. Visit https://apstudent.collegeboard.org/apcourse/ap-psychology/ for the complete updated AP PSYCH course curriculum framework.

| AP Psychology—Unit 1: Scientific Foundations of Psychology | |
|---|---|
| **Topic** | **Learning Target** |
| **Introducing Psychology** | ■ Recognize how philosophical and physiological perspectives shaped the development of psychological thought.<br>■ Identify the research contributions of major historical figures in psychology (Calkins, Darwin, Dix, Freud, Hall, James, Pavlov, Piaget, Rogers, Skinner, Washburn, Watson, Wundt).<br>■ Describe and compare different theoretical approaches in explaining behavior (structuralism, functionalism, early behaviorism, gestalt, psychoanalytical/ psychodynamic, humanistic, evolutionary approach, biological approach, cognitive approach, biopsychosocial approaches, sociocultural).<br>■ Recognize the strengths and limitations of applying theories to explain behavior.<br>■ Distinguish the different domains of psychology (biological, clinical, cognitive, counseling, developmental, educational, experimental, industrial-organizational, personality, psychometric, social, positive). |
| **Research Methods in Psychology** | ■ Differentiate types of research with regard to purpose, strengths, and weaknesses (experiments, correlational studies, survey research, naturalistic observations, case studies, longitudinal studies, cross-sectional studies).<br>■ Discuss the value of reliance on operational definitions and measurement in behavioral research. |
| **The Experimental Method** | ■ Identify independent, dependent, confounding, and control variables in experimental designs.<br>■ Describe how research design drives the reasonable conclusions that can be drawn. (For example, experiments are useful for determining cause and effect; the use of experimental controls reduces alternative explanations; random assignment is needed to demonstrate cause and effect; correlational research can indicate if there is a relationship or association between two variables but cannot demonstrate cause and effect.)<br>■ Distinguish between random assignment of participants to conditions in experiments and random selection of participants, primarily in correlational studies and surveys. |
| **Selecting a Research Method** | ■ Predict the validity of behavioral explanations based on the quality of research design. (For example, confounding variables limit confidence in research conclusions.) |
| **Statistical Analysis in Psychology** | ■ Apply basic descriptive statistical concepts, including interpreting and constructing graphs and calculating simple descriptive statistics (measures of central tendency; variation—range, standard deviation; correlation coefficient; frequency distribution—normal, bimodal, positive skew, negative skew).<br>■ Distinguish the purposes of descriptive statistics and inferential statistics. |
| **Ethical Guidelines in Psychology** | ■ Identify how ethical issues inform and constrain research practices.<br>■ Describe how ethical and legal guidelines protect research participants and promote sound ethical practice. [For example, those provided by the American Psychological Association, federal regulations, local institutional review board (IRB), and Institutional Animal Care and Use Committee (IACUC).] |

# Important Terms and Concepts Checklist

This section is an overview of the important terms, concepts, language, and theories that specifically target the key topics of Unit 1. Use this list of terms as a checklist to check your personal progress. As you study the topics, place a check mark next to each and return to this list as often as necessary to refresh your understanding.

After you finish the review section, you can reinforce what you have learned by working through the practice questions at the end of the chapter. Answers and explanations provide further clarification into the perspectives of the foundations of psychology.

| Term/Concept | Study Page | Term/Concept | Study Page | Term/Concept | Study Page |
|---|---|---|---|---|---|
| **applied research** | p. 28 | **experimental group** | p. 30 | **psychoanalytic** | p. 25 |
| **bar graph** | p. 38 | **experimental research** | p. 33 | **psychodynamic** | p. 25 |
| **basic research** | p. 28 | **experimenter bias** | p. 30 | **qualitative research method** | p. 32 |
| **behavioral psychology** | p. 26 | **field experiment** | p. 33 | **quantitative research method** | p. 32 |
| **bell-shaped curve** | p. 42 | **frequency distribution table** | p. 38 | **random sampling** | p. 30 |
| **biological psychology** | p. 27 | **Hawthorne effect** | pp. 33, 44 | **reliability** | p. 34 |
| **case study research method** | p. 33 | **histogram** | p. 38 | **representative sample** | p. 42 |
| **cognitive psychology** | p. 26 | **humanistic psychology** | p. 26 | **sample** | p. 30 |
| **confidentiality** | p. 44 | **hypothesis (alternative and null)** | pp. 29, 42 | **scatter plot** | p. 35 |
| **confounding variable** | p. 30 | **independent variable** | p. 29 | **scientific method** | p. 31 |
| **control group** | p. 30 | **inferential statistics** | p. 42 | **single-blind** | p. 30 |
| **correlation coefficient** | p. 35 | **informed consent** | p. 44 | **skewed distribution (positive and negative)** | p. 40 |
| **correlational studies** | p. 34 | **institutional review board (IRB)** | p. 44 | **sociocultural psychology** | p. 27 |
| **cross-sectional study** | p. 37 | **longitudinal study** | p. 37 | **statistical significance** | p. 42 |
| **debriefing** | p. 44 | **measures of central tendency (mean, median, mode)** | p. 39 | **survey research method** | p. 34 |
| **dependent variable** | p. 30 | **naturalistic observation** | p. 33 | **theory** | p. 30 |
| **descriptive statistics** | p. 37 | **normal distribution curve** | p. 42 | **Type I and Type II errors** | p. 43 |
| **double-blind** | p. 30 | **placebo** | p. 30 | **validity** | p. 34 |
| **empirical evidence** | p. 30 | **probability (chance)** | p. 43 | **variability (range, standard deviation, variance)** | p. 41 |
| **evolutionary psychology** | p. 25 | | | | |

# Chapter Review

The chapter review focuses on developing an understanding of psychology as a scientific study of mental processes. The origins of psychology, key contributors to the field of psychology, theories of psychology, and research methods in psychology will be examined and reviewed.

### Heads Up: What You Need to Know

For the AP PSYCH exam, as you work through this chapter, ask yourself these two essential questions: How does methodology of the research affect the outcome of the study? and How do ethical guidelines impact psychological research?

## The Origins of Psychology

It is generally agreed that psychology is the scientific study of behavior and mental processes. While psychology was not founded until the late 1800s, early written accounts of the study of the human mind were recorded with the Buddhists, ancient Babylonians, and Greek philosophers. In fact, the word *psychology* is derived from the ancient Greeks—*psyche* means mind and *logos* means study.

The Greek philosopher Socrates (c. 470–399 B.C.E.), and his student Plato (c. 428–347 B.C.E.) believed that the mind is separate from the body. Plato also proposed the idea of *nativism* (knowledge is innate). Aristotle (c. 384–322 B.C.E.) observed that "the *soul* (meaning psyche) is not separate from the body." He also proposed that humans are born not knowing anything, called *tabula rasa,* and that knowledge grows from the experiences stored in our memories.

The early reflections of ancient philosophers continue to be debated among modern-day psychologists, called *nature vs. nurture:* Is behavior biological, determined by genetic inheritance? Or is behavior determined by environmental factors? To help you arrive at your own conclusions about this important question, we will discuss various scientific viewpoints throughout this book.

The three early interpretations of the human mind that you should know for the AP PSYCH exam are *monism, dualism,* and *phrenology.*

**Monism.** Aristotle introduced the idea of *monism* (theory of oneness; the existence of the mind and the body as one), and modern scientific medicine concurs with Aristotle's findings. For example, if you feel scared, you may feel physical changes in your body (e.g., sweaty palms, racing heart, or unsettled stomach).

**Dualism.** French philosopher René Descartes (1596–1650) agreed with Socrates and Plato when he became interested in how the physical body relates to the mind. Philosophers, like Descartes, began asking, "Do thoughts cause brain activity or does brain activity cause thoughts?" Descartes answered the mind-body question with the idea of *dualism* (the mind is separate from the body).

**Phrenology.** German physician Franz Gall introduced the idea that personality and mental traits are determined by the shape of the human skull and the measurement of bumps and fissures on the skull. In the early 19th century, Gall proposed that certain areas of the brain have specific functions, and these areas reflect a person's tendency for certain personality traits. Although Gall's premise is still relevant today (i.e., mental functions are localized in the brain), his theory that personality traits are determined by the shape of a skull is considered a *pseudoscience* (not based on the scientific method) and lacks scientific proof.

## Timeline of Psychology

| Pre-Modern Psychology (Early Civilizations)<br>Psychology was viewed as a philosophy of the mind, not a science. | | | | | |
|---|---|---|---|---|---|
| **Date** | **Contributor** | **Contribution** | **Date** | **Contributor** | **Contribution** |
| **c. 320 B.C.E.** | Socrates<br>Plato | The mind is separate from the body. | **1796** | Francis Gall | Introduced phrenology |
| **c. 350 B.C.E.** | Aristotle | The mind and body are one. | **1853** | Dorothea Dix | Helped to establish the first hospital for the mentally ill |
| **1633** | René Descartes | Introduced a thesis on *dualism* (the mind is separate from the body) | **1859** | Charles Darwin | Published *On the Origin of Species,* which introduced the ideas for evolutionary psychology |
| **17th and 18th centuries** | Francis Bacon<br>John Locke | Introduced the concept of *empiricism* (knowledge comes from sensory experience) | | | |
| **Modern Psychology (Late 1800s to Present)**<br>**Psychology became known as a science of the human mind and behavior.** | | | | | |
| **1878** | G. Stanley Hall | First American to earn a doctorate in psychology | **1892** | G. Stanley Hall | Founded the American Psychological Association (APA) |
| **1879** | Wilhelm Wundt | Established first experimental laboratory in Germany | **1894** | Margaret Floy Washburn | First woman to receive a doctorate in psychology |
| **1883** | G. Stanley Hall | Established first experimental laboratory in America | **1900** | Sigmund Freud | Published *Interpretation of Dreams* |
| **1890** | William James | Published *The Principles of Psychology* | **1905** | Mary Whiton Calkins | Elected as first woman president of the American Psychological Association |

*Continued*

| Date | Contributor | Contribution | Date | Contributor | Contribution |
|---|---|---|---|---|---|
| **1905** | Alfred Binet | Introduced intelligence tests | **1932** | Jean Piaget | Published *The Moral Judgment of Children*, which led to his famous "stages of cognitive development" |
| **1906** | Ivan Pavlov | Published his findings of "classical conditioning" | **1939–1940** | Kenneth and Mamie Clark | Famously studied racial identity preferences in a "doll experiment." Results showed that children (white and black) had a tendency to view white dolls favorably and black dolls unfavorably. |
| **1913; 1920** | Carl Jung | (1913) Published *The Psychology of Dementia*<br><br>(1920) Departed from Freudian views and formed his own psychoanalytic theory | **1942** | Carl Rogers | Introduced the practice of "client-centered therapy" |
| **1920** | John B. Watson | Introduced his views of "classical conditioning" with Little Albert | **1952** | American Psychiatric Association | First edition of *Diagnostic and Statistical Manual of Mental Disorders* published |

## Key Contributors to Psychology

On the AP PSYCH exam, you should be able to identify the major contributors in the field of modern psychology.

| Key Contributions to Psychology | | |
|---|---|---|
| **Contributor** | **Field of Study (Theory)** | **Famous For** |
| **Mary Whiton Calkins** (1863–1930) | Self-psychology | Calkins was an American philosopher and psychologist who studied under William James. She was originally interested in experimentation and developed the "paired-associations technique" that describes a memory method of learning by associating one item to another. She then published papers on the "science of the self," which is now known as *self-psychology* (modern psychoanalytic theory). She became the first American woman to become the president of the American Psychological Association. Calkins was also a suffragist and fought for a woman's right to vote. |
| **Charles Darwin** (1809–1882) | Evolutionary psychology | Charles Darwin was a British biologist and naturalist who is known for his contributions to the science of evolution. He wrote *On the Origin of Species* (1859) and proposed an evolutionary approach to psychology based on his landmark theory that humans have social instincts that evolved by *natural selection* (as a result of a living organism's interaction with an environment, superior inherited traits adapt to survive if the environment favors the inherited traits). Darwin proposed that humans and animals descended from the same ancestry. He explained that the driving force of humankind's existence is centered in the concept of "survival of the fittest." Darwin's work on human behavior inspired psychologists like William James and Sigmund Freud. |

| Contributor | Field of Study (Theory) | Famous For |
|---|---|---|
| **Dorothea Dix** (1802–1887) | Mental health reform | Dix was an American pioneer in mental health reform to improve the treatment of mentally ill patients. She fought against inhuman conditions in mental institutions and felt that patients were treated with unusual cruelty. She argued for the moral treatment of the mentally ill, including "modesty, chastity, and delicacy." She was influential in passing the first mental illness legislation called "The Bill for the Benefit of the Indigent Insane." Dix also helped to establish the first type of mental hospitals, called *mental asylums*, in Pennsylvania. |
| **Sigmund Freud** (1856–1939) | Founder of psychoanalysis | Freud was an Austrian-born neurologist who founded *psychoanalysis* (the therapeutic treatment that emphasizes unconscious motives that control behavior). Freud wrote many essays and books that elaborated on his psychoanalytic process and developed a model of the psychic structure (id, ego, and superego). Freud formulated and established several theories and therapeutic techniques that are used in modern-day psychology, including unconscious processes, free association, transference, and defense mechanisms. Although the therapeutic effectiveness of some of his methodologies remains debatable (e.g., concepts of the Oedipus complex, hysteria, psychosexual development), Freud remains one of the most influential figures in psychology. Freud's work has influenced numerous psychologists (called *neo-Freudians*) including Carl Jung, Alfred Adler, Erik Erikson, Otto Rank, John Bowlby, Melanie Klein, and his daughter Anna Freud. |
| **G. Stanley Hall** (1846–1924) | Educational psychology | Hall was an American psychologist and educator whose professional contributions expanded the understanding of adolescent development (i.e., teens tend to be sensation seeking). He was the first president of the American Psychological Association (APA) and focused on developmental and evolutionary psychology. Although his basic stages of development were not popular, his studies laid the foundation for Jean Piaget's stages of cognitive development. Hall's studies included the inheritance of behavior, and *phylogenetic* (evolutionary development) and *ontogenetic* (original history of humans) perspectives of development. |
| **William James** (1842–1910) | Founder of functionalism; father of American psychology | James was an American philosopher and psychologist. He was known for writing *The Principles of Psychology* (1890), which outlines his theoretical viewpoints of consciousness, emotion, habit, and will. James became a leading contributor in the philosophical expansion of *pragmatism* (truth is measured by its practical consequences) and was a founder of *functional psychology* (emphasized the importance of rational thought instead of experimentation). James' theory of emotion, called the *James-Lange theory of emotion* (physical arousal triggers the experience of emotion), is one of the earliest theories to describe the process of emotion and is still an accepted view of emotion today. |

*Continued*

| Contributor | Field of Study (Theory) | Famous For |
|---|---|---|
| **Ivan Pavlov** (1849–1936) | Classical conditioning | Pavlov was a Russian-born physiologist and the pioneer of classical conditioning, originally called "conditional reflex." Pavlov conducted *stimulus-response* experiments. Through his experiments with dogs that salivated when they associated sound with food, Pavlov formed a conclusion that behavior is learned by repetition, association, and anticipation (also see John B. Watson). Dogs learned to involuntarily respond by salivating each time a buzzer rang at feeding time. The dogs were conditioned to respond by salivating to the bell, not to seeing or smelling the food. |
| **Jean Piaget** (1896–1980) | Theory of cognitive development | Swiss psychologist Jean Piaget was first a biologist who later became interested in the development of children. His theory of cognitive development is famous in the field of education. Piaget believed that children go through four distinct stages of thinking and mastering logical thought. The stages are determined by the child's ability to accomplish certain cognitive tasks. Piaget used naturalistic observation in his research design. The four stages of cognitive development are sensorimotor, preoperational, concrete, and formal operations. |
| **Carl Rogers** (1902–1987) | Humanistic psychology; client-centered therapy | Rogers was one of the founders of humanistic psychology and one of the most influential psychologists of the 20th century. He is well-known for his therapeutic approach to counseling, called *client-centered therapy*. This type of therapeutic treatment emphasizes a person-to-person relationship between the therapist and the client. |
| **B. F. Skinner** (1904–1990) | Operant conditioning | Skinner was a well-known American behavioral psychologist who developed the theory of operant conditioning. In *operant conditioning,* people learn from consequences. Skinner's experiments concluded that when people act in the environment, their behavioral responses produce a consequence of either a reinforced reward or a punishment. |
| **Margaret Floy Washburn** (1871–1939) | Animal psychology | Washburn was the first woman to receive a doctorate in psychology, proving that women could contribute to the field. Washburn studied animal behavior and examined over 100 animal species. She was also known for her studies of behavior and consciousness and wrote a book called *Movement and Mental Imagery* (1916) that linked mental processes and motor skills. |
| **John B. Watson** (1878–1958) | Classical conditioning | Watson was the founder of behaviorism. He applied Pavlov's stimulus-response to children and claimed that, based on his observations, all behavior is the result of reflexive reactions to stimuli. In his famous Little Albert experiment, Watson discovered that behavior occurs in the context of conditioning. |
| **Wilhelm Wundt** (1832–1920) | Experimental psychology | German physician Wilhelm Wundt is considered the founder of modern psychology and the father of experimental psychology. Prior to Wundt's contributions, psychology was a discipline within the field of medicine. Wundt established the first psychology laboratory when he wanted to scientifically study the structure of consciousness. He is known for introducing the term *introspection* as a technique to observe one's own consciousness. |

# Theoretical Approaches in Psychology

The AP PSYCH exam measures your knowledge of seven main domains in psychology. You should be able to identify, define, and respond to free-response questions regarding theoretical approaches.

**TEST TIP: The AP PSYCH exam does not explicitly focus on the approaches to psychology in the multiple-choice questions, but you should know the basics of each approach to compare and contrast in free-response questions.**

| Compare and Contrast Theories of Psychology | | | | |
|---|---|---|---|---|
| **Theory/Theorist** | **Main Ideas** | **Treatment** | **Advantages** | **Disadvantages** |
| **Evolutionary** (Charles Darwin) | Evolutionary psychology is a combination of biological and cognitive psychology. It focuses on how human behaviors have adapted for human survival when confronted with environmental pressures. Behavior, emotions, and thoughts are a result of natural selection in a modern society. People act, think, and feel due to biological processes that have modified the biological and cognitive processes of human beings. | Evolution-based therapies focus on strategies to improve a person's lifestyle (e.g., sleep, diet, stress, work) and compare these choices to those of our ancestors. | Evidence supports biological, cognitive, and anthropological inherited tendencies are adaptive in humans. | Evolutionary psychology is a theory; it is not an empirically based study that is studied in a laboratory.<br><br>The theory does not explain individual thoughts and behaviors very well. It only suggests that since cave-males might have acted a certain way, modern males might act that way, too. |
| **Psychoanalytic or Psychodynamic** (Sigmund Freud) | Psychoanalytic psychology focuses on unconscious motivations that stem from early childhood experiences and from the conflict between the id, ego, and superego. Mental illness is due to unconscious urges that can negatively affect emotions, thoughts, and feelings.<br><br>Psychodynamic psychology was inspired by followers of Freudian psychoanalytic principles. The main tenet emphasizes that unconscious processes underlie human behaviors and emotions. | Treatment focuses on uncovering unconscious processes that are manifested in a person's behavior and emotions. | Evidence shows that benefits are linked to the emotional development of one's internal resources and strengths. Uncovering childhood experiences impacts one's present behavior. Psychoanalytic or psychodynamic theory can identify and treat almost any mental disorder. | Psychoanalytic psychology is not an empirically based scientific theory. The unconscious has proven very difficult to study. |

*Continued*

| Theory/Theorist | Main Ideas | Treatment | Advantages | Disadvantages |
|---|---|---|---|---|
| **Behavioral** (Ivan Pavlov, John Watson, Edward Thorndike, B. F. Skinner) | Behavioral psychology focuses on how the environment shapes and controls behavior. Much of who and what we are can be reduced to reflexes and behaviors that are learned by either classical conditioning or operant conditioning.<br><br>Mental illness is the result of learning the maladaptive associations in stimuli, reinforcement, and punishment. | Treatment is focused on changing objectionable behavior (e.g., smoking). Examples include counter-conditioning, positive reinforcement, exposure, aversion, and desensitization. | Evidence demonstrates that behavioral psychology can be investigated, measured, and observed scientifically. Therefore, one advantage is that therapies are used to predict human reactions. | Behavioral psychology focuses too much on deterministic factors of behaviors based on studies. It is a simplistic view of psychology and sometimes overlooks underlying causes and biological functions. |
| **Cognitive** (Albert Ellis, Aaron Beck, Jean Piaget, Noam Chomsky) | Cognitive psychology focuses on the role of thoughts and mental processes that affect behavior. Thoughts aid in acquiring knowledge, information, memory, and perceptions.<br><br>Maladaptive behavior is the result of irrational, negative thoughts that can cause undesirable feelings and behaviors. | Treatment focuses on how to teach clients how to "think" in new, constructive ways. | Evidence shows that cognitive psychology has many practical and flexible applications. It is effective in treating anxiety, phobias, and post-traumatic stress. | The main disadvantage of cognitive psychology is that thoughts cannot be measured. The theory relies on inference and ignores behavioral approaches. |
| **Humanistic** (Carl Rogers, Abraham Maslow) | Humanistic psychology emphasizes the importance of understanding a person's subjective experience of the world.<br><br>Maladaptive thoughts, behaviors, and feelings are the result of obstacles that prevent a person from improving and growing. According to this approach, mental illness is the result of circumstances that block a person from growing toward their natural goodness and potential. | Treatment focuses on providing a therapeutic environment of unconditional positive regard, using active listening, and showing empathy for the client. | Humanistic psychology focuses on the subjective experiences of the client. It gives the client an experience of autonomy, free will, and an atmosphere of unconditional support. Evidence shows that clients tend to improve in an environment of support and respect. | The main disadvantage of humanistic psychology is that it assumes that people are intrinsically good and will choose a positive direction. Humanistic psychology is not scientifically based. |

| Theory/Theorist | Main Ideas | Treatment | Advantages | Disadvantages |
|---|---|---|---|---|
| **Biological** (Michael Gazzaniga, Oliver Sacks) | Biological psychology focuses on how the role of biological processes influences thoughts, emotions, and behavior. Human behavior is the result of bodily chemical reactions that take place between body parts such as glands, neurons, and specialized brain structures. Mental illness, according to this paradigm, is the result of chemical imbalances and malfunctioning parts of the nervous and endocrine systems. | Treatment focuses on psychoactive drugs to restore the brain's chemical balances. Other biomedical treatments include medical procedures such as electroconvulsive therapy, trans-cranial magnetic stimulation, and deep brain stimulation. | The main advantage of biological psychology is that evidence shows drug therapy is very effective. In addition, this approach is scientifically researched and studied because hormones, neurotransmitters, and electrical activity can be measured. | The main disadvantage of biological psychology is that it is a reductionist approach to the complexities of human behavior. For effective change to occur, drug therapy must be given in conjunction with psychological therapy. Drug therapy medications are sometimes imprecise, expensive, have side effects, and can be abused. |
| **Sociocultural** (Solomon Asch, Stanley Milgram, Muzafer Sherif, Leon Festinger) | Sociocultural psychology emphasizes how society and culture influence behavior. Humans are reflections of their roles in the social environment, groups, and culture.<br><br>According to sociocultural psychology, mental illness is the result of sociocultural conflicts and influences. | Treatment focuses on helping the client align with socially and culturally acceptable roles. | The main advantage of sociocultural psychology is that there is substantial evidence that measures how people act in different social situations. | The main disadvantage of sociocultural psychology is that the approach may be too narrow and may not consider the complexities of an individual's human behavior (e.g., cognitions). The approach is based on large data sets and what most people do in most situations, not on individual roles. |

## Professions in Psychology

Psychology has many fields of study, research, and clinical practices. Each branch focuses on the science of the mind and human behavior, and often branches overlap.

While the main goal on the AP PSYCH exam is to be able to identify the differences between the branches of psychology, we should first clarify the differences between a clinical psychologist and a psychiatrist. Although both deal with the treatment of psychological problems and often collaborate to treat patients, psychologists are not medical doctors and, therefore, cannot prescribe medication. Psychologists have a doctorate in philosophy (Ph.D.) or a doctorate in psychology (Psy.D.). Psychiatrists have a medical degree (M.D.).

This section will cover professions in psychology, not psychiatry.

| Professions in Psychology | |
|---|---|
| **Profession** | **Description** |
| **Clinical psychologist** | Clinical psychologists specialize in the diagnosis and treatment of emotional and behavioral disorders. Clinical psychologists frequently administer and interpret a battery of psychological tests (e.g., personality tests). They work in private practice, hospitals, colleges, government agencies, outpatient treatment centers, and prisons. |
| **Developmental psychologist** | Developmental psychologists study how people develop and grow throughout a life span. Some developmental psychologists specialize in a particular age group (e.g., child psychologists). Developmental psychologists work in public schools, university research, and private practice. |
| **Educational psychologist** | Educational psychologists focus on learning and cognitions of children through adulthood. They work in private practice as consultants, public schools, and educational centers. |
| **Forensic psychologist** | Forensic psychologists specialize in legal matters. Psychologists frequently conduct testing and interviews, evaluate competency for a person to stand trial, and offer expert clinical testimony in court cases (e.g., family custody issues). Forensic psychologists frequently work with the police or FBI in providing expert profiles of those persons who have committed a crime. |
| **Industrial/organizational psychologist** | Industrial/organizational psychologists apply psychological principles to businesses and organizations to improve the connection between employees and their work environment. A typical practice includes assisting employees with organizational change, training, development, and work performance. |
| **Neuropsychologist** | Neuropsychologists specialize in clinical work with individuals who may need cognitive, behavioral, or emotional rehabilitation. Neuropsychologists frequently work as part of a team to provide a battery of assessments and consult with other members of the team (e.g., physician, psychiatrist, clinical psychologist, or social worker). Children through adults who may have brain damage frequently see a neuropsychologist. Neuropsychologists work in private practice, treatment centers, or hospitals. |
| **Research (experimental) psychologist** | Research psychologists generally work at a university and conduct experimental research in specific areas of study of both humans and animals. There are two types of research psychologists: basic and applied researchers. *Basic researchers* conduct theoretical studies in controlled settings. **Basic research** is based on developing or expanding a theory. For example, basic researchers might draw conclusions about how memories are formed, but the results are not applied in real-world clinical settings. **Applied research** is based on developing practical intervention techniques in real-world scenarios. For example, *applied researchers* might study whether lecture-based learning or project-based learning is more effective. |
| **School psychologist** | School psychologists work with children and adolescents in a school setting to conduct testing, diagnosing, and identifying cognitive, social, and learning problems. |
| **Sports psychologist** | Sports psychologists specialize in sports-related therapy and work with teams and individuals to help athletes perform at their top levels. Sports psychologists help athletes with sports-related and personal-related issues. |

# Research Methods

As a high school student, you may be overwhelmed thinking about the myriad details involved in identifying the workings of empirical research scientists, but keep in mind that research is a systematic and logical method of explaining human behavior across broad and diverse issues. Because the process is systematic, we can walk you through the step-by-step procedures of the scientific method, introduce key concepts of research, explain the types of research methods, and review ethical considerations that may appear on the AP PSYCH exam.

## Key Terms and Concepts

All research studies have similar elements that you should be familiar with as you work through this section.

### Heads Up: What You Need to Know

On the AP PSYCH exam, you will need to know several important experimental concepts.

- Hypothesis, alternative hypothesis, and null hypothesis
- Independent variable, dependent variable, and confounding variable
- Experimental group, control group, and random assignment
- Population, sample, and random sampling
- Placebo
- Single-blind and double-blind
- Theory
- Empirical evidence

**Hypothesis.** A hypothesis is what the researcher predicts will happen. It is an educated guess or testable question. Use an if/then statement to remember the definition. For example, "if" students spend many hours studying for the AP PSYCH exam, "then" these students will score well on the exam. In research, the question becomes "how many hours" and "what is the definition of *score well.*" The hypothesis must be operationalized to measure these two variables. The hypothesis then becomes "If" students spend 40 hours studying for the AP PSYCH exam, "then" they will receive a score of 3 or above.

**Alternative hypothesis.** An alternative hypothesis predicts that there *will* be a significant change in the dependent variable. *Significance* is defined as the level of certainty in the results of the research that is not attributed to chance, accident, luck, or a confounding variable (see p. 42 for more about significance).

**Null hypothesis.** A null hypothesis is a prediction that there will *not* be a significant change in the dependent variable. Even if there is a change, the researcher cannot be certain what caused the change.

**Independent variable.** An independent variable (IV) is what the researcher acts upon or manipulates. Think of the independent variable as what the researcher changes (has control over) and the dependent variable as what changes because of that (the outcome). For example, in a sample experiment, the researcher may have participants drink caffeinated coffee to see if the coffee has an effect on being able to study longer. The *caffeinated coffee* is the independent variable.

**Dependent variable.** A dependent variable (DV) is the affected result from the independent variable that is tested and measured by the researcher. For example, in an experiment where participants drink caffeinated coffee to see if they can study longer, the *length of time* the participants can study is the dependent variable.

**Confounding variable.** In an experiment, a confounding variable is something that the experimenter didn't account for that can influence the dependent and independent variables. For example, in the experiment where participants drink caffeinated coffee to see if the coffee has an effect on being able to study longer, a confounding variable might be how much sleep the participants had the night before or their tolerance of caffeine.

**Random assignment.** Random assignment occurs when the researcher takes the total number of research volunteer (or animal) subjects and blindly or randomly places them into either the control group or experimental group so that each subject has an equal chance of being assigned to either group.

**Experimental group.** In an experiment, this group of people (or animals) receives the treatment (they are exposed to the independent variable).

**Control group.** In an experiment, the control group is the group of people (or animals) who do not receive the treatment (they are not exposed to the independent variable).

**Population.** In research, a population is the whole group of a particular study from which participants might be selected.

**Sample.** A sample is a "selected" number of participants from the population that is intended to represent the entire population being studied.

**Random sampling.** A random sampling is when each participant in the population has an "equal chance" of being chosen for the study.

**Placebo.** The control group can be called the placebo group because it does not receive the treatment. Placebo is something that has no real physical effect. It fools the volunteers in the *control group* into thinking that they received the treatment—for example, if the researcher is determining the effects of caffeine and gives the experimental group caffeinated coffee, but gives the control group decaffeinated coffee. Placebos are necessary for experiments to test the independent variable. If the participant receives a placebo, but reacts as if he or she did not receive the treatment, it is called a *placebo effect* (the person responds to the treatment even though he or she did not receive the treatment).

**Single-blind.** It is important for the researcher not to inform the experimental and control group participants which group they are in because the subjects might act unnaturally, adding a confounding variable. Not informing participants is called a single-blind technique.

**Double-blind.** Double-blind is a technique of not informing participants which group they are in, but also the researcher does not know the participants in each group. It is used to reduce the likelihood of **experimenter bias** (also known as **researcher bias,** the researcher's unintentional influence on the outcome of the results).

**Theory.** A theory is a generalized principle that connects concepts and explains phenomena. In research, a theory defines the variables, shows consistent relationships among the variables, and makes specific future predictions.

**Empirical evidence.** Empirical evidence is acquired by observation or experimentation. Empirical research is the process of working with a phenomenon that can be measured (which is sometimes difficult in psychology). For example, the feeling of *sadness* cannot be empirically studied, but the number of days missed from work or school due to sadness can be measured and studied.

## The Scientific Method

Earlier in the chapter, you learned that psychology was originally considered a branch of philosophy. When psychology became its own discipline that was separate from philosophy, it became a scientific field of study. Research psychologists investigate the human mind and human behavior, and, like other social science disciplines, researchers use the same type of experimental methods that other scientists use, such as the scientific method.

Each research method has advantages and disadvantages, and each research investigation answers questions, as well as raises questions. However, the scientific method helps researchers organize their observations of human behavior in real-life events, personal experiences, or in reproducing previous research studies.

The scientific method was developed in the 17th century when scientists like Francis Bacon and René Descartes began to question the theories of ancient scientists like Aristotle. The **scientific method** is the systematic organization of the process of experimentation. It is based on observation, forming a testable hypothesis, and the ability to reproduce the results to confirm the findings.

### The Steps of the Scientific Method

The basic steps of the scientific method are 1) make an observation, 2) state the problem by forming a question, 3) form a hypothesis, 4) make a prediction and gather evidence based on the hypothesis, 5) test the hypothesis, and 6) analyze the results and draw the conclusion to form a theory.

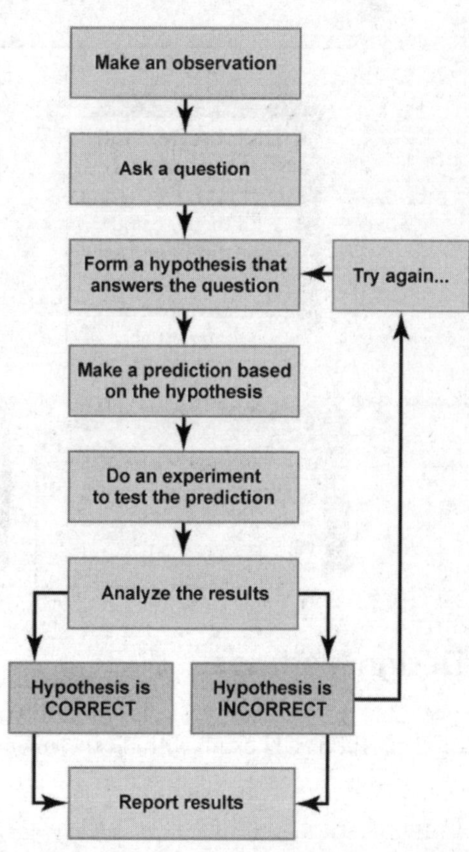


## Types of Research Methods

The goal of research is to explain, predict, and describe mental processes and behavior. Several types of research help to accomplish this goal, but each one has advantages and disadvantages that will be explained in this section.

Researchers start the investigation process by deciding on how to plan and conduct a valid experiment. The researcher must consider the following elements in deciding the type of research method, the specific research design, and how to approach the research design.

1. **Broad research method.** The researcher must select one of two *broad* research methods: experimental or descriptive (nonexperimental) research.
2. **Specific research design.** The researcher must select the *specific* design method: experiment, field experiment, correlational experiment, naturalistic observation, survey, or case study.

3. **How to approach the research.** The researcher must choose between a quantitative method of study and a qualitative method of study. Note: Some studies make use of both quantitative and qualitative studies.

Research methods can be conducted using quantitative and/or qualitative approaches. The **quantitative** approach is typically used in experimental research and is based on the statistical analysis of numbers. Research is conducted in an unbiased, objective manner. The **qualitative** approach is used in nonexperimental research and is based on observational analysis that is used to describe broad themes. In qualitative analysis, the researcher is biased and subjective.

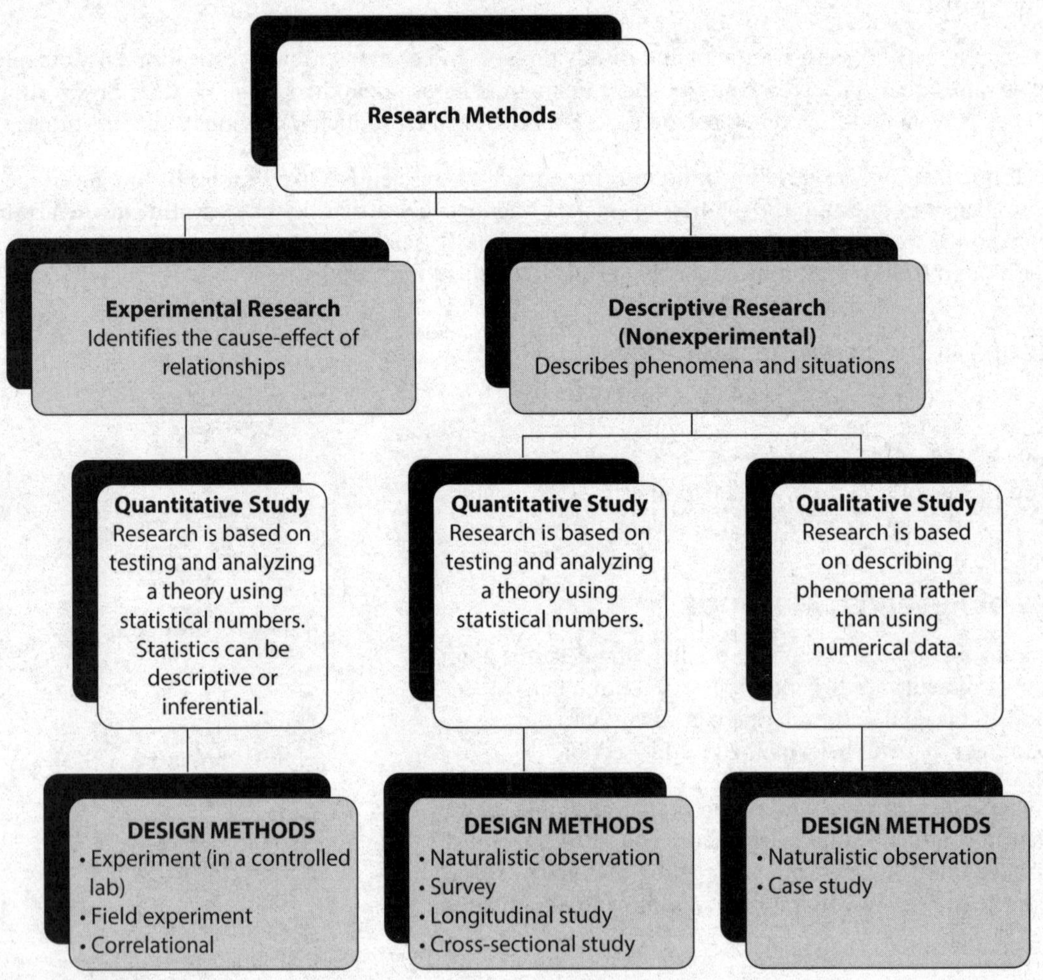


## Design Methods

The table that follows illustrates the subtypes of research methods (called design methods) that may appear on the AP PSYCH exam within experimental research or nonexperimental (descriptive) research.

**TEST TIP: Use the advantages/disadvantages and examples of each method on your free-response questions.**

| Experimental Research Design Methods | | | |
|---|---|---|---|
| **Method** | **Description** | **Advantages/Disadvantages** | **Example** |
| **Experimental** | The researcher manipulates an independent variable (IV) under controlled conditions to measure the effects on the dependent variable (DV).<br><br>The experimental method is straightforward. It is the practice of manipulating humans or animals (independent variable) and observing to see if there is a measurable change in their behavior (dependent variable). | **Experimental research** shows a relationship of cause and effect between the independent and dependent variables. However, experimental research is limited to a "controlled setting" (humans do not live in a laboratory). Therefore, the findings may not be representative of the general population. Henry Landsberger concluded that there is a *Hawthorne effect* (1955), suggesting that people change their behavior simply because they are being studied. | John B. Watson (1920) conducted the Little Albert experiment to prove classical conditioning works on humans. |
| **Field experiment** | The researcher introduces an independent variable (IV) and measures the dependent variable (DV) when random assignments of participants are not available. | One advantage is that because the research occurs outside of a controlled laboratory setting (in the field), participants act more naturally. Disadvantages include the following: (1) it's difficult to replicate; (2) it's difficult to control confounding variables that influence the results; (3) lack of random assignments can weaken the findings; and (4) ethical concerns—participants should have the right to know they are being observed. | Philip Zimbardo's Stanford Prison experiments (1971) to show the human response to captivity (prisoner and prison guard). |

| Descriptive (Nonexperimental) Research Design Methods | | | |
|---|---|---|---|
| **Method** | **Description** | **Advantages/Disadvantages** | **Example** |
| **Naturalistic observation** | The researcher observes humans or animals in their real-world natural environment and records the findings. | Researcher does not manipulate the conditions in a lab. Therefore, naturalistic observations can support the validity of experimental research that was conducted in a controlled laboratory setting. Two disadvantages: (1) People behave differently when they know they are being observed, but if they don't know they are being watched, it could be an ethical dilemma. (2) Each researcher may form a different conclusion from the same observation. | Konrad Lorenz (1935) animal imprinting.<br><br>Jane Goodall (1971) animal behavior. |
| **Case study** | The researcher studies a person or small group of people usually for a long period of time. It is an in-depth examination that uses observations and interviews to provide a detailed description of the behavior or problem. | Case studies can provide detailed analyses and advanced knowledge of uncommon or complex phenomena, but a case study has some limitations. The findings may not be representative of a larger or generalized group of people. | Sigmund Freud's principles of his theory of psychoanalysis (1961) were developed through case studies of his patients, specifically the case study of Anna O. |

*Continued*

| Method | Description | Advantages/Disadvantages | Example |
|---|---|---|---|
| **Survey** | The researcher collects a large number of samples by interviewing or using questionnaires to gather information about beliefs, behaviors, experiences, or attitudes. | Surveys and tests are easy and inexpensive to administer. Surveys can provide statistical findings, but several variables can affect the validity of the results. For example, there might be experimenter bias or poorly written questions, and participants might misinterpret the survey questions or not answer honestly. | The census survey systematically gathers and records information about the population of residents in the United States every 10 years. |

## Reliability and Validity

The design of the research is important to ensure quality data and reliable and valid results. When interpreting the results of quantitative and qualitative research data, the researcher organizes the information based on the observable data. In order to study cause-and-effect relationships, the study must show **reliability** and **validity.**

**Reliability** refers to the degree that the results of the study are dependable and can be repeated. That means that if other researchers perform the exact same study, under the exact same conditions, the results should be consistent. To ensure validity, the results of the research must first be reliable over time. For a study to be valid, you should ask, "Does the study give consistent results over time?" For example, there are different versions of the AP PSYCH exam. If you were to take each version of the exam and receive the same score each time, then it can be said that the AP PSYCH exam is a reliable test.

**Validity** describes the strength of the results. Validity is the key when analyzing and interpreting the results of a study because without validity, the results would not be scientifically significant. To maximize validity, any confounding variables must be reduced. For example, does the study clearly represent what it said it would measure? For example, if you score a 5 on the AP PSYCH exam, but could not pass any college-based introductory psychology courses, the AP PSYCH exam would not have validity.

## Correlational Studies

**Correlational studies** help to find the relationship between behaviors, events, or characteristics. Many psychological theories make specific predictions about the relationship between two variables. In each case, the researcher uses correlational studies as a statistical technique to explore the degree of strength in the relationship between the two variables. It measures the statistical relationship (the correlation) to see if the variables are connected, or not connected. For example, a social psychologist researcher may predict a relationship between the number of extracurricular activities and a score on a self-esteem survey.

Note: Naturalistic observation and survey method are types of correlational research.

### Correlation vs. Causation

Correlational research is sometimes used as a preliminary way to gather information when a cause-effect experiment is not possible. Let's look at another example. What is the relationship (correlation) between people who receive a college degree and their economic status? Is it true that the longer a person stays in college, the greater the salary? Two variables can correlate without causation. Keep in mind that just because two variables correlate, it does not mean that there is a *causal relationship* (cause-and-effect relationship).

Although there may be a correlation between the number of years of college completed and income, it does not mean that more years of college will *cause* a person to make more money.

The three possible relationships are positive, negative, or no correlation.

- **Positive correlation** – if both variables increase together.
- **Negative correlation** – if one variable increases, but the other variable decreases.
- **No correlation** – if no correlation exists between the two variables.

When researchers study correlations, they use a statistical formula to represent the two variables, called a **correlation coefficient.** The correlation coefficient represents the direction and strength of the relationship between the two variables. It is written as a decimal and ranges from +1.00 (perfect positive relationship) to –1.00 (perfect negative relationship). When there is no relationship, the correlation coefficient is 0.00. If there is a strong positive relationship, the correlation coefficient gets close to but never exceeds +1.00. When there is a strong negative relationship, the correlation coefficient approaches –1.00. If there is a weak relationship, the correlation coefficient would be closer to 0.00. The farther away from zero, the stronger the relationship. For example, a negative correlation of –0.72 is stronger than a positive correlation of +0.59.

Researchers transfer the collected data on graphs called *scatter plots* to see if there is a relationship. The line that summarizes the relationship is called the *line of best fit.* The closer the points are to the line of best fit, the stronger the correlation.

## Positive Correlation

If the patterns of the points are positively correlated, a trend line can be plotted on the points. Points appear to be plotted upward. A relationship is positive if one variable increases in value as the other variable increases in value. In the scatter plot below, notice that with a positive trend, the values are rising from left to right.

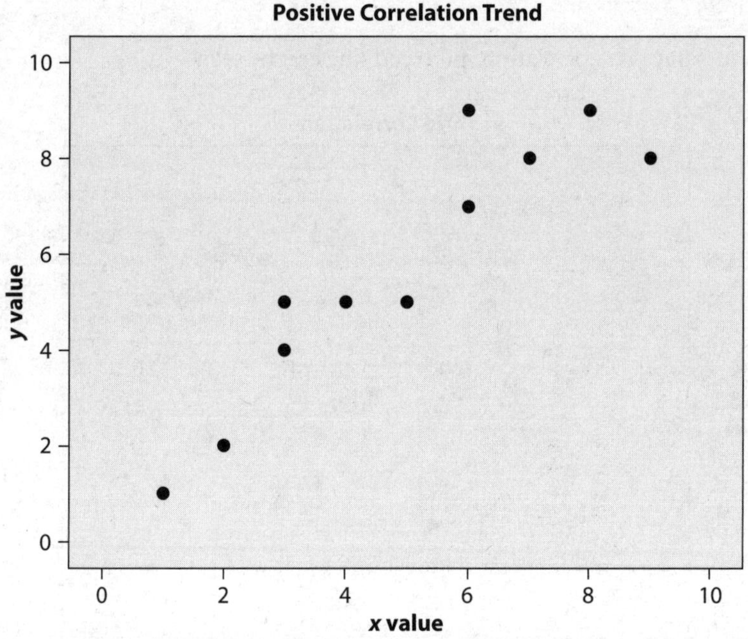

## Negative Correlation

If the patterns of the points are negatively correlated, a trend line can be plotted on the points. Points trend in a downward direction. A relationship is negative if one variable decreases in value as the other variable decreases in value. For example, there is a strong negative relationship between the number of hours spent playing video games and the number of hours spent doing homework. In the scatter plot below, notice that with a negative trend, the larger the *x* value, the smaller the *y* value, generally speaking.

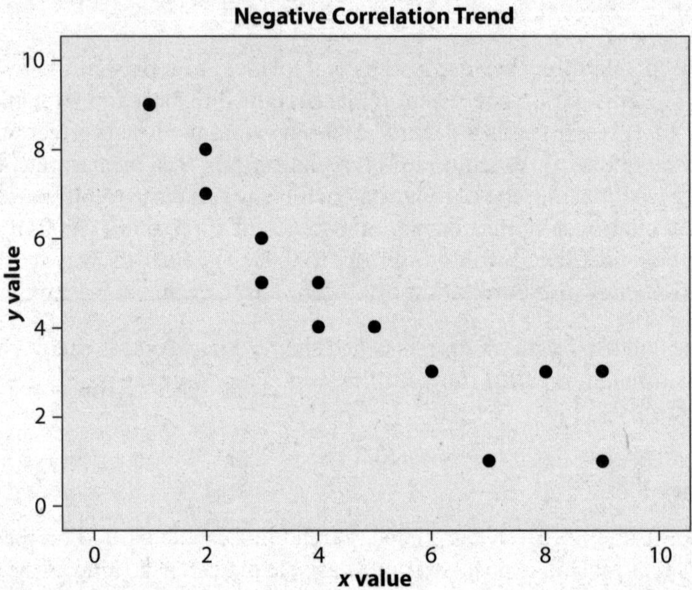


## No Correlation

If the patterns of the points have no correlation, no trend line can be seen.

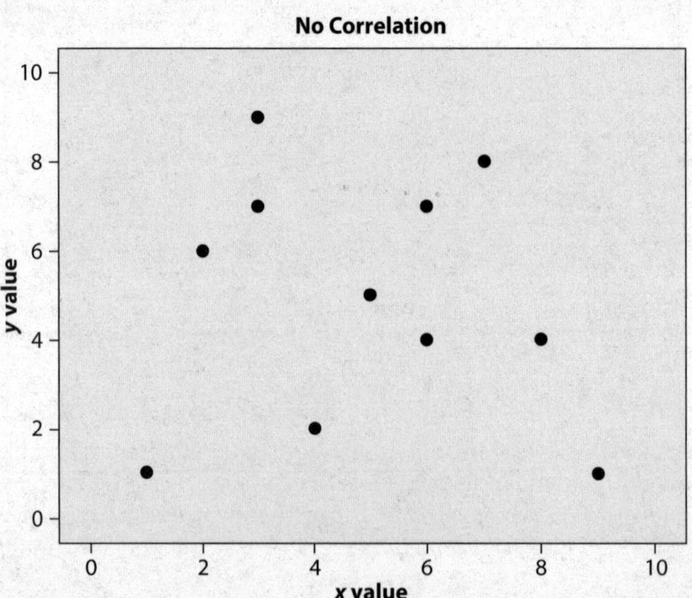

## Longitudinal Studies

A **longitudinal study** is when the researcher follows the same participant or same group (cohort) of participants for a long period of time. The researcher collects observations about the same variables at different ages of the person's life. For example, the researcher may interview the participant, give the participant a survey, or measure the dependent variable again at a later age. Longitudinal studies are especially beneficial when tracking the changes in development at different points in a person's life. The weakness of this type of study is that it is time-consuming, expensive, and some participants may drop out of the study.

## Cross-Sectional Studies

A **cross-sectional study** is when the researcher collects and compares participants or groups at a specific point in time (e.g., comparing variables such as the age at which a child's first words are spoken). It is a "snapshot" of their differences and similarities at a given point in time. Cross-sectional studies are useful to prove or disprove assumptions about characteristics at a specific period of time. For example, we can compare the differences in academic achievement between boys and girls during junior year. The weakness of cross-sectional studies is that the results do not determine cause and effect, the results may not be representative of the entire population being studied, and this type of study requires a larger sample population to be reliable.

# Statistics in Research

Statistics is a *method,* a way of working with numbers to answer puzzling questions and draw conclusions about both human and nonhuman phenomena. It describes numerical data and makes inferences about the data collected. Statistics is divided into two areas: descriptive statistics and inferential statistics.

The AP PSYCH exam looks beyond the step-by-step mathematical procedures and asks students to organize, describe, and analyze numerical data in graphs and charts. The exam draws on your understanding of the relationships of numbers so that you can make inferences and link the conclusions to real-world research methods.

| Compare and Contrast Statistics in Research | |
|---|---|
| **Descriptive Statistics** | **Inferential Statistics** |
| Describes the characteristics of a targeted sample population. | Makes generalizations about a population using inferences, estimates, and hypothesis testing from a targeted sample population. |
| Organizes and classifies information with numbers and graphs to draw conclusions about the sample population. | Compares, tests, and predicts the outcome. |
| Conclusions are presented in graphic tables, diagrams, and charts. | Conclusions are presented using probability scores. |
| Uses measures of central tendency (mean, median, and mode) and spread of range (range, standard deviation). | Uses hypothesis testing and analysis of variance. |

## Descriptive Statistics

**Descriptive statistics** is a method of organizing information with numbers and graphs to describe, categorize, and summarize data about the populations and phenomena being studied. Drawing conclusions from samples of a population helps to make general and specific statements about people, events, and situations. In this chapter, descriptive statistics is presented both graphically and numerically.

## Graphic Diagrams

One of the easiest ways to organize descriptive statistics is by using graphic diagrams. Diagrams help researchers analyze and compare statistical data. On the AP PSYCH exam, you may see a *frequency distribution table, bar graph, histogram,* or *scatter plot* (as seen above in correlational studies).

### *Frequency Distribution Table*

A **frequency distribution table** is used to organize data so that researchers can make sense of the entire range of scores. Generally, there is a column on the left (the data values) and a column on the right (the frequency), which indicates how many values are in the data set.

For example, a survey is taken in an English class at Kimberly High School to compare weather conditions to student absences. The class of 15 students was asked how many times they were absent during the snowy month of January. The results were recorded as follows: 1, 0, 4, 1, 1, 2, 0, 3, 4, 1, 6, 1, 2, 0, 1.

To organize the results, the teacher tallied and recorded the student responses using a frequency distribution table. Note: $x$ represents the number of days absent and $f$ represents their frequency.

| *x* | *f* |
|---|---|
| 0 | 3 |
| 1 | 6 |
| 2 | 2 |
| 3 | 1 |
| 4 | 2 |
| 5 | 0 |
| 6 | 1 |

### *Bar Graphs and Histograms*

Although frequency distribution tables are useful to gather and organize data, these tables do not provide you with a good visual picture of what the data actually mean. Researchers commonly transfer the information from a frequency distribution table to a **bar graph** or a **histogram.** While bar graphs and histograms may look similar, the AP PSYCH exam makes a clear distinction between the two. Bar graphs present categorical (also called *nominal*) information such as gender, age, or race. Histograms present numerical (also called *ordinal*) data such as percentages, scores, or quantities. Bar graphs are used to quickly compare frequencies, data, patterns, trends, and to draw conclusions. The bars (columns) can be either vertical or horizontal and can appear as single bars, a group of bars, or stacked bars. The bars should be labeled to indicate the differences between the variables.

Here are examples of a bar graph and histogram.

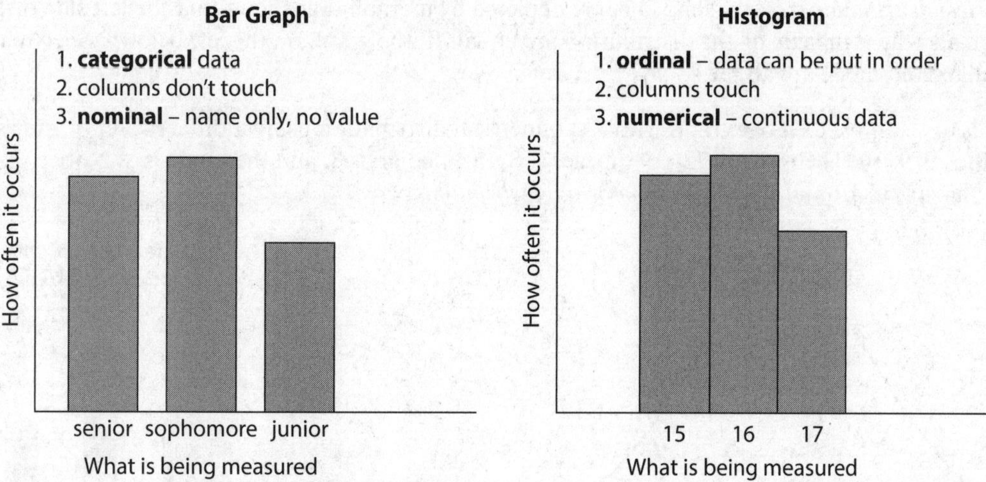


## Measuring and Interpreting Data

Before interpreting data, it must be measured and described.

### Measures of Central Tendency

A measure of central tendency explains how numbers tend to "bunch" around the middle of the data set. This tendency is sometimes called *regression to the mean.* It indicates the "center of a distribution." Any measure indicating a center of a distribution is called a **measure of central tendency.** The measures of central tendency are mean, median, mode, and range.

**Mean.** The *mean* is what is called the *average.* It is the most frequently used measure of central tendency. To determine the arithmetic mean, simply total the items and then divide by the number of items. For example, let's say that you earned 5, 5, 6, 6, 7, 8, 8, 8, 9, 10 on ten 10-point quizzes. The mean score is 72 ÷ 10 = 7.2 or 7 rounded off. Note: The mean is the only measure of central tendency that is affected by extreme scores.

**Median.** The *median* is the middle number of a group of numbers that is arranged in ascending or descending order (*if* there is an odd number of items in the set). If there is an even number of items in the set, their median is the arithmetic mean of the middle two numbers. The median is easy to calculate and is not influenced by extreme measurements. Let's use the same quiz results as an example: 5, 5, 6, 6, **7, 8,** 8, 8, 9, 10. Because there is an even number of quiz scores, you will need to add the two middle numbers and divide by 2: 7 + 8 = 15; 15 ÷ 2 = 7.5. The median is 7.5. (Note: Because the median is relatively unaffected by extreme scores, when measuring central tendency, it is best to use the mean because it is more stable when calculating extreme scores.)

**Mode.** The *mode* is the score that appears most often. In order to have a mode, there must be a repetition of a data value. Mode is not greatly influenced by extreme cases, but it is probably the least important or least used of the types of central tendency measures. Note: There can be more than one mode in a set. For example, using the same set of quizzes—5, 5, 6, 6, 7, **8, 8, 8,** 9, 10—the mode is 8 because that number appears most frequently.

### *Symmetrical Distribution*

A *symmetrical distribution* is a bell-shaped curve depicted by a graph that shows that the left side of the distribution and the right side of the distribution are equal. In the graph on the left below, notice that the mean, median, and mode are all the same.

Following is an example of a bar graph with a symmetrical distribution using a different set of quiz scores: 6, 7, 7, **8, 8,** 8, 9, 9, 10. The mean is 72 ÷ 9 quizzes = 8, the median is 8, and the mode is 8. Notice that the graph is symmetrical around the mean in a *normal distribution curve.*

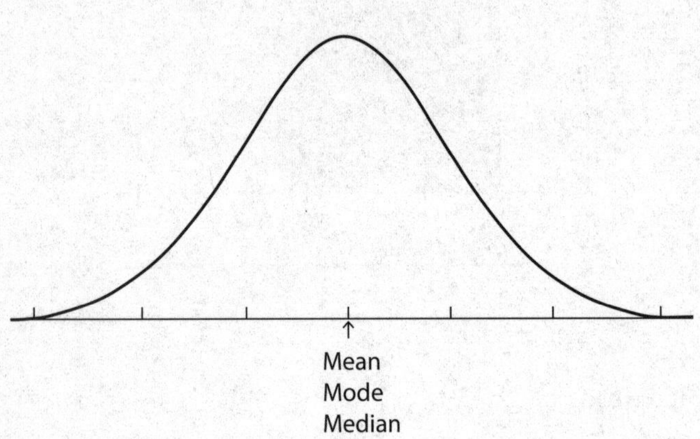


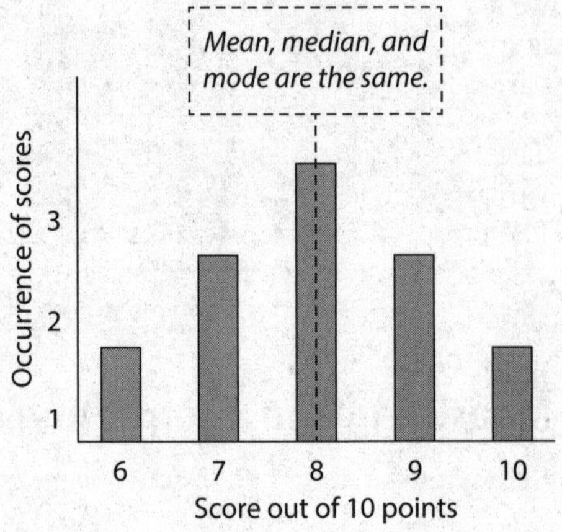


### *Skewed Distribution*

Now, let's say that the student was sick for a week and scored extremely low on the next quiz, receiving a score of 2 out of 10 possible points. Now the scores would be 2, 6, 7, 7, **8,** 8, 8, 9, 9, 10, making the mean 74÷ 10 = 7.4. Notice that the mode would still be 8, and the median would still be 8, but the mean would be 7.4. The student's grade would go from 80 percent to 74 percent, which in many schools is a drop from a B to a C.

When one or a few extreme scores cause the mean to shift negatively or positively, it is called an uneven or **skewed distribution.** The two types of skewed distributions are negative and positive. If the dotted line extends to the left of the cluster of scores, it is **negatively skewed** because one bad score decreases the mean. But let's say the student received extra credit on a quiz and received 4 bonus points, giving him a score of 14, making the scores 6, 7, 7, **8, 8,** 8, 9, 9 10, 14. The mode and median are still 8, but the mean is 86 ÷ 10 = 8.6. That extreme score of 14 would affect the mean, and the distribution would become **positively skewed.**

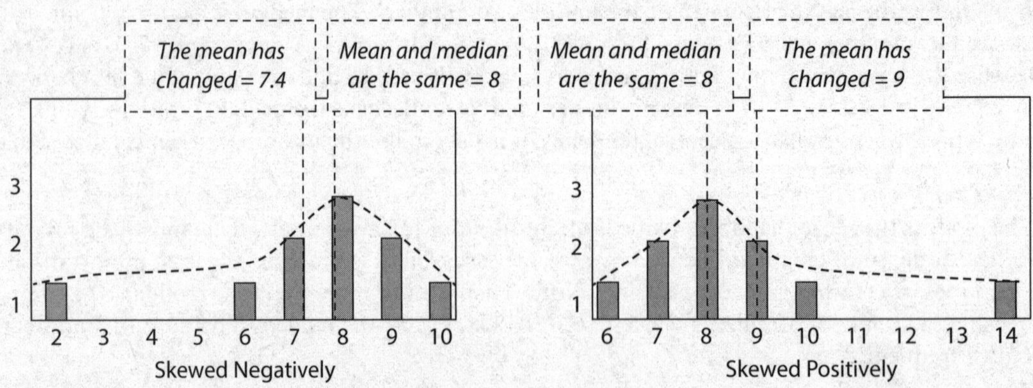

**TEST TIP: On the AP PSYCH exam, it's important to know that a small number of extreme scores will not affect the median or mode, but it will affect the mean.**

## *Statistical Variability*

**Variability** simply means how far apart or spread out numbers are from each other. If the set of scores is pretty close to each other, we say it has low variability. If a set of scores is spread out, then we say it has high variability.

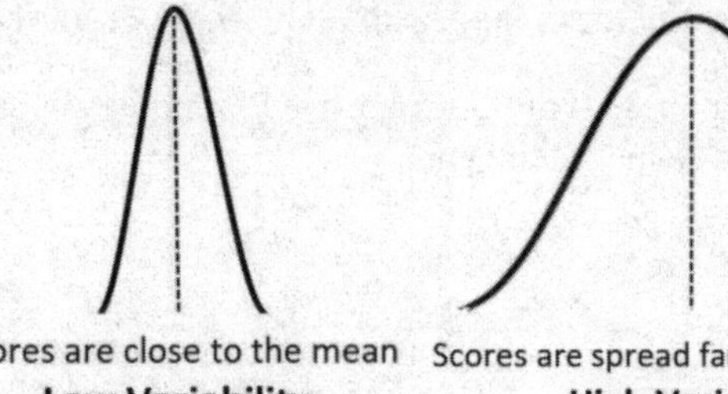

Scores are close to the mean
**Low Variability**

Scores are spread far from the mean
**High Variability**

The most common type of a measure of variability that you will see on the AP PSYCH exam is range. You have probably calculated the range of numbers many times in your life without knowing that you have calculated the statistical variability.

**Range.** The range for a set of data is the difference (or *variance*) between the largest and the smallest numbers in the set of data. To find the range, use this formula:

largest value – lowest value = range

For example, the range of the set of quiz scores 5, 5, 6, 6, 7, 8, 8, 8, 9, 10 is 5 because that is the difference between the highest value, 10, and the lowest value, 5.

The other concept related to variability is standard deviation.

## *Standard Deviation*

The **standard deviation** of a set of data is the measure how far data values of a population are from the mean or average value of the population. For example, instead of saying that the student quiz scores differ from each other, we say that they deviate from each other. Deviation does not happen randomly. There is almost always a pattern to how numbers deviate from each other, and the pattern of difference is called standard deviation.

- *Small standard deviation* indicates that the data values tend to be very close to the mean value (see the "Low Variability" graph above).
- *Large standard deviation* indicates that the data values are far from the mean value (see the "High Variability" graph above).

For example, two golfers have an average golf score of 90 for 18 holes played.

Golfer A is consistent, demonstrating a low variability, and a small standard deviation. Golfer A usually takes about 5 strokes to hit the ball in a hole. On some holes, she can hit the ball in the hole after only 4 strokes, and sometimes after 6 strokes.

Golfer B is inconsistent, demonstrating a high variability, and a large standard deviation. Golfer B sometimes takes 2 strokes to hit the ball in a hole, but other times takes 8 strokes.

The diagram that follows represents a set of data that has a *normal distribution.* This shape is also referred to as a **bell-shaped curve** or **normal distribution curve.** The standard deviation is the mean value of the set of data. Each vertical band has a width of one standard deviation. For normally distributed data, approximately 68% of all the data values within one standard deviation from the mean. You will find approximately 95.5% of all the data values within two standard deviations from the mean. At three standard deviations from the mean, approximately 99.8% of all the data values are found.

Note: See Chapter 8, "Unit 5: Cognitive Psychology," for another example of standard deviation and a normal bell curve in "intelligence."

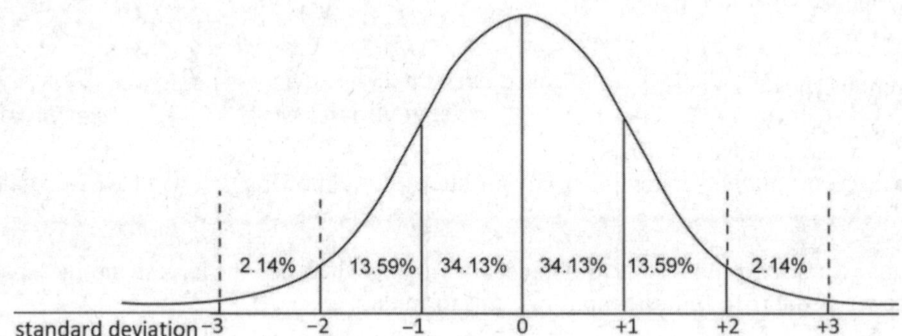


**TEST TIP: On the AP PSYCH exam, you will need to know the percentage of scores that fall within each standard deviation.**

## Inferential Statistics

**Inferential statistics** rests on a question: Can information gained from a small group sample be applied to infer information about a larger population? Because it is not possible to study everyone in a population, inferential statistics consists of techniques that allow researchers to study a smaller *representative sample* (whose characteristics must mirror the larger population) in order to make generalizations about a larger population.

### Statistical Significance

With the results, the researcher can make general statements and conclusions, but it depends on how much statistical confidence the researcher can place on those inferences. Researchers must use tests for *statistical significance* to approximate how often the experimental results could have happened by chance alone.

For example, let's look again at the hypothesis of giving caffeinated coffee to one group of participants and decaffeinated coffee (placebo) to another group of participants. The *alternative hypothesis* predicts that there will be a significant difference between the two groups. The *null hypothesis* predicts that there will not be a statistically significant difference. Statistical significance is the opposite of chance or accidental results due to confounding variables.

## Probability

**Probability** (or chance) is used to indicate the likelihood that a particular outcome will occur. It is represented by *p.* Thus, in research statistics we want the *p-value* to be as small as possible. If the *p*-value is less than 0.05, that means we are 0.95 or 95% certain that the difference was not due to chance. While no study is perfect, a 0.05 or 5% level of significance (or less) is often required as the minimum on all scientific studies to be considered statistically significant. These inferences are based on probability. A probability of 0.05 means that the experimental results would be expected to happen by chance no more than 5 times out of 100. Therefore, if the research has a *p*-value of less than 0.05, we can reject the null hypothesis and accept the alternative hypothesis. There will be a significant difference between the two groups (caffeinated and decaffeinated).

## Errors in Probability

Now, what if we are so excited (or heavily invested in a national coffee chain) that we mistakenly see a significant effect when one doesn't exist? It is called a false alarm, or **Type I error.**

| Inferential Statistics Hypothesis Testing | |
|---|---|
| **Type I error** | Type I errors are false alarms. The researcher concludes that the treatment does have an effect, when in reality there was no effect. The researcher notices that something occurred, when it didn't occur. For example, vaccines cause autism or chicken soup cures colds. |
| **Type II error** | Type II errors occur when the hypothesis test has failed to detect a real treatment effect. The researcher does not notice something significant that did happen. For example, Sildenafil was approved as a drug to help with heart problems, but was later removed when it was found to actually put extra strain on the heart. |

# Ethics in Research

While psychological research can be an exciting field, there are ethical obligations that researchers must follow in order to protect the rights of all study participants. The American Psychological Association (APA) has developed guidelines that govern the goals of scientific investigation for human and animal research.

To prevent unethical violations, like the Philip Zimbardo Stanford Prison experiments (1971) and the Stanley Milgram obedience studies (1963), psychologists must follow the APA Code of Ethics to "respect and protect civil and human rights." (Note: See Chapter 12, "Unit 9: Social Psychology," for a description of the Zimbardo and Milgram experiments.)

For any type of academic researcher, the researcher must first seek permission from an **institutional review board (IRB).** The researcher must submit a proposal to the IRB to review the research proposal and procedures to make sure that the study meets ethical guidelines.

For your reference, four of the APA research ethical standards are listed in the table that follows.

| Selected APA Research Ethical Standards | |
|---|---|
| **Informed consent** | Before the study, all participants must be given enough information for participants to make a well-reasoned decision about any potential harm or risk in the experiment. This helps prospective participants make a free and informed decision to participate, or not participate, in the study. However, by providing participants with information about the study, it might introduce a confounding variable, known as the *Hawthorne effect.* |
| **Fiduciary responsibility** | The researcher has a fiduciary (faithful) responsibility. This simply means that the researcher must be faithful to the good of the participants' physical and mental well-being. This takes priority over every other consideration. |
| **Right to decline** | Participants voluntarily take part in the research; there should be no coercion on the part of the experimenter. Participants also have the right to stop participation at any time during the study, for any reason. |
| **Confidentiality** | The researcher must take steps to protect information about the participants. Their identities must not be revealed. |
| **Debriefing** | Debriefing must occur after the study has concluded. It is when the researcher explains everything about the study and offers references for psychological support if needed. |

# Chapter Review Practice Questions

Practice questions are for instructional purposes only and may not reflect the format of the actual exam. The questions and explanations that follow focus on essential knowledge, course skills, and course content.

## Multiple-Choice Questions

1. Wilhelm Wundt studied the mind by developing which of the following psychological concepts?

   **A.** Stream of consciousness
   **B.** Nativism
   **C.** Tabula rasa
   **D.** Genotype
   **E.** Introspection

2. Which of the following approaches to psychology focuses on a person's unconscious thoughts?

   **A.** Psychodynamic
   **B.** Behavioral
   **C.** Social
   **D.** Cognitive
   **E.** Humanistic

3. Which of the following psychological terms most closely corresponds with the concept of "a false alarm"?

   **A.** Type I error
   **B.** Type II error
   **C.** Confounding variable
   **D.** Placebo effect
   **E.** Ordinal variable

4. Which of the following best explains when research participants have an equal chance of participating in either the control group or the experimental group?

   **A.** Random sample
   **B.** Representative sample
   **C.** Demographics
   **D.** Random assignment
   **E.** Sampling bias

5. Ms. Del Savio uses playing cards to place her research participants into groups. Those who draw black cards become part of the treatment group. Those who draw red cards become part of the placebo group. Which of the following best describes this research technique?

   **A.** Type I error
   **B.** Type II error
   **C.** Random assignment
   **D.** Ordinal variable
   **E.** Random sampling

6. Which of the following measures of central tendency is most affected by an extreme score?

   **A.** Median
   **B.** Mode
   **C.** Standard deviation
   **D.** Z-score
   **E.** Mean

7. A psychology teacher believes that warm-up activities will help her students score higher on unit tests. To test her hypothesis, the second-period psychology class is given a warm-up activity every day for one week, but the third-period psychology class is not given warm-up activities. The teacher then compares how the two classes performed on the unit test.

   In this scenario, which of the following research concepts best describes the warm-up activity?

   **A.** Independent variable
   **B.** Dependent variable
   **C.** Ordinal variable
   **D.** Correlation coefficient
   **E.** *p*-value

## Free-Response Question

**1 question**

**25 minutes**

**Directions:** It is suggested that you take a few minutes to plan and outline your essay. Write your response on lined paper. You must demonstrate your understanding of course skills and course content. Your essay is considered a first draft and may contain some grammatical errors that will not be counted against you. However, to receive full credit, your essay must demonstrate defensible content knowledge with substantive examples where appropriate.

---

Psychology research students posted a flyer on a males-only dormitory bulletin board at a coed college. The flyer offered a $5 gift card for students to participate in a research study that investigated headaches triggered by drinking frozen drinks.

- 37 males agreed to drink a 32-ounce cherry-flavored frozen drink from a straw in under 15 minutes.
- 37 males agreed to drink a 32-ounce orange juice at room temperature from a straw in under 15 minutes.

The researchers launched this study to settle a friendly wager. Researcher A believed that "brain freeze" wasn't a real phenomenon and that it only occurred in the presence of others. Researcher B believed that "brain freeze" was a real phenomenon. The participants were allowed to choose which group they would prefer based on their preference of the flavored drinks. After the 15-minute period, where both groups drank at the same time, participants were asked to compare their experiences with each other, inform the researchers if they experienced headaches, and report their experiences to the researchers.

The data was collected and analyzed: Of the participants who drank the frozen drink, 87 percent reported severe headaches, 13 percent reported no headache pain, and 0 participants reported mild headache pain.

**Part A**

Identify the following research concepts and how they might affect the validity of the study.

- Independent variable
- Placebo
- Demand characteristic
- Self-report bias
- Sampling bias

**Part B**

- Explain how a double-blind control could be applied to this study.
- Draw a bar graph representing a possible outcome of this study.

# Answers and Explanations

## Multiple-Choice Questions

1. **E.** *Introspection,* a form of self-examination that describes how personal observations are used to develop conscious thoughts, was developed by Wilhelm Wundt, choice E. It is often difficult to accomplish. For example, try to watch yourself read the next sentence. Are you *reading* or *watching* yourself read? It is difficult to do both at the same time. *Stream of consciousness* (choice A) was introduced by William James, who believed that thoughts are like a stream that is continuously flowing and changing. *Nativism* (choice B) describes the idea that people are born with hardwired abilities. It is a reference to Plato's belief that the mind is separate from the body. To help you remember this concept, think of nature vs. nurture. *Tabula rasa* (choice C) is translated as "blank slate," without preconceived ideas. It is a reference to Aristotle's theory of the psyche—that a young mind is pure. *Genotype* (choice D) is the genetic makeup (DNA sequence) of a cell that provides the genetic information about a person.

2. **A.** The *psychodynamic* approach in psychology is most concerned with unconscious processes, choice A. The *behavioral* approach (choice B) primarily focuses on symptoms (e.g., smoking, overeating). It does not necessarily focus on *why* someone smokes or overeats. The *social* approach (choice C) looks at *how* and *why* people do things in relation to other people. For example, a person might smoke or overeat to model other people. Do you know a high school student who works very hard to receive

good grades because he or she is modeling friends who might work hard? The *cognitive* approach (choice D) focuses on the role of thoughts that affect behavior. A cognitive therapist might ask a person who smokes or overeats to reflect on the first thoughts that occur when the craving begins. A *humanistic* approach (choice E) emphasizes the importance of a person's subjective experience of the world. Humanistic theory does not assume the client is ill, wrong, or needs to be fixed.

3. **A.** Errors in research design can occur when researchers find that the results of a study are statistically significant, but in reality, the results are not significant. *Type I error,* choice A, is also known as a "false alarm" error. Type I errors can occur when the researcher notices a change, but then realizes that there was no real effect in the variables. *Type II errors* (choice B) occur when there is a significant result, but the researcher fails to detect the effect of the treatment. In fact, many research findings have happened by accident. *Confounding variables* (choice C, also known as *lurking variables* or *research biases*) are unplanned factors that can lead to errors in research. Consider a study where a teacher gives her students caffeine to see if it helps them pay attention. In this situation, the confounding variable might be the amount of sleep a student got the night before. *Placebo effect* (choice D) is when the participants react to treatment because of their belief in the independent variable. For example, in the caffeine experiment, participants may react to the *belief* that the caffeine played a role in their increased attention. An *ordinal variable* (choice E) is any numeric variable that can be put in order, rank, or position in a series.

4. **A.** *Random sample* means that everyone in the population has an equal chance to be selected, choice A. *Representative sample* (choice B) is when the group of participants matches the ratio of demographics (e.g., gender, race, age) of the population from which it was chosen. *Demographics* (choice C) is a collection of data regarding a specific population group (e.g., age, wealth, education, geographic location). *Random assignment* (choice D) means once a researcher has selected participants, he or she will randomly assign the participants to an experimental group or a control group (placebo group). *Sampling bias* (choice E) happens when the sample population is selected for a study, but some participants are less likely to be included; the selections are not equal.

5. **C.** Random assignment, choice C, describes when a researcher uses a "chance" method to place participants into groups. This ensures that each participant has the same opportunity to randomly be placed into a group. A *Type I error* (choice A) occurs when the researcher believes something noteworthy has happened in the research results, but it is a false alarm. A *Type II error* (choice B) occurs when the researcher doesn't notice something noteworthy has resulted. *Ordinal variables* (choice D) are variables that can be ranked in order (e.g., height, weight, or SAT scores). *Random sampling* (choice E) is how a researcher randomly identifies and selects "representative" participants from the large population "prior to" the study. In this technique, participants can be "generalized" to the population.

6. **E.** The *mean,* choice E, is most affected by an extreme score. The mean is what most people think of as the *average.* It is how most grades are determined in school. When a student earns a set of scores, those scores are added and then divided by the number of scores to determine the average. For example, if a student scores 90%, 85%, and 95% on exams, the mean is 90%. However, if the student had a bad day and earned 10% on an exam, that one extreme score would change the mean to 67.5%. The *median* (choice A) is the middle number in a group of numbers. The *mode* (choice B) is the most frequent number in a group of numbers. *Standard deviation* (choice C) is the average difference of most scores from the mean. If most scores are clumped around the mean, the standard deviation is small. *Z-scores* (choice D) are the number of standard deviations away from the mean a score is. For example, the mean IQ score is 100. The standard deviation is 15. If a person has an IQ score of 130, that score of 130 would have a *z-score* of 2 because it is two standard deviations of 15 above the mean of 100.

7. **A.** *Independent variables* are what the researcher is studying. Think of independent variables as action verbs. In this case, the independent variable is the warm-up activity, choice A. A *dependent variable* (choice B) is what happens as a result of the independent variable. In this case, the dependent variable is how the students performed on the test. *Ordinal variables* (choice C) are variables that are numerically based and can be ranked in order. A *correlation coefficient* (choice D) represents the direction and strength of the relationship of two variables. It is a number between –1 and 1 that represents how closely two things relate to each other. For example, dark skies and nighttime are strongly correlated and probably have a correlation coefficient near, but slightly less than 1, because in rare cases it is light outside during night. A *p-value* (choice E) is a number that represents how much uncertainty there is in the results of a study. Studies with a $p$-value of less than 0.05 have less than 5% uncertainty, which means there is 95% confidence in the results.

## Free-Response Question

To achieve the maximum score of 7, your response must address each of the bullet points in the question.

### Sample Student Response

The *independent variable* is what an experimenter gives or applies to the participants. In this case, the independent variable is the type of drink, either frozen or not frozen. The *placebo* in this situation is the room-temperature drink. *Demand characteristic* is a concept when a research participant knows he is in a study and acts according to the perceived goals of the study. Because the participants knew what was being studied, they might have exaggerated their reports or the severity of their headaches. Some participants may have been able to cause their headaches by drinking the frozen drinks too fast.

*Self-report bias* is the idea that people are not accurate observers or analyzers of their own perceptions. This study may have had a self-report bias because the participants may not have been able to objectively notice, perceive, or describe their subjective experiences (e.g., pain) accurately.

A *sampling bias* applies to this study because only college-age males were recruited for the study. Females in the student population did not have an equal chance of being chosen for this study.

A *double-blind* procedure is when a researcher does not know anything about the participants and the participants do not know anything about the study. The chance of experimenters' bias is reduced in double-blind studies. This could have been a double-blind study if Researcher A had distributed the different drinks to the participants, and Researcher B had recorded the information from the participants. However, in this study participants were aware of the study and were allowed to select their preferred drink.

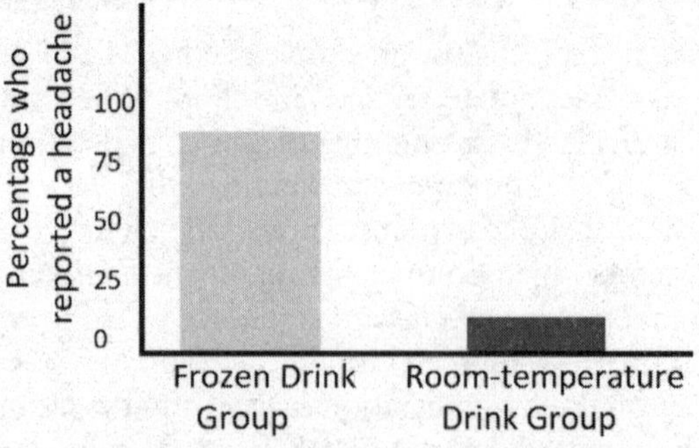

# Chapter 5

# Unit 2: Biological Bases of Behavior

AP Psychology Unit 2 explores how the biological structures of the brain are linked to all mental processes and human behaviors. The biological system operates and communicates to the brain to create thoughts, ideas, sensations, emotions, decisions, and behaviors.

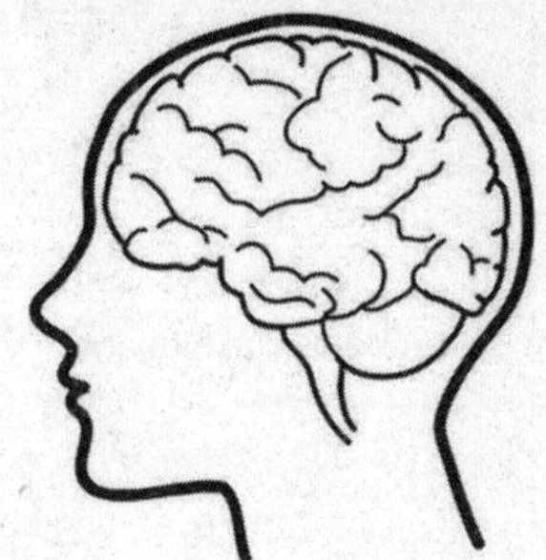

- Introduction to the Biological Bases of Human Behavior
- Key Contributors to the Biological Bases of Behavior
- The Endocrine System
- The Nervous System
- Genetics
- The Brain
- The Limbic System
- Consciousness
- Sleep and Dreams
- Drugs and Consciousness

## Overview of AP Psychology Unit 2

The overarching concepts for this chapter address neural communication, the brain, the nervous system, the endocrine system, genetic contributions to behavior, and consciousness. **The topics discussed in this unit will count toward 8–10 percent of your multiple-choice score.**

## AP Psychology Framework

Success on the exam depends on your ability to make connections to the major concepts described in the content topics of the *Course Framework for AP Psychology.* Remember that these concepts highlight the fundamental ideas that every student should take with them into the AP PSYCH exam and beyond.

Use the table below to guide you through what is covered in this unit. The information contained in this table is an abridged version of the content outlines with topic examples. Visit https://apstudent.collegeboard.org/apcourse/ap-psychology/ for the complete updated AP PSYCH course curriculum framework.

| AP Psychology—Unit 2: Biological Bases of Behavior | |
|---|---|
| **Topic** | **Learning Target** |
| **Interaction of Heredity and Environment** | ■ Discuss psychology's abiding interest in how heredity, environment, and evolution work together to shape behavior.<br>■ Identify key research contributions of scientists in the areas of heredity and environment (e.g., Darwin).<br>■ Predict how traits and behavior can be selected for their adaptive value. |
| **The Endocrine System** | ■ Discuss the effect of the endocrine system on behavior. |
| **Overview of the Nervous System and the Neuron** | ■ Describe the nervous system and its subdivisions and functions (e.g., central and peripheral nervous systems).<br>■ Identify basic processes and systems in the biological bases of behavior, including parts of a neuron. |
| **Neural Firing** | ■ Identify the basic process of transmission of a signal between neurons. |
| **Influence of Drugs on Neural Firing** | ■ Discuss the influence of drugs on neurotransmitters (e.g., reuptake mechanisms, agonists, antagonists). |
| **The Brain** | ■ Describe the nervous system and its subdivisions and functions in the brain (e.g., major brain regions, lobes, cortical areas, and brain lateralization and hemispheric specialization).<br>■ Identify the contributions of key researchers to the study of the brain (e.g., Broca and Wernicke). |
| **Tools for Examining Brain Structure** | ■ Recount historic and contemporary research strategies and technologies that support research (case studies, split-brain research, imaging techniques, lesioning, and autopsy).<br>■ Identify the contributions of key researchers to the development of tools for examining the brain (e.g., Sperry). |
| **The Adaptable Brain** | ■ Discuss the role of neuroplasticity in traumatic brain injury.<br>■ Identify the contributions of key researchers to the study of neuroplasticity (e.g., Gazzaniga).<br>■ Describe the various states of consciousness and their impact on behavior.<br>■ Identify the major psychoactive drug categories and classify specific drugs, including their psychological and physiological effects (e.g., depressants, stimulants, and hallucinogens).<br>■ Discuss drug dependence, addiction, tolerance, and withdrawal.<br>■ Identify the contributions of major figures in consciousness research (e.g., James and Freud). |
| **Sleeping and Dreaming** | ■ Discuss aspects of sleep and dreaming (e.g., neural and behavioral characteristics of the stages of the sleep cycle, theories of sleep and dreaming, and symptoms and treatments of sleep disorders). |

## Important Terms and Concepts Checklist

This section is an overview of the important terms, concepts, language, and theories that specifically target the key topics of Unit 2. Use this list of terms as a checklist to check your personal progress. As you study the topics, place a check mark next to each and return to this list as often as necessary to refresh your understanding.

After you finish the review section, you can reinforce what you have learned by working through the practice questions at the end of the chapter. Answers and explanations provide further clarification into perspectives of the biological bases of behavior.

| Term/Concept | Study Page | Term/Concept | Study Page | Term/Concept | Study Page |
|---|---|---|---|---|---|
| **acetylcholine (ACH)** | p. 63 | **dendrites** | p. 57 | **nervous system** | p. 55 |
| **action potential** | p. 60 | **dopamine** | p. 63 | **neural firing** | p. 61 |
| **activation-synthesis theory** | p. 79 | **EEG (electroencephalogram)** | p. 73 | **neurons** | p. 57 |
| **afferent signals** | p. 56 | **efferent signals** | p. 56 | **neuroplasticity** | p. 73 |
| **agonists and antagonists** | pp. 79–80 | **endocrine system** | p. 54 | **neurotransmitters** | pp. 59, 62–63 |
| **all-or-none principle** | p. 60 | **endorphins** | p. 63 | **norepinephrine** | p. 63 |
| **amygdala** | p. 71 | **excitatory (and inhibitory) neurotransmitters** | p. 62 | **parasympathetic nervous system** | p. 55 |
| **autonomic nervous system (ANS)** | p. 71 | **forebrain** | pp. 70–71 | **peripheral nervous system** | p. 55 |
| **axon** | p. 57 | **genetics** | p. 64 | **PET scan (positron emission tomography)** | p. 72 |
| **Broca's area** | pp. 53, 68 | **hindbrain** | p. 69 | **polygenic** | p. 52 |
| **CAT scan (computerized axial tomography)** | p. 72 | **hippocampus** | p. 71 | **pons** | p. 69 |
| **cell body** | p. 57 | **hypothalamus** | p. 71 | **reticular formation** | p. 70 |
| **central nervous system** | p. 55 | **limbic system** | pp. 71–72 | **reuptake** | p. 61 |
| **cerebellum** | p. 69 | **lobes (parietal, frontal, occipital, temporal)** | pp. 67–68 | **serotonin** | p. 63 |
| **cerebral cortex** | p. 67 | **long-term potentiation** | p. 60 | **sympathetic nervous system** | p. 55 |
| **cerebral hemispheres (left and right)** | pp. 66–67 | **medulla** | p. 69 | **synapse** | pp. 59–60 |
| **circadian rhythms** | p. 75 | **midbrain** | p. 70 | **terminal buttons** | pp. 57, 60 |
| **consciousness** | pp. 74–75 | **MRI (magnetic resonance imagining)** | p. 72 | **thalamus** | p. 71 |
| **corpus callosum** | p. 66 | **myelin sheath** | p. 57 | **Wernicke's area** | pp. 53, 68 |

# Chapter Review

The chapter review focuses on the biological underpinnings of psychology and human behavior. It may come as a surprise to study biology in a psychology course, but all of the topics covered in psychology are connected to biological influences. For an eye to see or for a brain to produce thoughts, there must be a cellular link between the brain and the body. The main biological topics that may appear on the AP PSYCH exam are neural processing, brain structures, and hormonal characteristics.

## Heads Up: What You Need to Know

For the AP PSYCH exam, ask yourself these three important questions as you continue to work through the topics in this chapter and develop an understanding of the biological perspectives of the brain: How can biology influence our behavior and mental processes? What happens when a particular neurotransmitter is absent from the body? and How do biological and environmental factors interact to influence our behaviors and mental processes?

# Introduction to the Biological Bases of Human Behavior

This chapter will study the *psychobiology* of human behavior (the study of the function of the brain in relationship to emotions, cognition, and the nervous system). Billions of cells in the human brain are inextricably interconnected to human behavior and have far-reaching effects on the psychological and physical mechanisms that encode, influence, and activate emotions, sensations, and mental processes. Human behavior is not only influenced by the biological structures of the brain, but also by evolutionary adaptive traits, heredity, and the environment.

Before we begin our discussion about the biological structures of the brain, let's start at the beginning and review some of the basic facts about evolution, heredity, and the environment.

## Key Facts about Evolution, Heredity, and the Environment

**Evolution.** The evolutionary approach to psychology identifies how humans have evolved and adapted from one generation to another over time. Evolution is based on Charles Darwin's landmark theory of *natural selection* published in *On the Origin of Species* (1859). Darwin studied the hereditary traits of finches in the Galapagos Islands and discovered that the average size of their beaks, bodies, and feeding behaviors adapted over time due to the environmental necessity of eating different food sources on the islands. The key claim to the Darwinian psychobiological approach is that the human brain continues to adapt over time for genetic and hereditary survival. This theory explains cognitive and behavioral changes in humans. For example, early humans pointed and grunted to communicate, but modern man has evolved over time and now communicates using a fairly sophisticated language system.

**Heredity.** Have you ever noticed that you have some of the same behavioral traits as a parent, grandparent, brother, sister, aunt, or uncle? It is likely that you have genetically inherited these adaptive traits from your family members. The psychological study of heredity identifies *specific genes* (encoded and inherited through DNA) that influence distinctive characteristics, called *traits,* of human behavior. Traits are the prevailing patterns of temperament, behavior, and emotion that can sway personality. They are the leading attributes of a person and have a tendency to remain the same throughout a lifetime. In researching hereditary traits, it is common for scientists to study fraternal and identical twins because the results are more reliable in comparing inherited vs. environmental factors that determine traits. For example, scientists have found that handedness, certain behaviors, mental disorders, learning disabilities, and substance abuse have a strong correlation to genetic inheritance. When traits arise from many genes, they are called **polygenic** (also see "Genetics," p. 64).

**Environment.** Are behavior, traits, and personality shaped by genetic inheritance or by environmental influences? The debate of genetic inheritability vs. learned influences, known as *nature vs. nurture,* is one of the oldest arguments in the history of psychology. Some scientists argue that certain behaviors are inborn (nature), while others argue that certain behaviors are learned experiences from the environment—family, society, geography, and culture (nurture). Researchers on both sides of the argument agree that neither nature nor nurture has a cause-and-effect relationship with behavior. While heredity may genetically influence the likelihood of a particular behavior, it may not be the *only* cause of that particular behavior. Studies have also shown that certain behavioral traits can only be expressed in a particular environment where nature and nurture must interconnect. For example, the "organism-environment interaction" is activated during the unique relationship of a mother's external interaction with her child's internal genetic predisposition. Hence, the child develops particular behavioral traits based on genetics and environmental influences of the mother.

## Key Contributors to the Biological Bases of Behavior

On the AP PSYCH exam, you should be able to identify the major research contributors in the field of psychobiology.

| Key Contributors to the Biological Bases of Behavior | | |
|---|---|---|
| **Contributor** | **Field of Study (Theory)** | **Famous For** |
| **Paul Broca** (1824–1880) | Left frontal lobe of the brain, "Broca aphasia" | Broca is best known for his research of a region of the frontal lobe, known as Broca's area. Broca's discovery was the first proof that a localized area is related to brain function. His research revealed that damage to the area could result in a speech disorder known as Broca aphasia (partial loss of language expression). |
| **Charles Darwin** (1809–1882) | Darwin's theory of evolution | Darwin's evolutionary approach is based on his landmark theory of natural selection (as a result of a living organism's interaction with an environment, superior inherited traits adapt to survive if the environment favors the inherited traits). Darwin explained that the driving force of humankind's existence is centered in the concept of "survival of the fittest." |
| **Michael Gazzaniga** (1939–) | Split-brain research | Gazzaniga led studies in learning split-brain cognitive functions. Gazzaniga and Roger Sperry studied the effects of split-brain surgery on perception, vision, and other brain functions; and how each hemisphere communicates with the other. After the surgery, participants were largely unaffected. In fact, some patients developed the ability to concentrate on two things at once (e.g., drawing two different shapes simultaneously). |
| **Roger Sperry** (1913–1994) | Split-brain research | Sperry discovered that the human brain is made up of two hemispheres that can consciously, and simultaneously, function independently. He was awarded a Nobel Prize for his research in the discovery of lateralization of brain functioning. His studies led to the medical discovery of continued normal brain functioning even when the corpus callosum is cut to reduce the number of seizures in patients. |
| **Carl Wernicke** (1848–1905) | Left temporal lobe of the brain, "Wernicke aphasia" | Wernicke related motor neuron damage to the left temporal lobe to a specific region of the brain. Known as Wernicke aphasia, damage may result in a language disorder. The person can speak fluently, but the words he or she says often make no sense and are often made-up words. |

# The Endocrine System

The brain is not the only structure in the body that can affect our thoughts, feelings, and motivations. The **endocrine system** is comprised of ductless glands that manufacture and release chemical messengers, called *hormones,* to regulate parts of the body.

**Why are hormones important to psychologists?** Hormones help the body maintain steady psychological and emotional states by balancing chemical and blood sugar levels. Hormones help the body's chemistry function and are responsible for many tasks such as breaking down food, managing stress, balancing emotions and mood (which affect behavior), balancing temperature, and sexual development. One of the reasons that your body changed during puberty was because hormones were at work sending chemical messengers to parts of your body.

**How do hormones alter mood and behavior?** The body has two types of glands: glands with ducts and glands without ducts. A duct is a passageway that carries substances to different parts of the body (e.g., saliva, sweat, tears, and breast milk). Hormones travel to their target tissue through ducts. Ductless glands can secrete hormones (that excite) into the bloodstream, and these hormones circulate throughout the body in the endocrine system, causing hormonal imbalances and behavioral changes.

The table that follows shows why the endocrine system can alter behavior. As you review the table, keep in mind that it is often tempting to think that only one hormone is responsible for a particular behavior. However, the mind-body connection is complex, and there are multiple explanations for shifts in one's behavior, mood, and desire.

**The Endocrine System**

| Gland | Function | Hormones |
|---|---|---|
| **Pituitary gland** | The pituitary gland is the "master" gland of the endocrine system that controls other glands by releasing (or inhibiting) hormones as needed to other parts of the body. It sits at the base of the brain near the hypothalamus. | Oxytocin—the trust, cuddle, or love hormone<br><br>Vasopressin—helps the brain manage social responsiveness |
| **Thyroid gland** | The thyroid gland controls a body's metabolism, energy, and protein synthesis. It sits at the base of the neck. | Thyroxine and triiodothyronine—control metabolism rate<br><br>Calcitonin—inhibits the release of calcium from the bones |
| **Adrenal glands** | Adrenal glands produce a variety of hormones, including adrenaline and cortisol. The glands are responsible for helping your body prepare for stress. When the sympathetic nervous system is triggered, an emergency "fight-or-flight" response is activated. These glands sit at the top of the kidneys. | Adrenaline (epinephrine)—the alert hormone that causes the body to respond to sudden stress<br><br>Cortisol—the hormone released in response to stress and levels of low blood sugar |
| **Gonads** | Gonads are sex glands that make reproduction possible. Males have testes and females have ovaries. Both testes and ovaries produce androgen and estrogen in different ratios. | Androgen (testosterone)—male hormone involved in energy, aggression, and sexual desire<br><br>Estrogen—female hormone related to energy and sexual desire<br><br>Melatonin—the sleep cycle hormone |

# The Nervous System

The Nervous System

Brain
Spinal Cord
Central Nervous System
Nerves
Peripheral Nervous System

Although the shapes and sizes of the human brain can vary, modern neuroscientists have been able to conclude that specific regions of the brain are linked to particular human behaviors. All human thoughts, feelings, and actions can be traced to electrical impulses within the neural network branches of the brain and body called the *nervous system.*

The human body has billions of networking cells called **neurons** (nerve cells) that communicate to the brain through the body's intricate nervous system. Neurons are the foundation of the nervous system. The nervous system is complex and manages the body's response to external stimuli. It is divided into two parts: the **central nervous system** (CNS) and the **peripheral nervous system** (PNS). The CNS is the command center and the PNS is an intricate network of nerves that connects the body to the CNS. The PNS contains the **autonomic** and **somatic** nervous systems. The autonomic nervous system is divided into a **sympathetic** branch and a **parasympathetic** branch. The sympathetic response reflects the body's reactions to stress (e.g., increased heart rate). The parasympathetic response reflects the body's reaction to relaxation (e.g., slower heart rate).

**TEST TIP: To help you remember the sympathetic and parasympathetic nervous systems, remember that *stress* begins with *s* (like the *s* in sympathetic) and relaxation begins with *r* (like the *r* in parasympathetic).**

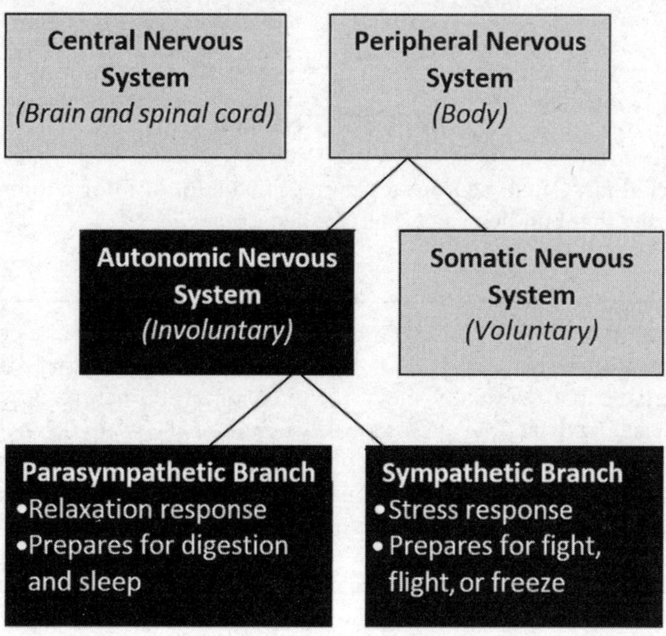

## Neural Signals

Think of the nervous system as a hive of bees. Individually, each bee is simple and expendable, just like a single neuron. Taken together with their complex communication system, bees can sustain entire food chains. In humans, the communication system functions with efferent and afferent impulse signals.

**Efferent signals.** The bees that *exit* the hive are like the efferent signals that *exit* the brain from the central nervous system (CNS) and go the peripheral nervous system (PNS). Efferent neurons send signals to the body's *motor* functions so the body will move. For example, if efferent signals are damaged due to a spinal cord injury, the brain may not be able to communicate to muscles, preventing body limbs from moving.

**Afferent signals.** When a bee returns to the hive, it is like an afferent signal *arriving* at the brain from the PNS. Afferent neurons send *sensory* signals from parts of the body (eyes, ears, nose, mouth, and skin) to the CNS's brain or spinal cord. For example, afferent signals take in sensory information (i.e., sight, touch, smell) and give the brain information about the external environment.

**TEST TIP: On the AP PSYCH exam, remember the letter "e" for efferent neurons exiting the brain and the letter "a" for afferent neurons arriving at the brain.**

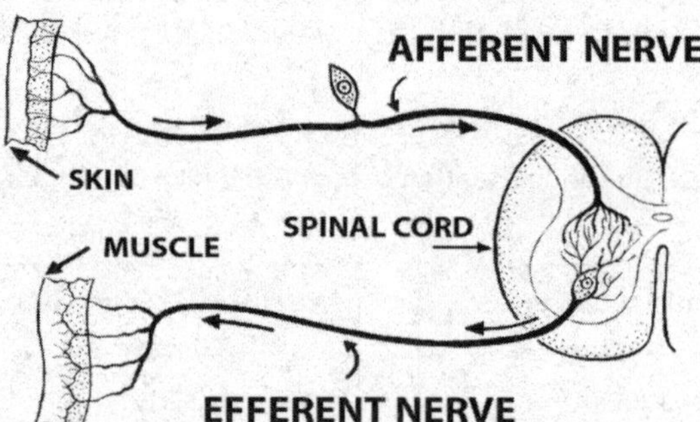


Each neuron does not act alone. Often, neurons team up so that a lot of information can be processed quickly and simultaneously; that bundle of neurons is called a *ganglion.*

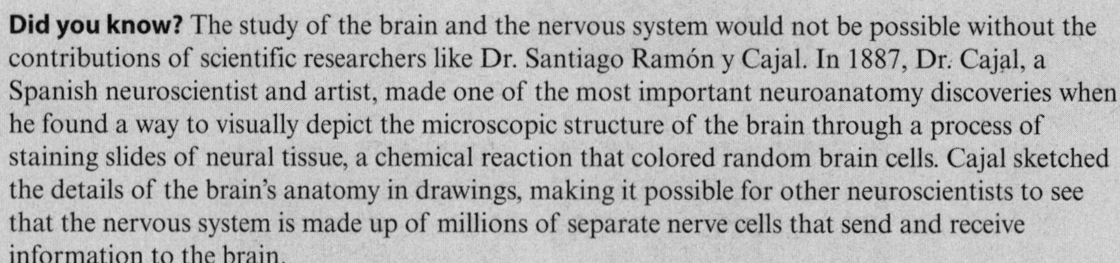

**Did you know?** The study of the brain and the nervous system would not be possible without the contributions of scientific researchers like Dr. Santiago Ramón y Cajal. In 1887, Dr. Cajal, a Spanish neuroscientist and artist, made one of the most important neuroanatomy discoveries when he found a way to visually depict the microscopic structure of the brain through a process of staining slides of neural tissue, a chemical reaction that colored random brain cells. Cajal sketched the details of the brain's anatomy in drawings, making it possible for other neuroscientists to see that the nervous system is made up of millions of separate nerve cells that send and receive information to the brain.

## Neurons

Neurons make up a remarkable forest of a billion nerve cells. Neurons consist of a cell body, dendrites, and an axon.

- **Cell body (soma).** The cell body is the central part (*nucleus*) of the neuron.
- **Dendrites.** Dendrites are the treelike branches extending from the cell body that receive messages from other cells. They are the starting point of neural activity. For example, dendrites transmit information when your eyes adjust to light after you turn on a lamp in the room or when you feel someone touch your arm with light pressure.
- **Axon.** The axon is a long nerve fiber that transmits neural impulses from the cell body to other nerve cells, muscles, or glands. It is the middle point of neural transmission. The axon is covered by a fatty substance called *myelin* or the *myelin sheath*. Myelin allows for the signal to move down the axon at greater speeds and insulates the cell from other neurons. *Myelination* is the process of coating the axon with myelin and is an important process in the development of fetuses and babies.
- **Axon terminal** (also called *end bulbs* or *terminal buttons*) are the end points of activity for a neuron. They are where the neural signal leaves one cell in the form of neurotransmitters to travel to another cell's dendrites.

**Parts of a Neuron**

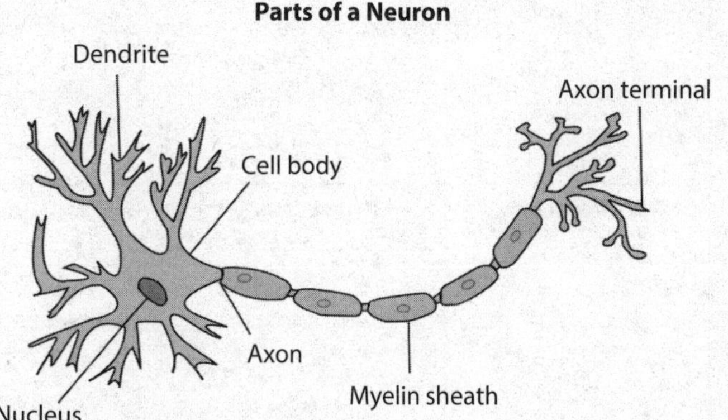


### Types of Neurons

The table that follows shows the common types of neurons that may appear on the AP PSYCH exam.

| Types of Neurons | | |
|---|---|---|
| **Term** | **Definition** | **Examples** |
| **Sensory neurons** | Sensory neurons are responsible for collecting sensory perceptions in the environment (from the eyes, ears, nose, mouth, and skin) to the brain. These neurons convert external stimuli into internal impulses, starting the process of sending afferent signals to the brain. | In Chapter 6, "Unit 3: Sensation and Perception," we will discuss the many types of sensory neurons, but two examples that you should be familiar with in this unit are nociceptors and proprioceptors.<br><br>Nociceptors are pain receptors. A nociceptor is a type of sensory neuron that starts the process of feeling pain by sending a signal to the brain to communicate a possible threat. Proprioceptors are sensory receptors that detect your body's movement and position. Proprioceptors tell your brain where your arms and legs are and what they are doing in relation to the surrounding environment. |

*Continued*

| Term | Definition | Examples |
|---|---|---|
| **Motor neurons** | Motor neurons control the contraction or relaxation of muscles and are the last stop of an efferent signal. | The human body has motor neurons that extend from toes to hips, but most of these neurons are microscopic. For these tiny neurons to receive a signal, the signal must be passed along by countless other neurons. Those countless other neurons are called interneurons (neurons that transmit impulses between the source and the destination). Note: In some cases, the source of one signal might end up being an interneuron for another signal. |
| **Mirror neurons** | Mirror neurons fire when watching certain movements of other people. These neurons may play an essential role in understanding why humans imitate one another. | For example, when playing tennis, if your opponent moves his or her body in a certain direction, mirror neurons are activated to estimate your opponent's intentions. In another example, researchers have theorized that mirror neurons are activated when a person empathizes with (shares the feelings of) another person. |
| **Feature detectors** | Feature detectors are neurons that sort and respond to very specific stimuli with specific individual features. | Examples of feature detectors include mirror responses to specific movements and shapes. For example, feature detector neurons might be stimulated by a single vertical line, but may not be activated by the capital letter "I." Although the two are very similar, the capital letter "I" has specific features (e.g., header, footer), rather than the simple stimulus of a straight line. |

## Heads Up: What You Need to Know

On the AP PSYCH exam, you should know the difference between neurons and glial cells. *Glial cells* are nerve cells, but they don't carry nerve impulses like neurons do. Neurons send and receive electrical and chemical signals to and from the brain, but glial cells do not. It's important to note that neurons would not be able to function without glial cells, but both glial cells and neurons can receive and send neurotransmitters and hormones to other glial cells, other neurons, and to glands throughout the body. Glial cells play an important role in communicating, supporting, nourishing, and protecting neurons. Glial cells have multiple forms that have different functions. For example, the *astrocyte cell* provides nutrients to the neurons and maintains the cell environment. The *oligodendrocyte cell* protects the neurons by creating myelin sheaths around the axons. The *microglia cell* scavenges pathogens and removes dead cell waste.

## Overview of the Nervous System

The chart below will distinguish between important nervous system terms.

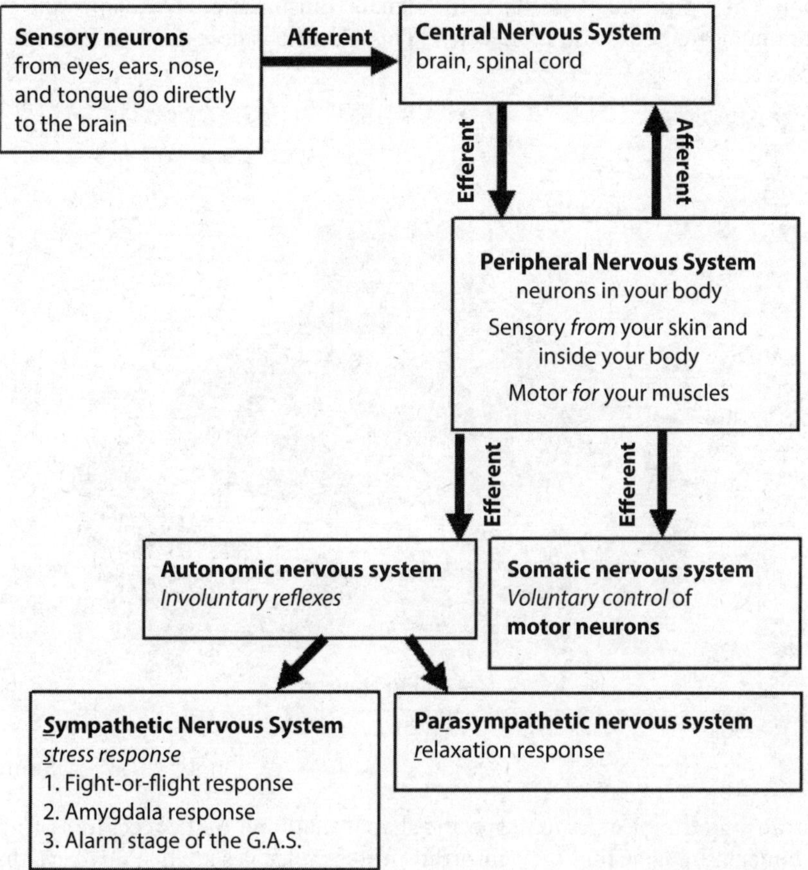


## Neurotransmission

### Key Facts about Neurotransmission

**Neurotransmitters.** A neuron's main job is to communicate. It can literally send hundreds of messages in 1 second using chemicals called neurotransmitters (chemical messengers that are stored in tiny bubbles called *vesicles* and released to carry signals to other cells in the body). Neural signals are transmitted from one end of a neuron to another through dendrites (the bushy antenna), but neuron cells never touch each other. The space between the neurons is called a *synapse.*

**Synapse (aka synaptic gap, synaptic cleft, synaptic chasm).** A synapse is the space between neurons (the axon of the sending neuron and dendrites of the receiving neuron). Neurons pass neurotransmitter molecules back and forth to cross the synapse, resulting in neurotransmission.

The neuron that sends chemicals across the synapse is called the *presynaptic* cell, and the neuron that receives the chemical is called the *postsynaptic* cell. It is important to note that a neuron cannot "sort of" send a signal or "sort of" create an electrical action potential. It is either activated 100 percent, or not at all; this is called the *all-or-none principle.*

**Long-term potentiation** is a long-lasting improvement in signal transmission between two neurons (synapses) based on the response of a postsynaptic cell. As the signals transmit more frequently, the synapse gets smaller so they communicate better and more often. This increase is necessary for learning and memory formation.

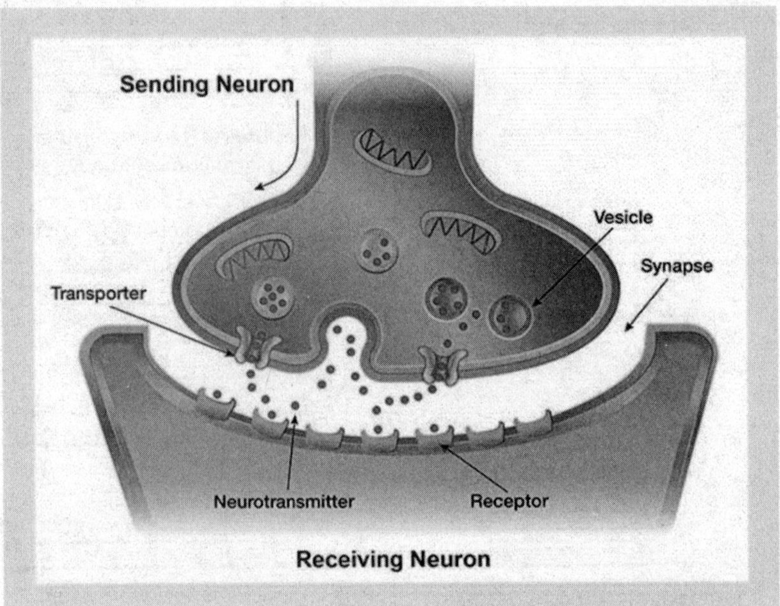


Source: Drugabuse.gov

**Receptors.** Neurotransmitter molecules have specific shapes that bind to the receptors of a receiving neuron in a key-lock mechanism. Imagine that the neurotransmitter molecules are like tiny keys that fit inside the locked dendrites. In these receptor sites, if the exact keys unlock enough of the fitted locks (receptor sites), then the nerve cell body (soma) will inform the axon *end bulb* (small knobs at the end of the axon; also called *terminal buttons*) to let the chemicals enter.

Think of the cell body as the brains of the cell. It must make a decision based on whether enough good information was received. If so, the neuron will create an electrical impulse, called an action potential.

**Action potential.** This action potential is an electrochemical impulse that runs down the long axon tube. The electrochemical impulse is extremely fast. It can travel faster down an axon that is insulated with a *myelin sheath* (fatty substance that is made by the glial cells that acts just like the rubber insulation around a copper wire).

Note: All cell membranes are electrically charged by *ions* (a charged molecule due to the loss or gain of one or more electrons) present inside and outside the cell (*extracellular* and *intracellular* space). Sodium ions ($Na+$) and chlorine ions ($Cl+$) exist in large quantities in extracellular space. Potassium ions ($K+$) exist in intracellular space.

## How Neurons Fire

"Neurons that fire together, wire together."

Now that you have studied the key facts of neurotransmission, let's put all of this information together to help you understand the process of how neurons fire. First, it's important to understand that the term "firing" means "action potential." The process of neurons firing begins with the stimulation of an electrical charge—an action potential.

**TEST TIP: Neurons either fire by transmitting an electrical impulse along the axon, or they don't fire. For the AP PSYCH exam, remember that it's either an all-or-none response. There is no in-between stage.**

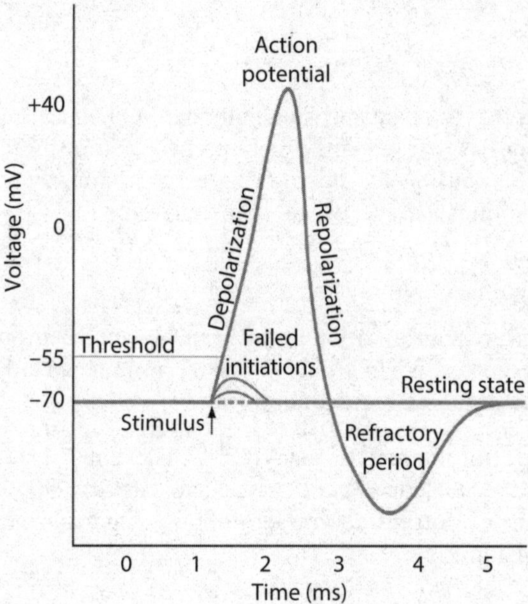


**RESTING STATE:** At this stage, the neuron is prepared to activate and communicate its message, but it is waiting for the electrical charge of the action potential. If the postsynaptic cell receives enough stimulation, the neuron will fire to transmit a signal down the length of the axon.

**ACTION POTENTIAL:** At this stage, atoms (ions) that are positively charged blast into the axon. Notice that the electrical charge briefly changes inside from negative to positive and outside from positive to negative. The impulse travels from the dendrites down the axon to the terminal branches. The action potential continues to change as it moves down the length of the axon.

**REFRACTORY PERIOD:** The action potential stops at the end of the axon and end bulbs. For a brief moment, the neuron is recharging and cannot fire. During this time, potassium channels reopen and sodium channels close.

## What Happens After Neurons Fire?

After presynaptic neurons release molecules across the synapse, (1) some molecules bind to receptors, (2) some molecules are chemically destroyed by enzymes, and (3) many molecules are quickly reabsorbed into the presynaptic neurons, returning back to the axon terminal for later use. This reabsorption is called **reuptake.** It is kind of a "molecule recycling" that allows neurotransmitters to be used again. Neurotransmitters return to the *vesicle* (a little bubble or sac that holds the neurotransmitters). While reuptake is happening, sodium ions (Na+) are being pumped back out of the axon so that they are reseparated from the potassium ions (K+). This separation is called *polarization.* Therefore, when a neuron fires, it is *depolarized;* when it is recharging by pumping the sodium out, it is *repolarizing.*

## Heads Up: What You Need to Know

On the AP PSYCH exam, you should be able to describe the impact of chemical substances transmitting neural impulses from one neuron to another through neurotransmitters.

Neurotransmitters don't just signal the next neuron to fire. In fact, it is just as important for a postsynaptic neuron to get the signal to *not* fire. For example, if you are reading a book and quickly reach for a snack, what if all of the motor neurons connected to your arm muscles suddenly receive an afferent signal to flex? Your arm would freeze. Half of your motor neurons receive a signal to inhibit the action potential, while the other half receive a signal to increase the action potential. Neurotransmitters are classified by these functions: **inhibitory** or **excitatory** action potentials that lie on a spectrum.

## Types of Neurotransmitters

There are literally hundreds of neurotransmitters, but that is a relatively small number of chemicals to explain all of the possible thoughts, feelings, and memories that humans experience. Neurotransmitter imbalances can affect every cell in your body and are responsible for making you feel a certain way. Imbalances can cause symptoms of anxiety, mood disorders, fatigue, weight gain, and more.

## Influence of Drugs on Neurotransmitters

All drugs change the way neurons send, receive, and process information in the brain. When a neuron is activated, it releases neurotransmitters that bind to receptors. When it binds to its receptor, it can either block or activate other neurons, causing chemical changes in the brain and body.

The table that follows illustrates seven important neurotransmitters for the AP PSYCH exam and shows you some of the drugs that can alter the function of an excess or deficiency of these chemicals. To help you stay focused, use the acronym SNAGGED to remember the neurotransmitters: **s**erotonin, **n**orepinephrine, **a**cetylcholine, **G**ABA, **g**lutamate, **e**ndorphins, and **d**opamine.

Remember, if you study smart, you won't get *snagged.*

| Influence of Drugs on Neurotransmitters | | | | |
|---|---|---|---|---|
| | | Effects on Human Behavior | | |
| Neurotransmitter | Function | Excess Is Linked To | Deficiency Is Linked To | Drugs That Help To Balance |
| **Serotonin** | Controls mood, appetite, anxiety, impulsivity, and aggression.<br><br>Unlike other psychoactive drugs that activate on the postsynaptic cell, serotonin acts on the pre-synaptic cell.<br><br>Serotonin molecules work by recycling the serotonin neurotransmitter after it delivers its message to the receptors. SSRIs (selective serotonin reuptake inhibitors) restrict the return (reuptake) of serotonin back to the presynaptic cells. If the serotonin molecules are not able to be returned back to the presynaptic cells, they will remain in the synapse and receptor sites. The more serotonin in the synapse and receptor sites, the greater the feeling of well-being. | Sense of sedation | Depression | SSRIs that activate a feeling of well-being.<br><br>SSRI common psychoactive drugs: Prozac, Zoloft, Paxil, Celexa, Lexapro, and Luvox. |
| **Norepinephrine/ Epinephrine** | Both serve as hormones and stimulate the nervous system.<br><br>Norepinephrine stimulates a part of your brain that controls alertness, energy, and attention. It can trigger the body's "fight-or-flight" response.<br><br>Epinephrine balances arousal with relaxation. | Rapid heartbeat, high blood pressure, and a feeling of anxiety or panic | Migraine headaches, sleep disorders, bipolar disorder, hypoglycemia, and headaches | Common epinephrine drugs include EpiPen (for severe allergic reactions) and bronchial dilators (asthma).<br><br>Common norepinephrine drugs treat attention deficit disorder (ADD) and low blood pressure (hypotension). |
| **Acetylcholine (ACH)** | Stimulates muscle and motor movements, attention, memory, sleeping, and emotions. | Convulsions | Alzheimer's disease | |
| **GABA (Gamma Amino Butyric Acid)** | The most common "inhibitory" neurotransmitter.<br><br>Calms and soothes. Regulates anxiety and sleep. | Excessive drowsiness | Anxiety or involuntary motor actions (tremors) | Common drugs include benzodiazepines (Valium and Ativan for anxiety and Ambien and Lunesta for insomnia). |
| **Glutamate** | The most common "excitatory" neurotransmitter.<br><br>Regulates learning, memory, and cognition. | Anxiety | Hallucinations, coma, or even death | |
| **Endorphins** | Inhibitory neurotransmitters that are linked to pain relief and pleasure. | "Runner's high" | Low tolerance for pain; fatigue | |
| **Dopamine** | Neurotransmitter inhibitor that regulates motor movements, motivation, emotions, alertness, and learning. | Psychoses (e.g., hallucinations and delusions), uncontrolled muscle movements, "tics" | Apathy, Parkinson's disease | Antipsychotics are antagonists that help with schizophrenia.<br><br>L-Dopa is an agonist that helps with Parkinson's disease. |

# Genetics

Before we look into the structures of the brain, let's look at how the brain is formed. The brain, like everything else in the body, develops according to genetic instructions. In fact, 70 percent of your genes are expressed in the formation and functioning of the brain.

## Key Facts about Genetics

**What is a gene?** A *gene* is an inherited characteristic from your parents. Humans have between 20,000 and 25,000 genes. Genes are made up of *DNA*. A gene is a specific segment of DNA located within a *chromosome* that determines each trait (see figure at right). Every person has two copies of each gene, one inherited from each parent.

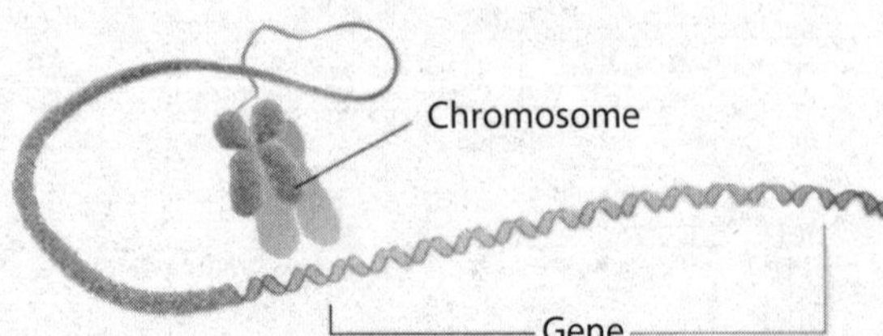


Source: U.S. National Library of Medicine

**What is DNA?** DNA is deoxyribonucleic acid. DNA is the carrier of genetic information. An important aspect of DNA is that it can make copies of itself.

**What is a chromosome?** In the nucleus of each cell, the DNA molecule is packaged into thread-like structures called *chromosomes.* A chromosome has many genes composed of DNA. All of the different chromosomes together are called a *genome.*

**What is genotype?** All of the genes of an individual are called a *genotype.* A genotype is the genetic makeup of a person.

**What is a phenotype?** A *phenotype* is the physical characteristics of a person. Because each person has the same set of genes, any observable trait variances are due to the differences in genes.

**How many chromosomes do people have?** Humans have 23 pairs of chromosomes (23 by the male sperm cells and 23 by the female egg cells) for a total of 46. Twenty-two of these pairs, called *autosomes,* look the same in both males and females. The 23rd pair of chromosomes, called the sex chromosomes, is different because the 23rd pair decides whether the person is biologically male or female. If you genetically inherit an X and a Y from your parents, you are male. If you inherit two X chromosomes, you are female. Males are XY and females are XX.

## Genetic Disorders

Particular disorders and conditions can run in families, especially if more than one person in the family has the condition. The karyotype can be used to diagnose genetic medical conditions.

| Genetic Disorders | |
|---|---|
| **Disorder** | **Description** |
| **Color blindness** | Most cases of color blindness are caused by the inheritance of a recessive trait on the X chromosome. Genes for the trait of color blindness are on the X chromosome. If a male inherits an X chromosome with a defect, he is color blind. If a female inherits an X chromosome with a defect, she has another X chromosome to work with. |
| **Turner syndrome** | Turner syndrome symptoms include females who do not develop ovaries, do not go through puberty, and develop infertility. The condition is present when a female has one normal X chromosome and a second X chromosome that is damaged or missing. |
| **Klinefelter's syndrome** | Symptoms such as lower testosterone production, developing female sex characteristics, and infertility are all indicators of Klinefelter's syndrome. The condition is due to a male having an extra X chromosome, XXY. |
| **Sickle cell anemia** | A condition where red blood cells, which carry oxygen through the body, develop abnormally. |
| **Huntington's disease** | Huntington's disease is a slow degenerative disease of the nervous system that can be inherited from a defective HTT gene. Symptoms include tremors and forgetfulness. Think of it as a blend of Parkinson's and Alzheimer's. |
| **Down syndrome** | Down syndrome is the result of an extra copy of chromosome 21. This occurs when there are three copies instead of two. Children with down syndrome have distinctive facial structures, short stature, and lower cognitive abilities. |

**Did you know?** The reason that medical professionals need to know a patient's medical and psychiatric family history is because certain conditions can be inherited (e.g., psychiatric conditions like bipolar disorder, schizophrenia, alcoholism, major depression, and anxiety). However, it's always important to keep in mind that genetic inheritance is not necessarily a person's destiny. The brain is shaped by our genes, but it is also shaped by our experiences in the environment. This is called **brain plasticity,** which means the brain can modify, reorganize, and regenerate itself. Certain genes can be switched off or on when certain environmental factors are present. This environmental effect on genetic expression is called *epigenetics*. If genes influence how one interacts with the environment and the environment can affect which genes are turned on, then we can say that genes and the environment are *bidirectional*.

# The Brain

The human brain is the control center for the nervous system and has more than 100 billion nerves that communicate with the body. Scientific research shows how we use all of our brain nearly all of the time, even when sleeping. That makes sense because the brain is a network of neurons whose sole purpose is to communicate. The body's sensory organs input information to the brain, and the brain outputs information by sending neurons (electrical impulses) along the spinal cord to parts of the body.

## Key Facts about the Human Brain

- The human brain is the largest compared to all vertebrates relative to body size.
- The average weight of the brain is 3.3 pounds.

- The brain needs a constant supply of oxygen.
- The brain is about 60 percent fat. It is the fattest organ in the body.
- Dehydration can have a negative impact on brain function because the brain, like all of our organs, is dependent upon water to function well.
- All brain cells are not alike.
- The brain has about 100 billion neurons.
- Each neuron in the brain can transmit about 1,000 nerve impulses per second.
- The brain can generate about 23 watts of power when awake.

## Cerebral Hemispheres

The human brain has two *cerebral* (another word for brain) *hemispheres:* left and right. The two hemispheres are connected by a thick band of neural fibers called the **corpus callosum.** Some self-help authors have attempted to simplify the concept of personality into two categories of hemispheres—left-brained and right-brained—but these studies have not been well-received in the professional psychology community. Both sides of the brain are involved in every brain process of personality.

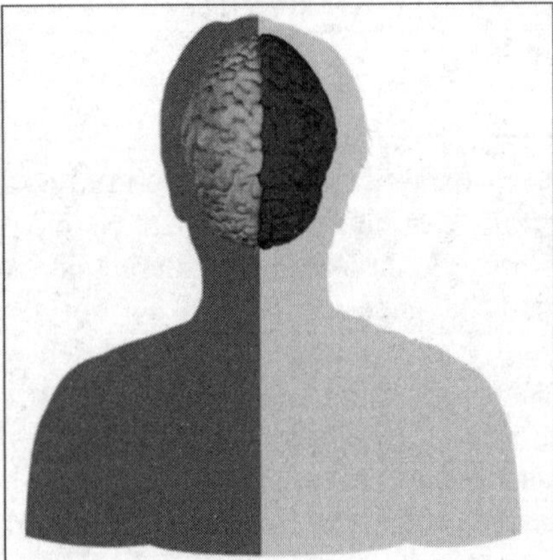


Source: Alzheimer's Association

**Did you know?** "Split-brain surgery" has been performed to treat people with extreme and uncontrollable epileptic seizures (see the research of Sperry and Gazzaniga). It is a surgical procedure that cuts all or part of the corpus callosum to prevent the seizures from spreading from one half of the brain to the other. An interesting observation occurred in patients who had this surgery. Since language centers are in the left hemisphere, when patients *saw* something (right hemisphere), they could draw the object with their "left hand," but couldn't *say* it because there is no language center.

**TEST TIP: When studying for the AP PSYCH exam, it is important to remember that the left side of the brain processes language and logic.**

**Author's side note:** Although you may not need to know this term for the AP PSYCH exam, *contralateral control* means that the left hemisphere controls the right side of the body and the right hemisphere controls the left side of the body. Some southpaws (left-handed people) say "Only left-handed people are in their right minds!"

## Cerebral Cortex

The **cerebral cortex** is the only part of the body that can study itself because 76 percent of brain mass is in the cerebral cortex and it contains three-quarters of all synapses. Think of the cerebral cortex as the apple skin of the brain. It is thin and tightly stretched across the surface of the forebrain so that it covers every nook and cranny of the forebrain. It is often referred to as "gray matter" because it's darker tissue that is gray in color; the nerves in this area lack insulation, causing the rest of the brain to appear white. The *gyri* are bumps on the brain, and *sulci* are the crevices on the brain. In fact, it is the sulci that are the dividing lines between the lobes, just like natural landforms are the divisions between nations.

### The Brain's Four Lobes

The brain's cerebral cortex has four major divisions, known as *lobes:* frontal lobe, parietal lobe, temporal lobe, and occipital lobe.

**Lateral Views of the Brain**

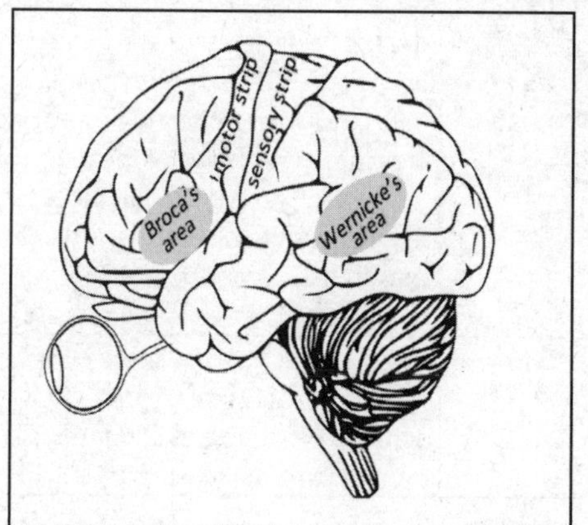


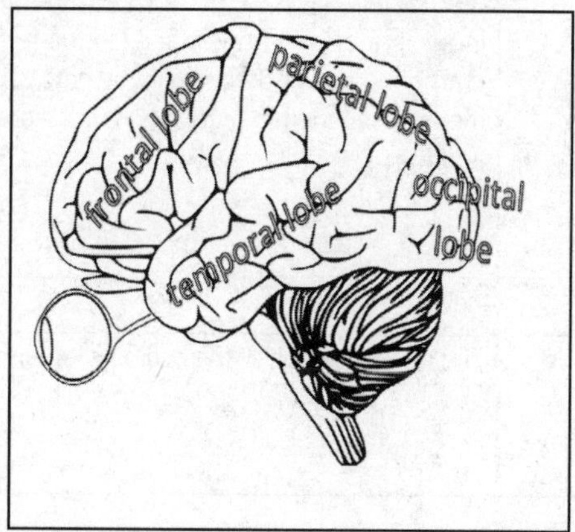


Source: https://pixabay.com/vectors/brain-diagram-anatomy-biology-40377/

The four lobes are actually eight lobes because there are four in each hemisphere, but scientific literature refers to them as four lobes. *Traumatic brain injuries* (TBIs) can cause damage to the lobes. TBIs are severe brain injuries caused by a traumatic event such as a violent blow to the head from an automobile crash, a fall, a sports-related injury, or an injury that a war veteran might experience from explosives. Symptoms of TBI could be temporary or permanent.

| The Four Lobes of the Brain | | |
|---|---|---|
| **Lobe** | **Description** | **What Might Happen If Damaged** |
| **Frontal lobe** | The frontal lobe is the part of the brain that contains the prefrontal cortex, which is responsible for personality, problem solving, moral judgment, and executive functioning. It is not fully developed until 25 years old. If you understand this sentence, it is because your prefrontal cortex is working. Your frontal lobe contains the motor strip that is involved in all purposeful motor movements. Think of the motor strip as a proportional map of your body's muscles on the surface of a strip of your frontal lobe. If a certain area on that strip was stimulated with a small electric charge, the corresponding muscle would contract. | The left frontal lobe contains Broca's area, a region of the brain that controls speech production. Damage to Broca's area can result in changes in personality, decision making, and a speech disorder known as Broca aphasia. Although the speaker is clear about what he or she is saying, the words spoken are very slow, deliberate, and several words are omitted (e.g., a 2-year-old's telegraphic speech). |
| **Parietal lobe** | The parietal lobe is divided into two regions. One region is responsible for sensation and perception, and the other region integrates sensory visual input. The parietal lobe registers and provides sensation from the skin of the peripheral nervous system (PNS) and contains a sensory strip called a somatosensory cortex that is a proportional map of the sensitive areas of your body's skin. For example, even though your hand is much smaller than your thigh, your hand is much more sensitive to touch. As such, your hand is a larger area on the sensory strip. | Damage to the parietal lobe could result in a sensory impairment causing you not to feel things accurately—which would impair self-care skills like dressing or washing. |
| **Temporal lobe** | The temporal lobe processes sensory input into derived meanings so that you can remember the input. It helps you understand language, process visual memories, and understand some emotions. (Remember, the **l**eft hemisphere processes **l**anguage and **l**ogic.) | Effects from damage to the temporal lobe depend on where the damage exists. Damage to the right side can cause impairment to sounds and shapes. Damage to the left side can cause difficulty in remembering or speaking. Wernicke's area is on the left side of the temporal lobe. It is the region of the brain that processes spoken language. If Wernicke's area is damaged or a person has a problem recalling spoken language, it is called Wernicke's aphasia. |
| **Occipital lobe** | The main function of the occipital lobe is to receive and interpret visual stimuli from the eyes. | One result of damage to the occipital lobe on both sides is cortical blindness. It is when someone experiences blindness as a result of brain trauma in the occipital lobe. |

**TEST TIP: All parts of the brain communicate in some way with all other parts of the brain. When you are writing your response to a free-response question, make sure to mention as many brain parts as possible and also mention *how* the parts communicate and help each other. While each lobe focuses on a certain task, they all communicate with each other and share information. The occipital lobe, for example, primarily performs visual processing signals from the eyes, but it also communicates with the temporal lobe, which is responsible for hearing and language. For example, if you see a bear, your occipital lobe must communicate with your hippocampus so you can remember what you are seeing.**

## Brain Structure

The structure of the brain is grouped into the *lower brain* (also known as the **hindbrain**), the **midbrain,** and the **forebrain.**

### Heads Up: What You Need to Know

The AP PSYCH exam will probably not ask you to identify every internal structure and tissue of the brain. However, you should be able to identify and describe important general terms like the medulla, pons, cerebellum, the four lobes, Wernicke's area, and Broca's area.

### The Lower Brain (Hindbrain)

The lower brain connects the spine to the higher brain and the brainstem. It is often called the "primitive" part of the brain because it coordinates the body's functions that are vital to survival (e.g., breathing, heart rate, and blood pressure). It regulates these functions automatically and flawlessly to keep you alive—but it is far from primitive.

The lower brain has three main regions: the *medulla,* the *pons,* and the *cerebellum.* Each of these three regions helps to coordinate specific functions in the body.

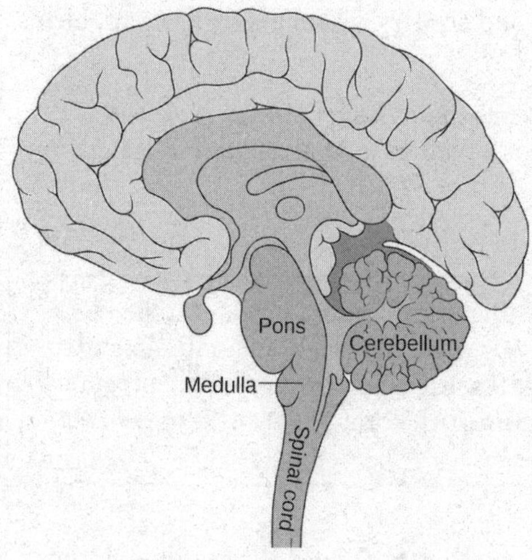


Source: Patrick J. Lynch, medical illustrator; C. Carl Jaffe, MD, cardiologist

**Medulla [oblongata].** The medulla is an important part of the brain—and your entire body. It controls automatic vital life functions such as breathing, circulation, and swallowing.

**Pons.** The pons is located near the medulla and does many of the same vital tasks. The pons is a relay station between the medulla and the rest of the brain.

**Cerebellum.** The cerebellum's nickname is the "little brain" because it is able to function by itself. It extends out from the rear of the brainstem and plays a vital role in coordinating physical movements. It is responsible for posture, balance, muscle coordination, practiced motor movements, and *implicit* (unconscious) memories. Practiced motor movements can be thought of as *procedural memories* (a type of unconscious memory that helps you perform certain tasks without your conscious awareness), like walking or playing a musical instrument. If damaged, it can impede walking.

## Heads Up: What You Need to Know

On the AP PSYCH exam, you might be asked about the importance of *reflexes* and *ventricles* in relationship to the lower brain. As mentioned above, the lower brain handles many unconscious functions. So, it makes sense that the lower brain, which includes the spinal cord, is where reflexes are processed. A *reflex arc* is a loop where a sensory neuron sends an afferent signal to the spinal cord or brainstem; then it sends an efferent signal to motor neurons. Of course, the higher parts of your brain become aware of the reflex, but this only occurs after you have flinched, ducked, or blinked.

*Ventricles* are hollow cavities in the brain filled with fluid (cerebrospinal fluid) that help to protect the brain by providing a cushion if there is a physical trauma. Imagine your brain as a blob of Swiss cheese and the ventricles as weirdly shaped holes deep inside. On the AP PSYCH exam, it is important to remember that research studies have concluded, through MRI imaging, that individuals with schizophrenia and autism frequently have enlarged ventricles of the brain.

## The Midbrain

The midbrain region is the smallest portion of the brain and is associated with important unconscious reactions that control responses to eye and hearing (auditory) input. The midbrain's job can be summed up as awareness and arousal, not the consciousness of one's own thoughts, but the consciousness of the input from the environment. Damage to the midbrain can cause movement disorders, vision and hearing problems, and memory problems.

An important part of the midbrain is the **reticular formation,** known as the *reticular activating system (RAS);* the RAS helps motor control activity of the body. If there is a change in your surroundings or your emotions, or if there is an emergency, your body activates its RAS.

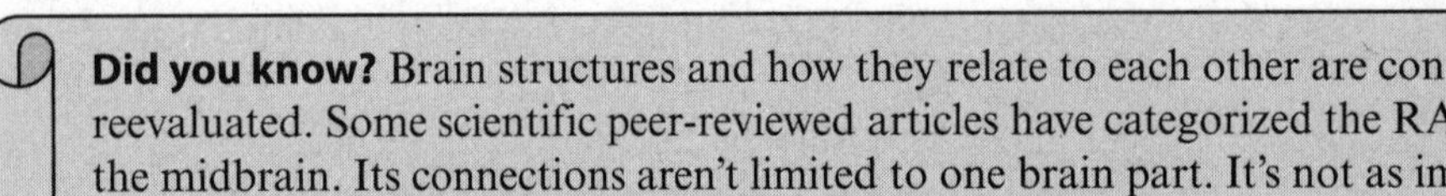

**Did you know?** Brain structures and how they relate to each other are constantly being studied and reevaluated. Some scientific peer-reviewed articles have categorized the RAS in the hindbrain and the midbrain. Its connections aren't limited to one brain part. It's not as important to remember where it's located, but rather to remember that the RAS is a part of the brain's network. In fact, the word *reticular* means *net.*

## The Forebrain

The forebrain is the biggest part of the brain. It is where thoughts, consciousness, and emotions occur. The forebrain has three regions: the basal ganglia, the thalamus, and the hypothalamus.

**Basal ganglia** (remember that a ganglia is a group of neurons that works together) is a set of structures that directs intentional movements. That makes sense because unthinking reflexes happen in the lower brain. Remember also that dopamine is the neurotransmitter most associated with intentional movement. Parkinson's disease, which is centered in the basal ganglia, is when a lack of dopamine affects the ability to move smoothly. Another dopamine-rich area is the *nucleus accumbens*—the pleasure center of the brain. That makes sense because dopamine is also the reward and one of the pleasure chemicals of the brain.

**TEST TIP: On the AP PSYCH exam, you should be able to explain for a possible free-response question that too little dopamine is associated with Parkinson's disease and too much dopamine is associated with psychotic thoughts. A dopamine agonist, like L-Dopa, might help with Parkinson's disease and antipsychotic drugs are dopamine antagonists.**

**Thalamus.** The thalamus serves as a "router" for all of the information that flows to and from the forebrain, including senses (vision, hearing, taste, and touch). If the thalamus has significant damage, it can cause a person to be in an unresponsive, vegetative state.

**Hypothalamus.** The hypothalamus is the master control center for basic biological needs: hunger, thirst, sexual function, and body temperature. It also affects sleep, hormone release, and emotions. If the hypothalamus is damaged, it can cause insomnia, problems with body temperature, problems with adrenal glands, or a thyroid dysfunction.

**Did you know?** Many parts in the forebrain have a twin. The brain has two hemispheres, so we don't have a hippocampus, we have two hippocampi, two amygdalae, and so on.

## The Limbic System

The **limbic system** is at the center of reflexes for survival instincts. For example, if the body becomes aroused due to extreme stress or trauma, the limbic system becomes activated. The two brain regions of the limbic system are the hippocampus and the amygdala.

**Hippocampus.** The hippocampus is part of the limbic system that regulates emotions and forming long-term memories. The hippocampus has been called a seahorse-shaped structure. In fact, the word hippocampus means "seahorse." Hippopotamus means "river horse." If this fun fact will help you remember on the AP PSYCH exam, good because that is what the hippocampus does.

**Amygdala.** The amygdala processes and stores reactions to fearful events, aggression, and disgust. It facilitates the storage of emotional experiences in your memory. This makes sense because remembering things that scared us helps us avoid unsafe situations.

It was originally thought that the limbic system was the boundary between the lower brain and the more advanced forebrain. However, since the brain is a network, it doesn't make sense to think of it as a boundary. Instead, the limbic system should be seen as a relay station between the medulla, which causes the heart to beat faster, and the cerebral cortex, which perceives and thinks about situations as dangerous.

The limbic system acts like a librarian and organizes episodic memories in the cerebral cortex and helps you remember to respond to extreme stress or trauma by releasing hormones that communicate to the body. Because the limbic system controls the **autonomic nervous system** (ANS), when under extreme stress the **sympathetic nervous system** is activated by the hypothalamus, causing the body to be in a heightened state of arousal. This action prepares the body for a fight, flight, or freeze response. (More about this in Chapter 10, "Unit 7: Motivation, Emotion, and Personality.")

## Brain Imaging

Before modern technology, scientists were left to study the brain primarily by autopsy and by lesioning. *Lesioning* is purposefully removing or disabling part of the brain for scientific study. Researchers could then study components of the brain to make assumptions about cognition, behavior, thoughts, and feelings. Today, brain imaging has radically advanced, and there are a number of safe techniques employed by research facilities throughout the world. Scientists can zoom in on a cubed millimeter and can even view brain activity while a person is thinking.

The two categories of brain imaging are *structural* and *functional.* You might remember these terms from Chapter 4, "Unit 1: Scientific Foundations of Psychology," which discusses the theoretical approaches of Wilhelm Wundt and William James. Structural imaging is used to determine what is in the brain structures and look for abnormalities in the brain. Functional imaging is used to determine what the brain is doing at any given moment.

| Structural Imaging | | | |
|---|---|---|---|
| **Type of Imaging** | **What It Does** | **Advantages** | **Disadvantages** |
| **CAT scan**<br>Computerized Axial Tomography | CAT scans are also called CT scans (computed tomography). The imaging uses an X-ray to produce two-dimensional pictures of the brain structures and soft tissues. | A CAT scan is inexpensive, fast, and can help determine if there are deformities in the shape or structure of the brain (strokes, blood clots, tumors, or hemorrhage). | CAT scans, compared to other imaging tests, deliver a higher dose of radiation. CAT scans are not as detailed as other scans. |
| **MRI**<br>Magnetic Resonance Imaging | MRIs use magnets and radio waves for computer three-dimensional images of the brain. | MRIs do not expose the patient to radiation. The MRI is more detailed and can usually detect more abnormalities than the CAT scan. | MRIs are more expensive than CAT scans, take much longer, and many people who are claustrophobic fear the enclosed space and loud noises. |
| **Functional Imaging** | | | |
| **Type of Imaging** | **What It Does** | **Advantages** | **Disadvantages** |
| **fMRI**<br>Functional Magnetic Resonance Imaging | FMRIs are a type of MRI that uses magnets to align the protons in brain tissue. | The fMRI doesn't use radiation and has virtually no health risks. It provides a high-resolution image as the brain thinks, feels, and reacts. | Bulky and expensive. It requires a team of people to operate it. One of the biggest complaints is that the fMRI can only look at blood flow in the brain. |
| **PET scan**<br>Positron Emission Tomography | A PET scan uses trace amounts of a radioactive substance that passes through blood vessels of the brain to produce a map of the brain. | A PET scan can distinguish between benign and malignant cancer tissues. It is relatively painless, so doctors can make more accurate diagnoses and target treatment plans. | Pregnant women cannot undergo PET scans since they have radioactive elements. PET scans are expensive and require injecting radioactive material into the blood. |

| **EEG** Electroencephalogram | EEGs measure electrical activity on the surface of the brain. By placing electrodes on the head, the EEG measures the brain waves such as alpha, beta, theta, and delta. | An EEG is a direct measure of epileptic pathophysiology. It is very quick to respond to changes in the brain's electrical activity and is inexpensive. | Measures only the surface of the brain (cerebral cortex). |
|---|---|---|---|

## The Adaptive Brain

Our brains are truly amazing and adaptable. The father of neuroscience, Santiago Ramón y Cajal, recognized nonpathological changes in the structure of the brain, but most early neuroscientists believed that adult neurons were fixed and could not be altered. It wasn't until the 1970s that neuroscientists acknowledged the existence of possible changes in our brain's neural networks and connectivity, called neuroplasticity.

**Neuroplasticity** is the brain's ability to adapt and reorganize in response to environmental influences. This dynamic process allows neurons and neural networks in the brain to change their connections (and therefore change a person's behavior) in response to new input from the environment. It can take place at any time during a lifetime. For example, when we learn a new language, we form new pathways in the brain. Sensory input of learning tasks can change the structure and function of neurons to help cells become functionally reconnected. Exercise is one of the most effective ways to stimulate neuroplasticity and *neurogenesis* (creating new neurons). Neurogenesis is a phenomenon of neuroplasticity that new neurons in adult brains can generate.

For survivors of traumatic brain injury, neuroplasticity is an important breakthrough in treatment. The extraordinary physiological changes in the brain can help survivors create new pathways and rewire the brain as a result of interactions with new circumstances in the environment. Neuroplasticity can directly influence how the brain responds after a brain injury, and the brain can spontaneously rewire itself. Survivors of strokes and dementia have also been able to improve due to neuroplasticity and neurogenesis.

# Consciousness

Psychologists vary on their views regarding the nature of consciousness. It is a complex and long-explored concept in psychology that has been historically challenging for researchers to study using scientific experimental measures. For the purpose of the AP PSYCH exam, we will focus on defining consciousness, introducing the stages of consciousness, and discussing specific aspects of unconscious behaviors—sleeping and dreaming.

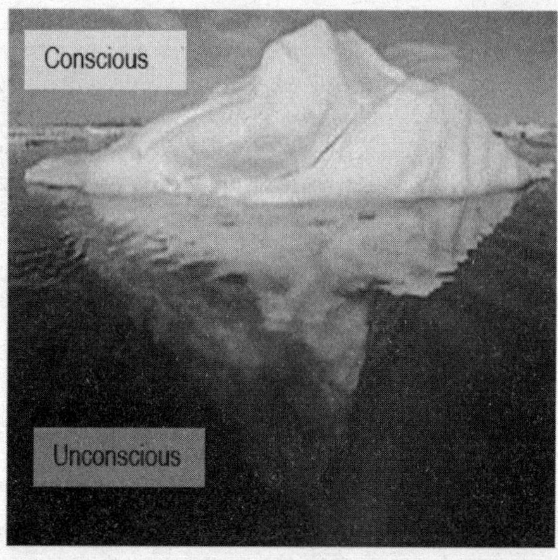


## Consciousness vs. Unconsciousness

The image of an iceberg is a metaphor to visually reflect on the two parts of the mind. The conscious is represented by what we can see on the surface, and the huge mass of ice beneath the water is associated with what is underneath the surface—unconscious thoughts, feelings, and motivations.

| Compare and Contrast Consciousness and Unconsciousness | |
|---|---|
| **Consciousness** | **Unconsciousness** |
| In simplistic terms, *consciousness* is a waking state of awareness—our thoughts, feelings, memories, and perceptions. The levels of consciousness lie on a spectrum spanning from maximum alertness and concentration to minimal alertness and concentration. When you consciously perform a task, you are able to mentally focus your attention, integrate information, and respond to environmental experiences. Note: *Altered states of consciousness* produced by temporary experiences (e.g., meditation, hypnosis, or psychoactive drugs) can change your normal conscious awareness.<br><br>Another way to look at consciousness is to introduce a model in psychology called *theory of mind*. Theory of mind suggests that most people are not only aware that they can think, but also that others can think. It is the ability to insightfully recognize internalized mental states (knowledge, beliefs, intentions, etc.). For example, close your eyes and focus your awareness on the brilliant colors of a rainbow—red, orange, yellow, green, blue, indigo, and violet. If you were able to visualize this image, then you have conscious inner awareness.<br><br>Consciousness occurs gradually starting in early childhood. For example, a baby isn't mindful that mommy might not want to wake up for a 4:00 a.m. feeding. The baby will not reach the conscious stage of development until about 4 years old (see Chapter 9, "Unit 6: Developmental Psychology"). Theory of mind is important to a child's development so that the child will consciously develop prosocial skills, foster moral standards, solve problems, and empathize with others. | Just like consciousness, the term *unconsciousness* is complex and has been extensively researched as a psychological state of mind. In general, most theorists would agree that the unconscious refers to the absence of inner awareness of one's mental processes, behaviors, feelings, and actions.<br><br>Many of the ideas about the unconscious began with the founder of psychoanalysis, Sigmund Freud, and his followers. In Freud's early writings, he suggested that the unconscious mind was motivated by instincts, urges, fears, wishes, dreams, and fantasies. *Psychodynamic theory* (a branch of psychology that deals with unconscious mental processes that determine personality and motivation) has suggested that powerful unconscious internal forces arise from early childhood experiences and, if left unattended, continue to influence our emotions, decisions, and defenses. |

**Did you know?** A Freudian slip is when you say or do something that is believed to be linked to the unconscious mind. It may reveal something that you unconsciously fear or desire. It sneaks past your conscious guardian and may reveal something deep inside. It's like when you say one thing, but really mean your mother (Freud emphasized the important role of the mother).

## Levels of Consciousness

In order to study consciousness, researchers have established different levels of a person's responsiveness to external stimuli from the environment. The states of consciousness are a broad spectrum between conscious and unconscious awareness.

| Levels of Consciousness | | |
|---|---|---|
| **Stage** | **Description** | **Examples of How Each Stage Can Impact Behavior** |
| **Conscious** | What you are aware of right now or at any given moment. | The conscious mind is alert, awake, and responsive to the environment, just like you are aware that you are now reading this book. |
| **Preconscious** | Information that is stored in your memory and can be accessed at any time, but that you are not thinking about at that exact moment. | If you are asked your phone number, you are retrieving the phone number from preconscious into conscious thought. |
| **Subconscious** | The subconscious handles information below your level of awareness. *Priming* (the process of preparing) and the *mere-exposure effect* (which occurs when you repeatedly encounter a stimulus and then develop a preference for it merely because you have had frequent exposures) are examples of information stored in the subconscious. | When you are able to perform a task without thinking, your subconscious is at work. For example, how you remember to play a video game that you haven't played in many years. |
| **Unconscious** | Deep human drives that are unconsciously activated in life through actions, feelings, emotions, and behaviors. | The unconscious mind can overrule the conscious mind and make decisions without "thinking" about the outcome. |
| **Nonconscious** | The nonconscious are functions you are not aware of doing, but are necessary for human survival. | When your body organs function automatically, without knowledge (e.g., heartbeat, respiration, blinking), your nonconscious is at work. |

## Sleep and Dreams

This section will continue the discussion of consciousness and explore other states of consciousness—sleeping and dreaming. Before we discuss these topics, it's important to explain how our internal biological clock can impact sleep.

## Circadian Rhythms

Have you ever noticed that you learn more efficiently at a certain time of day, or that your body changes the way it feels throughout the day? The body's internal clock fluctuates in energy regularly throughout the day because it is biologically synchronized by a 24-hour sleep cycle, called a **circadian rhythm.** Circadian timing impacts every aspect of your daily life. Studies have shown that the body's natural functions like appetite, digestion, hormone secretion, and heart rate all follow the timing of circadian rhythms during our sleep, and that our thinking is sharpest when we are at the peak of the circadian arousal. Circadian rhythm is the reason for jet lag. If you travel, you may have trouble falling to sleep. Incidentally, did you know that our thinking and alertness is at its lowest performance between 2:00 p.m. and 5:00 p.m.? This is due to circadian rhythms.

## Sleep

Humans need sleep more than they need food or water. Though most of us are not consciously aware when we sleep, our brains and minds are always active. How do we know that the brain is active? Because scientists have studied sleep brain activity using an EEG, **e**lectro**e**ncephalo**g**raph, which measures the electrical activity of the brain's surface, the cerebral cortex.

The brain's electrical activity can be divided into four distinct patterns of *brain waves.* It is important to note that everyone experiences these waves during all stages of sleep.

| Stages of Sleep | | | | |
|---|---|---|---|---|
| **Stage** | **Brain Wave** | **Description** | **EEG Frequency** | **Brain Wave Patterns** |
| **Awake** | Beta waves | The person is awake and aware, like you are right now as you are reading this book.<br><br>Low amplitude, high frequency | 14+ Hz; there are more than 14 peaks of a brain wave every second. | 1 second |
| **NREM 1**<br>Stage 1 | Alpha waves | The person is very relaxed, meditating, daydreaming, or hypnotized; halfway asleep.<br><br>Less amplitude and variability | Small, irregular waves: 8–12 Hz. Approximately 10 peaks of a brain wave every second. | 1 second |
| **NREM 1 and 2**<br>Stages 1 and 2 | Theta waves | The person is asleep, but not deeply. The brain wave patterns are mostly theta, but can go back and forth between theta and alpha.<br><br>Higher amplitude, lower frequency | During this stage, sleep spindles can occur (sudden increases in wave frequencies): 4–7 Hz. Approximately 6 peaks of a brain wave every second. | 1 second |
| **NREM 3**<br>Stages 3 and 4 | Delta waves | The person is in a deep sleep. It is the deepest level of normal sleep. When delta waves are present, the person might drool due to *cataplexy*. Cataplexy is when the muscles are inhibited to the point of having no muscle tone. If you sleep on your side, there is a good chance that you will drool on your pillow.<br><br>Highest amplitude, lowest frequency | 2–4 Hz, approximately 3 peaks of brain waves every second. | 1 second |
| **REM** | | The person's eyes move back and forth, called *rapid eye movement;* the autonomic nervous system is activated. During this stage, the person is hard to wake. Note: The first REM period occurs after approximately 60 to 85 minutes of non-REM sleep.<br><br>Low voltage, random, and fast | During this stage, brainwaves are fast, irregular, and resemble a mix between alpha and beta. | 1 second |
| **KEY TO THE TWO BASIC STATES OF SLEEP**<br><br>REM – Rapid eye movement. Most of the brain is awake except the prefrontal cortex.<br><br>NREM – Non-REM sleep helps the body recover from fatigue. | | | | |

## The Sleep Cycle

Older textbooks might still suggest there are four stages of non-REM sleep, but newer textbooks have combined stages 3 and 4 into NREM 3. Sleep starts at NREM 1 to NREM 2, then NREM 3. Here's where it gets interesting: After about an hour of NREM 3, you might enter REM directly, or you might go "back" into NREM 2, then NREM 1, and then REM. At the beginning of the night you should have more NREM 3 and less REM. As morning approaches, you should have little or no NREM 3 and mostly experience REM. Notice that the periods of REM sleep get longer toward the morning.

This cycle of going down and up through the stages of sleep takes place about every 90 minutes, four to seven times per night. The graph that follows shows a typical sleep cycle. While it is important to know that the whole brain is active during sleep, the brain structure that is most involved in transitioning from consciousness to sleep is the *superchiasmatic nucleus.* Its nickname is the *sleep switch,* which makes sense because it sits atop the *optic chiasm.* That is where the two optic nerves cross, which means the optic chiasm responds to light and dark cycles of day and night.

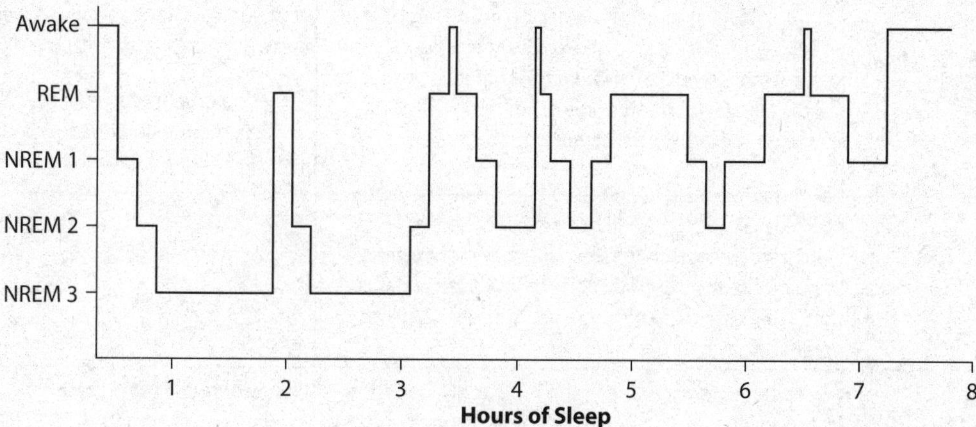


## Sleep Disorders

Many people believe that 8 hours of sleep are essential to feel refreshed and alert. This is untrue. Although restorative sleep is important to maintain physical and mental health, some adults can function well on 6 hours of sleep, while others need about 10 hours of sleep each day. Sleep requirements are unique to each person.

**What happens if you are sleep deprived?** Research indicates that cognitive performance declines, memory is impaired, the immune system is weakened, and many people have episodes of irritability and moodiness. If you have ever stayed up late for a few nights, you may have experienced some of these symptoms. Severe sleep loss is a serious risk to your health and quality of life, and in some cases can cause episodes of hallucinations.

Some of the common sleep disorders that you should be familiar with for the AP PSYCH exam are insomnia, parasomnia, nightmares, sleep apnea, and narcolepsy.

| Sleep Disorders | | |
|---|---|---|
| **Disorder** | **Description** | **Treatment** |
| **Insomnia** | Insomnia, also called sleeplessness, is the most common sleep disorder. People with insomnia have difficulty falling asleep and/or staying asleep. It is defined as a person's distress and dissatisfaction with sleep, not by the number of hours that a person sleeps, or how long it takes to fall asleep. | Behavior modification such as reducing caffeine (stimulant) consumption, exercising regularly, practicing relaxation techniques, and maintaining regular sleep patterns. |
| **Parasomnia** | Parasomnia behaviors normally take place during the waking state, but can also occur while the person is sleeping (for example, walking or talking in your sleep). *Somnambulism* is a term for sleepwalking and usually happens in NREM 3. | Lifestyle changes such as avoiding sleep deprivation, maintaining good sleep hygiene, and reducing stress. |
| **Nightmares** | Nightmares are actually pretty rare in adults and teens and are only considered a disorder if the dreams cause enough distress to keep the person from adequate sleep. Nightmare disorders are recurrent episodes that cause intensely disturbing dreams that involve fear and anxiety. Nightmares only occur during REM because the brain is active enough to create a story.<br><br>Night terrors are different from nightmares because they usually occur in NREM 3 and often target children. The person who experiences night terrors has intense fears and will awaken in a state of panic—often accompanied by a scream. Another name for night terrors is *incubus attacks.* | Relaxation techniques and/or cognitive behavioral therapy that focuses on goals that address the thoughts, emotions, and behaviors associated with the nightmares.<br><br>Other treatments can consist of stress management techniques, hypnotherapy, psychotherapy, and prescribed medications. |
| **Sleep apnea** | Sleep apnea is when breathing repeatedly stops and starts while sleeping. It can last a few seconds or a few minutes, and can cause loud snoring. The throat muscles and airway become *cataplexic,* and the airway collapses on itself to prevent breathing. Once that happens, the unconscious mind will wake up just enough for muscle tone to reestablish. Then a person goes deeper into sleep and the cycle repeats. Aside from noisy breathing and snoring, the real problem with sleep apnea is a person does not get their four to five periods of 20-minute REM sleep, causing the person to be sleep deprived. | Behavior modification techniques include weight loss, changing sleep positions, ceasing smoking, avoiding alcohol, avoiding sleep aids, and using a prescribed continuous positive airway pressure (CPAP) device. |
| **Narcolepsy** | Narcolepsy is the uncontrollable tendency to fall asleep in an NREM stage any time during the day. It involves the inability to regulate sleep-wake cycles and is related to a lack of hypocretin (a neuropeptide that regulates arousal and wakefulness). | Prescribed medications and behavior modification can improve symptoms, but there currently is no cure. |

## Dreaming

Dreams are images, stories, sensations, and emotions that occur involuntarily during REM sleep. There are numerous theories about dreams, but for the AP PSYCH exam, it is important to be familiar with the biological approach to dreams that occur during REM sleep. REM dreams have a narrative quality and are almost nonstop during REM sleep.

The **activation-synthesis theory,** a biological approach to dreaming, suggests that dreams are a byproduct of the brain's attempt to interpret what is occurring when the brain cells fire randomly during REM sleep. Remember that during REM sleep, brain cells are activated (turned on), which activates memories and sensations. Since the frontal cortex is shut down during REM sleep (the part of the brain that controls higher levels of thinking and helps us make logical sense of things), the images and stories in dreams appear to be hazy, primitive, and disconnected.

Perhaps dreams are more than a biological response to brain cells firing. Perhaps dreams are random bits of perception and emotion that our minds try to organize into a story that makes sense unconsciously. Sigmund Freud believed that dreams came from a person's past and are the "royal road" into the unconscious mind. Freud's first book, *The Interpretation of Dreams,* suggested that a person shouldn't simply look at the obvious story of a dream, called *manifest content.* Instead, a person should look at the parts of the story represented in the hidden content from his or her past. Carl Jung, originally a follower of Freud and author of *Memories, Dreams, Reflections,* believed that dreams not only express a person's personal past, but also a person's future. Jung believed that dreams are symbolic images seeking to communicate important information that the conscious mind does not yet fully understand.

## Drugs and Consciousness

*Psychoactive drugs,* both legal and illegal, are covered in this unit because drugs change one's consciousness.

### How Drugs Affect the Brain

Drugs alter the chemistry of the brain and the body and cause an altered state of consciousness. Drug molecules that alter brain activity are so small that they reach the brain by passing through the *blood-brain barrier,* which prevents harmful contaminants from entering the brain. These molecules imitate or block neurotransmitters in the brain. Mind-altering drugs that manipulate neurotransmitters, and therefore neural activity, are called *agonists* and *antagonists.* An agonist is a drug that is chemically similar to a neurotransmitter and "picks the lock" of the receptor site by mimicking the neurotransmitter. An antagonist is a drug that blocks the receptor site so the natural neurotransmitter can't do its job.

**Agonists and Antagonists**

Agonists - Drugs that occupy receptors and activate them.
Antagonists - Drugs that occupy receptors but do not activate them.
Antagonists block receptor activation by agonists.

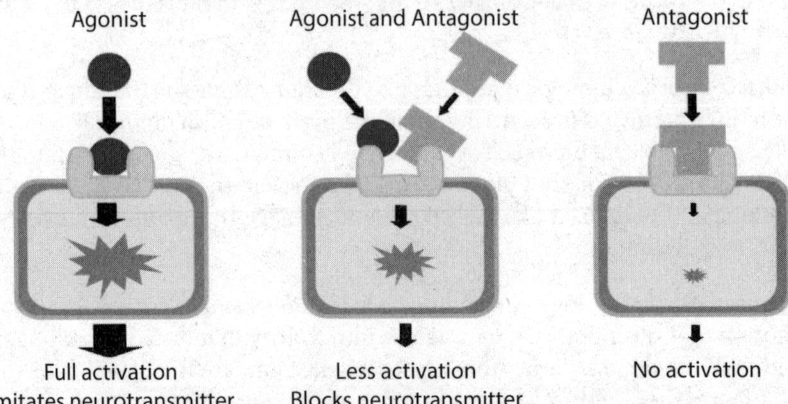


**FUN FACT: There are only three chemical bodily experiences you can enjoy: serotonin, dopamine, and endorphins. Everything else causes a reaction involving these chemicals.**

## Psychoactive Drugs

Any chemical substance, even aspirin, can alter neurotransmitters, affecting your brain's chemistry. The physiological and psychological chemical reactions are associated with distinctive altered states of consciousness that can change your thoughts, perceptions, and mood.

The table that follows shows the most common types of psychoactive drugs. The main classifications are stimulants and depressants. *Stimulants* (sometimes called "uppers") speed up the central nervous system, make a person feel more alert and energetic, and suppress appetite. If depressants inhibit stress, stimulants appear to excite and energize the reward circuits of the brain by over-exciting dopamine mechanisms. This eventually leads to the brain producing less natural dopamine. *Depressants* (sometimes called "downers") inhibit certain parts of the central nervous system that are associated with stress and anxiety reactions. Hence, a person taking a depressant might feel very relaxed and may not be as sensitive to outside stimulation. This sense of pleasure, called *euphoria,* can result, causing the person to want to take the depressant again. This can lead to the reduced production of the brain's natural relaxation chemicals (i.e., dopamine, serotonin, endorphins). Depressants inhibit the part of the brain that controls judgment; thus, users cannot accurately evaluate the risk of certain behaviors when taking depressants.

| Psychoactive Drugs | | | |
|---|---|---|---|
| **Drug** | **Classification** | **Effects** | **Medical Usage** |
| **Caffeine** | Stimulant | Produces feelings of wakefulness and alertness. Usually found in coffee, tea, and colas. While it can be physically addicting with mild withdrawal symptoms such as a headaches, most people have a psychological dependence on caffeine. | Treatment of migraine headaches |

| Drug | Classification | Effects | Medical Usage |
|---|---|---|---|
| **Nicotine** (tobacco) | Stimulant | Triggers feelings of calm, alertness, and feelings of increased sociability. Usually found in cigarettes and e-cigarettes and is very addictive. The withdrawal symptoms are very unpleasant, which makes quitting very difficult. | Induce vomiting (emetic) |
| **Cocaine** | Stimulant, local anesthetic | Cocaine and its more concentrated derivation, "crack," make people feel euphoric, full of energy, and full of confidence. It is extremely addicting. | Local anesthetic |
| **Methamphetamine** (crystal meth) | Synthetic stimulant | Designed to "wake up" part of the brain, produce extreme euphoria, and lower inhibitions. It is a derivation of amphetamines. It is extremely addicting and demands frequent use to maintain homeostasis. | Pharmaceutical varieties, such as Adderall and Ritalin, are used for treating ADHD. |
| **MDMA** (ecstasy) | Stimulant, hallucinogen | This "party drug" produces excitation and euphoria, and increases empathy for others. Using this drug can lead to risky sexual behaviors and is very addictive. | Currently being tested to help with symptoms of PTSD |
| **Alcohol** | Depressant, sedative | The effects of alcohol (beer, wine, liquor) are often the same as those of a psychoactive substance. Produces feelings of sociability and reduced anxiety. Note: Some energy drinks have concentrations of alcohol. | Antiseptic, solvent |
| **Barbiturates** | Depressant, sedative | The effects sought are anxiety reduction and feelings of euphoria. | Sedation, sleep aid, anticonvulsant, and reduction of high blood pressure |
| **Anti-anxiety** | SSRI (serotonin-norepinephrine reuptake inhibitor) | Anti-anxiety medications are widely used and abused. While very effective for anxiety, these medications can cause drowsiness and slurred speech. Examples are benzodiazepines (e.g., Valium, Xanax, and Klonopin) and non-benzodiazepines (e.g., Benadryl, Vistaril, Ambien, and Lunesta). | Anti-anxiety and insomnia |
| **Opiates** | Narcotic | The effects sought are pain relief, euphoria, and relaxation. Examples are opium, morphine, heroin, OxyContin, fentanyl, methadone, and codeine. Opiates are the most physically addictive of all drugs because they work as an endorphin agonist. This means that they trick postsynaptic cells into feeling a sense of euphoria. This leads to the lack of production of the body's natural endorphin molecules. | Painkiller and cough suppressant (codeine) |

*Continued*

| Drug | Classification | Effects | Medical Usage |
|---|---|---|---|
| **Hallucinogens** | Hallucinogen | Known as psychedelics, the effects sought are exhilaration, altered perceptions of reality, and insightful experiences. Some people use hallucinogens because they want to "think" differently. Examples are marijuana (THC), LSD (acid), PCP (angel dust), peyote (mescaline), and psilocybin (magic mushrooms). | While rarely prescribed, hallucinogens (e.g., Ketamine) are used for the treatment of depression. Marijuana is used to aid in the side effects of chemotherapy, treatment of glaucoma, and reducing the frequency of seizures. |

## Drug Dependence

Although some psychoactive drugs are approved for pharmaceutical use, psychoactive drugs are called *controlled substances* for a reason. Psychoactive drugs can be highly addictive and cause drug dependence and should only be prescribed by a doctor.

Our society is faced with serious problems related to physical and psychological drugs. Physical dependence means that the body depends on the drug to feel normal and achieve homeostasis. Since drugs mimic or block a neurotransmitter, if drugs are taken regularly, the body will reduce or stop production of that neurotransmitter and deplete the natural production of dopamine, serotonin, or endorphins that help the body to feel good. Once the high of the drug wears off, the resulting feeling is very unpleasant, causing the user to immediately reach for another dose. Just like *myopia* (nearsightedness, discussed in Chapter 6, "Unit 3: Sensation and Perception"), a drug-induced myopia is the unintended side effect of drug use that reduces the ability to think of long-range consequences. The person will often focus on the physical pleasure that occurs when taking the drug. Hence, the physical body progressively adapts to the drug and develops a physical tolerance to the drug.

*Tolerance* means that the person becomes less affected by the same dosage and needs a greater dose to achieve the same effect as the previously smaller dose. Once tolerance is established, the person becomes addicted because the body cannot function without the drug. If the drug is stopped, the body's withdrawal symptoms ensue. Withdrawal symptoms are painful and uncomfortable (e.g., fever, body aches, chills, and nausea) and can even be life threatening. Withdrawal happens when the body cannot get the substance that it has come to expect as part of its normal functioning. The psychological withdrawal symptoms can include distress, insomnia, agitation, anxiety, depression, and fatigue.

### Heads Up: What You Need to Know

On the AP PSYCH exam, you should remember the term *neuroplasticity* (see p. 73). While drugs obviously have physiological effects, the mental effects such as psychological dependence are quite powerful. The plasticity of the brain can change due to stressors and environmental influences of drug use. Therefore, it is possible to change the dopamine pathway in the midbrain in response to chronic drug use. Just the "expectations" from the sound of a bottle opening or the click of a lighter can stimulate a physiological reaction and cause a person to want to use the drug. Note: *Placebos* (substances with no therapeutic effect) can also cause the same physical reaction in those who are physiologically dependent.

# Chapter Review Practice Questions

Practice questions are for instructional purposes only and may not reflect the format of the actual exam. The questions and explanations that follow focus on essential knowledge, course skills, and course content.

## Multiple-Choice Questions

1. Which of the following processes occurs when a neuron creates an action potential?
   - **A.** Reuptake
   - **B.** Reaching dendritic threshold
   - **C.** Long-term potentiation
   - **D.** Depolarization
   - **E.** Neurogenesis

2. During a workplace confrontation, Andy was angry and punched a hole in the office wall. Which of the following brain structures was most active when Andy exhibited this physical act of anger?
   - **A.** Thalamus
   - **B.** Hypothalamus
   - **C.** Cerebellum
   - **D.** Hippocampus
   - **E.** Pons

3. The occipital lobe is most active during which of the following scenarios?
   - **A.** Listening to your teacher give a lecture
   - **B.** Smelling someone's perfume
   - **C.** Watching your teacher write on the board
   - **D.** Feeling a dog lick your hand
   - **E.** Distinguishing between the taste of a lemon and of a grapefruit

4. Which of the following is most true of the pituitary gland?
   - **A.** It controls the endocrine system and is controlled by the hypothalamus.
   - **B.** It controls the hypothalamus and is controlled by the endocrine system.
   - **C.** It controls the thalamus and controls the endocrine system.
   - **D.** It is part of the limbic system.
   - **E.** It is the source of our primitive urges.

5. Which of the following neurological structures allows charged ions to cross a cell membrane to facilitate an axon returning to a resting state?
   - **A.** Vesicle
   - **B.** Sodium pump
   - **C.** Receptor site
   - **D.** End bulb
   - **E.** Myelin

6. The cerebellum allows a person to perform which of the following functions?
   - **A.** Remember one's name
   - **B.** Regulate hunger and thirst
   - **C.** Activate the sympathetic nervous system
   - **D.** Run without thinking
   - **E.** Activate the parasympathetic nervous system

7. According to the homunculus model of the sensory strip, the average person is likely to evaluate a unique texture with their hand because
   - **A.** the cortex prefers tactile sensations
   - **B.** there is more surface area of the cortex dedicated to afferent information from the fingers
   - **C.** the fingers bypass the thalamus and go directly to the parietal lobe
   - **D.** there are many interneurons in the pathway between the fingertips and the sensory strip
   - **E.** it is the only sense that is not contralateral

## Free-Response Question

**1 question**

**25 minutes**

**Directions:** It is suggested that you take a few minutes to plan and outline your essay. Write your response on lined paper. You must demonstrate your understanding of course skills and course content. Your essay is considered a first draft and may contain some grammatical errors that will not be counted against you. However, to receive full credit, your essay must demonstrate defensible content knowledge with substantive examples where appropriate.

Winston is a sophomore with an amazing singing voice. He is planning to perform a new song in front of the entire student body, but he just started learning the lyrics of the song the night before. When Winston takes his position on the stage, he finds himself standing completely still and feeling terrified. His mind goes blank and he can't think of the words to the song.

Explain how the following concepts relate to the scenario and how each might help Winston or hinder Winston's efforts to perform.

- Cortisol
- Amygdala
- Beta waves
- Sympathetic response
- Hypothalamus
- Inhibitory postsynaptic potential
- Serotonin

# Answers and Explanations

## Multiple-Choice Questions

1. **D.** If polarization means separated, *depolarization* means not separated. In this case, the charged depolarized ions mix to create electricity—action potential, choice D. None of the other answer choices occur when a neuron creates an action potential. *Reuptake* (choice A) is when a neuron absorbs the neurotransmitter it previously purged to stimulate the next, postsynaptic, cell. It does this to reload. It happens as the axon repolarizes itself and expels the sodium ions. *Dendritic threshold* (choice B), like absolute threshold and differential threshold, asks a question: "Has the correct amount and correct type of stimulation occurred?" In this case, "Have enough neurotransmitter molecules stimulated the receptor site on the dendrite?" *Long-term potentiation* (choice C) is when neurons become better at communicating with each other by narrowing the space between them (synapses). It is happening right now as you learn the vocabulary in this chapter. *Neurogenesis* (choice E) means growing new neurons.
2. **B.** The *hypothalamus* has many nicknames: the gas pedal, the primitive urge area, and the physical manifestation of the id. Thus, Andy's urge to physically lash out originated in his hypothalamus, choice B, but it was his frontal lobe, or superego, that did not stop him from punching the wall. The *thalamus* (choice A) is the router of the brain and takes incoming, afferent signals from your senses

(eyes, ears, mouth, skin, but not nose), and directs those signals to the appropriate parts of the brain. The *cerebellum* (choice C) is where automatic behaviors, or procedural memories, are stored, such as walking, chewing gum, and, for most teens, checking their phones for messages. The *hippocampus* (choice D) is the memory organizer part of the brain. The *pons* (choice E) is part of the hindbrain and is most involved with life functions, sleep, and connecting the medulla to the rest of the brain.

3. **C.** The *occipital lobes*—remember you have two, one for each hemisphere—are responsible for receiving afferent signals from your eyes and turning them into vision, choice C, such as watching your teacher write on the board. Choice A is not correct because *listening* would involve the temporal lobe(s). *Smelling* someone's perfume (choice B) would involve the olfactory bulb. *Feeling* a sensation on your skin (choice D) is done by the parietal lobe(s), specifically the sensory strip. *Taste* (choice E) is also interpreted by the parietal lobe(s).
4. **A.** The pituitary gland is the "master gland" of the endocrine system. It controls and organizes the other glands of the body such as the testes, ovaries, and adrenal glands, and is controlled by the hypothalamus, choice A. The pituitary gland does not control the hypothalamus and is not controlled by the other glands of the endocrine system (choice B). The pituitary gland does not control the thalamus and does not control the other glands of the endocrine system (choice C). The pituitary gland is not part of the limbic system, which controls basic emotions and drives (choice D). The pituitary gland is not the source of our primitive urges (choice E); that is the hypothalamus. However, the pituitary gland plays a part in carrying out the hypothalamus' urges.
5. **B.** Sodium pumps, choice B, are channels through which ions (sodium) flow across the membrane and out of the axon. Vesicles (choice A) are molecule-filled bubbles in the axon terminal that burst open to release the neurotransmitter to the neuron on the other side of the synapse (post-synaptic cell). Receptor sites (choice C) are on the dendrite and receive neurotransmitter molecules from the presynaptic neuron. An end bulb (choice D) is the end of an axon and is shaped like a bulb; it is also called an axon terminal or terminal button. Myelin (choice E) is the fatty insulation produced by glial cells that coats the axon and helps signals travel faster down the axon.
6. **D.** The cerebellum is called the little brain and is responsible for initiating automatic behaviors such as running without thinking, choice D. Such automatic behaviors are also known as implicit memories and procedural memories. Remembering one's name (choice A) is an explicit memory and is not stored in the cerebellum. The hypothalamus regulates hunger and thirst (choice B). The cerebellum can act as an "on" switch for the sympathetic nervous system (choice C), which is arousal, and can be thought of as similar to the fight-or-flight reflex and an amygdala response. The cerebellum does not activate the parasympathetic nervous system (choice E).
7. **B.** The homunculus model is a representation of how a person would look if their body were proportional to the amount of brain space dedicated to that body part. The legs would be very small on the model because the brain does not have a lot of surface area on the cortex to handle incoming signals from the legs. The fingers on the model would be disproportionately huge because humans have a lot of surface area in the parietal lobe(s) dedicated to relatively small parts of the body; thus, the answer is choice B. Choice A is incorrect; the cortex is the whole surface of the brain and different regions "prefer" different functions. Choice C is incorrect because afferent signals from the body do not bypass the thalamus; they go through the thalamus. Choice D is incorrect because even though there are many interneurons in the pathway between the fingertips and the sensory strip, this is not the reason why people prefer to feel textures with their fingertips. Choice E is incorrect; the sense of touch is not the only sense that is contralateral. *Contralateral* means that afferent signals from the left side of the body are processed by the right hemisphere of the brain.

## Free-Response Question

To achieve the maximum score of 7, your response must address each of the bullet points in the question.

## Sample Student Response

*Cortisol* is one of the body's stress response hormones that is released when the body feels extreme stress. It shuts down unnecessary functions and directs energy to fighting, running away, or freezing. In this scenario, cortisol hindered Winston by causing him to "freeze." This prevented Winston from remembering the lyrics of the song. The *amygdala* is a limbic system brain structure that is involved with processing innate survival responses, such as fear. When Winston's amygdala was activated by stage fright, he was hindered and unable to perform. *Beta waves* are patterns of electrical activity on the surface of the brain that correspond with Winston's ability to concentrate. If Winston's brain activity was dominated by beta waves, this might have helped his ability to focus because he would have been able to concentrate on the lyrics. A *sympathetic response* is part of the autonomic nervous system and responds to stress by preparing to run away, fight, or freeze. The sympathetic response reduced salivation in Winston's mouth, hindering him from singing because he could not sing with a dry mouth. The *hypothalamus* is a region in the brain that controls how the nervous and hormonal systems interact in the body. It is in charge of primitive urges such as the desire to run or to eat. If Winston's hypothalamus was contributing to his urge to run away, he would be hindered from performing because he would be distracted by intense fear. *Inhibitory postsynaptic potential* makes a postsynaptic neuron less likely to fire. This might help Winston because neurons that are associated with stress might be inhibited, and thus allow him to relax. *Serotonin* is a neurotransmitter that regulates the transmission of messages between nerve cells in the brain. It is associated with a feeling of well-being and happiness. Feelings of anxiety and stress may have depleted serotonin levels in certain synapses and caused Winston to have a change in mood and anxiety.

Chapter 6

# Unit 3: Sensation and Perception

AP Psychology Unit 3 explores how external environmental input gathered by sensations and perceptions affects mental processes and behaviors.

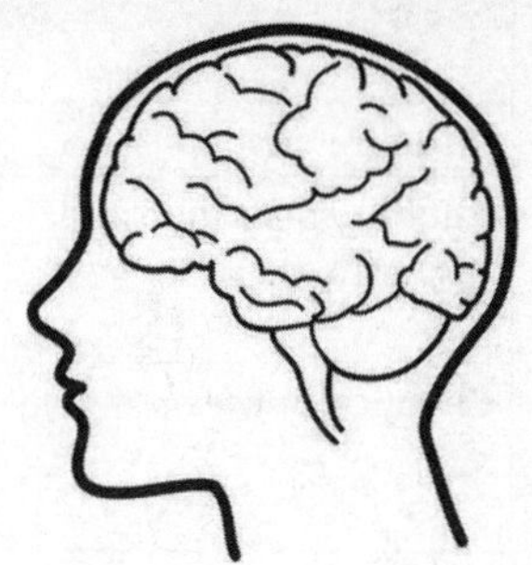

- Sensation and Perception Overview
- Key Contributors to Sensation and Perception
- Principles of Sensation
- Sensory Receptors
- Sensation—Balance and Movement
- Principles of Perception

## Overview of AP Psychology Unit 3

The overarching concepts for this chapter address visual and auditory perceptions and sensations. **The topics discussed in this unit will count toward 6–8 percent of your multiple-choice score.**

## AP Psychology Framework

Success on the exam depends on your ability to make connections to the major concepts described in the content topics of the *Course Framework for AP Psychology.* Remember that these concepts highlight the fundamental ideas that every student should take with them into the AP PSYCH exam and beyond.

Use the table below to guide you through what is covered in this unit. The information contained in this table is an abridged version of the content outlines with topic examples. Visit https://apstudent.collegeboard.org/apcourse/ap-psychology/ for the complete updated AP PSYCH course curriculum framework.

| AP Psychology—Unit 3: Sensation and Perception | |
|---|---|
| **Topic** | **Learning Target** |
| **Principles of Sensation** | ■ Describe general principles of organizing and integrating sensation to promote stable awareness of the external world (e.g., gestalt principles, depth perception, top-down processing, and bottom-up processing).<br>■ Discuss basic principles of sensory transduction, including absolute threshold, difference threshold, signal detection, and sensory adaptation.<br>■ Identify the research contributions of major historical figures in sensation and perception (Fechner, Hubel, Weber, and Wiesel). |
| **Principles of Perception** | ■ Discuss how experience and culture can influence perceptual processes (e.g., perceptual set, context effects, schema).<br>■ Discuss the role of attention in behavior. |

*Continued*

| Topic | Learning Target |
|---|---|
| **Visual Anatomy** | ■ Describe the vision process, including the specific nature of energy transduction, relevant anatomical structures, and specialized pathways in the brain for each of the senses (e.g., vision process, concepts related to visual perception, and theories of color vision).<br>■ Explain common sensory conditions (e.g., visual and hearing impairments, synesthesia). |
| **Visual Perception** | ■ Explain the role of top-down processing in producing vulnerability to illusion. |
| **Auditory Sensation and Perception** | ■ Describe the hearing process, including the specific nature of energy transduction, relevant anatomical structures, and specialized pathways in the brain for each of the senses (e.g., hearing process). |
| **Chemical Senses** | ■ Describe taste and smell processes, including the specific nature of energy transduction, relevant anatomical structures, and specialized pathways in the brain for each of the senses (e.g., taste and smell). |
| **Body Senses** | ■ Describe sensory processes, including the specific nature of energy transduction, relevant anatomical structures, and specialized pathways in the brain for each of the body senses (e.g., touch, pain, vestibular, and kinesthesis). |

## Important Terms and Concepts Checklist

This section is an overview of the important terms, concepts, language, and theories that specifically target the key topics of Unit 3. Use this list of terms as a checklist to check your personal progress. As you study the topics, place a check mark next to each and return to this list as often as necessary to refresh your understanding.

After you finish the review section, you can reinforce what you have learned by working through the practice questions at the end of the chapter. Answers and explanations provide further clarification into how sensation and perception can interpret information about the environment to impact behavior.

| Term/Concept | Study Page | Term/Concept | Study Page | Term/Concept | Study Page |
|---|---|---|---|---|---|
| **absolute threshold** | pp. 91–92 | **conductive hearing loss** | p. 100 | **kinesthetic sense** | p. 103 |
| **accommodation** | p. 95 | **cornea** | p. 95 | **law of Prägnanz** | p. 106 |
| **afterimage** | p. 94 | **depth cues** | p. 107 | **lens** | p. 95 |
| **amplitude** | p. 97 | **depth perception** | p. 107 | **McGurk effect** | p. 107 |
| **attention** | pp. 103–104 | **difference threshold** | p. 92 | **monocular cues** | pp. 108–109 |
| **binocular cues** | pp. 107–108 | **fovea** | p. 95 | **Müller-Lyer illusion** | p. 107 |
| **blind spot** | p. 95 | **frequency theory** | p. 99 | **myopia** | p. 97 |
| **bottom-up processing** | p. 104 | **gate-control theory** | pp. 101–102 | **opponent process theory** | p. 94 |
| **cochlea** | p. 98 | **gestalt principles** | pp. 105–106 | **optic nerve** | p. 95 |
| **color blindness** | p. 96 | **hyperopia** | p. 97 | **perception** | p. 89 |

| Term/Concept | Study Page | Term/Concept | Study Page | Term/Concept | Study Page |
|---|---|---|---|---|---|
| **perceptual constancy (size, shape, color)** | pp. 104–105 | **sensory adaptation** | p. 91 | **top-down processing** | p. 104 |
| **pitch** | pp. 97–98 | **sensory habituation** | p. 91 | **touch (tactile)** | pp. 100–102 |
| **place theory** | p. 99 | **sensory receptors** | p. 93 | **transduction** | p. 90 |
| **Ponzo illusion** | p. 107 | **sight (vision)** | pp. 93–97 | **trichromatic theory** | p. 94 |
| **pupil** | p. 95 | **signal detection theory** | p. 93 | **tympanic membrane** | p. 98 |
| **retina** | p. 95 | **smell (olfaction)** | p. 102 | **vestibular sense** | pp. 102–103 |
| **rods and cones** | p. 95 | **sound (auditory)** | pp. 97–100 | **visual illusions** | pp. 106–107 |
| **sensation** | pp. 89, 91–93 | **taste (gustation)** | p. 102 | **Weber's law** | pp. 92–93 |
| **sensorineural hearing loss** | p. 100 | **timbre** | p. 97 | | |

# Chapter Review

Many AP psychology students have asked why they need to study sensation and perception. Every day, the external environment floods our internal thoughts with representations from the world around us. It may surprise you, but our eyes do not actually see and our ears do not actually hear. It is through the process of sensing and perceiving that humans can see, hear, taste, smell, and feel. Sensory information is encoded and processed through one's perceptions of the world. Because our thoughts develop from our perceptions and our perceptions develop from our sensations, it is important to study these two key concepts in preparation for the AP PSYCH exam.

### Heads Up: What You Need to Know

For the AP PSYCH exam, ask yourself these two important questions as you continue to work through the topics in this chapter and develop an understanding of sensation and perception: How do we process the information we receive from our environment? How does our interpretation of the information we receive from the environment influence our behaviors and mental processes?

## Sensation and Perception Overview

Before we continue the chapter review, let's formally define the two main topics of this chapter: sensation and perception. **Sensation** is the automatic process of sensory receptors receiving information (visual, auditory, and other sensory stimuli) and transmitting the information to the brain through the central nervous system. **Perception** is the active process of selecting, organizing, and interpreting sensory information to formulate an internalized view of the world. Keep in mind that perceptions are not automatic.

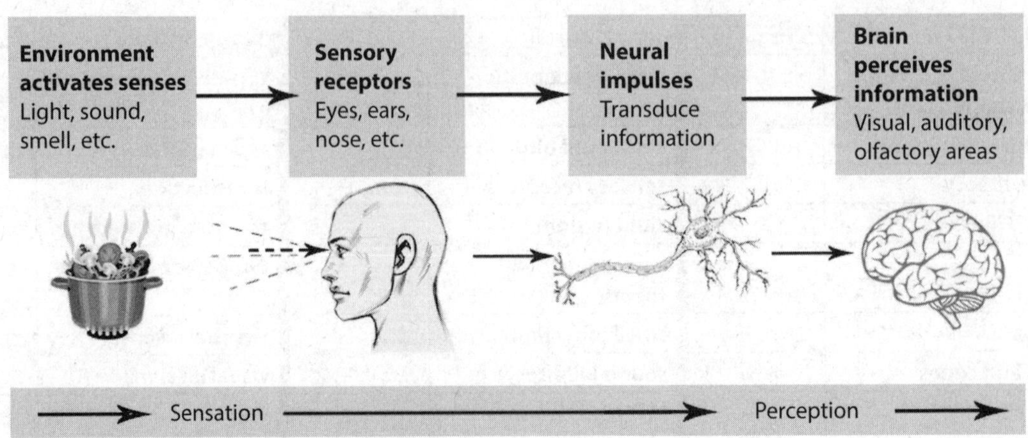


## Heads Up: What You Need to Know

Sensations provide the raw information of the environment to the brain using *sensory receptors* and perceptions provide a reflection of those experiences (e.g., the ability to see, hear, smell, taste, and feel). But how are sensations transmitted to our brain so that we can perceive them? A key concept in understanding the process of converting sensory stimulations into perceptions is called **transduction.** This concept frequently appears on the AP PSYCH exam. Transduction transforms environmental energy into neural signal impulses that link physical senses to specific locations in the brain. For example, when you see something, it is transduced to the visual cortex of the brain.

# Key Contributors to Sensation and Perception

On the AP PSYCH exam, you should be able to identify the major research contributors.

| Key Contributors to Sensation and Perception | | |
|---|---|---|
| **Contributor** | **Field of Study (Theory)** | **Famous For** |
| **Gustav Fechner** (1801–1887) | Psychophysics | Fechner was known as a sensory physiologist who invented psychophysics (the science of quantitative relations between sensations and stimulus). Fechner laid the groundwork for experimental psychology. |
| **David Hubel** (1926–2013) | Visual cortex | Hubel was a co-winner (with Torsten Wiesel) of a Nobel Prize for their contributions to information processing in the visual cortex. Hubel hypothesized that the development of the brain is shaped by eye activity. He suggested that eye disorders could avoid serious impairments if diagnosed and treated in early childhood. Hubel and Wiesel expanded the scientific knowledge of sensory processing. |
| **Ernst Weber** (1795–1878) | Experimental psychology | Weber is known for the *Weber-Fechner law* that quantifies perception of change in a given stimulus. He introduced the concept of the "sense of touch" and is considered one of the founders of experimental psychology. |
| **Torsten Wiesel** (1924–) | Visual cortex | Wiesel is a Swedish neurophysiologist who received the Nobel Prize in Physiology, together with David Hubel, for their discoveries in information processing in the visual cortex. |

# Principles of Sensation

Let's examine why sensation and perception can fluctuate in different people. To help us take a closer look, this section will cover some of the concepts related to sensation—sensory adaptation, sensory habituation, absolute threshold, differential threshold, and signal detection theory.

Thinking is an action that involves creating and manipulating mental representations.

## Sensory Adaptation and Sensory Habituation

The diminishing sensitivity to stimuli is called **sensory adaptation.** As you learned in Chapter 5, humans naturally adapt to environmental changes for survival—this includes sensory adaptations. Sensory adaptation is when your sensory nerve cells become less responsive to stimulus. When you are consistently exposed to a stimulus, your nerve cells may fire less frequently, and therefore, do not perceive the same. For example, can you feel the shirt or blouse that you're wearing right now? When you put clothing on in the morning, you may feel it on your body, but as the day progresses, the sensitivity fades.

**Sensory habituation** is similar to sensory adaptation, but it is a reduced response to something that previously prompted a stronger response. Sensory habituation is a *learned behavior* because your brain stops attending to repeated stimuli. For example, when you were younger, you were probably easily startled when you heard loud noises. Now, you may notice the same loud noise, but do not react to it the same way as you once did.

**TEST TIP: Sensory adaptation is not noticing stimuli; sensory habituation is not reacting to stimuli.**

## Thresholds

Perceiving information from the environment can be complex because perception has a different threshold for each person. Have you ever noticed that one person might be sensitive to certain sounds, smells, or tastes, while another person is not sensitive? For example, if you've ever played your favorite song too loud and your parents asked you to turn down the volume, your parents' perception of noise might cause them to be sensitive to the sound of your music selections.

In another example, one of the common symptoms of autism spectrum disorder is that a person diagnosed with the disorder often experiences a hypersensitivity to input from the environment (noise, lights, foods, or textures). This does not mean that a person with autism has more sensory neurons; rather, the sensitivity may result from how the brain perceives the information. Similarly, a person who is diagnosed with the rare phenomenon of *synesthesia* (stimulation of one sensory organ leads to an involuntary experience in a second sensory organ) can experience two different perceptions of the same stimulus. For example, the person may be able to audibly *hear* color. Although ears do not sense light waves, the brain processes the signals from the eyes as sight and sound.

### Absolute Threshold

Gustav Fechner coined the term **absolute threshold** to refer to the most sensitive and weakest stimulus. To determine the lowest and highest scales of absolute threshold, scientists expose research participants to progressively greater, and more intense, stimuli. The table that follows illustrates the measures of absolute thresholds.

| Measures of Absolute Thresholds | | |
|---|---|---|
| **Sense** | **Action** | **Approximate Minimum Stimulation** |
| **Visual** | Seeing | The equivalent of seeing a candle flame 30 miles away on a clear day (although there is debate on the accuracy of this given the numerous confounding variables involved). |
| **Auditory** | Hearing | The equivalent of hearing the ticking of a clock 20 feet away in a quiet room. |
| **Olfactory** | Smelling | The equivalent of smelling a musty odor from a water leak in a two-bedroom house. |
| **Gustatory** | Tasting | The equivalent of tasting salt dissolved in 2 gallons of water. |
| **Tactile** | Touching | The equivalent of feeling the wing of a bee falling on your cheek from a distance of approximately 0.4 inch. |

Absolute threshold introduces the idea of reliability. Is what you're sensing reliable and consistent over time? If you can only hear something one out of five times, did you really hear it? For example, consider the dimmest light you could possibly see (e.g., the dimmest star in the sky on a clear night). Absolute threshold is the minimum amount of stimuli needed to *reliably detect* a particular sense (e.g., light, sound, taste, or smell). If you see a star in the sky one out of ten times, you may wonder if you are actually seeing the star, or if you are confused by seeing *phosphines* (the phenomenon of seeing light without light entering the eye) that you sometimes see when you rub your eyes. Therefore, absolute threshold is determined when the stimulus can be noticed more than half the time it is presented.

## Difference Threshold

The **difference threshold** (also known as *just noticeable difference,* or JND) explains the smallest change in intensity (minimum difference) that a person can detect between any two stimuli for 50 percent of the time. For example, did you notice that the letters in "difference threshold" in the first sentence of this paragraph have a slightly larger font?

### *Weber's Law*

Psychophysicist Ernst Weber (pronounced *Vayber*) discovered the threshold for perceiving individual differences, called **Weber's law** (sometimes called Weber-Fechner law). In the diagram at right, for example, in a quiet car, if you turn up the radio one notch, it will correspond with your perception of a similar increase in sound coming out of the speakers. However, a stronger stimulus needs to be changed more than a weaker stimulus for a person to notice the difference. When music is soft, a small change will be noticed; when it is loud, a larger change is needed.

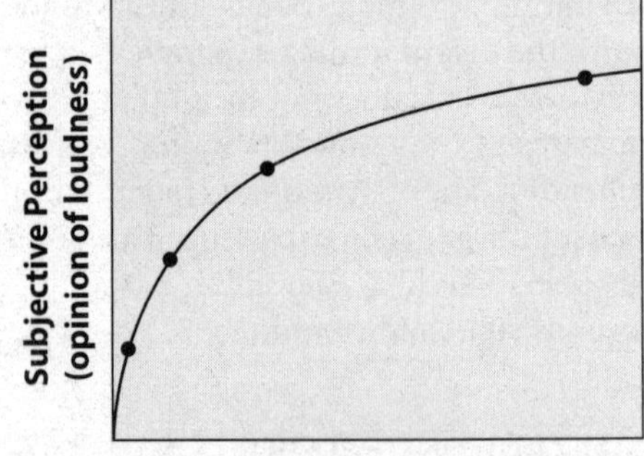


Weber's law explains why you may not have noticed the difference in the font, or why you may not notice when your headlights are on in the daytime. Weber's law quantifies the perception of change—the size of the difference threshold is proportional to the size of the original stimulus. The change in a stimulus that will be just noticeable is a constant ratio of the original stimulus. This includes all senses (i.e., seeing, hearing, smelling, tasting, and touching). For example, the constant for noticing weight is 0.05. Therefore, if you are lifting a 100-pound weight, you would not notice an additional 1 pound of weight, but you would notice if you were lifting 6 additional pounds of weight. For example, if you are listening to music at a low volume or a high volume, you would probably not notice a very slight change. The change would have to be significant in order to notice it.

## Signal Detection Theory

Most concepts in psychology are not as precise as Weber's law with a logarithmic equation. Confounding variables frequently influence experimental results. **Signal detection theory** explains that the intensity of a stimulus (called a *signal*) not only depends on the strength, but also on the person's psychological state of mind, motivation, and expectations. Signal detection takes into account the person's *motivation to notice*. For example, consider walking past a sink full of dirty dishes, but not noticing the dirty dishes. When your mom asks you if you noticed the dirty dishes, you don't remember seeing them. Even though light bounced off the dishes and crossed your eye's retina, you might not have perceived the dishes, and therefore, not detected the signal. In another example, in Chapter 4, "Unit 1: Scientific Foundations of Psychology," we discussed a researcher who predicts a significant difference between the control group and the experimental group. If the researcher notices something that is not in the results, it is a false alarm error or Type I error. The researcher did not perceive the error in the results.

The relationship between a physical stimulus and a sensory response is more than a precise mathematical equation. Absolute threshold is not constant; it can be changed based on a variety of variables. When studying sensory responses, it's always important to consider the human psychological elements. The relationship between the intensity of the stimulus and the participants' perception is called *psychophysical* (the relationship between physical stimuli and the psychological response).

# Sensory Receptors

The human body has many types of **sensory receptors** that detect and respond to sensory stimuli. This section will discuss the forms of sensory receptors that are presented on the AP PSYCH exam: sight, sound, touch, smell, and taste.

Note: The sensory receptors in this section are listed according to energy or chemical senses. The first three senses—sight, sound, and touch—respond to energy sensory stimuli. Smell and taste respond to chemical sensory stimuli, rather than energy.

## Sight (Vision)

All light is electromagnetic radiation, and radiation comes from different wavelengths, frequencies, and energies. The shorter the wavelength, the higher the energy. Ultraviolet radiation (UV) is light on the electromagnetic spectrum with wavelengths shorter than the minimum that the human eye can see. The ability to see objects in our environment is the process of receiving electromagnetic radiation so that our eyes can respond to visible light waves by converting the electromagnetic energy into neural signals.

We see the colors of objects because light reflects off objects using a visible spectrum. The seven colors are different light wavelengths that bounce off objects. The wavelengths of reflected light determine what we see. For example, the black ink of the words in this sentence absorb all of the light, so they appear dark against the paper that reflects most light into your eyes. When all of the colors of the light are mixed together, you see white.

The colors differ in wavelength, and the following figure illustrates the relative wavelengths for all forms of electromagnetic energy. Notice that the shortest wavelength is violet and the longest wavelength is red.

**Visible Spectrum**

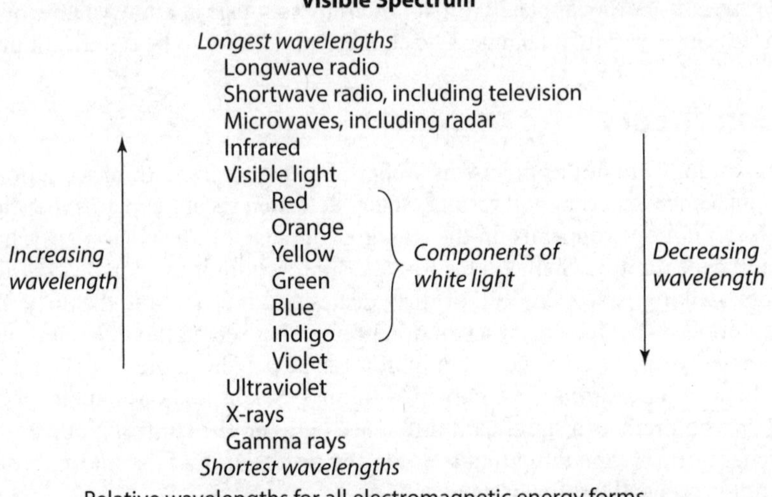


Relative wavelengths for all electromagnetic energy forms.

**TEST TIP: The mnemonic Roy G. Biv will help you remember the spectrum of colors (red, orange, yellow, green, blue, indigo, and violet).**

## Theories of Color Vision

Two theories that explain color vision are **trichromatic theory** and **opponent process theory.** Trichromatic happens in the retina, and opponent process happens in the brain.

| Trichromatic Theory of Color Vision (Young and Helmholtz) | Opponent Process Theory (Ewald Hering) |
|---|---|
| In **trichromatic theory,** there are three types of cells (cones) that, when stimulated, send signals to the brain. The brain processes these signals into what we see as color. The three cones respond to different wavelengths of radiation.<br>■ short wavelengths = blue<br>■ medium wavelengths = green<br>■ long wavelengths = red<br>The mix of afferent signals sent from the cones in different ratios can produce the perception of any color. Our idea of yellow comes from the stimulation of both red and green cones.<br><br>Advantage: It is based on how cones work. | In **opponent process theory,** there are neural circuits that, when excited, cannot process certain colors because the processes are inhibited. For example, when blue circuits are active, you cannot simultaneously see yellow. You can see opposites next to each other, but not at the same exact spot.<br>■ blue and yellow are opponent pairs<br>■ red and green are opponent pairs<br>■ black and white are opponent pairs<br><br>Advantage: Theory explains afterimages. An *afterimage* is what happens when one side of the pair is excited for a long time. The rebound of seeing the opposite is called the afterimage. |

## Anatomy of the Human Eye

On the AP PSYCH exam, it is important to describe the major structures of the eye and their functions. Remember, sensations are the raw material of thought, and they are sensed by organs, like the human eye.

Light enters the eye through the **cornea,** the outer transparent coating of the eye. The cornea protects the eye's interior (like a car's windshield). The light then passes through the **pupil,** the small opening in the center of the iris. The **iris** regulates the amount of light that enters the eye by dilating and contracting. The **lens** is behind the pupil and has many thin layers that help the eye to focus. It is transparent tissue that bends to focus by changing its shape; this is known as **accommodation.** As a person ages, the lens loses its ability to accommodate for near vision. That's why many older adults wear glasses. The lens focuses the incoming image onto the retina. The **fovea,** in the center of the retina, is densely packed with cones to give us the ability to see color and fine details (e.g., letters on this page). The **retina** is the whole back of the eye's surface (like a movie screen) that has sensory receptors for vision.

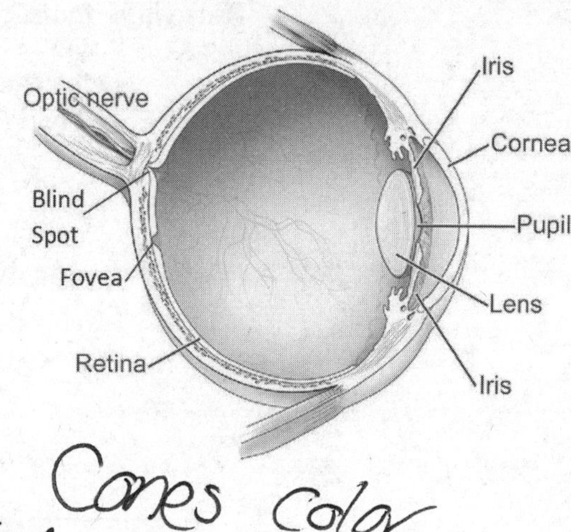


Have you ever held a flashlight on a part of your body (e.g., hand, mouth, or nose) and noticed that light is able to pass through the flesh? It's similar to light energy passing through to the back of the eye. If you follow light energy into the human eye, you would be able to see that light makes its way through the outer layer of the retina to the back of the retina where there are light-sensitive receptor cells (*photoreceptors*) called **cones** and **rods.** Since rods and cones are neurons, when they are stimulated, in this case by light, an action potential is created which is the beginning of the neural signal that is processed by the brain.

**Cones:** Cones are light-sensitive receptor cells that are concentrated in the center of the retina. Cones help you see color and fine details, such as when you're reading. Cones function in the daylight or in a room that has good lighting. You can't read or see color out of the corner of your eye because that image would be projected somewhere on the periphery of retina and not concentrated where there is a dense group of 100 million cones.

**Rods:** Rods are light-sensitive receptor cells in the retina that detect black, white, and gray. Rods help you see in dim light or twilight and help you to see movement out of the corner of your eye. There are about 7 million rods at the fovea in the center of the visual field.

Let's recap the process. Light passes through the cornea, but only a certain amount of light is let in because the iris will cause the pupil to be small enough for comfort. The lens pinpoints the image onto the fovea so the cones can process the color and fine details while everything else in the visual field is projected onto the retina.

However, there is a certain part of the retina that has no rods, called the **blind spot.** This is where the optic nerve passes through the optic disc.

Once the electromagnetic radiation that we call visible light (ROYGBIV) stimulates the rods and cones, the neural signal needs to go somewhere. If enough rods are stimulated, they will signal a bipolar cell, which will then send the signal to a ganglion cell, which will then form strands of rope to form the **optic nerve.** The optic nerve carries information to the lateral geniculate nucleus, which is part of the thalamus, where the information is transmitted and distributed throughout the brain. Remember, the thalamus acts as a router to transmit afferent signals throughout the brain. The nerve fibers from each side of the retina go to the right and left hemispheres. This plays an important role in depth perception. The area of the brain where the two optic nerves cross is called the *optic chiasm*.

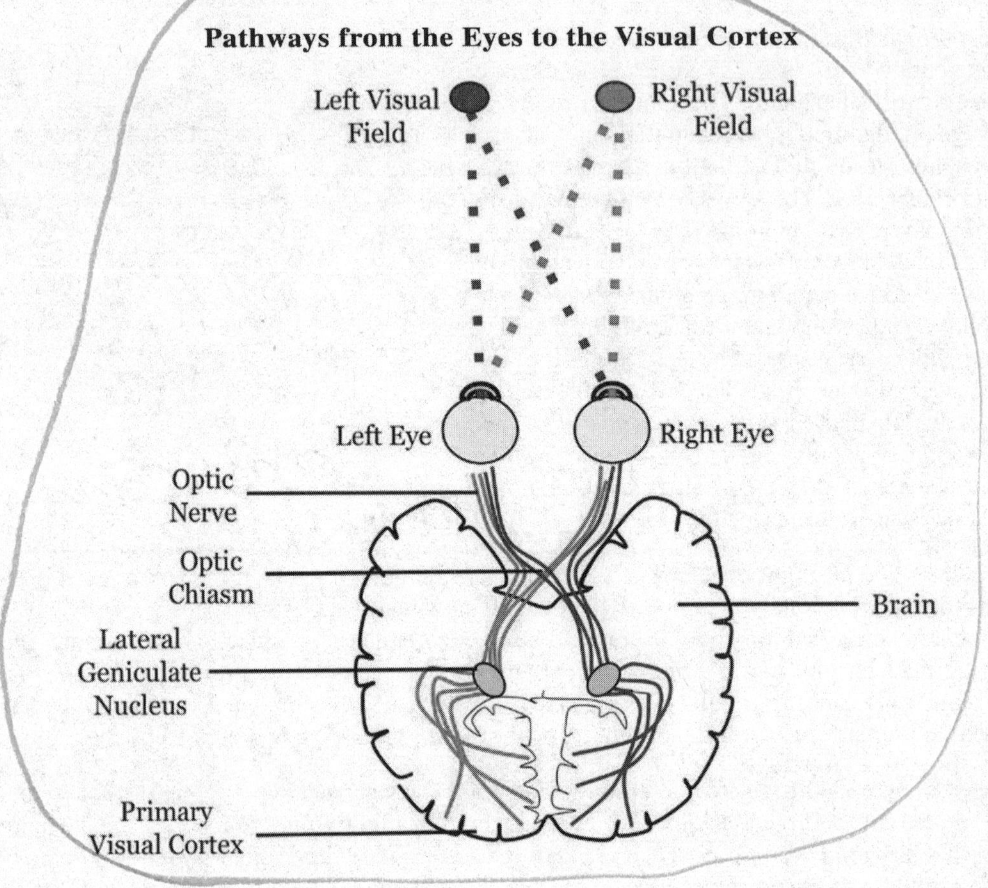


**Light flow:** ganglion → bipolar → receptor (rod or cone)

**Neural signal flow:** thalamus ← optic nerve ← ganglion ← bipolar ← receptor

**Did you know?** The gene for *color blindness* is carried by the Y chromosome, and therefore color blindness almost always affects men. Color blindness is the inability to distinguish certain colors from one another. It makes it difficult to see the differences in colors when selecting clothing and other objects (e.g., fruits and vegetables). For example, a person with color blindness may not be able to see the difference between a red and a green traffic light, so people with color blindness learn to adapt to the differences.

The cells that detect light, rods and cones, may be responsible for the deficiency. The three types of cones that see color (red, green, and blue) signal the brain to determine color perception. Scientists suggest that color blindness occurs when one or more of the color cone cells is absent or not functioning properly.

## Nearsighted vs. Farsighted

The distance from the lens to the retina can sometimes be either too short or too long for a person to focus. If the image is not focused, it will be blurry. Nearsighted vision is called **myopia** and occurs when the eye focuses distant images in front of the retina (instead of on the retina). People who are nearsighted perceive near objects clearly, but distant objects become blurry. Farsighted vision is called **hyperopia** and occurs when close images focus behind the retina (instead of on the retina). People who are farsighted perceive far objects clearly, but near objects become blurry.

**TEST TIP: On the AP PSYCH exam, you will see more questions about the eye and vision than any of the other senses (sound, smell, taste, or touch).**

# Sound (Auditory)

Similar to light, sound exists in our mind through perception. Sound is a perception-based sensation of vibrating air molecules that transduce into neural signals to the brain.

## How to Measure Sound

Sound is measured by its frequency and intensity. *Frequency* is the number of vibration waves per second measured in hertz (Hz). *Intensity* is how loud the sound measures in decibels (dB). The three dimensions of sound are pitch, loudness, and timbre.

| Perception of Sound | Sensation of Energy | Description |
|---|---|---|
| **Pitch** | Frequency | Humans can *sense* the *frequency* of the sound wave, but *perceive* pitch. In frequency, if the sound wave has a frequency of 100 waves per second, then 100 pulses per second move up the auditory nerve signals to the brain. The cycles per second are measured in *hertz* (Hz).<br><br>**Pitch** (high or low sounds) is determined by frequency. The higher the frequency, the higher the sound. Humans can hear an impressive range of pitches. For example, humans can hear very deep, low sounds that correspond to a frequency of 30 Hz (e.g., whale burp) and can hear as much as 20,000 Hz (e.g., mouse fart). In addition, humans are very sensitive to the changes in the sound. Remember how the Weber's constant for noticing change in weight was 0.05? For pitch, the constant is 0.003. This is the reason that humans love music and notice the different types of cries from a baby. |
| **Loudness** | Amplitude | The loudness of sound is determined by the measure of **amplitude.** Humans *sense* the amplitude of the sound wave, but *perceive* loudness. Amplitude is how high the wave reaches by the force (pressure) of the air molecules. It is measured in decibels (dB). |
| **Timbre** | Shape of the wave | All instruments, voices, and sources of sound have a mix of waves. **Timbre** (pronounced *tamber*) is the distinctive "quality" of a sound that distinguishes it from pitch and loudness. This makes them sound different to the perceiver. A violin and a trumpet might play the same notes, at the same pitch (number of waves per second) and the same loudness (height of waves), but they sound different because the mix of waves each sound has is perceived differently by each individual. |

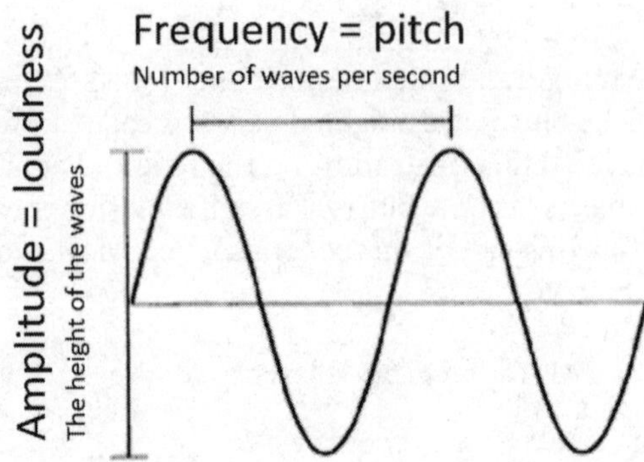


**Did you know?** In space, no one can hear you scream. Sound travels in waves and causes molecules to vibrate and collide with each other, but in space the molecules are too far apart. To hear sounds, there must be a medium (e.g., air pressure, water, or a solid object). In space, there is no air, so sound has no way to travel.

## Anatomy of the Ear

The ear consists of three major parts: the outer ear, middle ear, and inner ear. The ear and all of its parts have one job: to move sound vibrations through the outer ear to the inner ear, where they can be transduced into neural signals to the brain.

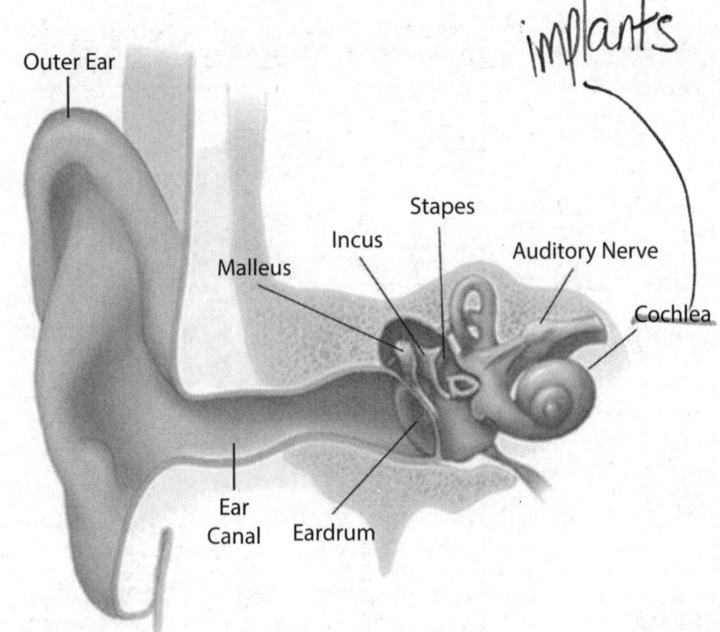


Source: National Institutes of Health

Sound waves enter the outer ear and move through the ear canal to the eardrum. The ear canal acts like a cave and helps to echo sound toward the eardrum **(tympanic membrane).** The eardrum vibrates from the incoming sound waves and sends these vibrations to three small connected bones in the middle ear (called the *ossicles*). The three tiny bones are *malleus* (hammer), *incus* (anvil), and *stapes* (stirrup). The movement sends a signal to the **cochlea** in the inner ear and causes fluid to move in the inner ear. As the wave of fluid moves through the snail-shaped cochlea, it stimulates thousands of tiny hair-like cells. (Note: The hair-like cells are similar to seaweed that flutter when waves touch them.) This movement converts vibrations into nerve impulses that are carried to a precise location in the brain.

**Did you know?** The hair-like cells in the inner ear are sensory receptors that are the cause for most hearing loss. These tiny cells are very sensitive, delicate, and fragile. The human ear has about 16,000 of these cells in the cochlea. If a cell loses sensitivity to soft sounds, it can still respond to loud sounds. But what is a loud sound? What is a loud sound to one person may not be loud to another person (see "How to Measure Sound," earlier in this chapter).

## Place Theory and Frequency Theory

Different theories describe how we can recognize a high or low frequency or pitch when we are hearing the sound. Two theories of frequency and pitch are place theory and frequency theory.

**Place theory** suggests that we hear distinct pitches because various sound waves activate specific areas in the cochlea's basilar membrane. Therefore, the brain can recognize pitch by its location. **Frequency theory** provides a good explanation for how we hear low tones. It suggests that we do not experience sound waves; rather, it is the frequency of movement of the basilar membrane that determines tone and allows us to detect pitch. The hair-like cells vibrate the same number of times per second and communicate to the brain using frequencies that match the type of pitch. The number of times the hair-like cells are stimulated determines if the sound is loud or soft.

**Did you know?** The number of times a neuron fires accounts for the intensity of a signal. If a neuron fires 500 times per second, your brain perceives the message as loud or painful, called *temporal coding*. Therefore, one neuron can send different signals, depending on how often it fires, recharges, and fires again.

## Hearing Loss and Deafness

Hearing loss is described as when a person is not able to hear as well as someone with normal hearing. The loss can be mild, moderate, severe, or profound and affects about 48 million people in the United States. Did you know that more than 90 percent of children who are born with hearing loss are born to hearing parents? Early identification of children with hearing loss is essential to developing communication skills because even a mild hearing loss can cause a child to miss as much as 50 percent of classroom instruction.

Hearing loss may impact at least one in five people (ages 12 and over) living in the United States. Over half of the people older than age 75 have hearing loss, and one-third of the people ages 65 to 74 have hearing loss.

### *Types of Hearing Loss*

The causes of hearing loss or deafness can result from trauma, tumors, infection, and other disorders. Treatment depends on the degree or type of hearing loss. The two types of hearing loss that you should be familiar with on the AP PSYCH exam are conductive and sensorineural.

**Conductive hearing loss** is when the sounds are not conducted by the outer and/or middle ear. The vibrations are not transduced into neural signals to be transmitted to the cochlea in the inner ear. This causes the reduced volume of sound that can be moderate to severe. The causes of conductive hearing loss include fluid in the ears, foreign objects in the ears, chronic allergies, ruptured eardrum, or impacted ear wax. Treatment options include hearing aids, medications, or surgery.

**Sensorineural (nerve) hearing loss** is when sound reaches the inner ear, but it is not being relayed to the precise location in the brain to interpret the sensory information. The cause of sensorineural hearing loss can be neurological damage to the inner ear (auditory nerve) due to chronic loud noises (e.g., explosions), tumors, head trauma, viral infections, or aging. Some diseases or infections that can cause hearing loss include chicken pox, mumps, meningitis, sickle cell disease, Lyme disease, diabetes, and syphilis. Treatment includes hearing aids, but one of technology's most amazing miracles, a *cochlear implant,* can surgically transduce sound direction into neural signals that can be understood.

## Touch (Tactile)

**Touch** is perceived through contact with the body onto an external object. Internal sensory receptors of touch include four distinct senses: cold, warmth, pressure, and pain. Although cold, warmth, and pressure can turn into pain, pain is the physical discomfort of touching something unpleasant. The sense of touch is also called *tactile sense* or *cutaneous sense*.

Your skin is the largest organ of your body and is composed of several layers. The top layer is the epidermis, the second layer is the dermis, and the bottom layer is the subcutaneous tissue. The sense of touch is regulated by a network of nerve endings and sensory receptors in the skin called the *somatosensory system*.

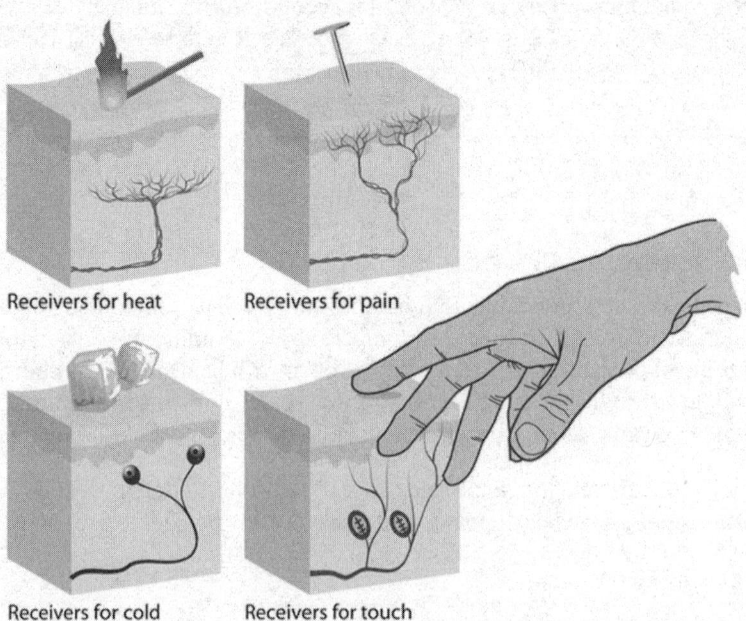


Sensory organs of the skin

Source: © 2019 iStockphoto LP

When your brain receives tactile information from sensory receptors, you will notice that some of your body's nerve endings are more sensitive to touch than others. For example, you can perceive water about 110 degrees Fahrenheit as hot, but you cannot perceive hot water that is much higher than 110 degrees because you perceive pain instead of heat.

## Pain

Tactile stimulation can carry a great deal of pleasure, but it can also carry a great deal of pain. Pain is a chemical reaction, a psychological experience, and an emotional reaction.

### *Gate-Control Theory*

**Gate-control theory** suggests that pain can be blocked. Nerves from all over your body are connected to the spinal cord. The spinal cord has many gates that receive messages when a part of the body feels pain. If the gates are open, then the pain messages pass through to the brain and you will most likely experience a high level of pain. If the gates are closed, fewer messages pass through to the brain and you will most likely experience less pain.

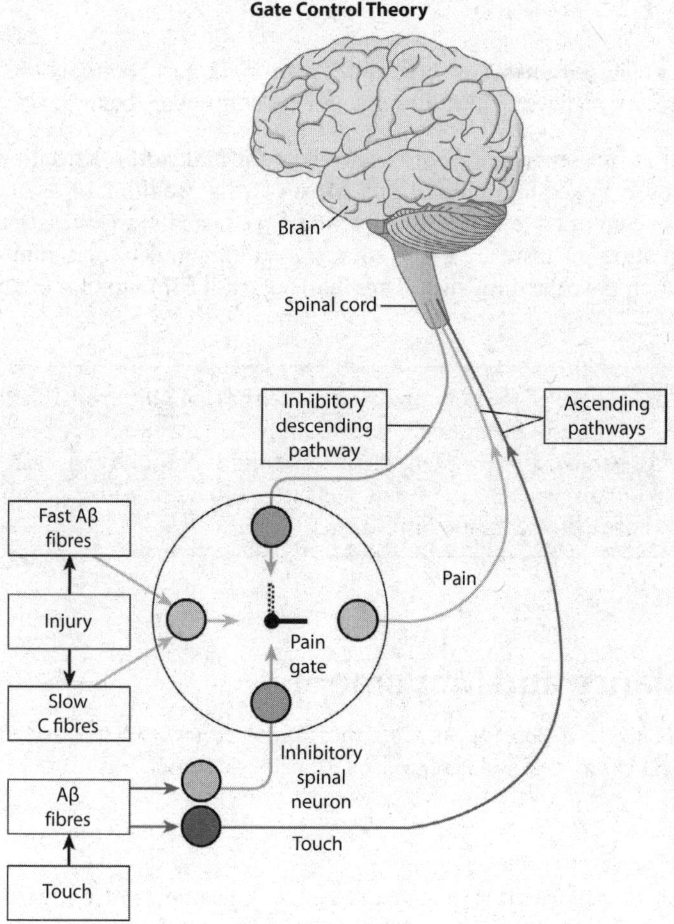


Credit: Peter Gardiner / Science Photo Library

The spinal cord contains a neurological gate in the *dorsal horn* that can block pain signals. According to the theory, nonpainful pressure closes the gate to the pain. For example, pain may be relieved when nonpainful pressure is applied to a part of the body when experiencing pain. This suppresses the pain and prevents the pain sensation from traveling up the spinal cord to the brain (*inhibitory interneurons*). For example, you might notice that putting ice on an injury helps to reduce pain. Imagine that the sensation of cold forces itself through the gate and blocks the pain from passing through to the brain. The brain itself has no pain receptors. In fact, many brain surgeries are done when the patient is awake.

### Smell (Olfactory)

**Smell (olfaction)** has an important role in human behavior. It is our most primitive sense and is interlinked with the sense of taste. Molecules of an odor become airborne when they pass from a solid or liquid form to a gaseous state. When those molecules become airborne, they travel to olfactory receptor cells that are transduced from the olfactory bulb into neural signals. The neural signals bypass the brain's thalamus and go directly to the amygdala and hippocampus. This is why smells trigger memories and emotions so vividly. Humans are able to distinguish over 10,000 blends of smell substances.

### Taste (Gustation)

The sensory receptors for **taste (gustation)** are cells called *taste buds.* Taste buds are the tiny bumps located on your tongue. Taste bud receptors have a short lifespan and are continually being replaced about every 10 days.

Taste is the most limited of our senses and is often mistaken for many other sensations (e.g., smell, texture, temperature) that are closely linked to our emotions. Most of what we think of as taste is actually perceived as smell. For example, we cannot taste the flavor of orange. We taste its sweetness, but smell the flavor of orange. The five basic qualities of taste are sweet, sour, salty, bitter, and savory (sometimes called *umami,* which corresponds to a rich flavor). Many dishes are made up of a combination of these tastes.

**Did you know?** Humans are genetically predisposed to disliking bitter-tasting foods. Researchers believe humans are sensitive to bitter tastes because it has an evolutionary purpose—our ancestors found it necessary for human survival. Our ancestors found that food that tasted good was generally good for humans, whereas food that was bitter often contained poisonous or mind-altering molecules that elicited a subtle bitter taste.

## Sensation—Balance and Movement

Before we move on to the topic of perception, it's important to review two sensory concepts that frequently appear on the AP PSYCH exam: vestibular sense and kinesthetic sense.

### Vestibular Sense

**Vestibular sense** is a sense of balance. It is the sensory system's awareness of body balance and special orientation. The vestibular sense is located in the structures of the inner ear that orient balance, equilibrium, and proprioception. For example, vestibular imbalance related to a severe inner ear infection can cause dizziness, motion sickness, and disorientation. Think of vestibular sense as something that tells you where your head is in relation to the ground. Humans have three semicircular canals in each ear located near the cochlea of the inner ear. These horseshoe-shaped organs are filled with gel-like fluids and tell the brain when the head moves in a circular motion (e.g., when you nod, look down, or look from right to left). As your head moves, the fluid remains parallel to the ground from a tilting action. If the canal moves but the fluid does not move, it can cause an imbalance.

### Kinesthetic Sense

**Kinesthetic sense** is the feeling of movement. It is sensory input that provides the brain with information about the body to control movements. Kinesthetic sense helps us to perceive body position, weight, or the movements in muscles and joints. Can you close your eyes and bring your finger to your nose? If so, that is your kinesthetic sense. It is based on *proprioception* (the awareness of the position and movement of your body), which is a feedback loop from your muscles to your brain. When your brain flexes your bicep, your bicep moves. As your muscle flexes, it sends a signal back to your brain that your brain interprets as the location of your arm.

## Principles of Perception

In the previous two sections, we reviewed the process of *sensing* (receiving information from the environment and transmitting that information to the brain). This section will cover how the brain actively organizes and integrates the sensory information to construct a person's perception of the world. Perception is the conscious awareness of taking sensory stimuli from the outside world and forming an internal representation of that information. Perception affects attention, motivation, learning, and expectations.

### Attention

**Attention** is an awareness of the world around you and is a central part of perception. Without attention, perception is not possible. The ability to maintain attention to focus on a stimulus can vary depending on different elements (e.g., personal motivation, emotion, environmental distractions, and the complexity of the stimulus). Human senses receive an estimated 11 million bits of information per second, but we can only consciously process about 40 bits per second. *Selective attention* is when the brain selectively filters out large amounts of sensory information to help us pay attention and react to specific stimuli.

**TEST TIP: The *cocktail party phenomenon* is an example of selective attention and has frequently appeared on the AP PSYCH exam. Imagine lots of people at a party who have formed into several conversational groups. In a noisy room, a person in one group can focus on a single conversation and filter out what is being said in other groups. However, if the person's name is spoken out loud in another group, the person instantly notices the stimuli of his name.**

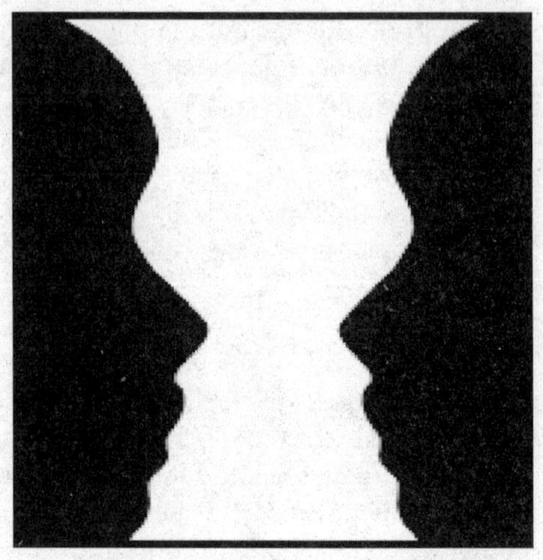

For example, look at the image at right. Do you see two faces or a vase? In black, you see two faces looking directly at one another. In white, you see a curved vase. If you noticed both images, which one did you pay attention to first? Psychologist Edgar Rubin created this image to test visual perception.

## Top-Down Processing

Sensory experiences are organized and interpreted differently by each individual. Most people organize perceptions by prior knowledge and experiences, called **top-down processing.** Top-down processing is automatic, unconscious, and based on prior experiences. Reading this sentence proves this point because a competent reader does not read each letter of a word (and sometimes not even each word). Competent readers usually read schematic groups of words to understand the meaning of a sentence. In fact, top-down processing sensations are turned into perceptions so effortlessly and unconsciously that they can influence your thoughts, called embodied cognitions. *Embodied cognitions* occur when unconscious perceptions trigger bodily reactions, which in turn affects how and what the brain thinks.

## Bottom-Up Processing

Bottom-up perceptual processing is when the brain must assemble each individual sensation into a recognizable whole (e.g., whole to parts, and parts to whole). For example, in the TV show "Chopped," chefs are given ingredients (parts) and must envision a dish (whole) to prepare. This process might be how babies perceive the world until they can establish enough experience to develop a library of perceptual sets. Visual bottom-up processing requires that the brain notice individual 2-D and 3-D shapes, known as **geons,** and assemble them into recognizable objects.

### Perceptual Constancy

**Perceptual constancy** (sometimes called *object constancy*) is the tendency to see familiar objects as unchanging. It is the ability to perceive an object as the same even when the illumination and retinal image change. Perceptual constancy is a good example of top-down processing (e.g., when the mind holds perception the same even when sensory information changes). In perceptual constancy, we perceive objects as a constant shape, size, or color despite their differences.

**Size constancy** is the tendency to perceive a change in an object within a reasonable range. Consider walking closer to someone. As you get closer to the person, the image of the person becomes larger on your eye's retina. You know that a person can't increase in size when you get closer, but your mind can perceive a larger size when the person gets closer.

**Shape constancy** is the tendency to associate an object to a certain shape even though it transforms when the angle is changed. It is similar to size constancy because it uses distance.

In the three images below, did your eyes deceive you? Did you first see each door as a rectangular shape? The second and third doors change shape and size, called *size and shape constancy.* The image that is on your retina is a trapezoid, but your brain knows things simply don't change shape, so you perceive a rectangle.

**Color constancy** affects a person's ability to recognize colors. It is the tendency to perceive objects as retaining their color, even though colors are different under different lighting and at different angles. For example, when lights are dimmed in a room, we still know our red shirt is red although it now looks different.

## Gestalt Principles

Gestalt is another top-down processing concept. **Gestalt principles** state that the mind unconsciously sees patterns (or rules) that people follow to make sense of the world. It is based on the premise that "the whole is greater than the sum of its parts." Humans see objects as groupings of similar elements by recognizing patterns. This means that we don't perceive individual elements of an object; rather, we perceive and group elements together as a whole. From a *nativist perspective,* gestalt principles suggest that humans are born with the ability to see patterns. From an *environmental perspective,* gestalt principles suggest that humans learn these patterns as the brain rewires itself based on experiences.

The table that follows illustrates how the eye creates a whole gestalt from parts to bring order into perception.

| Gestalt Laws of Perceptual Organization | | |
|---|---|---|
| **Gestalt Principle** | **Description** | **Example** |
| **Proximity** | Proximity is how we organize and group objects that are near each other. In the image, you should automatically see a group of four dots and a group of two dots, not a group of six. | ● ●    ●<br>● ●    ● |
| **Similarity** | Similarity is how we group and organize objects that look the same. In the image, you should automatically see two groups, not one group of alternating dots. | ○●○●○● |

*Continued*

| Gestalt Principle | Description | Example |
|---|---|---|
| **Continuity** | Continuity is how we organize lines to minimize sudden changes. In the image, you should automatically perceive an arrow pointed in the right direction, even though it is composed of broken lines.<br><br>According to the environmentalist perspective, humans are prewired to see the arrow based on evolutionary beginnings. | |
| **Closure** | Closure is how we group and organize lines (or circles) to create whole figures. Although we *sense* broken circles, we *perceive* closed circles because of our schema of the alphabet. | Psychology |
| **Common fate** | Common fate is how we group objects together that appear to be going in the same direction. Notice that we sense that all four cars are not traveling in the same direction, but we perceive the cars all traveling to the right. If you look carefully, notice that the third car is facing left, not the right. | |
| **Phi-phenomenon** | Phi-phenomenon is how we group objects together with lights. Lights that blink in the same rhythm are perceived as motion. For example, if the "lighted bulb" (third position) turns off just before the fourth bulb lights up, you would perceive motion. | |
| **Figure ground** | Figure ground is how we group objects so that the mind is only able to concentrate on one object at a time (e.g., perceiving figures out of the background). Notice that you will only be able to see the white vase or the two black faces. You cannot see both simultaneously. | |

## Visual Illusions

**Visual illusions** are perceptual distortions of our senses. In illusions, the length, position, or direction of the object is misinterpreted from how we normally organize and interpret sensations. To understand visual illusions, let's first explore the **law of Prägnanz** (also known as the law of simplicity), which suggests that our brain organizes the world in the simplest possible form. It is a central law of gestalt psychology. When a pattern is viewed, it can be viewed as simple and complete, rather than complex and incomplete.

However, when our brain sees a visual illusion that it may not understand, it becomes a *binding problem*. The problem is that humans don't know exactly how the mind binds things together so we are able to see unified objects in our visual world. Researchers know that our mind follows rules for connecting objects to something that can be perceived. The laws are followed 99.99 percent of the time and work so well that most of us are not consciously aware of them. On rare occasions, the laws don't work, resulting in illusions.

The two illusions that follow are examples of your mind trying to apply a rule that doesn't fit that particular stimulus.

### Ponzo Illusion

The **Ponzo illusion** is a geometrical-optical illusion that suggests that the mind judges an object's size based on its background. When drawing two identical lines across a pair of converging lines, notice the upper line appears longer due to linear perspective.

### Müller-Lyer Illusion

The **Müller-Lyer illusion** is an optical illusion based on the gestalt principles of convergence and divergence. The lines at the sides appear to lead the eye either inward or outward to create an illusion of length.

## McGurk Effect

While optical illusions are by far the most common, there are also auditory illusions, such as the McGurk effect. The **McGurk effect** is a perceptual phenomenon that shows an interaction between hearing and seeing in speech perception. The illusion occurs when one sound is paired with the visual part of another sound, leading to the perception of a third sound. For example, the mind blends sounds (e.g., *ga*) with the visual component of the lips (pronouncing *ba*). The mind then combines the two to perceive the sound *da*. This is an example of an *illusory conjunction*. Therefore, an illusory conjunction is when your brain incorrectly combines sensations into an illusion.

## Depth Perception

**Depth perception** is the ability to see three dimensions and to accurately determine the distances of objects. We live in a three-dimensional world, but the image on our retina is only two dimensions. If the image on our retina is only two dimensions, how can we walk around without bumping into solid objects? Without depth perception, we would not be able to move around in our daily activities. The world would appear flat.

**Depth cues** help us to perceive three-dimensional space. The cues are elements in the environment and messages from the body that give us information about distance and space. Depth cues include eyes (binocular and monocular cues), auditory cues, and bodily cues (muscular cues).

### Binocular Cues

Because we have **binocular vision** (we see with two eyes), let's first review the two depth cues that require both eyes to work: retinal disparity and muscular convergence.

| Binocular Depth Cues | |
|---|---|
| **Depth Cue** | **Description** |
| **Retinal disparity** | Retinal disparity explains small discrepancies in images on the right and left retinas. The disparity of the images on the actual retina depends on the eye(s) functions. When you read this sentence, you see only one of each word, but you have two eye signals traveling to your occipital lobe. Why? Well, your brain analyzes the difference (disparity) between the two signals. If the difference between two images is vast, then what you are looking at is very close. Don't believe it? Close one eye then the other while reading this book. Do you notice the big difference? Now look across the room and close one eye at a time. It should be a small difference because the objects are farther away. |
| **Muscular convergence** | Muscular convergence explains a neuromuscular cue that turns the eyes inward as the object moves toward you. The brain uses this information to judge distance. Remember the word *proprioception* (the awareness of the position and movement of the body) from earlier in this chapter? It is when your muscles send a message to your brain to let you know the position of your body. The muscles that make your eye move perform in the same way. The muscular signals help the brain to know the distance of objects. |

## Monocular Cues

**Monocular cues** help us to judge how close or far away an object is. The retinal disparity and muscular convergence of looking straight ahead at an object are very slight, so we need monocular cues to judge the distance of objects. This means that even people with only one eye can still perceive depth, though not as well as with two eyes. Note: Monocular depth cues are referred to as external cues because the information comes from outside of our body and not from the brain.

| Monocular Depth Cues | |
|---|---|
| **Depth Cue** | **Description** |
| **Relative size** | Relative size explains how objects that are farther away appear smaller. |
| **Height in visual field** | Height in the visual field explains that objects that are placed higher are perceived as farther away. |

| Depth Cue | Description |
|---|---|
| **Interposition** | Interposition explains that an object appears closer if it is partially blocking the view of another object. |
| **Linear perspective** | Linear perspective explains how converging lines that meet at a single vanishing point can make an object appear smaller. For example, if you have taken an art class, you know that two parallel lines (e.g., two railroad tracks) can appear farther away when the two lines converge. Larger objects appear closer and smaller objects appear distant. |
| **Atmospheric perspective** | Atmospheric perspective explains that objects that are farther away appear blurry because smog and air molecules distort our vision. |
| **Light and shadow** | Light and shadow explain how dimmer lights on an object make it appear to be farther away than brighter lights. The placement and angles of shadows give us cues about the shape and depth of objects. |
| **Texture gradient** | Texture gradient explains how texture contributes to depth perception. Objects that are farther away appear smoother in texture than objects that are closer. |
| **Motion parallax** | Motion parallax is the phenomenon that faraway objects appear to move slowly (e.g., a plane in the sky), but close objects appear to be moving fast (e.g., lines on a road). |

**Did you know?** Many pirates wore patches over one eye, but not for the reasons that you might think. Pirates did not have a string of amazing eye injury coincidences. Rather, pirates wore eye patches to keep one eye *dark adapted*. When the pirates had to go below the ship's deck where it was dark, the pirates shifted their patches to the opposite eye because it was already adapted to darkness.

# Chapter Review Practice Questions

Practice questions are for instructional purposes only and may not reflect the format of the actual exam. The questions and explanations that follow focus on essential knowledge, course skills, and course content.

## Multiple-Choice Questions

1. Which of the following represents the idea that one can perceive sensory input in multiple ways?

   **A.** Synesthesia
   **B.** Plasticity
   **C.** Transduction
   **D.** Differential threshold
   **E.** Myopia

2. Which of the following parts of the eye is most involved in sensing visual fine details, such as reading?

   **A.** Cochlea
   **B.** Rods
   **C.** Fovea
   **D.** Sclera
   **E.** Iris

3. Which of the following best describes the minimum amount of stimulation needed for a person to notice the stimuli?

   **A.** Differential threshold
   **B.** Absolute threshold
   **C.** Fechner's law
   **D.** Weber's law
   **E.** Retinal disparity

4. Which of the following is most related to the concept of afterimages?

   **A.** Helmholtz theory
   **B.** Trichromatic theory
   **C.** Optic chiasm
   **D.** Doppler effect
   **E.** Opponent processing theory

5. High-amplitude sound waves are correlated with

   **A.** timbre
   **B.** high pitch
   **C.** low volume
   **D.** low pitch
   **E.** high volume

6. Which of the following is an example of a monocular depth cue?

   **A.** Opsins
   **B.** Retinal disparity
   **C.** Feature detectors
   **D.** Ossicles
   **E.** Atmospheric cues

7. The three semicircular canals help to provide which of the following types of sensation?

   **A.** Cutaneous
   **B.** Tactile
   **C.** Gustatory
   **D.** Vestibular
   **E.** Olfactory

## Free-Response Question

**1 question**

**25 minutes**

**Directions:** It is suggested that you take a few minutes to plan and outline your essay. Write your response on lined paper. You must demonstrate your understanding of course skills and course content. Your essay is considered a first draft and may contain some grammatical errors that will not be counted against you. However, to receive full credit, your essay must demonstrate defensible content knowledge with substantive examples where appropriate.

Ms. Valencic introduced her students to concepts in the sensation and perception unit, but the students were struggling with the idea that what they perceive is not always what they sense.

Ms. Valencic decided to try a visual lesson to illustrate her ideas. She played a video that contained many visual illusions that distort the perception of objects. The volume on the video was very low and some students weren't sure what they heard. One student claimed she knew there was sound coming out of the speakers because she could feel the music as "goosebumps." Another student said the video was damaged because it was blurry, but denied that it was due to poor eyesight. A few students noticed that some of the illusions in the video weren't clear if they closed one of their eyes. In addition, the illusion at the end of the video amazed most the students with a colorful afterimage effect. Students understood the idea that it is not the eyes that are fooled by illusions, it is the brain. Ms. Valencic felt confident that she succeeded in teaching students about the concepts of sensation and perception by showing the video.

Using the scenario above and your knowledge of sensation and perception, respond to the following.

- Explain why absolute threshold must be measured using multiple trials when confounding variables are present.
- Describe a possible relationship between studying synesthesia and self-report bias.
- Identify one operational definition example of sensory adaptation.
- Identify a testable hypothesis in diagnosing myopia.

Explain how each of the following concepts helps the brain transform sensations into perceptions.

- Retinal disparity
- Opponent processing theory
- Top-down processing

# Answers and Explanations

## Multiple-Choice Questions

1. **A.** *Synesthesia* is a condition where a person perceives sensory input in multiple ways, such as hearing color, choice A. *Plasticity* (choice B) refers to the idea that the brain can grow and change itself based on environmental conditions. *Transduction* (choice C) is the process of converting environmental energy, such as light, into neural energy, such as your thoughts. *Differential threshold* (choice D) refers

to the minimum amount of change in a stimulus a person can notice. For example, did you notice that this sentence used 1 percent less ink than the one above it? No, that is not true, but hopefully you are paying more attention now. *Myopia* (choice E) describes nearsightedness, which means the image the lens is attempting to focus on falls short of the retina, so one perceives near objects clearly, but distant objects become blurry.

2. **C.** The *fovea* is the center of the retina. It is where the cones (which sense color) are centered. Cones have the ability to distinguish fine detail, such as the words you are reading now, choice C. The *cochlea* (choice A) is the snail-shaped structure in the ear that holds the structures that transduce vibrations into sound. *Rods* (choice B) are spread out all over the retina and are responsible for seeing in dim light and out of the corner of your eye. But since the cones are concentrated in the center of the retina (the fovea), a person cannot read or see color out of the corner of the eye. *Sclera* (choice D) is the hard covering of the whole eye. The *iris* (choice E) is the colored ring of muscle. When the iris expands and contracts, it opens the pupil.

3. **B.** The *absolute threshold,* choice B, is the smallest amount of stimulation a person can notice more than 50 percent of the time. For example, if a person can see an object 1 out of 10 times, the result might be due to chance. *Differential threshold* (choice A) is the minimum change in stimulation a person can notice. Imagine your mom tells you to turn down the TV, but you turn it down only one unit lower. She doesn't notice the small change in volume. *Fechner's law* (choice C) suggests that in order to double the perception of loudness, there must be triple or quadruple the sensation of amplitude. This means that sensation and perception do not increase at the same rate. *Weber's law* (choice D) is related to the differential threshold. If a person is perceiving a slight stimulus, it will not take much for that person to notice a change. If a person is perceiving a large stimulus, like a sunny day, it will take a lot to make that person notice an increase in brightness. *Retinal disparity* (choice E) is the difference between the signals of the right and left retina.

4. **E.** Afterimages are what people see after they have been staring at an image for quite a while. The *opponent processing theory*, choice E, suggests that when certain neurons consistently fire, the neurons that are opposite in function are inhibited. Therefore, when a person stops staring, there is a rebound effect. The neurons that are inhibited start firing and the others that have been firing take a break. The *Helmholtz theory* (choice A) refers to the researcher Hermann von Helmholtz, who found three types of color receptors (cones) in the eye. The *trichromatic theory* (choice B) is another name for the Helmholtz theory because Helmholtz found three cones. The *optic chiasm* (choice C) is the part of the brain where the optic nerves cross so that images from the right side of the retina go to the left side of the occipital lobe. The *Doppler effect* (choice D) refers to the perception that sound changes in frequency and volume as it approaches the listener.

5. **E.** *Amplitude* refers to the height of the top of the wave on the *y*-axis. The higher the peak, the more we perceive sound as loud, choice E. *Timbre* (choice A) refers to the shape of the wave and the purity of the sound. *High pitch* (choice B) is a perception based on high frequency. The frequency of waves can be objectively measured and whether it seems high or low is the opinion of the listener. *Low volume* (choice C) is associated with waves that are vertically short (or low amplitude). *Low pitch* (choice D) is associated with few waves per second and is perceived as a deep sound.

6. **E.** *Atmospheric cues,* such as smog or humidity, are depth cues and can blur images that are far away even when seen with one eye, choice E. *Opsins* (choice A) are light-sensitive chemicals present in certain neurons in the back of the eye. *Retinal desparity* (choice B) is when the brain compares the differences (disparity) between the signals from the eyes (retinal). Because the brain compares the signals from two eyes, it is not a monocular depth cue. *Feature detectors* (choice C) are individual

neurons in the occipital lobe(s) that react to specific simple stimuli. *Ossicles* (choice D) are the three small bones of the middle ear.

7. **D.** The *vestibular* sense is the sense of balance. People exist in a three-dimensional world and have three semicircular, fluid-filled structures in each ear to determine in which direction the head is moving, choice D. The *cutaneous* sense (choice A) is the sensation of touch. The *tactile* sense (choice B) is also the sensation of touch. The *gustatory* sense (choice C) is the sensation of taste. The *olfactory* sense (choice E) is the sensation of smell.

## Free-Response Question

To achieve the maximum score of 7, your response must address each of the bullet points in the question.

### Sample Student Response

A *confounding variable* is anything that might interfere with the results of a study. If a study was performed to determine the minimum amount of stimulation a person could notice, it might be possible that the participant's own body sent a signal to the brain such as a ringing in the ears or random muscle spasms at the exact same time the test was being done. If there was such a muscle spasm, it would be difficult to say with certainty that the person experienced a sense of stimulation. So, several instances of the test are done to eliminate possible confounding variables. It is only with the multiple trial-and-error format that *absolute threshold* can be determined. *Synesthesia* is when a brain uses more than one association area to process incoming signals from a sense organ, such as hearing color. Since one cannot compare his or her experiences to anything different, a person with or without synesthesia might not know they have it and might not be able to explain or describe it to someone else. This would explain how the self-report bias might make it difficult to identify and study synesthesia.

*Sensory adaptation* is based on a constant stimulus being noticed less as time progresses. Operationalization means taking an abstract concept such as perception and changing it so it can be measured. So, for example, sensory adaptation could be operationalized by assigning a number that corresponds with the sensation of the pressure of one's socks. If the participant reports the pressure is at a zero, then sensory adaptation has occurred. *Myopia* is a term for nearsightedness. A doctor might say that <u>if</u> a person cannot read the second line of an eye chart at 20 feet, <u>then</u> that person has myopia and needs glasses.

*Retinal disparity* is the difference between the signals that the right and left eyes send to the brain. If each eye senses information and sends the brain a signal about what it senses, the brain will compare those signals. If the difference is larger, the object is closer. *Opponent processing theory* is a theory of color vision that suggests that while a certain part of the brain is processing red, it cannot simultaneously process green. This means while we might sense the light waves for red and green at the same time, we can only perceive red or green in a certain space at a certain time. *Top-down processing* is the idea that the brain matches incoming sensations against what it already knows the object is and perceives that image or sound as a whole concept it already knows. For example, the ears sense the individual notes of the song "Twinkle, Twinkle, Little Star," but the brain perceives the song "ABC" because it was played in a classroom.

# Chapter 7

# Unit 4: Learning

AP Psychology Unit 4 explores the theoretical models of learning, including classical conditioning, operant conditioning, and learning by observation in social and cognitive learning.

- Key Contributors to Learning
- Learning Theories
- Classical Conditioning
- Operant Conditioning
- Cognitive and Social Learning

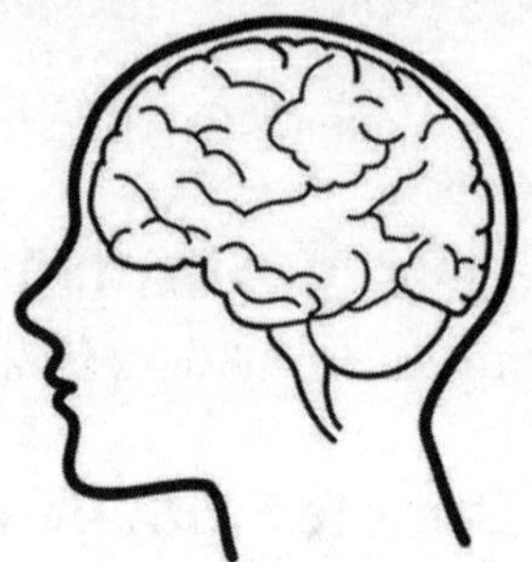

## Overview of AP Psychology Unit 4

Chapter 7 covers a range of topics related to how people learn and how learning outcomes are influenced by conditioning. **The topics discussed in this unit will count toward 7–9 percent of your multiple-choice score.**

## AP Psychology Framework

Success on the exam depends on your ability to make connections to the major concepts described in the content topics of the *Course Framework for AP Psychology.* Remember that these concepts highlight the fundamental ideas that every student should take with them into the AP PSYCH exam and beyond.

Use the table below to guide you through what is covered in this unit. The information contained in this table is an abridged version of the content outlines with topic examples. Visit https://apstudent.collegeboard.org/apcourse/ap-psychology/ for the complete updated AP PSYCH course curriculum framework.

| AP Psychology—Unit 4: Learning | |
|---|---|
| **Topic** | **Learning Target** |
| **Introduction to Learning** | ■ Identify the contributions of key researchers in the psychology of learning (Bandura, Pavlov, Rescorla, Skinner, Thorndike, Tolman, Watson, and Garcia).<br>■ Interpret graphs that exhibit the results of learning experiments.<br>■ Describe the essential characteristics of insight learning, latent learning, and social learning.<br>■ Apply learning principles to explain emotional learning, taste aversion, superstitious behavior, and learned helplessness.<br>■ Provide examples of how biological constraints create learning predispositions. |

| Topic | Learning Target |
|---|---|
| **Classical Conditioning** | ■ Describe basic classical conditioning phenomena (e.g., acquisition, extinction, spontaneous recovery, generalization, stimulus discrimination, higher-order learning, unconditioned stimulus, unconditioned response, neutral/conditioned stimulus, and conditioned response).<br>■ Distinguish general differences between principles of classical conditioning, operant conditioning, and observational learning (contingencies). |
| **Operant Conditioning** | ■ Predict the effects of operant conditioning (e.g., positive reinforcement, negative reinforcement, positive punishment, and negative punishment).<br>■ Predict how practice, schedules of reinforcement, other aspects of reinforcement, and motivation will influence quality of learning. |
| **Social and Cognitive Factors in Learning** | ■ Suggest how behavior modification, biofeedback, coping strategies, and self-control can be used to address behavioral problems. |

## Important Terms and Concepts Checklist

This section is an overview of the important terms, concepts, language, and theories that specifically target the key topics of Unit 4. Use this list of terms as a checklist to check your personal progress. As you study the topics, place a check mark next to each and return to this list as often as necessary to refresh your understanding.

After you finish the review section, you can reinforce what you have learned by working through the practice questions at the end of the chapter. Answers and explanations provide further clarification into the perspectives of learning.

| Term/Concept | Study Page | Term/Concept | Study Page |
|---|---|---|---|
| **acquisition** | p. 120 | **learned helplessness** | p. 128 |
| **aversive conditioning** | pp. 121–122 | **observational learning** | p. 128 |
| **avoidance learning** | p. 122 | **operant conditioning** | pp. 122–126 |
| **biological preparedness** | p. 124 | **punishment (negative and positive)** | p. 125 |
| **chaining** | p. 127 | **reinforcement (negative and positive)** | p. 124 |
| **classical conditioning** | pp. 118–122 | **reinforcement schedules** | pp. 125–126 |
| **cognitive learning** | pp. 126–128 | **reinforcers (primary and secondary)** | p. 125 |
| **conditioned response** | pp. 119, 121 | **shaping** | p. 127 |
| **conditioned stimulus** | pp. 119, 121 | **Skinner box** | p. 123 |
| **discrimination** | p. 122 | **social learning** | pp. 117, 128–129 |
| **emotional conditioning** | pp. 121–122 | **spontaneous recovery** | p. 120 |
| **extinction** | p. 120 | **taste aversion** | pp. 117, 122 |
| **generalization** | p. 122 | **Thorndike's law of effect** | pp. 116, 123 |
| **higher-order conditioning** | p. 120 | **token economy** | p. 125 |
| **insight learning** | p. 128 | **unconditioned response** | pp. 119, 121 |
| **instrumental learning** | p. 123 | **unconditioned stimulus** | pp. 119, 121 |
| **latent learning** | p. 127 | | |

# Chapter Review

A big question in the field of psychology is how learning should be defined. The answer has been debated for years, but most psychologists agree that learning is a "relatively permanent" change in knowledge or behavior that can only take place through experience. The term "relatively" is an important part of this definition because if everything is permanently learned, then school or even this book would be pointless.

For the AP PSYCH exam, you should remember that learning is based on experience. Simply getting older does not increase learning, but it is through a person's experiences over time, and through the reinforcement of these experiences, that learning is possible.

## Heads Up: What You Need to Know

For the AP PSYCH exam, ask yourself these two underlying questions as you work through the topics in this chapter and develop an understanding of learning: How do people learn? and How do our experiences influence our behaviors and mental processes?

**TEST TIP: When researching terms for the AP PSYCH exam, keep in mind that numerous psychology textbooks may identify units, chapters, and concepts differently. As you research the concept of "learning," refine your search by using specific keywords related to learning: *behaviorism, the learning approach,* and *conditioning.***

## Key Contributors to Learning

On the AP PSYCH exam, you should be able to identify the major contributors in learning research.

| Key Contributors to Learning | | |
|---|---|---|
| **Contributor** | **Field of Study (Theory)** | **Famous For** |
| **Ivan Pavlov** (1849–1936) | Classical conditioning | Pavlov was a pioneer in classical conditioning, stating that behavior is learned based on repetition, association, and anticipation (see also John Watson).<br><br>Pavlov conducted *stimulus-response* experiments. Dogs learned to involuntarily respond, by salivating, each time a bell rang at feeding time. The dogs were conditioned to respond to the bell, not to seeing or smelling the food. |
| **Edward Thorndike** (1874–1949) | Law of effect | Thorndike's research helped to lay the foundation for educational psychology. His research led to the development of operant conditioning within behaviorism (i.e., learning from the consequences of our behavior).<br><br>Thorndike's experiments concluded that responses that produce a good outcome will be likely to happen again, and responses that produce a discomforting outcome will not happen again. |

| Contributor | Field of Study (Theory) | Famous For |
|---|---|---|
| **John B. Watson** (1878–1958) | Classical conditioning | Watson applied Pavlov's stimulus-response manipulation to children and claimed that based on his observations, all behavior is the result of inner reactions to stimuli. |
| **Edward Tolman** (1886–1959) | Latent learning; cognitive mapping | Tolman was known for contributing to the concept of *latent learning* (behavior that is learned later when the right motivations occur). Tolman challenged Watson's assumption of classical conditioning and proposed that people had the ability to learn even if there is no reinforcement. Based on Tolman's experiments, animals (rats) were able to create cognitive maps.<br><br>Tolman's experiments concluded that humans learn cognitively by being active, not passive, learners; this is known as *cognitive mapping*. |
| **B. F. Skinner** (1904–1990) | Operant conditioning | In *operant conditioning*, people learn from operating in the environment.<br><br>Skinner's experiments concluded that when people function in the environment, their behavioral responses produce a consequence of either a reinforced reward or a punishment. |
| **John Garcia** (1917–2012) | Taste aversion (the Garcia effect) | Garcia discovered a conditioned taste aversion learning, called the *Garcia effect* (a survival mechanism that causes a person to have a learned connection between taste aversion and illness). |
| **Albert Bandura** (1925–) | Social learning theory | Bandura's *social learning theory* (1977) has had a significant impact in the development of learning experiences. Whereas the behavioral model of development emphasizes environmental influences on learning and conditioning, Bandura's theory emphasizes the value of learning through observation. This theory stresses the importance of observing and modeling the behaviors, attitudes, and emotional reactions of others to advance learning.<br><br>Bandura's experiments concluded that children learn aggression by observing, modeling, and imitating adult behavior. |
| **Robert Rescorla** (1940–) | Contingency theory | Rescorla studied the nature of associative learning. He proposed an alternative explanation for Pavlov's classical conditioning (stimulus-response) theory that emphasized a level of contingency. For learning to occur, contingent associations must occur between the conditioned and unconditioned stimuli.<br><br>Rescorla's experiments concluded that before the conditioning, the participant may be surprised by the unconditioned stimuli, but after conditioning, the participant is no longer surprised. For example, *A* is contingent on *B* when *A* depends on *B* and vice versa. |

# Learning Theories

On the AP PSYCH exam, it is important to be able to compare and contrast three noteworthy learning theories: classical conditioning, operant conditioning, and social-cognitive learning.

| Learning Theories | | |
|---|---|---|
| Learning is the process by which experience relatively changes a person's knowledge and/or behavior. | | |
| **Classical Conditioning** | **Operant Conditioning** | **Social-Cognitive Learning** |
| Stimulus-response learning | Rewards or punishment learning | Observation learning |
| (Ivan Pavlov and John Watson) | (B. F. Skinner and Edward Thorndike) | (Albert Bandura) |

The first published theories on learning were from Plato and Aristotle. Plato suggested that people are innately born with some knowledge (called *nativism*), and Aristotle suggested that people are born knowing nothing about the world (called *tabula rasa*) and we become who we are based on experiences.

The most direct form of learning is the ability to form mental associations, called *conditioning.* The two main types of conditioning are **classical** (Pavlov and Watson) and **operant** (Skinner and Thorndike) conditioning.

# Classical Conditioning

Russian scientist **Ivan Pavlov** is the most famous researcher of classical conditioning. He borrowed from Plato's view that people are innately born with knowledge, but could learn by associating one *stimulus* (something in the environment that prompts a response) to another. Pavlov's contributions in learning came about by chance. He was studying digestion in dogs when he accidently discovered that the salivation reflexes in dogs could be triggered by something other than food or the smell of food. Pavlov called his findings *reflexive conditioning* (sometimes referred to as *Pavlovian conditioning*).

## Reflex Response

Pavlov didn't teach the dogs to drool. All dogs, and presumably most humans, are innately born (unconditioned) with the involuntary production of saliva. Drooling is a **reflex response** (automatic action by the nervous system) when certain stimuli are present. Pavlov simply taught the dogs a new reason to drool.

Think about the conditions that must be present for a dog to drool. It is likely that the senses of sight and smell will trigger a dog to drool when presented with food, but what about the sense of sound? Pavlov's experiments proved that other bodily senses could also stimulate a reflex response. By introducing a new stimulus (sound) right before the smell of food, Pavlov discovered that reflex responses could be learned.

# How Classical Conditioning Works

Unconditioned Response (Salivation)

Unconditioned Stimulus (Food)

At this first unlearned stage, the dog is presented with food t(US), which triggers the innate reflex to salivate (UCR).

No Response

Neutral Stimulus (Bell Ringing)

At this stage, a bell is rung (NS), which causes no response from the dog.

Neutral Stimulus (Bell Ringing)

Unconditioned Stimulus (Food)

Unconditioned Response (Salivation)

Now, a bell is rung (NS) as the dog is presented with food (US), which causes the dog to salivate (UR).

Conditioned Stimulus (Bell Ringing)

Conditioned Response (Salivation to the Bell)

Finally, a bell is rung (CS) each time the food is presented until the dog salivates (CR) even when the food is not presented. Note: The sound of the bell becomes the conditioned stimulus (instead of the food) to trigger a conditioned response (salivation).

**KEY**

US – Unconditioned stimulus
NS – Neutral stimulus
CS – Conditioned stimulus
UR – Unconditioned response
CR – Conditioned response

| | **Conditioned Stimulus** | **Unconditioned Stimulus** | **Unconditioned Response** | **Conditioned Response** |
|---|---|---|---|---|
| Natural untrained dogs | | Food ⟶ | Drool | |
| During training | Sound + | Food ⟶ | Drool | |
| After training | Sound ⟶ | | | Drool |

**Did you know?** Most textbooks show that Pavlov rang a bell to produce a conditioned stimulus. However, Pavlov's written records show that he used a variety of stimuli, including a tuning fork. He banged the tuning fork against a solid object to make the precise sound of a bell.

## Pavlov's Other Conclusions

### Heads Up: What You Need to Know

On the AP PSYCH exam, you will need to identify some of Pavlov's other conclusions: acquisition phase, extinction phase, spontaneous recovery, and higher-order conditioning.

Pavlov's process of classical conditioning drew several other conclusions, as detailed in the following table.

| Pavlov's Other Conclusions | |
|---|---|
| **Acquisition** | Acquisition is the initial learning, or training, when the association between the unconditioned stimulus and the neutral stimulus is created. Pavlov found that the training must be reinforced for a period of time to be conditioned. Otherwise, it fades and becomes extinct. For example, when students attend school the first week, it means nothing to hear the sound of the school bell (neutral stimulus) at the end of class and the teacher directs the students to close their notebooks (unconditioned stimulus). After repeated occurrences of the bell ringing at the end of class with the teacher's directions, the bell alone (without the teacher's directions) prompts the students to respond by closing their notebooks. This is because conditioning has taken place. |
| **Extinction** | Extinction occurs when the conditioned response (CR) gradually weakens over time and eventually stops. For example, when the students in class close their notebooks and reach for their backpacks, that sound predicts the sound of the bell and leaving the class. However, if the teacher exclaims, "I dismiss you, not the bell!" the teacher is extinguishing the paired association. |
| **Spontaneous recovery** | Spontaneous recovery refers to the reappearance of a learned conditioned response after it is extinguished. The recovered response, however, is usually weaker and shorter in duration than the conditioned response. For example, if Pavlov did not present the meat for a whole day, the dog would stop salivating. If the dog salivates the next day, it is spontaneous recovery. |
| **Higher-order conditioning** | Most of us are not mere collections of simple associations between conditioned stimuli and unconditioned stimuli. Rather, we have complex associations between stimuli. Consider a dog who learned to drool at the sound of a bell. What if a buzzer was presented before the bell? The dog would eventually learn a new association. Pavlov conditioned the dog to salivate at the sound of a bell, and then he paired the sound of the bell with the lighting of a light. The dog soon started salivating when a light was turned on. Therefore, higher-order conditioning (sometimes called second-order conditioning) occurs when a previously conditioned stimulus is paired with a new conditioned stimulus. |

## Examples of Classical Conditioning in Everyday Life

Examples of these conditioned learnings can be observed in day-to-day experiences. What if you did not realize that you were getting the flu and drank an orange soda because you were hot. A short time later, you vomited, an **unconditioned response** (UR), due to the flu, an **unconditioned stimulus** (US). Now, you cannot drink orange soda because the smell of it makes you feel nauseous. In this case, the orange soda is the transition from a **neutral stimulus** (NS) to a **conditioned stimulus** (CS). The nausea you now feel after smelling orange soda is a **conditioned response** (CR) because it occurs without the flu. *Stimulus generalization* occurs when smelling similar orange candy causes nausea. *Stimulus discrimination* occurs when grape soda does not produce nausea.

## Emotional Conditioning

American psychologist John B. Watson expanded Pavlov's stimulus-response manipulation, discovering that all behavior is the result of internal emotional "gut" reactions to stimuli, called *conditioned emotional responses.* For example, what if we say that emotions are merely physiological nervous system reactions and that chemical reactions are reflexes. Does that mean that emotions can be conditioned? According to Watson, the answer would be absolutely yes. Think of the high-pitched whine of a dentist's drill. Your physical body might not blink, flinch, or drool, but you might have a chemical reaction that your mind interprets as a feeling.

To illustrate, let's take a look at an experiment that Watson and his partner Rosalie Raynor conducted with a young child known as "Little Albert." Little Albert liked white lab rats. When the boy was playing with a rat, Watson snuck up behind him and startled Albert by hitting a hammer against a metal rod to produce a loud noise. The boy cried when he heard the loud noise. Watson repeated this experiment until the boy began to fear white rats. According to classical conditioning, the loud noise is the **unconditioned stimulus** (US) and crying is the **unconditioned response** (UR). White rats are the **conditioned stimulus** (CS) and crying at the sight of white rats is a **conditioned response** (CR). (Note: Although this experiment violated today's ethical standards, it is an important experiment to prove that reflexes and emotions can be conditioned to learn and unlearn a stimulus.)

**Did you know?** Little Albert was conditioned to fear anything that appeared white and fluffy (generalization), such as bunnies, a white fur coat, and even Santa Claus.

### Key Facts about Emotional Conditioning

Conditioned emotional responses are learned fears that can often develop into *phobias* (fears that persist even though no realistic threat exists). The three emotional conditioning concepts that you should know for the AP PSYCH exam are aversive conditioning, discrimination, and generalization.

**Aversive conditioning.** An *aversive* stimulus that is presented with a targeted behavior is meant to decrease the probability of a particular behavior. *Aversion conditioning* is a type of avoidance learning that trains a person to respond negatively to the stimulus.

For example, a person loves to eat tacos, but after eating a beef taco, the person becomes sick with violent bouts of nausea. Thereafter, the person might experience an aversion to beef tacos and associate the aroma of a beef taco (stimulus) with the response of feeling nauseous. Therefore, the person might avoid eating beef tacos for a very long time. Why is aversive conditioning important in psychology? Because research shows that aversive conditioning can be effective in the treatment of addictions and bad habits. For example, when *Antabuse* (a drug to treat alcoholism) is given to a person before drinking, the person begins to associate an unpleasant sickness with drinking alcohol. Therefore, the person may stop drinking alcohol to avoid the feeling of nausea.

### Heads Up: What You Need to Know

When is it okay for a person to avoid learning? On the AP PSYCH exam, you should be familiar with **avoidance learning** (also called escape learning), where a person learns to avoid an aversive stimulus.

American psychologist John Garcia demonstrated that animals could develop an aversion to taste and avoid the food as a means of survival, called **taste aversion.** Garcia first experimented with rats and later with coyotes. While working with ranchers to protect flocks of sheep, Garcia exposed countless coyotes to a poisonous bait. When the coyotes ate the bait, they became sick to the point of throwing up. Coyotes soon learned to be "bait shy" and would avoid eating sheep. Garcia called this type of conditioning *aversive conditioning* so that coyotes would learn to stay away from ranchers' herds. This type of aversive learning was soon called the *Garcia effect* (a survival mechanism that causes a person to have a learned connection between taste aversion and illness).

The findings of Garcia's experiment suggest that people tend to associate sickness with a particular odor or taste of food as a form of *biological preparedness* that activates the sympathetic nervous system to respond negatively for the sake of survival.

**Discrimination.** *Discrimination* is the ability to differentiate between a conditioned stimulus and other stimuli. For example, perhaps Little Albert was not fearful of black rats, only white rats; or a person who has an aversion to beef tacos might love beef burritos. In both of these examples, discrimination makes it possible for a person to make a distinction between stimuli.

**Generalization.** *Generalization* is when a person has a tendency to respond to all stimuli that are similar to the original conditioned stimulus. For example, if Little Albert continued his aversion to white rats, and also became fearful of *all* white and furry animals, then he made a generalization based on his fear of white rats. Another example is the person who became ill from eating beef tacos. If the person starts to feel nausea from the smell of other beef foods, the person has made a generalization and associates sickness with *all* beef products.

## Operant Conditioning

American psychologist B. F. Skinner studied the complex relationships between environmental stimuli-responses and introduced a new method of learning called *operant conditioning.* Skinner believed that operant conditioning was the basis of all learning, and his viewpoints about learning have strongly influenced the American educational system.

As discussed in the previous section, classical conditioning is when an association is made by an *involuntary* reflex response, but operant conditioning is when a consequence occurs after a *voluntary* behavior. In **operant conditioning,** people learn from operating in the environment and soon develop behavior patterns that result in consequences. Behavior patterns produce a consequence of either a *reinforced* reward or a *punishment.*

Skinner's ideas about operant conditioning were based on Edward Thorndike's principles of the law of effect.

## Thorndike's Law of Effect

This brings us back to Aristotle's idea of *tabula rasa,* which means people are born knowing nothing and that the environment and certain conditions shape us to be who we are in the world. American psychologist Edward Thorndike proposed a principle of learning behavior to illustrate Aristotle's point, the **law of effect.** Thorndike stated that "responses that produce a satisfying effect in a particular situation become more likely to occur again in that situation, and responses that produce a discomforting effect become less likely to occur again in that situation." According to the law of effect, the consequence of a preceding action will influence a future action.

**Instrumental learning.** Thorndike experimented by putting cats in puzzle boxes, where they had to figure their way out of the boxes by pressing a lever. At first, the cats' responses were instinctual and the cats couldn't figure out how to get out of the boxes; so when one cat found the trick of opening the box, Thorndike attributed it to a lucky coincidence. But it was what happened after that response that intrigued Thorndike. When he put the "lucky cat" back into the puzzle box, the cat got out of the box sooner than the first time, and with each subsequent effort the escape time was shorter. Hence, Thorndike concluded that the cat learned from the consequences of its behavior, called *instrumental learning.*

**Thorndike's Puzzle Box**

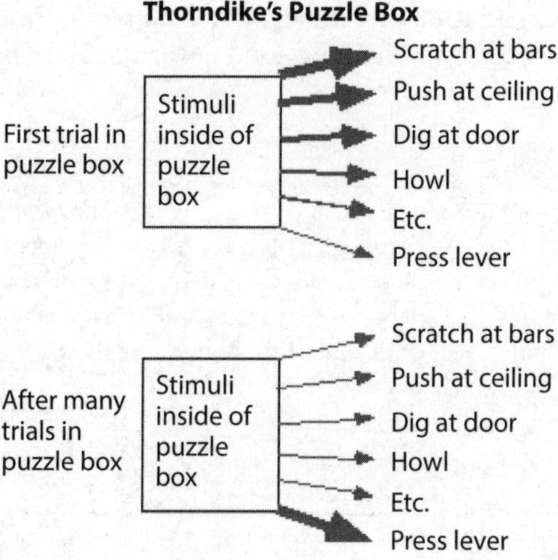


## B. F. Skinner's Operant Conditioning

Almost 50 years later, B. F. Skinner continued Thorndike's research in operant conditioning. Skinner was not only interested in observing learned behavior, he was also interested in the *cause* of behavior and its consequences. Skinner removed all *confounding variables* (anything that might have an effect on the dependent variable) to achieve experimental control. This procedure of only introducing one variable (the independent variable) allowed Skinner to identify the cause of behavior. To conduct his experiments, Skinner used an operant conditioning chamber, called a **Skinner box,** that was similar to Thorndike's puzzle box. The Skinner box contained a lever that a caged animal might press to gain a reward or avoid a punishment.

## Heads Up: What You Need to Know

On the AP PSYCH exam, you will need to identify Skinner's two main types of operant conditioning responses to increase or decrease behavior: reinforcement and punishment.

| Skinner's Four Quadrants of Operant Conditioning | | |
|---|---|---|
| | **Reinforcement (Increases behavior)** | **Punishment (Decreases behavior)** |
| **Positive (+) (Add stimulus)** | Add a pleasant stimulus to **INCREASE** or maintain behavior | Add an unpleasant stimulus to **DECREASE** behavior |
| **Negative (–) (Remove stimulus)** | Subtract an unpleasant stimulus to **INCREASE** or maintain behavior | Subtract a pleasant stimulus to **DECREASE** behavior |

## Reinforcement

When Skinner reinforced an animal after a behavior, this increased the probability that the animal would repeat the behavior. Reinforcement is either positive or negative. While animals can be taught to repeat a wide range of behaviors, some associations can be reinforced more easily than others. **Biological preparedness** explains that some associations are innate. For example, a pigeon can be trained to peck for a food reward easier than it can be trained to flap for a food reward because pecking is more closely associated with eating than flapping.

| Reinforcement | Description | Example |
|---|---|---|
| **Positive reinforcement** | Positive reinforcement is anything that strengthens the probability of a behavior by providing a reward. When Skinner's animals accidentally knocked the lever, a food pellet would immediately drop next to the hungry animal. The animals quickly learned to push the lever to receive food. Positive reinforcement (+) can be applied to good behavior. | Something pleasant is given for good behavior. Consider a mother who says, "If you clean your room, you can play video games." The reinforcement with an enjoyable activity as a reward is called the *Premack principle.* |
| **Negative reinforcement** | Negative reinforcement is anything that strengthens the probability of a behavior because it terminates an unpleasant experience. Negative reinforcement is not a punishment; it is actually a desirable consequence because it stops or reduces something unpleasant. Negative reinforcement is when you subtract (–) an unpleasant stimulus once the desired response occurs. | Something is taken away to increase good behavior. Think of your alarm clock. The sound of an alarm in the early morning hours may be annoying, but when you hit the stop button, the consequence is that the alarm goes off and you can start your day on time. The *removal* or *subtraction* of the unpleasant alarm sound is a negative reinforcement. The behavior of turning off the alarm clock stops the unpleasant sound and increases the chance that you will behave similarly in the future. |

**Primary and secondary reinforcers.** A *primary reinforcer* is something that is biologically rooted and does not need to be learned. For example, in the lowest level of *Maslow's hierarchy pyramid* (human basic needs to complex needs) food, water, shelter, oxygen, and sex are primary physiological needs that all humans experience as essential. A *secondary reinforcer* is something that is learned through primary reinforcers. Examples of secondary reinforcers (also called conditioned reinforcers) are money, class grades, applause, and attention. Note: Exchanging money for food is an example of a secondary reinforcer, called **token economy** (a behavior modification procedure based on the principles of operant conditioning).

## Punishment

Punishment is the opposite of reinforcement. Punishment is a concept of operant learning that refers to any change that happens after a behavior. It decreases the probability that a behavior will occur again. Punishments can be positive or negative.

| Punishment | Description | Example |
|---|---|---|
| **Positive punishment** | Positive punishment results when an *unpleasant* stimulus occurs after an undesired behavior. Positive punishment does not mean the punishment is good or pleasurable. | Something "bad" results from an undesired behavior (e.g., detention, a long lecture, or extra homework). |
| **Negative punishment** | Negative punishment is when a *pleasant* stimulus is removed (taken away) after an undesired behavior. Conditioning by negative reinforcement is also called *omission training*. | Something is taken away after an undesired behavior (e.g., cell phone is taken away). |

**Did you know?** Most educators and psychologists favor reinforcement instead of punishment because punishment is significantly less effective as a learning tool than reinforcement. According to Skinner, punishment does not teach you something; it only informs you about what not to do. Although some punishments can be effective, punishment does not encourage desirable behavior. Research from longitudinal studies have shown that children whose parents use physical punishment are, on average, less likely to receive high test scores compared to children whose parents do not use physical punishment.

# Reinforcement Schedules

In operant conditioning, some responses are aided by a process called **reinforcement schedules.** Reinforcement schedules act as the rules that define when and how to increase reinforcement (or decrease punishment) in order to reach the desired behavior after a specific number of responses. For example, when training dogs, training employees, or raising kids, it is important to know *when* to reinforce or punish to achieve the desired goals.

The following table will help you compare and contrast reinforcement schedules for the AP PSYCH exam.

**Compare and Contrast Reinforcement Schedules**

| Reinforcement Schedule | Description | Examples |
|---|---|---|
| **Continuous reinforcement** | Reinforcement after every correct response. It is great for quick learning, but the behavior quickly becomes extinguished because once the pattern of behavior-reward is broken and the behavior does not pay off, the learning stops. | Many families bring home new dogs. The dog is trained to receive treats at every occurrence of a trick. However, as time goes on, the owners soon get bored and don't give treats, even when the dog does the behavior. Thus, the dog stops the behavior and the behavior becomes extinguished. |
| **Fixed-ratio schedule** | Reinforcement after a brief pause between each set of responses. It has a high response rate. | ■ The dog will get a treat after a specific number of behaviors.<br>■ A frozen yogurt store offers a "punch card" where your tenth purchase is free. |
| **Fixed-interval schedule** | Reinforcement after a period of time. Response rate increases as time for reinforcement approaches. | ■ The dog will get a treat after a specific time has passed.<br>■ A paycheck is given every 2 weeks and is not linked to behavior. |
| **Variable-ratio schedule** | Reinforcement after a varying number of responses. It is resistant to extinction because the animal or person doesn't know when another reward is coming. The pattern is unpredictable. The belief is "It might happen if I try just one more time." | ■ The dog will get a treat after a random number of behaviors.<br>■ Playing slot machines because they are unpredictable. |
| **Variable-interval schedule** | Reinforcement after varying lengths of time. | ■ The dog will get a treat after a random amount of time has passed.<br>■ Pop quizzes because they occur randomly and independent of behavior.<br>■ The weather because it occurs randomly and independent of behavior. |

# Cognitive and Social Learning

## Cognitive Learning

How many vocabulary words do you think the average AP Psychology student knows? Do you think those words were learned by reward and punishment? Do you think the student received a reward (treat) each time a new vocabulary word was memorized? No, probably not. So, how is something as complex as language learned if it is not due to classical or operant conditioning?

Conditioned behavior is not just demonstrated by rewards and punishments; there is evidence to support that cognitive processes are at work even when there are no obvious rewards. The mind is constantly learning even when it appears to be passive, called cognitive learning. **Cognitive learning** is a type of learning based on mentally processing internal and external information that is acquired, interpreted, stored, and later retrieved.

## Shaping

The principles of operant conditioning have been used to guide behavior toward a desired result. The **learning curve** (rate of a person's progress in gaining new behavior or skills) validates that people (and animals) don't usually learn on the first try; rather, the desired outcome can be gradually attained by shaping behavior.

**Shaping** is a method of reinforcing behavior until the learner attains the desired behavior. The first time a person or animal tries a behavior it may not be successful, but after successive tries the learner gradually achieves the targeted behavior. To help you remember this concept, think of the phrase "You're getting warmer" as the learner gets closer to the desired outcome.

Other terms that are related to shaping are *successive approximation* and *differential reinforcement.* That means each attempt is successively closer to approximating the desired behavior. Once an organism (humans and animals) learns a behavior, that behavior can be linked with other behaviors, known as **chaining.**

**TEST TIP: On the AP PSYCH exam, the terms *shaping* and *successive approximation* are similar terms. To save you time, study these terms at the same time.**

## Latent Learning

**Latent learning** describes learning when the right motivation or incentive is present. American psychologist Edward Tolman theorized that people are active, not passive, learners, and that people actively form mental pictures about their physical environment, called *cognitive mapping.* Tolman believed that humans learn by cognition, and when the right conditions are present and it is beneficial to demonstrate such behavior, learning is possible even with no reinforcement. For example, imagine a 5-year-old child who has learned table manners, but refuses to demonstrate polite table manners until a formal dinner occasion with her grandparents, aunts, uncles, and cousins.

**Did you know?** Superstitions and phobias can arise when a person learns the wrong connection between a behavior and the reward or punishment. For example, if a high school baseball player wears a specific pair of socks and then hits two home runs at a game, the player might wear the same pair of socks at future games for positive reinforcement. In contrast, if the player performs badly by striking out three times (punishment) while wearing a specific pair of shoes, the player might not wear the same shoes again in the future. According to Skinner and other strict behaviorists, all superstitions and phobias are simply the misapplication of rewards and punishment.

### Insight Learning

**Insight learning** refers to cognitive learning that is immediate and clear as a result of understanding all elements of a problem. Insight learning is not trial-and-error testing; it is the sudden realization of a solution by applying what you already know to a situation. The four stages of insight learning are preparation (gather information), incubation (unconsciously sort out), insight (sudden solution), and verification (confirm the insight). Insight learning is difficult to study because it cannot be observed, measured, or reliably replicated. An example would be struggling with a math, chemistry, or physics problem and then suddenly understanding the solution. Insight learning is sometimes called the "aha moment." In scientific research by German psychologist Wolfgang Kohler, pigeons and chimpanzees demonstrated insight behavior that was observed as a sudden flash of understanding in order to receive treats.

### Learned Helplessness

An important exception of learning to avoid unpleasant situations is called **learned helplessness.** It is the passive resignation that a person (or animal) learns when he or she is unable to avoid situations from which there is no control, leaving the person with feelings of helplessness, hopelessness, and depression. According to behaviorists, whenever a person (or animal) does not learn, the fault is with the system of rewards and punishments. In certain sad cases, a person cannot figure out how to receive reinforcement or avoid the punishment; and when that happens, the person is no longer motivated to learn. For example, in an experiment, dogs that were strapped in a harness and given repeated shocks learned a sense of helplessness because they could not escape the punishment.

## Social Learning

**Social learning** is a cognitive process that refers to people learning new behaviors from one another by observing what is modeled, and then imitating the behavior. Children imitate behavior through socialization by learning gender roles, self-reinforcement, and *self-efficacy* (belief in the ability to do things on their own). Imitating and rehearsing are powerful learning tools, especially when rewards or punishments are imposed. On the AP PSYCH exam you should be familiar with observational learning.

### Observational Learning

**Observational learning** (also called modeling) results when people learn by watching the behavior of others and making mental notes about the good or bad consequences. American psychologist Albert Bandura theorized that four conditions must be present for modeling behavior: attention, retention, reproduction, and motivation. For example, even though you are "motivated" to play tennis and pay "attention" to the skills of professional tennis players on television, it is likely that you won't be able to commit the same "attention" to "reproduce" the same skills of a professional tennis player like Serena Williams. Imitation requires the physical and mental ability to reproduce the behavior that you are observing.

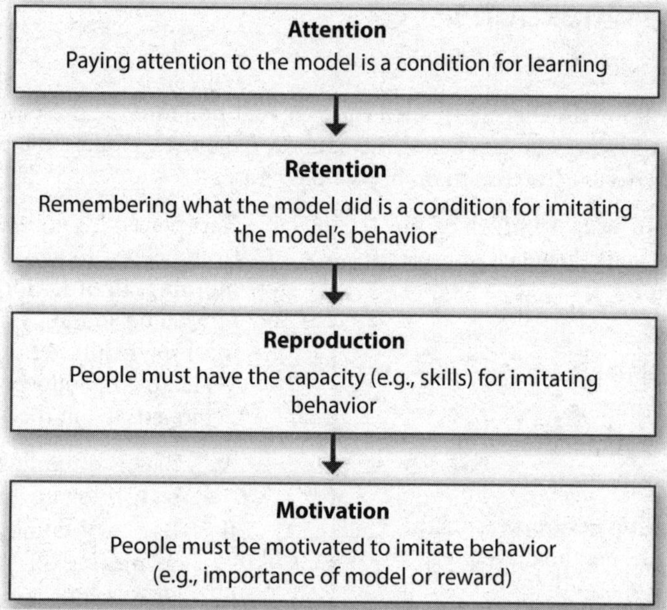


### Heads Up: What You Need to Know

On the AP PSYCH exam, you should be familiar with Albert Bandura's **social learning theory.** Bandura explains how people learn from one another by observing, imitating, and modeling behaviors. In Bandura's "Bobo doll experiment," quiet, well-behaved preschool children observed an adult who repeatedly punched and knocked down an inflated doll. Children imitated this behavior and later played aggressively.

## Chapter Review Practice Questions

Practice questions are for instructional purposes only and may not reflect the format of the actual exam. The questions and explanations that follow focus on essential knowledge, course skills, and course content.

## Multiple-Choice Questions

*Questions 1–3 refer to the following scenario.*

A teenager feels annoyed when she hears her mom's car pull into the driveway. She becomes annoyed because for the last 3 years she has heard the sound of the car's engine immediately before her mom walks into the house to ask the teen to do household chores.

1. According to John B. Watson, which of the following best represents the teen's annoyance for having to do chores?

   **A.** Punishment
   **B.** Unconditioned response
   **C.** Conditioned stimulus
   **D.** Unconditioned stimulus
   **E.** Conditioned response

2. Which of the following best represents the sound of the car entering the driveway?

   **A.** Conditioned response
   **B.** Unconditioned response
   **C.** Conditioned stimulus
   **D.** Unconditioned stimulus
   **E.** Punishment

3. Which of the following represents the voice of her mom telling her to do chores?

   **A.** Conditioned response
   **B.** Unconditioned response
   **C.** Conditioned stimulus
   **D.** Unconditioned stimulus
   **E.** Punishment

4. Whenever the dog, Rudy, whines, his owners give him a doggie treat to stop his whining. As a result, Rudy is a very noisy and whiny dog. Rudy is responding to which of the following schedules of reinforcement?

   **A.** Variable-interval schedule of reinforcement
   **B.** Variable-ratio schedule of reinforcement
   **C.** Fixed-interval schedule of reinforcement
   **D.** Fixed-ratio schedule of reinforcement
   **E.** Continuous reinforcement

5. Bart placed his alarm clock across the room from his bed to help him wake up in the morning. In order for him to stop the screeching sound of the alarm going off, he must physically get out of bed to turn it off. Which of the following operant principles is demonstrated in this situation?

   **A.** Bart is obtaining positive reinforcement by turning off his alarm.
   **B.** Bart is obtaining negative reinforcement by turning off his alarm.
   **C.** Bart is suffering from positive punishment from the loud noise.
   **D.** Bart is suffering from negative punishment from the loud noise.
   **E.** Bart has associated the loud noise with waking up.

6. Reinforcers _______ and punishers _______ the future occurrence of the behavior that led to these respective consequences.

   **A.** increase; increase
   **B.** decrease; decrease
   **C.** increase; decrease
   **D.** decrease; increase
   **E.** relate; associate

7. Sheila wants to teach her new puppy to come to her on command, so she rewards the puppy when it looks at her. She then rewards the puppy when it takes one step toward her, even though it has not yet walked to Sheila. Which of the following training methods is Sheila using?

   **A.** Positive punishment
   **B.** Differential reinforcement
   **C.** Reflexive conditioning
   **D.** Negative reinforcement
   **E.** Negative punishment

## Free-Response Question

**1 question**

**25 minutes**

**Directions:** It is suggested that you take a few minutes to plan and outline your essay. Write your response on lined paper. You must demonstrate your understanding of course skills and course content. Your essay is considered a first draft and may contain some grammatical errors that will not be counted against you. However, to receive full credit, your essay must demonstrate defensible content knowledge with substantive examples where appropriate.

Ms. Smilowitz wanted to teach her AP psychology students about positive punishment and positive reinforcement. She developed an experiment that was similar to the original operant conditioning experiments performed by B. F. Skinner. The sample size was two lab rats that were clones and acquired from a biological supply company. The rats were trained in two different mazes. Both rats were trained in two separate boxes to find the end of a maze.

Rat #1 was squirted with water every time it made a wrong turn in the maze. Rat #2 was rewarded with food every time it made a correct turn in the maze. To make the punishments and reinforcements more impactful, Rat #1 (the punished rat) would be awoken at random times for training exercises. In order to keep it hungry, Rat #2 was not allowed to eat regularly. The hypothesis was that after 10 routines, Rat #1 (the one that learned by punishment) would complete the maze faster than Rat #2 (the one that learned by reinforcement).

**Part A**

- Identify each of the following in this study.
  - Independent variable
  - Dependent variable
  - Confounding variable

**Part B**

- Explain how learning is operationally defined by the researcher.
- Identify one example of experimental control.
- Explain how this experiment could be modified to prevent experimenter bias.
- Identify one ethical concern of this experiment.

# Answers and Explanations

## Multiple Choice Questions

1. **B.** According to Watson, emotions are nervous system chemical reactions that can be conditioned. The feeling of annoyance is an *unconditioned response,* choice B. A *punishment* (choice A) occurs after an undesired behavior. Therefore, the feeling of annoyance is not a punishment. A *conditioned stimulus* (choice C) can be taught to induce the natural response of another stimulus. An *unconditioned stimulus* (choice D) is anything that will cause a reflexive response without learning. A *conditioned response*

(choice E) is the same as an unconditioned response; the difference is that a conditioned response only occurs when a conditioned stimulus is presented.

2. **C.** The sound of the car is not naturally scary, happy, or annoying. The teenager learned that the sound of the engine precedes the sound of her mom's voice telling her to do chores. Thus, the engine sound is a *conditioned stimulus,* choice C. A *conditioned response* (choice A) is the same as an *unconditioned response* (choice B); however, a conditioned response only occurs when a conditioned stimulus is presented. An *unconditioned stimulus* (choice D) is anything that will cause a reflexive response without learning. *Punishment* (choice E) falls under operant conditioning, and this question refers to classical conditioning.
3. **D.** Any sound (mom's voice) that precedes an automatic reflex of annoyance is an *unconditioned stimulus,* choice D, because a person does not have to learn that a sound leads to an automatic feeling. A *conditioned response* (choice A) is the same as an unconditioned response; however, a conditioned response only occurs when a conditioned stimulus is presented. *Unconditioned responses* (choice B) are just reflexes that are caused by stimuli. A *conditioned stimulus* (choice C) is something that needs to be learned and is connected to an unconditioned stimulus. *Punishment* (choice E) is what is done to a person or animal after a behavior.
4. **E.** *Continuous reinforcement* is giving a treat or removing something unpleasant every time a behavior occurs, choice E. *Variable interval* (choice A) means randomly receiving a reinforcement after varying lengths of time. Imagine giving Rudy a treat after 4 hours, then 15 minutes, then 7 hours, and then 3 hours. Rudy would not learn when to expect the treat. *Variable ratio* (choice B) means that reinforcement is given after a random number of behaviors. *Fixed interval* (choice C) means that reinforcement is given after a period of time, such as every 4 hours. *Fixed ratio* (choice D) means that reinforcement is given after a certain set of behaviors. For example, Rudy would have to roll over three times to get one treat.
5. **B.** *Negative reinforcement,* choice B, is the removal of something unpleasant after doing the right behavior. Bart got out of bed and the annoying sound of the alarm clock was eliminated. Bart is not receiving a reward for turning off his alarm, so this is not *positive reinforcement* (choice A). Neither *positive punishment* (choice C) nor *negative punishment* (choice D) apply because punishment happens after a behavior. The sound of the alarm is not punishment for sleeping. This question is about behavior, not reflexes, so choice E is incorrect.
6. **C.** Re<u>in</u>forcers <u>*in*</u>*crease* the likelihood of a behavior occurring again and punishers *decrease* the likelihood of the behavior occurring again, choice C. Therefore, choices A, B, and D are incorrect. Positive reinforcement increases the chance of a behavior happening again because the person receives a reward. Negative reinforcement increases the chance of a behavior happening again because it takes away something unpleasant when the correct behavior is performed. Punishments, both negative and positive, decrease the chance of a behavior happening again. The words in choice E (*relate* and *associate*) are pointing toward stimulus-response classical conditioning; therefore, choice E is incorrect.
7. **B.** Rewarding someone or something for getting close to the desired behavior is using *differential reinforcement,* choice B. *Positive punishment* (choice A) adds an aversive stimulus. In the case of positive punishment, the word "positive" is used to denote adding (**+**) something unpleasant like extra homework for bad behavior. *Reflexive conditioning* (choice C) is a classical conditioning term. Because the puppy is doing a behavior (operant conditioning) and not a reflex (classical conditioning), choice C is incorrect. *Negative reinforcement* (choice D) is subtracting (–) something bad after the correct behavior is performed. *Negative punishment* (choice E) is subtracting (–) something pleasant after a bad behavior is performed.

## Free-Response Question

To achieve the maximum score of 7, your response must address each of the bullet points in the question.

## Sample Student Response

The *independent variable* is what is changed, moved, or controlled by the experimenter to cause an outcome. In this case, the independent variable is the consequence that was given to each rat, either a reward or punishment. The *dependent variable* is the result of the independent variable. In this case, the dependent variable is how much time it took the rats to complete the maze. A *confounding variable* is anything other than the independent variable that the experimenter may not have taken into account. In this case, Ms. Smilowitz used separate boxes, which might mean one maze was easier to maneuver than the other.

To *operationally define* a concept means to identify the operational process in a way that the concept can be measured. In this case, the teacher operationally defined learning as the *amount of time* it will take each rat to finish the maze. By using rats that have no genetic differences, the teacher attempted to achieve *experimental control* by eliminating the confounding variable of genetic differences between the two rats. *Experimenter bias* can occur consciously or unconsciously. If bias is conscious, the experimenter is partial to the results in some way. If bias is unconscious, the experimenter doesn't know that he or she is somehow adding a confounding variable. To avoid bias, the experimenter could have recruited another person to record the results of the study. *Ethical concerns* should always be addressed when conducting a research design experiment. One of the most obvious ethical concerns in this study was the mistreatment of the rats by restricting access to food for Rat #2.

Chapter 8

# Unit 5: Cognitive Psychology

AP Psychology Unit 5 explores the principles and theoretical models of memory processing, problem solving, intelligence, and language acquisition.

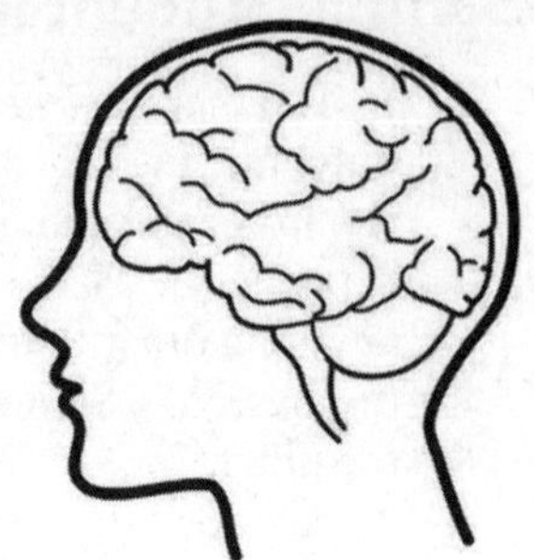

- Key Contributors to Cognitive Psychology
- Cognition
- Memory
- Forgetting
- Amnesia
- Thinking, Reasoning, and Problem Solving
- Intelligence
- Language

## Overview of AP Psychology Unit 5

The overarching concepts for this chapter address cognition, the mental activity involved in thinking, processing memories, intelligence, and language communication. **The topics discussed in this unit will count toward 13–17 percent of your multiple-choice score.**

## AP Psychology Framework

Success on the exam depends on your ability to make connections to the major concepts described in the content topics of the *Course Framework for AP Psychology.* Remember that these concepts highlight the fundamental ideas that every student should take with them into the AP PSYCH exam and beyond.

Use the table below to guide you through what is covered in this unit. The information contained in this table is an abridged version of the content outlines with topic examples. Visit https://apstudent.collegeboard.org/apcourse/ap-psychology/ for the complete updated AP PSYCH course curriculum framework.

| AP Psychology—Unit 5: Cognitive Psychology | |
|---|---|
| **Topic** | **Learning Target** |
| **Introduction to Memory** | ■ Compare and contrast cognitive processes (e.g., effortful vs. automatic processing, deep vs. shallow processing, selective vs. divided attention (task switching), and metacognition).<br>■ Describe and differentiate psychological and physiological systems of memory (e.g., short-term, implicit, long-term, sensory, prospective, and explicit memory; physiological systems).<br>■ Identify the contributions of key researchers in cognitive psychology (e.g., Chomsky, Ebbinghaus, Köhler, Loftus, and Miller). |

| Topic | Learning Target |
|---|---|
| **Encoding** | ■ Outline the principles that underlie the construction and encoding of memories. |
| **Storing** | ■ Outline the principles that underlie effective storage of memories. |
| **Retrieving** | ■ Describe strategies for retrieving memories. |
| **Forgetting and Memory Distortion** | ■ Describe strategies for memory improvement and typical memory errors. |
| **Biological Bases for Memory** | ■ Describe and differentiate psychological and physiological systems of short- and long-term memory. |
| **Introduction to Thinking and Problem Solving** | ■ Identify problem-solving strategies as well as factors that influence their effectiveness.<br>■ List the characteristics of creative thought and creative thinkers. |
| **Biases and Errors in Thinking** | ■ Identify problem-solving strategies as well as factors that create bias and errors in thinking. |
| **Introduction to Intelligence** | ■ Define intelligence and list characteristics of how psychologists measure intelligence (e.g., abstract vs. verbal measures, speed of processing, fluid intelligence, crystallized intelligence, Flynn effect, stereotype threat, and savant syndrome).<br>■ Discuss how culture influences the definition of intelligence.<br>■ Compare and contrast historic and contemporary theories of intelligence (e.g., Spearman, Gardner, and Sternberg).<br>■ Identify the contributions of key researchers in intelligence and testing (Binet, Galton, Gardner, Spearman, Sternberg, Terman, and Wechsler). |
| **Psychometric Principles and Intelligence Testing** | ■ Explain how psychologists design tests, including standardization strategies and other techniques to establish reliability and validity.<br>■ Interpret the meaning of scores in terms of the normal curve.<br>■ Describe relevant labels related to intelligence testing (e.g., gifted; intellectual disability). |
| **Components of Language and Language Acquisition** | ■ Synthesize how biological, cognitive, and cultural factors converge to facilitate acquisition, development, and use of language.<br>■ Debate the appropriate testing practices, particularly in relation to culture-fair test uses. |

## Important Terms and Concepts Checklist

This section is an overview of the important terms, concepts, language, and theories that specifically target the key topics of Unit 5. Use this list of terms as a checklist to check your personal progress. As you study the topics, place a check mark next to each and return to this list as often as necessary to refresh your understanding.

After you finish the review section, you can reinforce what you have learned by working through the practice questions at the end of the chapter. Answers and explanations provide further clarification into perspectives of the cognitive processes.

| Term/Concept | Study Page | Term/Concept | Study Page | Term/Concept | Study Page |
|---|---|---|---|---|---|
| amnesia | p. 145 | Gardner's theory of multiple intelligences | pp. 154–155 | reliability | p. 155 |
| artificial concept | p. 148 | heuristics | p. 150 | repression | p. 145 |
| Atkinson-Shiffrin model | pp. 141–142 | iconic memory | p. 142 | retrieval | pp. 140, 146–147 |
| bottom-up thinking | p. 149 | inductive reasoning (informal) | p. 149 | ruminative thinking | p. 151 |
| Chomsky's universal language acquisition theory | p. 160 | intelligence | pp. 151, 158 | Sapir-Whorf hypothesis | p. 160 |
| chunking | p. 146 | language | pp. 159–161 | schema | p. 140 |
| cognition | p. 138 | levels of processing model | p. 141 | semantic learning | p. 146 |
| cognitive bias | p. 151 | long-term memory (LTM) | pp. 142–143 | semantic memory | p. 143 |
| convergent thinking | p. 150 | memory distortion | pp. 145–146 | sensory memory | pp. 141–142 |
| correlate | p. 155 | mnemonics | p. 147 | short-term memory (STM) | p. 142 |
| critical period | p. 161 | non-declarative memory (implicit) | p. 143 | standard deviation | p. 157 |
| declarative memory (explicit) | p. 143 | normal distribution curve | pp. 157–158 | standardization | p. 155 |
| deductive reasoning (formal) | pp. 148, 149 | parallel processing model | p. 141 | Stanford-Binet intelligence test | p. 153 |
| divergent thinking | p. 150 | priming | p. 146 | Sternberg's triarchic theory of intelligence | pp. 152, 154 |
| Ebbinghaus forgetting curve | p. 143 | problem solving | pp. 150–151 | storing | p. 139 |
| echoic memory | p. 142 | procedural memory | p. 143 | top-down thinking | pp. 148, 149 |
| elaborative rehearsal | p. 147 | prototype | p. 148 | validity | pp. 155–156 |
| encoding | pp. 139–140 | psychometrics | p. 151 | Wechsler Adult Intelligence Scale (WAIS) | pp. 152, 154, 156–157 |
| Flynn effect | p. 156 | reconstructive memory | p. 140 | Yerkes-Dodson law | p. 151 |
| forgetting | pp. 143–144 | rehearsal | p. 146 | | |

# Chapter Review

Cognitive psychology is the study of the mind's thinking processes. It focuses on scientific and empirical approaches to human memory, thought, intelligence, and language.

## Heads Up: What You Need to Know

For the AP PSYCH exam, ask yourself these two essential questions as you continue to work through the topics in this chapter and develop an understanding of cognition: What roles do memory and learning play in our behaviors? and What is intelligence, and how can we study it to understand it?

## Key Contributors to Cognitive Psychology

On the AP PSYCH exam, you should be able to identify the major contributors in the field of cognitive research.

| Key Contributors to Cognitive Psychology | | |
|---|---|---|
| **Contributor** | **Field of Study (Theory)** | **Famous For** |
| **Alfred Binet** (1857–1911) | Binet-Simon intelligence test | Binet developed the first practical intelligence test to assess mental abilities, not "learned" information. The test is called the Binet-Simon Test. |
| **Noam Chomsky** (1928–) | Universal language acquisition theory | Chomsky was the first to theorize that language is innate and all humans are prewired to learn language even if it's not taught. |
| **Hermann Ebbinghaus** (1850–1909) | Memory, "forgetting curve" | Ebbinghaus is known for his systematic experiments of memory and learning. He was the first to describe a forgetting curve that shows that people forget 80 percent of newly learned material within 24 hours. |
| **Francis Galton** (1822–1911) | Inherited intelligence traits, "eugenics" | Galton is known as the father of *psychometrics* (the science of measuring mental faculties). He is known for developing theories of inherited intelligence traits by studying twins and coined the word *eugenics* (selective breeding to produce preferred traits). |
| **Howard Gardner** (1943–) | Multiple intelligences theory | Gardner redefined intelligence by developing the theory of multiple intelligences whereby humans have a variety of intellectual strengths. |
| **Wolfgang Köhler** (1887–1967) | Problem solving<br><br>Gestalt psychology | Kohler proved that animals (chimpanzees) can think and solve problems. He was also a key figure in the study of perception and behavior, called Gestalt psychology (the whole is greater than its parts). |
| **Elizabeth Loftus** (1944–) | Memory distortions (eyewitness and false memories) | Loftus proposed the idea that eyewitness memories can be unreliable and flawed. |

*Continued*

| Contributor | Field of Study (Theory) | Famous For |
|---|---|---|
| **George A. Miller** (1920–2012) | Information processing theory | Miller developed the **information processing theory** (the mind receives information, processes it, stores it, locates it, and then responds to the information). Miller was also one of the first to suggest that humans can only hold 5–9 chunks of information at a time. |
| **Charles Spearman** (1863–1945) | Spearman's theory of intelligence | Spearman theorized that intelligence is based on a statistical technique to evaluate the performance of mental abilities by two factors: general ability (G-factor) and specific abilities (S-factors). |
| **Robert J. Sternberg** (1949–) | Triarchic theory of intelligence | Sternberg theorized that intelligence arises from a balance of three types of mental abilities: analytical, practical, and creative. |
| **Lewis Terman** (1877–1956) | Stanford-Binet test | Terman revised and standardized the Binet-Simon Intelligence Test. The Stanford-Binet test is now the most widely used intelligence test. |
| **David Wechsler** (1896–1981) | Wechsler Adult Intelligence Scale (WAIS) | Wechsler was the developer of the Wechsler Adult Intelligence Scale (WAIS) and the Wechsler Intelligence Scale for Children (WISC). |

## Cognition

**Cognition** is how the brain *thinks.* It is defined as "the study of mental processes and human memory, including perceiving, remembering, reasoning, solving problems, and using language." The cognitive thinking process has to do with receiving sensory input and then integrating, processing, and categorizing the information in order to make sense of the world. For example, our cognition helps us to remember concepts from our textbooks, create new technology, solve problems in the world, and much, much more.

The diagram that follows will help you understand how basic cognitions work. This model is a *serial processing model,* which means that information flows sequentially through a series of steps. External information from the world is transmitted through our senses (sensory input) to the internal mental processes that store information in our memory. Subsequently, the formation of thoughts is integrated and categorized into our consciousness.

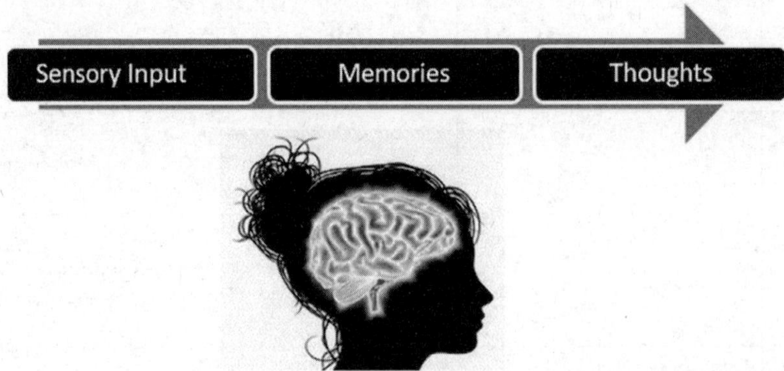


## Memory

Without memory, there is no past, only today and the future. Like a computer organizes information, our thinking brain programs information to collect, encode, store, and retrieve information in our memory.

**The Stages of Memory**

| Encoding | Storing | Retrieving |
|---|---|---|
| Information is converted and recorded into the memory. | Information is saved and maintained in the memory. | Information is recovered and brought into awareness when needed. |
| **Types of encoding: acoustic, visual, semantic** | **Types of memory stores: sensory, short-term memory (STM), and long-term memory (LTM)** | **Types of retrieval: recall and recognition** |

## Encoding and Storing

**Encoding** simply means putting new information into the mind. It is the first step to creating memories, but if the information is not encoded correctly, you probably won't be able to recall it later. **Storing** means that all of the information (input) starts in the sensory organs, where it transduces energy into neural signals that are encoded and stored in the brain.

The human mind is limited in its processing speed, storage capacity, and, perhaps most importantly, storage accuracy. Humans cannot encode memories like a librarian puts a new book on the shelf to be retrieved later. Instead, imagine that your brain's internal librarian receives an incoming book, rips out all of the pages, and places each page in a pile to organize the pages by content. For example, if you encode a new memory of a fire truck, your internal librarian organizes the fire truck by the color red, and places the tires in a tire pile, and the sound of the siren in an auditory pile.

For the AP PSYCH exam, you should be able to compare and contrast some of the cognitive processes of encoding.

| Compare and Contrast the Cognitive Processes of Encoding | |
|---|---|
| **Effortful Processing** | **Automatic Processing** |
| *Effortful processing* is a type of encoding that takes a conscious effort and requires attention. These are things that you make an effort to remember. For example, how you take the information you are currently thinking about and encode it so that it goes into long-term memory. While there is no magic answer, one clear idea is that studying must be *active*. Encoding cannot be a passive act, where you simply read a vocabulary word and expect to remember it. You must actively think, question, talk about, and *paraphrase* (reword in your own words) the information to encode it in your memory. | *Automatic processing* is the unconscious encoding of day-to-day incidental information (i.e., implicit/procedural memories that you don't intentionally think about). Automatic encoding is involuntary and occurs without your effort or attention. For example, walking, bicycling, or remembering the lyrics to your favorite song. |

*Continued*

| Deep Processing | Shallow Processing |
|---|---|
| *Deep processing* is a way of learning, whereby you make the information more meaningful to store it at a deeper level. The brain processes lasting memories when the memories are meaningful and are encoded with a depth of understanding. | *Shallow processing* is a cognitive encoding process that uses only the surface features of information processing. The consequence of shallow processing is the short-term retention of the information. The two types of shallow processing are structural and phonemic. *Structural processing* encodes visual and physical input. *Phonemic processing* encodes auditory input. |
| **Selective Attention** | **Divided Attention** |
| *Selective attention* is the ability to focus encoding cognitive processes on specific tasks. The brain filters out unattended sensory input and only focuses on encoding specific information. For example, you are writing a class research paper while at the local public library, but do not pay attention to the conversations going on around you at the library. | *Divided attention* or "multi-tasking" is actually *task switching*. Although it is possible to do many implicit/procedural tasks at the same time because these actions do not require attention, it is impossible to concentrate on two things simultaneously. Task switching actually reduces cognitive performance and is not a very good study strategy. |

Other factors that you should be familiar with for the AP PSYCH exam that can influence encoding and storage are serial position effect, primacy effect, and recency effect.

When encoding, where a memory is placed in a series (or list) affects how well it is encoded. This is called the *serial position* effect. The ability to encode and retrieve words at the beginning of a series (or list) is called the *primacy effect.* The ability to remember the last words (or the most recent words) is called the *recency effect.*

## Retrieving

**Retrieval** means bringing old memories back to the consciousness. Our internal librarian doesn't just randomly reassemble pages, it does so according to a scripted mental plan, called a **schema** (a scripted framework or blueprint of a concept that your internal librarian fills in with details). Note: In Chapter 9, "Unit 6: Developmental Psychology," we will discuss the concept of schema as described by Jean Piaget. Piaget suggests that schemas are mental representations that children use to *assimilate* or *accommodate* new learnings.

In the previous fire truck example, if you retrieve the information about the fire truck, your internal librarian sorts the information from the pile of papers, reassembles them, and hands the information off to your working memory. It might not be the exact memory of the fire truck, but it is often very similar. This process is called *reconstructive memory.*

**Reconstructive memory.** The human mind is not a computer in processing speed, storage capacity, and perhaps most importantly, storage accuracy. Humans cannot encode a memory as a librarian might store a new book on the shelf to be later retrieved. For example, when you want to retrieve the memory of the fire truck, your internal librarian grabs papers from each subject and reassembles the contents in your working memory. The assembly might not be exactly like the original fire truck, but it is close. The internal librarian doesn't just randomly reassemble pages, it does so according to a mental plan in the scripted schema.

## Information Processing Models of Memory

Memory, like a lot of concepts in psychology, cannot be observed or measured. So, we must rely on scientific models to help us understand and study memory.

### Parallel Processing Model

An important model to remember for the AP PSYCH exam is the **parallel processing model.** It is a *computational model,* which means that our brain's system of memories consists of many elements working at the same time. The brain simultaneously processes several stimuli at once to encode, store, and retrieve memories.

The parallel processing model performs multiple operations below the level of consciousness. Think of it this way: For you to memorize or encode a word, your mind must process the sound of the word, the spelling of the word, and the meaning of the word. Your brain does not accomplish this in a step-by-step manner. It processes all of the information simultaneously below the level of consciousness without your awareness.

### Levels of Processing Model

Another model of memory is the **levels of processing model.** As mentioned in the "Compare and Contrast the Cognitive Processes of Encoding" table above, the brain treats the information differently based on how deeply the information is encoded. The information must be encoded with "meaning" for accurate retrieval. Information cannot be easily retrieved from a side of a spectrum where information is shallowly processed, is not well connected to other information, and does not have much meaning. On the other side of the spectrum, information that is deeply processed, is well connected, and has meaning can be retrieved much easier. For example, thinking of synonyms requires the thinker to find and make meaningful connections. Making those connections will then link the concept to other concepts, which, of course, allows for deeper processing.

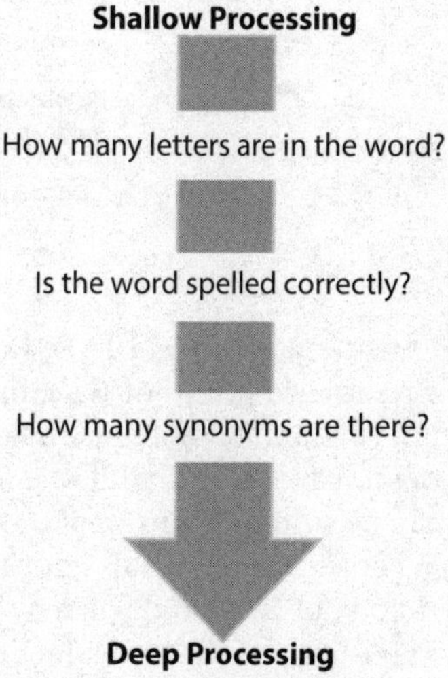

**Shallow Processing**

How many letters are in the word?

Is the word spelled correctly?

How many synonyms are there?

**Deep Processing**

### Atkinson-Shiffrin Model

On the AP PSYCH exam, make sure that you are familiar with the **Atkinson-Shiffrin model.** In contrast to the parallel processing model, it is a serial position model because information must pass sequentially through each memory stage. It is the most widely accepted approach to information processing. Computer technology provides us with a new framework for understanding mental processes; in this information processing theory, the brain processes and interprets information in sequential steps.

#### *Key Facts about the Atkinson-Shiffrin Model*

According to the Atkinson-Shiffrin model, there are three interacting stages of memory: sensory memory, short-term memory, and long-term memory.

**Sensory memory,** or *sensory register,* is known as temporary memory storage from which memories are processed into the short-term memory. Sensory memories are held for up to 2 seconds. Information flows in and immediately flows out. It is categorized by two subsections: iconic memory and echoic memory. **Iconic memory** is like an instant replay that allows you to re-see something that happened less than 1 second before. **Echoic memory** allows you to re-hear sounds that happened up to 2 seconds before. Have you ever been daydreaming in class and not listening to the teacher? But to your surprise, when the teacher calls on you, you are able to repeat exactly what the teacher said. That's echoic memory. Your brain didn't process the information, only the sounds.

**Short-term memory (STM),** also called **working memory.** Fortunately, people are able to retain sensory memories in short-term or long-term memories. Most of what you see is not processed because you do not give it your attention. However, if you pay attention to sensory input (what you see, hear, taste, smell, or touch), then information will go from your sensory register to your STM. In STM, you *consciously* work on ideas, conversations, and problems. Short-term memory has a limited capacity. As the following diagram illustrates, humans can only hold about seven (plus or minus two) points at one time. When STM is filled to capacity, new items can push out existing items, called *displacement.*

**Atkinson-Shiffrin Model of Information Processing**

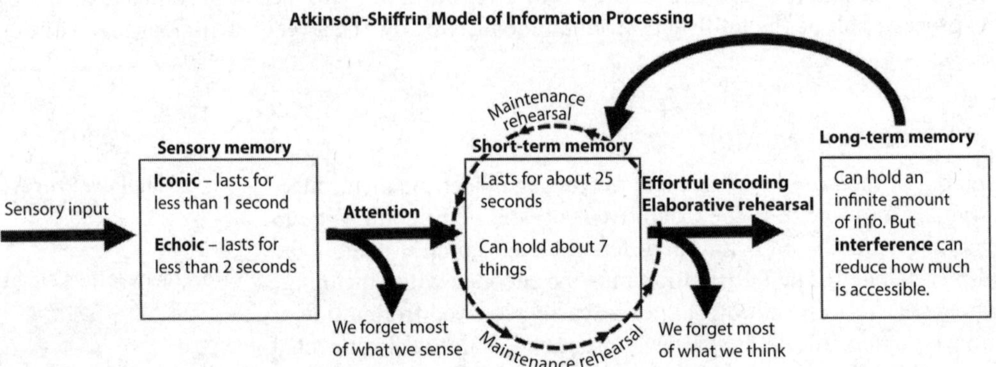


**Long-term memory (LTM).** Long-term memory is like a dry-erase board, where memories can be stored for a prolonged period of time, but it allows for memories to be easily revised or erased. In fact, LTM can hold information for a lifetime. The problem with the study of long-term memories is that memories cannot be observed or measured. Experts can theorize, but they really don't know how much or how long something can be stored. For example, as you are reading this sentence, can you think of your friend's e-mail address? When you think of this information, it is called retrieval. However, soon the e-mail address will disappear from your STM and you may wonder where the address went. How you encode and retrieve information is important for understanding the storage of LTM.

**Did you know?** The first time you read a book out loud in class may be slower than the second time. Why? One reason is because your implicit memory unconsciously conditions and stores the words in your memory. Did you know that episodic memories are easier to forget than semantic memories? This is because new episodes (experiences) happen every moment of every day.

Many years ago, cognitive psychologists theorized that LTM was one storage system. Now, studies show that LTM is divided into subdivisions: declarative memory and non-declarative memory.

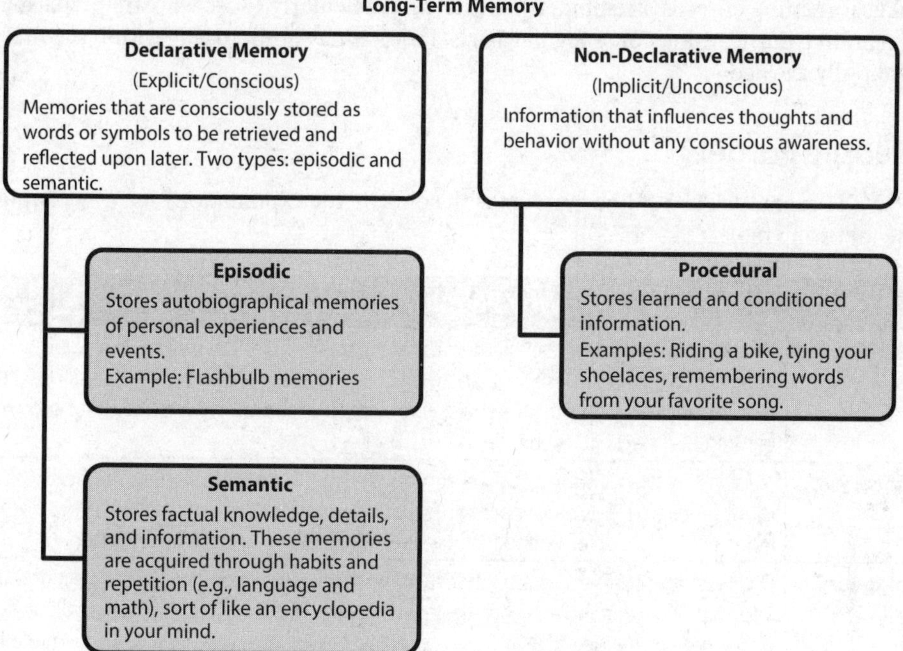


# Forgetting

Forgetting and memory slips are common among everyone—people forget where they put their keys, forget a phone number, or forget someone's birthday. Let's illustrate a research experiment to help you understand how easy it is for people to forget.

## Experiment

Researcher Hermann Ebbinghaus (1885) was interested in how people learn, remember, and forget. He used the basic tasks of recognition, recall, and relearning to determine the rate at which something is forgotten after it is initially learned. *Recognition* involved remembering information that was previously learned. *Recall* involved identifying how many items could be remembered from a list of items. *Relearning* involved learning a second time and was as tedious as the first time learning.

Ebbinghaus developed a mathematical formula and used "nonsense" syllables in his experiment so that there were no prior associations to the words. The results of his experiment are known as the **Ebbinghaus forgetting curve.** He was able to hypothesize that memory retention declined immediately after learning, but the results depended on the strength of memory and the amount of time that passed since learning.

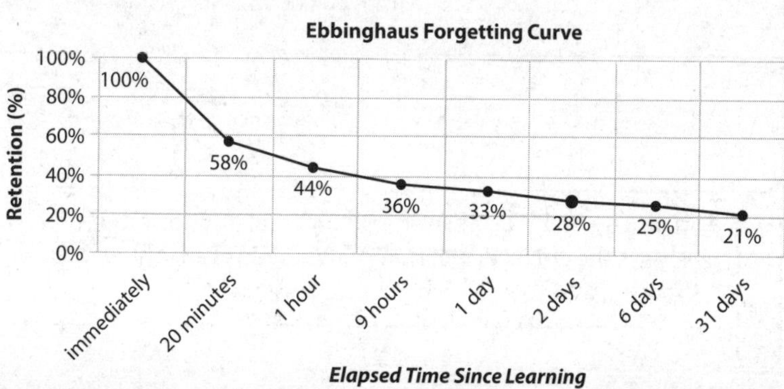

The Ebbinghaus forgetting curve is a reminder to all of us, particularly those who are preparing for an exam, that we must reinforce our learnings on a regular basis. Relearning should occur within the first 30 days after something is initially learned.

## Why Do People Forget?

For the AP PSYCH exam, you should be familiar with some of the explanations for why people forget, as detailed in the following table.

| Why People Forget | |
|---|---|
| **Encoding failure** | One answer to why we can't remember something might be an *encoding failure,* which means the information was never linked to the memory in the first place. The link can fail for a number of reasons, so if you want to store the information permanently, you should use some of the techniques listed in this chapter. |
| **Trace decay theory** | Trace decay theory suggests that memory decays (weakens) over time in short-term memory if it is not rehearsed. This theory proposes that information lasts about 15 to 25 seconds and then fades away. If the information is not rehearsed, it will eventually be forgotten. |
| **Displacement theory** | Displacement theory suggests that short-term memory has a limited capacity and when new information enters the memory, the new information takes the place of the old information. It can be likened to the idea of using a computer to revise a class paper. If you are limited to a 200-word essay and write a first draft with 200 words, then want to add more information, you must revise the essay by inserting the new written information and deleting old existing information to keep within the 200-word limit. |
| **Interference** | Interference means that new memories tend to impair the retrieval of older memories. Interference can be retroactive, proactive, or a negative transfer. Retroactive interference means that new learning interferes with the retrieval of old learning. The word *retro* means going backward. Therefore, imagine new information going backward in time to interfere with the older memorized information. For example, imagine that you changed schools and are now playing baseball for the new school's varsity team. Because you have been busy learning the new team's plays, you have difficulty remembering the plays that your former team ran.<br><br>*Proactive* interference occurs when old, previously learned information prevents new information from being retrieved. The memory can be disrupted (or interfered with) by what was previously learned.<br><br>In *negative transfer,* information is unable to be retrieved because it is conflicting. Think of negative transfer as learning hockey skills, but not being able to transfer these memories to learning golf skills. |

**Did you know?** The answer to the penny question in Experiment 1 is choice A. The penny in choice A shows the correct direction of Abraham Lincoln and the correct placement of "In God We Trust, "Liberty," and "1976."

# Amnesia

Amnesia is one of the more fascinating topics in psychology. Memories enter the brain through the senses. Failure to retrieve memories can be caused by a number of reasons, including brain injury, disease, psychological trauma, or drug and alcohol abuse. It is important to note that amnesia rarely affects non-declarative memories, which are made up of *procedural* or *implicit* memories. These types of memories answer the question "how." For example, procedural or implicit memories remember how to tie shoes, walk, or any other skill that is automatic. Amnesia usually affects declarative memories, which are made up of *explicit memories* that help you to remember the "what," "when," "who," and "where."

## Key Facts about the Types of Amnesia

**Childhood amnesia.** Perhaps the most common form of amnesia is a form that everyone has, but few people notice, *childhood (infantile) amnesia.* This is the idea that few people have any memories before age 5. If a person claims to remember early childhood memories before the age of 5, it may be a confabulation from sources such as family stories, old photographs, or a vague schema. Sigmund Freud suggested that childhood amnesia was due to the repression of traumatic events in early childhood, but more recent scientific research suggests that formation of new neurons in the hippocampus that helps to organize new learnings also clears old memories.

**Repression.** Repression of memories is a type of psychogenic amnesia. That means that the mind protects itself by blocking certain unpleasant memories as a way to guard itself from the content of uncomfortable thoughts.

**Source amnesia.** Another common type of amnesia is *source amnesia.* This simply means that although you may remember that George Washington was the first president, you cannot remember when you learned that fact.

**Retrograde amnesia.** When most people think of amnesia, they are probably imagining *retrograde amnesia.* This is when a person cannot remember something in their past. Retrograde amnesia may be caused by a concussion and memories are lost at the time of the head injury.

**Anterograde amnesia.** Anterograde amnesia is far less common and far more interesting, such as the cases of Henry Molaison and Clive Wearing. In both cases, the two men suffered brain damage to the hippocampus and were unable to form new memories. These two men were stuck at a point in time in their lives because their brain "librarian" could not encode or reconstruct memories. Note: Anterograde amnesia seems to affect only declarative or explicit memories, not procedural memories.

# Memory Distortion

**Memory distortion** is an inaccurate recall of facts and can occur when information is remembered incorrectly. Elizabeth Loftus' research on memory distortion supports the idea that humans are not good at remembering details. In fact, her work with eyewitness testimony in courts shows that such testimony is quite flawed and has led to many wrongful convictions. Memories are constructed based on a *schema* or script, and misinformation is easily woven into our memories without us noticing that some of the memories contain false information. Eyewitnesses are often unreliable because the memory might be affected by the wording of questions, biases, the time exposed to the event, post-event information, and stress. When accurate and false information are presented together, a person might unconsciously absorb the false detail into the accurate retrieval cues. This is similar to the idea of *confabulation.* Confabulation means that people weave false information into their episodic memory without conscious awareness.

## Strategies for Retrieving Memories

How you encode and retrieve is important for remembering information. For example, how do you remember key information when studying for the AP PSYCH exam? You may not be able to encode the exact wording of this book when you are studying, nor will you be able to retrieve all of this information during the AP PSYCH exam. However, you will hopefully be able to retrieve the gist of the information to be successful on the exam.

This is called **semantic learning** (or *principle learning*), which focuses on the *main ideas* behind what is being learned. The word "semantic" actually means "meaning," and that is how we consciously (explicitly) organize our memories—according to meaning, not details. Consider the word "ice." What pops into your mind—cold, cream, or skates? Each word retrieves a memory, which opens up more connections to related concepts. This is an example of semantic networks.

### Key Facts about Techniques for Retrieving Memories

On the AP PSYCH exam, you should know that there are techniques to increase the number of memories that you hold in your memory.

**Priming.** The process of unconsciously encoding and retrieving a memory begins with *priming* (the activation of certain associations to recall information). Nearly anything can prime a person to recall connected ideas from schematic long-term memories. For example, priming memories can be mood and context dependent.

- *Mood dependent.* Have you ever been so anxious and stressed out that all you can remember are the things that you must do? This is *mood congruent memory,* which means that when you are feeling anxious, you will more easily retrieve other memories associated with being anxious.
- *Context dependent.* Similarly, *where* you are might prime you to retrieve memories. Right now, you might not be able to remember much about the 4th grade, but if you were to walk into your elementary school right now, you would probably recall more associations to memories from the 4th grade than you would while reading this book.

**Chunking.** To improve your capacity to hold more short-term memories, use a memory technique called chunking. For example, you might have difficulty remembering a 10-digit phone number, but you can combine or chunk individual numbers together so they take up less space in your STM. For example, think of your area code as one unit (three digits combined into one) instead of three separate numbers. The three digits are chunked into one unit, leaving you two more spaces in your STM. You can then also chunk the prefix and chunk the last four digits, so the whole phone number takes up just three spaces in your STM.

**Rehearsal.** Thoughts in your STM will vanish in less than 25 seconds unless you repeat them over and over again. This repetition is called *rehearsal.* The thought in your mind needs to be restored, just like a computer needs to be restored when it's in sleep mode. Once you start thinking about the thought again, your STM reboots itself. If you repeat this process over and over again, the thought will stay in your STM indefinitely, called *maintenance rehearsal* (this is represented by the dotted circle around the short-term memory box in the diagram on p. 142). But remember, when you stop repeating a thought, the 25-second clock starts again.

**Elaborative rehearsal.** What does the information you would like to remember remind you of, sound like, or look like? You should elaborate with details of what you want to encode, called *elaborative rehearsal* (a method used to increase retention by relating memories to well-known associated information).

While there is no magic bullet in retrieving information to take the AP PSYCH exam, one clear idea is that studying must be *active,* not passive. You must actively think, question, talk about, and paraphrase information in your own words. Rewording is not rewriting. Rewriting is passive because you are rewriting material that was already written by someone else; you are not actively thinking about the material. Paraphrasing information in your own words and adding ideas to the information will help to remind you of the details of each topic.

Each idea is a *node,* and each node connects to other ideas, which allows us to retrieve other connecting ideas. Consider what you had for breakfast 2 weeks ago. Chances are that your breakfast was not encoded in such a way that it was linked to other nodes. To link any new idea to other nodes, you need to engage in elaborative rehearsal. That means you need to "think about" and relate your new ideas to old ideas. Elaborative rehearsal processes information at a deeper level because you are attending to and thinking about related ideas. For example, you might remember associated bits of information (similar feelings, surroundings, people, etc.).

**Mnemonics.** Remember how we said we might use techniques to increase the capacity of the working memory? Mnemonic devices are memory hacks that allow us to store a web of associations into our semantic networks. It's a relatively easy process, as illustrated in the following table.

| Mnemonic Device | Description | Example |
|---|---|---|
| **Acronym** | One of the most commonly used mnemonics is a technique to remember names or phrases by using the first letter of each word to form a "memorable" word. | To remember the four lobes of the brain, use the phrase "**F**reud **t**ore his **p**ants **o**ff."<br>**F**rontal<br>**T**emporal<br>**P**arietal<br>**O**ccipital |
| **Method of loci** | *Method of loci* (or memory palace) is a visual memory filing system used to recall an unlimited number of items; creating vivid images is especially effective. It requires you to visualize yourself moving through a familiar location while placing what you need to remember in certain locations. | To use this method to remember a list of things, you would imagine a familiar place, like your home. You might imagine the first item on the list to be placed in the closet near the front door, the second item on the counter, the third item in the refrigerator. This might be especially effective if you were to pair the locations with a well-used routine like coming home, putting your coat away, putting the keys on the counter, and getting a snack from the fridge. |
| **Peg method** | The *peg method* associates the numbers 1 to 10 with words that rhyme. This system is ideal for remembering information that must be recalled in a particular order. | Create a mental image of pegs hanging. Then associate each number for 1 to 10 with a rhyming word (e.g., 1 is gun, 2 is shoe, 3 is tree, etc.). Any new information is superimposed on the number-rhyme list. If you want to recall the first item, then you might visualize it being fired from a gun, and so on. |

# Thinking, Reasoning, and Problem Solving

## Thinking

Thinking is an action that involves creating and manipulating mental representations.

### Heads Up: What You Need to Know

The idea that you can think about your own mental processes, or "think about thinking," is called **metacognition.** It is important that you remember this term for the AP PSYCH exam. As you think about your mental processes, you are aware of your thoughts to clarify, modify, and reinforce your comprehension of sensory input.

### How People Think

When you are asked "What are you thinking about?" you can normally respond by saying what's on your mind, but how does thinking work? Thinking is part of our information processing system, and as information from the environment enters our brains, we mentally group and categorize the input. In the previous section, you learned that memories are reconstructed according to *schemas* (mental representations). Well, thinking is constructed according to schemas and is grouped by patterns of thoughts—known as concepts or general ideas.

For example, think of a bird. Did you think of the general idea of a bird, or the specific characteristics of a bird, like its tail feathers or talons? It is likely that you did not think about the bird's specific features or some of the unusual types of birds, like a penguin. Most people first think of a general schema that is a blend of all birds, before thinking of the specific details about a specific bird.

Hence, people think by organizing information into categories of different general concepts. Concepts can be categorized by features, prototypes, or hierarchies. People can organize thoughts by placing information into categories with certain features. Something with a specific set of features is known as an **artificial concept.** For example, a circle is an artificial concept because it cannot be anything other than a circle. In the example about a bird, if you thought of a crow, eagle, or robin, you thought of the **prototype** of a bird (a common example of something) because these are common American birds. If you thought of a bird as an animal that can fly (vs. a bird that can walk), you thought of the *hierarchy* of the bird family. A bird is a species of animal family and is classified as flying or walking, and within the classification of flying birds there are thousands of birds. Note: In our thinking process, the more closely the object matches the concept, the easier it is to recognize it within the mental category.

## Reasoning

Reasoning is a thinking process that involves evaluating information to reach a valid conclusion. For the AP PSYCH exam, we will focus on two different methods of reasoning: formal reasoning and informal reasoning.

**Formal reasoning (deductive reasoning)** is a type of thinking that involves **top-down thinking** (general information reaches a specific conclusion). Formal reasoning applies a logical *algorithm* (formula of a step-by-step process) to reach a conclusion. For example, think of using formal reasoning as an approach to solve a complex math problem. Hopefully you will follow an algorithm to solve the question. It is slow, but it allows for precise thinking supported by evidence derived from the algorithm before you form a conclusion. Formal reasoning is increasingly important in our data-driven world. For example, you wouldn't want the AP PSYCH Reader to grade your essays by using intuition. It is important that formal reasoning is used so that the AP PSYCH algorithm will find all possible points before forming a conclusion about your score.

**Informal reasoning (inductive reasoning)** is a type of thinking that involves intuitive thought, or **bottom-up thinking.** This type of reasoning begins with *specific* facts to arrive at a *general,* but logical, conclusion. Sometimes the facts are weak and may lack adequate specific evidence. For that reason, the conclusions may or may not be true. Informal reasoning will often use shortcuts when processing multiple elements of information, but these shortcuts, while usually dependable, can lead to errors in thinking. For example, you are passing someone in a school hallway and the person says, "Good morning." However, based on your previous experiences, your brain anticipated that the person would say, "What's up?" If your shortcut-driven response is "Nothing" because you didn't think to collect all of the information by listening to each specific word, your response would have been incorrect. In this case, your reasoning was intuitive based on what you thought the person would say.

**Bottom-Up Thinking**

Inductive reasoning begins with the senses, "gut feelings of intuition," and works up to the brain.

**Top-Down Thinking**

Deductive reasoning begins in the higher-level thinking brain where thoughts originate and works down to the senses in the body.

| Compare and Contrast Informal and Formal Reasoning | |
|---|---|
| **Informal Reasoning** | **Formal Reasoning** |
| **Inductive reasoning** starts with a set of facts and specific clues before forming a general conclusion. | **Deductive reasoning** starts with general information and then looks for clues that prove a specific conclusion. |
| **Intuitive.** Decisions are based on unconscious, flexible thought processes. | **Logical.** Decisions are based on logical reasoning and permanent rules. |
| **Bottom-up thinking** that begins with the senses. | **Top-down thinking** that begins with higher-level thinking. |
| **Heuristic** methods are used as a shortcut to find the logical answer that will probably be correct. | **Algorithms** are employed by using a step-by-step process, like a formula, to find the correct answer. |

### Heads Up: What You Need to Know

On the AP PSYCH exam, you should be familiar with the term **heuristics.** It is a mental "rule of thumb" that people use for problem solving and decision making; it is based on intuition. It does not guarantee the correct solution, but when it works, the results are derived quickly. Daniel Kahneman and Amos Tversky suggested that heuristics is a type of "fast unconscious thinking" that when employed will often result in the correct decision. Heuristics helps to inform decision making by focusing on the most significant aspects of the problem.

### Creative Thought

Creativity is the ability to think about something in a new way—"outside the box" thinking. The approaches creative thinkers use to gain new insights include reexamining existing problems or ideas, taking chances, challenging social norms, trying new ideas that others believe impossible, and refusing to accept limitations.

For the AP PSYCH exam, you should be familiar with the two thought processes that creative individuals use to solve problems: divergent thinking and convergent thinking.

**Divergent thinking** is a type of creativity where a person views a problem and explores multiple new solutions. For example, how many ideas can you come up with for studying?

**Convergent thinking** is a type of creativity where a person views a problem and narrows the solution to the single most efficient way to solve the problem. For example, convergent thinking would be ignoring the infinite ways to study and choosing the most simplistic method—using this study guide.

**Lateral thinking** is similar to divergent thinking, but instead of using the same process, it is "thinking outside the box" from a different perspective using new ideas (or new processes).

Factors that inhibit creativity are functional fixedness and a preconceived mental set. *Functional fixedness* is the opposite of creativity. It is a cognitive bias that limits a person's creativity. The person is unable to see that a traditional idea can be used in different ways. *Mental set* is a type of rigid bias, where a person's mind is stuck in a particular schema.

## Problem Solving

Problem solving research identifies big and small thinking challenges that we must solve in everyday scenarios. **Problem solving** refers to using thoughts and actions to meet a desired objective.

Three basic methods that are used in problem solving are algorithms, trial and error, and heuristics. An *algorithm* is a formula that breaks up the problem into smaller systematic steps that guarantees a solution. **Trial and error** is the process of experimenting with various methods until finding the correct solution. As discussed earlier in this chapter, **heuristics** is a mental "rule of thumb" that people use for problem solving and decision making; based on intuition, heuristics speeds up the problem-solving process, but is vulnerable to mistakes. Various heuristics are used in different situations. For example, a person can use the solution that is most easily remembered, called an *availability heuristic.* Other examples are when a person can work a problem in reverse, starting with the solution and then working back through the problem; a person can brainstorm; or a person can use the "rule of thumb" estimation to approach the problem.

## Key Facts about Bias and Errors in Problem Solving

To solve problems effectively and efficiently, we must use reasoning. As mentioned earlier, though a person can unconsciously perform many things simultaneously, the human brain is limited and can only consciously think of one thing at a time. Therefore, we use mental shortcuts (heuristics) to get around our brain's limitations. However, using such shortcuts can sometimes lead to errors in problem solving.

**Yerkes-Dodson law.** When the body is aroused (a sympathetic response) due to stress, creative problem solving can initially be more productive. However, when the stress level reaches its threshold, thinking becomes inhibited, leading to errors in problem solving. This stress response is called the *Yerkes-Dodson law.* As the level of stress increases, problem solving performance decreases (also see Chapter 10, p. 202).

**Ruminative thinking.** Problem solving errors can occur when a mood-congruent memory causes a person to become trapped in an emotional loop of stress-related thoughts, called *ruminative thinking*.

**Cognitive bias** is a mental shortcut that enables a person to make quick decisions; however, these quick decisions can often lead to mistakes in reasoning. Cognitive biases frequently occur when a person has an involuntary belief that deviates from rational thought.

There are numerous cognitive biases because people are very creative in how they can make mistakes in thinking that influence the outcome of solving problems. For the AP PSYCH exam, review the examples listed in the table that follows.

| Cognitive Biases | |
|---|---|
| **Anchoring bias** | The tendency to jump to conclusions by thinking of an improbable, but scary, solution rather than the reasonable outcome. For example, many people are afraid of flying, even though driving is more dangerous, and therefore choose to take a long car ride instead of flying. |
| **Availability bias** | The tendency to rely on readily available information and find a solution that is easy. For example, when you lose your keys, you probably keep looking in the same location because that is where the keys were found in the past. |
| **Confirmation bias** | The tendency to look for information that confirms an existing belief. For example, consider how people choose to view news sources that agree with their opinion. |
| **Hindsight bias** | The tendency to see past events as predictable, called the "I knew it all along" effect. For example, after watching a football game, a fan might claim that he knew the coach's decision would be wrong even if the fan didn't think so originally. |
| **Overconfidence bias** | The tendency for a person to place too much faith in his or her own opinion even if there is no reasonable explanation. For example, a gambler tends to continue betting even though he or she has lost the last ten hands at a poker game. |
| **Self-serving bias** | The tendency to make decisions based on what allows people to feel good about themselves. For example, you are biased to take credit for your success, but place blame on others for your failures. |

# Intelligence

Human intelligence has been described by many theorists, but for the purpose of the AP PSYCH exam, **intelligence** can be summed up in one word: **psychometrics** (the measure of the mind). The American Psychological Association (APA) describes intelligence as measurable *intellectual functioning.* It refers to standardized intelligence quotients (IQs) that test a person's general intelligence in reasoning and problem-solving skills.

## Theories of Intelligence

As with many fascinating subjects in psychology, intelligence cannot be directly observed—it must be quantitatively measured. Even the best standardized tests only measure a representation of intelligence. Although tests are not an exact science, one of the main advantages of intelligence tests is that they are accurate in predicting a person's cognitive strengths and weaknesses and future academic achievements.

Because contemporary psychologists recognize that IQ tests are not innate representations of a person's intelligence, they rely on other theories to guide their understanding of intelligence. As you will notice in the table that follows, some theories emphasize different abilities and multiple dimensions of intelligence.

Use the following list of theories of intelligence as a quick reference guide for the AP PSYCH exam.

| Theorist | Theory of Intelligence | Description |
|---|---|---|
| **Alfred Binet**, revised by Lewis Terman | Stanford-Binet test | The Stanford-Binet test is a popular test to measure cognitive abilities in five areas: knowledge, quantitative reasoning, visual-spatial processing, working memory, and fluid reasoning. |
| **David Wechsler** | Wechsler Adult Intelligence Scale (WAIS) | The Wechsler Adult Intelligence Scale is considered to be one of the best intelligence tests and assesses a range of intellectual abilities in verbal comprehension, reasoning, working memory, and processing speed. |
| **Charles Spearman** | General intelligence | Spearman's theory proposes that intelligence is measured by a general ability, the *g* factor. |
| **Raymond Cattell** | Fluid vs. crystallized intelligence | Cattell was known for his distinction between *fluid intelligence* (biologically influenced intelligence) and *crystallized intelligence* (learning-based intelligence). |
| **Robert Sternberg** | Triarchic theory of intelligence | Sternberg suggests a three-pronged *triarchic* theory of intelligence: analytical, creative, and practical. |
| **Howard Gardner** | Multiple intelligences | While most other tests emphasize math and linguistics, Gardner's theory expands intelligence to include (1) linguistic-verbal, (2) logical-mathematical, (3) spatial, (4) bodily-kinesthetic, (5) musical, (6) interpersonal, (7) intrapersonal, and (8) naturalistic. |
| **Daniel Goleman** | Emotion intelligence (EQ) | Emotional intelligence is a controversial form of intelligence in the field of psychology. It is similar to Gardner's multiple intelligences and highlights the importance of intrapersonal and interpersonal intelligence (e.g., self-awareness, empathy, cooperation, and self-control). |

**TEST TIP: On the AP PSYCH exam, you may be asked to compare fluid intelligence and crystallized intelligence. *Fluid intelligence* is the innate ability to reason and solve complex problems logically without previous learnings. Fluid intelligence—for example, solving puzzles—is not based on a person's education. *Crystallized intelligence* is what a person has learned in a lifetime through learning, education, and knowledge. As a person learns, crystallized intelligence increases. For example, learning basic arithmetic will help you learn more advanced math skills like algebra and calculus.**

## Stanford-Binet Test (Ages 2 to 85)

The **Stanford-Binet test** is one of the most widely used tests to assess intelligence. It is used to measure general verbal and nonverbal intelligence, including fluid reasoning, knowledge, quantitative reasoning, visual-spatial processing, and working memory.

Alfred Binet (and Theodore Simon) developed the basis for the first modern intelligence test. The test actually began as an aptitude test, but was later revised to become an IQ test. The test was created in the early 1900s in France to help educate French schoolchildren according to their abilities. The idea was to compare how well a child could perform compared to other children of the same age. This introduced the concept of testing based on *mental age* (average intellectual performance) vs. *chronological age* (age in years). Mental age is based on the level of "age-ranked" questions a person can answer and is a good measure of a person's abilities.

American psychologists immediately saw the merit in Binet's test, and Lewis Terman, who worked at Stanford University, revised Binet's ideas and applied them to intelligence testing, called the Stanford-Binet Intelligence Scale. If you can remember a bit of elementary school math, you might remember that a quotient is the number that is the result of dividing two numbers. The Stanford-Binet Intelligence Scale divides a person's mental age by the chronological age to get a quotient. Then the quotient is multiplied by 100 to get what was commonly known as an *IQ score.* Note: On the AP PSYCH exam, you should memorize the following IQ formula:

$$IQ = \frac{\text{mental age}}{\text{chronological age}} \times 100$$

| IQ score | Percentile |
|---|---|
| 130+ = very superior | 97th percentile |
| 90–109 = average | 50th percentile |
| 69 and below = extremely low | 2.275 percentile |

So, if a 7-year-old can do all of the things she should be able to do based on her age, then 7 divided by 7 equals 1. Multiply 1 by 100 and her IQ becomes 100, which is average. If a child can do all of the tasks of a 10-year-old, but is actually only 8 years old, her IQ would be 125 (i.e., 10 ÷ 8 = 1.25; 1.25 × 100 = 125). While Terman claimed that his formula could help identify gifted adults, the formula begins to break down in validity as age increases. For example, what can a 45-year-old do that a 44-year-old can't?

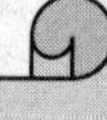

**Did you know?** Francis Galton, who was famous for being Charles Darwin's cousin as well as for several scientific advancements, was the first to take the abstract concept of intelligence and measure it scientifically. He suggested that people with enhanced physical abilities would have higher mental abilities. Galton's assumption was an obviously flawed assumption, but it gives us perspectives about the scientific advancements made in the field of psychology.

## Wechsler Adult Intelligence Scale (WAIS)

The **Wechsler Adult Intelligence Scale (WAIS)** developed by David Wechsler is used to statistically measure verbal and performance abilities, including verbal comprehension, perceptual organization, working memory, and processing speed. Each subtest is scored separately to help pinpoint strengths and weaknesses. For example, if a person does well on performance subtests but is weak on verbal subtests, this may indicate a language disability. The *Wechsler Intelligence Scale for Children (WISC)* is another statistical method to assign an IQ score for children ages 6 to 16.

## Sternberg's Triarchic Theory of Intelligence

Robert **Sternberg's triarchic theory of intelligence** is similar to Greek philosopher Aristotle's view illustrating intelligence in three components: analytical, creative, and practical. Whereas most IQ tests only look at analytical abilities, Sternberg felt that practical and creative needed to be included in assessing intelligence. These categories demonstrate a level of commonsense intelligence, and success is uniquely defined within the limits of culture and society.

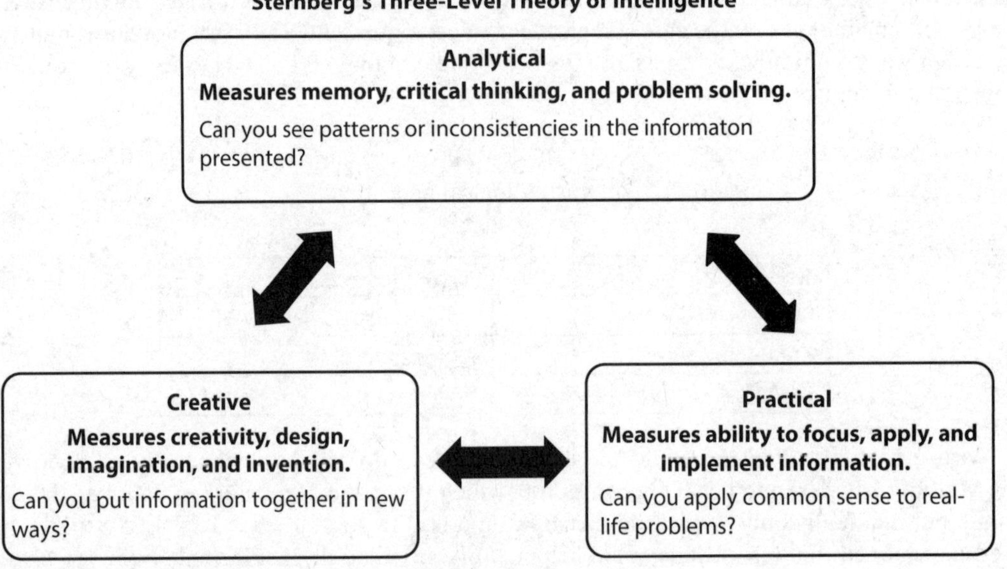


## Gardner's Theory of Multiple Intelligences

Howard Gardner created a theory known as multiple intelligences, which proposed a pluralistic view of the mind. Gardner believes that intelligence has roots in evolutionary history, and that humans are much like their ancestors, who had a variety of intellectual strengths to cope with environmental challenges. While most other tests emphasize linguistics, logics, and math, **Gardner's theory of multiple intelligences** outlines eight types of intelligences that are not typically considered when examining competencies.

1. **Linguistic-verbal ability:** The ability to think using words and language to express meaning (poets, authors, journalists, and speakers).
2. **Logical-mathematical ability:** The ability to carry out mathematical operations (scientists, engineers, and accountants).

3. **Spatial ability:** The ability to think three-dimensionally (architects, artists, and engineers).
4. **Bodily-kinesthetic ability:** The ability to solve problems using the body and physical skills (surgeons, craftspeople, dancers, and athletes).
5. **Musical ability:** The ability to be sensitive to pitch, melody, rhythm, and tone (composers, musicians, and sensitive listeners).
6. **Interpersonal ability:** The ability to understand others, a people person who has good conversational skills and knows how to interact with others (teachers, mental health professionals, salespeople, and politicians).
7. **Intrapersonal ability:** The ability to understand oneself and effectively direct one's life (theologians and psychologists).
8. **Naturalist ability:** The ability to observe patterns in nature and understand natural and human-made systems (farmers, botanists, ecologists, and landscapers).

## How Is Intelligence Measured?

What if you take a quick break from this book and find an intelligence test online. Will it show you are a genius? Maybe, but psychological tests must meet certain criteria to be accepted. Tests must be standardized, reliable, and valid.

**Standardization.** In order for test scores to have meaning, tests must be standardized. For example, the number of questions that you answer correctly on an intelligence test has no meaning unless your score is directly compared with other scores within the same representative group (e.g., the same age group) to determine the norms. Standardization starts with giving a sample pretest before the test is actually administered as an official test. In order to make the comparisons, the test-makers spend countless hours to establish detailed instructions, outline procedures, and administer pretests to a sample population. Revisions are made as necessary to determine the norms of a high, median, and low score. For example, to score AP PSYCH exam free-response essays, AP Readers use a sample essay to create a standardized scoring rubric. Essays are then scored using a standardized norm.

**Reliability.** Reliability refers to the level of accuracy, dependability, and consistency of a test over time. For example, if you take an intelligence test and then are reexamined at a later date with another form of the same test, the test results must be the same to be reliable. The *split-in-half* method helps to ensure testing correlation. A good test must **correlate** (show a relationship) with another version of the test to be reliable. For example, if a test-taker usually does better on one part of a test than another part of the test, the test is not correlated with itself. The higher the correlation, the higher the reliability.

**Validity.** Validity is the most important issue in the formation of a test. Just because a test is reliable does not mean that it is valid. A test can have high reliability but low validity. Validity means that the test measures what it was intended to measure (or predict). For example, do you think that the AP PSYCH exam will measure your overall knowledge of psychology or measure your ability to recall a narrow set of vocabulary terms?

There are several types of validity that you should be familiar with for the AP PSYCH exam.

| Types of Validity | |
|---|---|
| **Content validity** | Content validity is when the test has relevant and pertinent elements that are representative of the construct. For example, does the test ask about all the things that fall into the area that the test should be asking? What if the AP PSYCH exam only asked about neural activity? Then it would have low content validity. |
| **Construct validity** | Construct validity is the degree to which the test accurately measures what it was designed to measure. For example, how can the abstract idea of intelligence be translated into something that can be measured? |
| **Criterion validity** | Criterion validity measures how well the test correlates with the outcome. Does the test match an independent measure? For example, if a student is a genius on an online test but consistently misspells the word "intelligence," the online test has low criterion validity. |
| **Predictive validity** | Predictive validity is the measure of how well a test predicts future performance. For example, the SAT has a high predictive validity if the data set is large enough. If 100,000 people take the SAT, those who score higher will, on average, do better in college. Note: Predictive validity tests lose their accuracy as the data set gets smaller or if it is used to predict a single individual. |
| **Face validity** | Face validity is when the construction of the test is consistent in meaning and interpretation. For example, the AP PSYCH exam curriculum is divided into units. Does the exam have a proportional number of questions to match the curriculum goals? |

There are nearly infinite data points that might relate to intelligence—age of parents, zip code, the number of books in the home, etc. *Factor analysis* is a statistical technique that attempts to find relationships within data. Misusing statistics can be tempting because humans have a tendency to jump to conclusions and confuse correlation with causation. A *correlation* shows a relationship between variables, but it does not necessarily *cause* something to result. For example, there might be a correlation between the number of books read and economic status, but we cannot be sure if one causes the other.

**TEST TIP: On the AP PSYCH exam, you may be asked about the Flynn effect phenomenon. The *Flynn effect* shows a rise in average fluid and crystallized IQ test scores in the past century. Each generation of Americans seems to be more intelligent than the previous one. This is called the Flynn effect. While we can see a relationship between advancements in the world and higher test scores, researchers have not determined why this phenomenon exists.**

## Distribution of Scores

Standardized tests are calculated using the concept of **normal distribution** (a normal curve that shows the bell-shaped pattern of scores). Some of the adults who take intelligence tests will perform very well and others will perform very poorly, but most adults will perform about the same as everyone else. For example, most scores for the Wechsler Adult Intelligence Scale fall close to the average; only a few are found at the extremes.

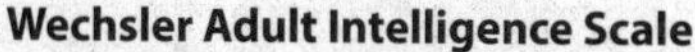


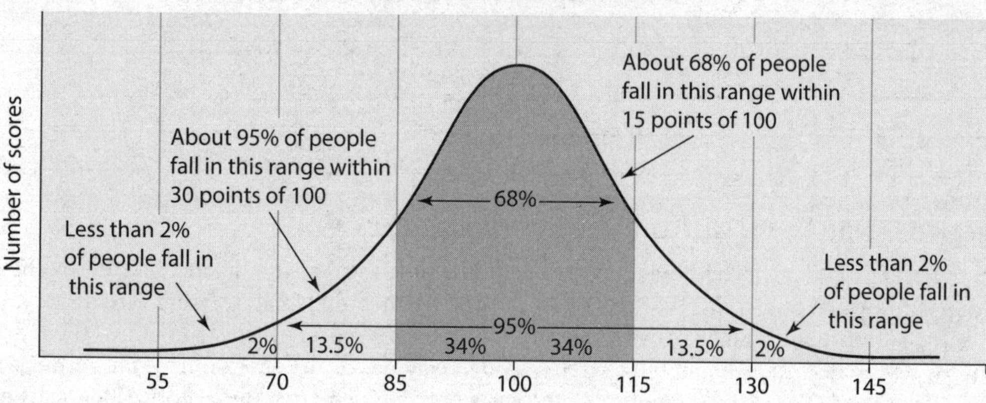


**IQ Score**

| **Standard Deviation** | −3 | −2 | −1 | 0 | +1 | +2 | +3 |
|---|---|---|---|---|---|---|---|
| **Percentile** | 0.1% | 2.3% | 15.9% | 50% | 84.1% | 97.7% | 99.9% |

## The Normal Curve

The normal curve describes how a set of scores is spread out from the average. The measurement of a normal curve isn't restricted to intelligence. Think of a person's height. Most people are of average height, a few are tall, and even fewer are extremely tall. Scores fall into categories, or how far they deviate from the *mean* (middle). **Standard deviation** is a unit to show how far away a score is from the mean. For example, the mean for the Wechsler Adult Intelligence Scale is 100 and the standard deviation is 15. Therefore, an IQ score of 115 is one standard deviation above the mean. As you can imagine, most scores fall between one standard deviation below the mean and one standard deviation above the mean, so most scores are between 85 and 115.

Look at the graph above. Notice that there are two numbers that read 34 percent. If you add them together, the result is 68 percent of the scores that fall within one standard deviation from the mean. Look to the right on the graph. Do you see that only about 2 percent of the population scores two standard deviations above the mean? Now look at the percentiles. Do you see that a person with an intelligence score of 100 is in the 50th percentile? That make sense because half of any scores in a normal distribution are above the mean and half are below the mean. Therefore, an IQ score is determined by finding out how far the test-taker deviates from the norm.

**TEST TIP: On the AP PSYCH exam, you will not be required to memorize math calculations. However, you will need to know that the average IQ score is 100 and the standard deviation is 15.**

| IQ Scale | |
|---|---|
| **IQ Score** | **Classification** |
| 130+ | Superior (extremely above average) |
| 120–129 | Superior (well above average) |
| 110–119 | High Average |

*Continued*

| IQ Score | Classification |
|---|---|
| 90–109 | Average |
| 80–89 | Low Average |
| 70–79 | Borderline (well below average) |
| 69 and below | Extremely low (intellectually deficient) |

## Intelligence—Nature vs. Nurture

What are the genetic and environmental influences on intelligence? Was intelligence shaped by the genetic instructions that formed our brains (nature) or by the environment in which we were raised (nurture)? This question is too simplistic. It's analogous to asking, "What makes music, the instrument or the musician?" It is difficult for researchers to estimate the degree to which genetics or the environment has influenced intelligence. The closest comparisons that psychologists have studied are monozygotic (identical) twins who were raised together and those separated at birth. Often, this type of research poses an unethical dilemma with too many confounding variables to claim causality, but researchers have claimed that IQ scores of separated twins can have large differences if the environmental differences are large.

Several studies show that identical twins raised in the same home have intelligence scores that are very similar. This seems logical because if the genetics and the environment are similar, then the IQ scores should be similar. Another study compared 25 mentally challenged children living in an orphanage who were eventually adopted with 26 mentally challenged children who were never adopted. The study revealed that those children who were adopted raised their IQ scores by an average of 29 points, while the children who were not adopted lost an average of 26 IQ points.

In summary, research suggests that both nature and nurture shape intelligence, and researchers will continue to debate which has the greater influence. Even if family members are raised in the same environment and have received the same education, they may still have differing aptitudes.

## Intellectually Gifted

What is the IQ of a genius? People with high intelligence have scores that are at least one standard deviation above the mean, which is an IQ above 119. People who are geniuses have a score of two standard deviations above the mean, scoring above 130 on IQ tests. This suggests that a genius scores higher than 98 percent of those in a representative sample. *Child prodigies* show amazing abilities, but often their abilities seem to level off as they reach adulthood. *Savant syndrome* is having a genius-level ability in a narrowly defined area, such as remembering dates.

## Intellectually Disabled

Early studies of intellectual disabilities have been based on the idea that a person can be stuck at a certain mental age, rather than chronological age. Modern ideas suggest that a person must meet two criteria to be classified as an intellectually disabled person: The person must have an IQ of two standard deviations below the mean, and the person must also demonstrate fairly low functioning in societal norms of adaptive behavior (communication, self-care, social skills, health, and safety). This brings up the idea of criterion validity because a low score might not be correlated with low functioning. *Down syndrome,* for example, which results from having an extra 21st chromosome, is the most recognizable form of an intellectual disability. A variety of chromosomal and genetic abnormalities can cause intellectual disabilities. Intellectual disabilities can be caused by external or environmental factors as well. For example, traumatic brain injuries, poisoning (including addiction), and physical and/or emotional deprivation can all cause the brain to react in a way that inhibits what we would call normal brain functioning.

## Bias and Stereotype in Testing

Bias and stereotype in testing refer to factors surrounding the test that may impact higher or lower score results (e.g., race, ethnic minority groups, or gender). A negative bias occurs when the criterion group scores lower than average, and a positive bias occurs when the criterion group scores higher than average. The topic of cultural bias continues to be controversial in the field of psychological testing. Traditionally, intelligence tests have been culturally biased and have reflected the cultural values and experiences of the creators of the test. More specifically, critics argue that white, middle- to upper-class Americans have an unfair testing advantage. For this reason, test developers have reevaluated test questions and now apply culture-fair testing practices. For example, the SAT has been criticized for administering a "white preference test," and the College Board has removed several items from the test that may have been biased based on the vocabulary. The predictive validity of the SAT remains the same for men and women, minorities, and the rich and the poor.

# Language

Language and thinking are interconnected. Language is the expression of thoughts through words and symbols that are arranged according to the structure of grammar.

### Heads Up: What You Need to Know

Russian psychologist Lev Vygotsky provided a rich foundation for understanding the meaningful relationship between thinking processes and language. Language is not just an instrument of communication; it is the center of *all* learning. For example, Vygotsky studied the relationship between second-language acquisition and thinking. He concluded that in order to acquire the knowledge of a second language, a person must *think* before any new concepts can be formulated. Therefore, if someone is learning English as a second language, the person must have a solid command of the primary native language in order to think about and understand the concepts, rules, and conventions of English.

Try to have a thought without words. Before you rush and say it is possible, let's define "words." A word is a symbol of meaning. Whether you are seeing the words on this page, feeling the words in Braille, or listening to words on an audio recording, the sights, textures, and sounds of words all carry meaning. Therefore, language is a system of communicating thoughts with symbols.

**Did you know?** Language is often confused with the ability to speak, but language is not speech. The ability to use language does not hinge on hearing or speaking words. Language is a communication system based on native rules and symbols (grammar and words) that carry *meaning.* For example, deaf children who fully participate in expressive and receptive sign language at home show the same cognitive development advances as hearing children.

## Language Acquisition

Psychologists view **primary language acquisition** (the unconscious acquisition of language) as an innate, built-in ability that is shaped by cognitive and sociocultural influences.

### Key Facts about Important Language Acquisition Theories

Although the AP PSYCH exam will focus on primary language acquisition, it is important to differentiate *primary language acquisition* from *secondary language acquisition.* Primary language acquisition is an unconscious process. Infants are not consciously aware of learning how to speak or how to apply the rules of grammar. Children will often repeat words just because it "sounds and feels right" when the words are formed together. On the other hand, when people learn a second language, they must consciously participate in the learning experience to study the rules, conventions, and patterns of the second language.

Most psychologists agree that there are certain patterns that occur when early language skills emerge, but there is some disagreement about why language develops. Noam Chomsky is one of the most influential linguistic scholars that you should be familiar with for the AP PSYCH exam.

**Chomsky's universal language acquisition theory.** Noam Chomsky theorized that language is innate in that humans will naturally develop language even if not taught. He suggested that infants are neurologically prewired to learn language and called this instinctive ability to learn language the *language acquisition device.* For example, infants and toddlers intuitively know how to combine a noun with a verb to form grammatically correct phrases. Chomsky is considered a *nativist* (someone who supports the idea that mental structures are innate, rather than learned). The fact that deaf babies will babble sounds they have never heard supports this theory.

**Sapir-Whorf hypothesis.** Edward Sapir (who studied the languages of indigenous people) and Benjamin Whorf (who was dedicated to proving Sapir's hypothesis) theorized that our native language (the language we are born into) shapes or determines what kinds of thoughts we think in an unalterable way. These thoughts impact cognition, called *linguistic determinism.* Linguistic determinism suggests that language limits human knowledge because thoughts cannot be altered. On the other hand, *linguistic relativism* suggests that thoughts can be altered. People of different cultures have different thought processes. Linguistic relativism suggests that how you think can be changed, expanded, or modified relative to the cultural experiences of the person.

### Stages of Language Acquisition

All children experience primary language acquisition during different stages of development, from pre-linguistic to linguistic, but what can infants think and at what age can they think? To study this question, research psychologists look at what words a baby speaks. Notice that each of the stages below involves a child producing language, called *active mastery.* Children might know more words and grammar rules than they can produce. Understanding words and grammar rules, but not being able to produce them is called *passive mastery.*

- **Eye contact (0–12 months).** Infants first communicate by making eye contact and gestures. Early vocalizations start with sounds of *cooing* (vowel sounds).
- **Babbling (3–12 months).** Babbling sounds begin that sound like patterned speech of consonant-vowel strings (*phonemes*); for example, "da-da-da-da."

- **Holophrase (8–24 months).** First words are spoken by 12–18 months and are usually familiar nouns—objects or persons—called *holophrases,* like "mama," "dog," and "juice." A holophrase expresses a complete and meaningful thought.
- **Telegraphic speech (18–24 months).** Toddlers speak in two-word phrases, like "juice spill," known as *telegraphic speech.* Telegraphic speech is an early form of speech and can be observed when a toddler selectively omits or simplifies words in a phrase to communicate his or her message. The sentence consists of just enough words to get the meaning across. Notice that a toddler can use the correct *syntax* (words are arranged in the correct grammatical order).
- **Fast mapping (2–5 years old).** As toddlers learn new vocabulary, they begin fast mapping to figure out the meaning of words. *Fast mapping* is a mental process whereby young children are able to use the "context" of a word or phrase and accurately arrive at the word's meaning.
- **Overgeneralization (4–5 years old).** Overgeneralization is when young children misapply grammar rules. For example, a 4-year-old child adds the suffix "ed" to an irregular verb and says, "Mommy, I *runned* really fast."

**TEST TIP: On the AP PSYCH exam, it is important to remember the term *critical period.* It refers to a time in a person's life (especially in early childhood) when it's optimal to acquire certain developmental skills. In language acquisition, all children experience a critical period when it is most advantageous to learn verbal skills in their native language. If children do not interface with language in early childhood, they may demonstrate a limited range of language fluency, predominantly with grammar systems.**

# Chapter Review Practice Questions

Practice questions are for instructional purposes only and may not reflect the format of the actual exam. The questions and explanations that follow focus on essential knowledge, course skills, and course content.

## Multiple-Choice Questions

1. Based on his gut feelings, Rodrigo has decided which college to attend. Which of the following decision-making processes did Rodrigo use?

   **A.** Deductive reasoning
   **B.** Bottom-up thinking
   **C.** Top-down thinking
   **D.** Algorithm
   **E.** Schema

2. A woman has the tendency to believe that air travel is unsafe because she remembers seeing recent footage of plane crashes. Which of the following cognitive phenomena best explains this scenario?

   **A.** Representative bias
   **B.** Availability heuristic
   **C.** Survivor bias
   **D.** Anchoring bias
   **E.** Hindsight bias

3. Which of the following stages of language development best describes a 2-year-old who says, "More drink" and "Where dog" when speaking to his mother?

   **A.** Fast mapping
   **B.** Telegraphic speech
   **C.** Overgeneralization
   **D.** Mental model
   **E.** Holophrase

4. In the organization of thoughts, which of the following best describes how our brains might categorize the number 2?

   **A.** Algorithm
   **B.** Prototype concept
   **C.** Artificial concept
   **D.** Morpheme
   **E.** Linguistic relativity

5. Which of the following creative thinking terms best describes the inability to see that an object can be used in a way that is different from how it was originally designed to be used?

   **A.** Lateral thinking
   **B.** Convergent thinking
   **C.** Divergent thinking
   **D.** Functional fixedness
   **E.** Over-confidence bias

6. Juan is trying to teach his grandmother how to use a new electronic device, but his grandmother has difficulty grasping the concept of new technology. She says that she keeps thinking about the operations of older machines and continually forgets Juan's instructions. What cognitive function best describes this thinking process?

   **A.** Elaborative rehearsal
   **B.** Retroactive interference
   **C.** Retrograde amnesia
   **D.** Maintenance rehearsal
   **E.** Proactive interference

7. Which of the following IQ scores is one standard deviation above the mean?

   **A.** 115
   **B.** 15
   **C.** 130
   **D.** 100
   **E.** 85

## Free-Response Question

**1 question**
**25 minutes**

**Directions:** It is suggested that you take a few minutes to plan and outline your essay. Write your response on lined paper. You must demonstrate your understanding of course skills and course content. Your essay is considered a first draft and may contain some grammatical errors that will not be counted against you. However, to receive full credit, your essay must demonstrate defensible content knowledge with substantive examples where appropriate.

---

James is a middle-aged man who feels pretty foolish because he can't seem to figure out how to upload a video onto his cell phone so that he can electronically transfer the video to his television screen. He is frustrated and lost the cables that connect his phone to the TV. James has seen his teenage son accomplish this task several times, but can't seem to master what he calls "new technology."

Describe how the following concepts might affect James' ability to solve this problem.

- Algorithm
- Sapir-Whorf hypothesis
- Proactive interference
- Context-dependent learning
- Availability heuristic
- Top-down thinking
- Levels of processing model

# Answers and Explanations

## Multiple-Choice Questions

1. **B.** *Bottom-up thinking,* choice B, starts with the senses, like "gut feelings" and intuition. In this case, the soon-to-be college student used his gut feelings to make his decision. Bottom-up thinking is similar to inductive reasoning. Rodrigo did not use higher-level thinking processes (choices A, C, and D) in deciding which college to attend. *Deductive reasoning* (choice A) and *top-down thinking* (choice C) are similar logical reasoning processes. They begin with consciously gathering data from general information and then forming a specific logical conclusion. An *algorithm* (choice D) is the logical step-by-step process of problem solving. It is similar to following a specific formula to solve a problem. A *schema* (choice E) is a set of ideas about a given topic.

2. **D.** *Anchoring bias,* choice D, is a cognitive phenomenon, but not a heuristic or problem-solving strategy. It is when rare, but emotionally powerful, events seem more likely than common events. The woman in this scenario is relying too heavily on her fear of a plane crash, and these powerful thoughts have become anchored to an unlikely event. *Representative bias* (choice A) can lead to false conclusions because it is an oversimplified decision-making process. For example, if you hear that a person loves books, and are asked whether that person is a Marine Corps sergeant or a librarian, you will probably predict that the person is a librarian, using quick decision making without doing a thorough investigation. Statistically, you might be wrong, because there are far more Marine Corps sergeants than librarians. *Availability heuristic* (choice B) is a problem-solving strategy in which a person uses the solution that most easily springs to mind or one that they are accustomed to using. *Survivor bias* (choice C) focuses on historical information, rather than the information that is available today. For example, great-grandparents may overlook a logical conclusion if they focus on information that was valid in the past but is no longer suitable in today's world. *Hindsight bias* (choice E) occurs every time a person exclaims, "I knew it!"

3. **B.** *Telegraphic speech,* choice B, is the first sentences that toddlers speak. To remember telegraphic speech, think of a message sent by text—short sentences that are quick and to the point. Sometimes words are omitted, but the meaning is clear. *Fast mapping* (choice A) is when children ages 2–5 years old arrive at a word's meaning by using the context of another word. *Overgeneralization* (choice C) is when a child misapplies the rules of grammar, such as saying, "He runned fast." A *mental model* (choice D) is not relevant to language acquisition; it is an explanation for a person's thought process. *Holophrases* (choice E) are the first one-word utterances a baby speaks.

4. **C.** *Artificial concept,* choice C, is a thought that is defined and organized by precise rules. As such, the number 2 can only be defined by the mathematical rules. An *algorithm* (choice A) is a step-by-step method for solving a problem. A *prototype concept* (choice B) is an ideal example for a typical concept, from which all other forms are developed. *Morpheme* (choice D) is not a thinking process; it is a language term that describes the smallest unit of meaning that can exist by itself. *Linguistic relativity* (choice E) is not a thinking process; it is the idea that the language a person is raised with shapes the types of thoughts he or she can have.
5. **D.** Imagine that a person's mind is fixated and has only one function. *Functional fixedness,* choice D, is the inability to see that there are multiple ideas for any given situation. It is the opposite of creativity. *Lateral thinking* (choice A) is a type of creative thinking that involves solving problems in a new and unusual way. *Convergent thinking* (choice B) is a type of creative thinking that narrows the solution to the single most efficient way to solve the problem. *Divergent thinking* (choice C) is a type of creative thinking where a person creates a new solution to an existing problem by exploring multiple new solutions. *Over-confidence bias* (choice E) is an error in thinking in which a person, with limited information about the task or abilities, believes that it is possible to do the task.
6. **E.** *Proactive interference,* choice E, is when information from one's past prevents the memory retrieval of new information. *Elaborative rehearsal* (choice A) is a method of memory encoding in which information is stored in the long-term memory by associating memories to related and familiar information. (Hopefully, this is what you are doing as you read this explanation.) *Retroactive interference* (choice B) is a reason why people forget; it is when new learning interferes with the retrieval of old learning. *Retrograde amnesia* (choice C) is when a person can't remember what happened before a certain point. *Maintenance rehearsal* (choice D) is when a person attempts to keep information in his or her long-term memory by repeating it over and over.
7. **A.** The established mean for intelligence scores is 100. The established standard deviation is 15. Therefore, one standard deviation above the mean would be 100 + 15 = 115, choice A. Choice B, 15, is not one standard deviation above the mean; it is the established standard deviation for intelligence scores distribution. Choice C, 130, is two standard deviations above the mean of 100. Choice D, 100, is simply the mean score for any given representative sample of the population. Choice E, 85, is one standard deviation below the mean.

## Free-Response Question

To achieve the maximum score of 7, your response must address each of the bullet points in the question.

## Sample Student Response

An *algorithm* is a step-by-step process for finding a solution. If James is not following the directions that came with his cell phone or not using a step-by-step guide found on the Internet, he might not be able to find a solution. The *Sapir-Whorf hypothesis* suggests that the language in which we are raised shapes, and may even limit, the thoughts we can have. As a result, James' native language not only might not have the knowledge of technical words, it might not allow him to comprehend the problem. *Proactive interference* is when previously learned information prevents the processing of newer information. For example, James' understanding of how to connect older technology, like a DVD player, to the TV is interfering with his ability to understand how to connect his cell phone to the TV. *Context-dependent learning* is the idea that learning is best when encoding and retrieval both occur in similar settings.

If James has learned all of his connectivity knowledge in his son's room, but now must remember this in his living room, he might have trouble recalling how to connect the devices.

An *availability heuristic* is a problem-solving shortcut where a person uses the solution that is most easily remembered or accessed in the mind. James' idea to use the power cord to connect his phone to the TV is the solution that easily comes to his mind, but without the power cord, this shortcut won't work. He needs to find another way. *Top-down thinking* is the idea that a person starts problem solving by perceiving or thinking about the big picture, rather than each individual piece of the problem. If James was thinking from the top down, then he might only think of the whole process of connecting and not of the individual solutions so that a phone can send a signal. *Levels of processing* is the idea that the deeper we think about things, or the more mental connections we make with the information, the better we can remember and use the information. If James simply skimmed the directions to connect the cell phone to the TV, rather than thoroughly reading the instructions, he might not be able to follow the directions.

Chapter 9

# Unit 6: Developmental Psychology

AP Psychology Unit 6 covers the study of physical, cognitive, social, and moral behavior through a lifespan.

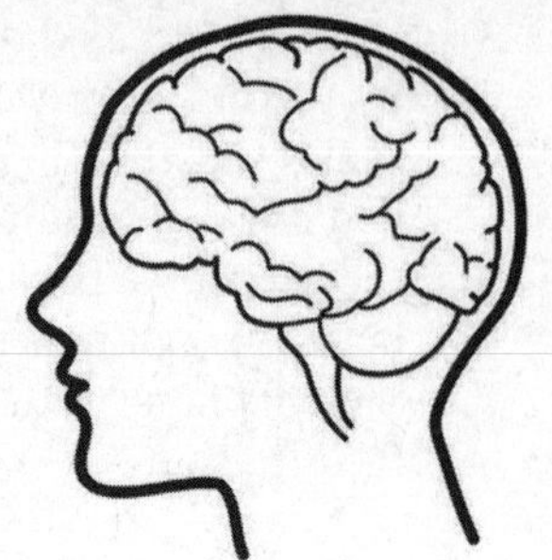

- Key Contributors to Developmental Psychology
- Lifespan and Physical Development
- Social Development
- Maturationism and Critical Period
- Cognitive Development
- Adolescent Development
- Adulthood and Aging
- Moral Development
- Gender and Sexual Orientation

## Overview of AP Psychology Unit 6

The overarching concepts for this chapter analyze the physical, cognitive, psychological, social, and moral stages of a person's development from birth through adulthood. **The topics discussed in this unit will count toward 7–9 percent of your multiple-choice score.**

## AP Psychology Framework

Success on the exam depends on your ability to make connections to the major concepts described in the content topics of the *Course Framework for AP Psychology.* Remember that these concepts highlight the fundamental ideas that every student should take with them into the AP PSYCH exam and beyond.

Use the table below to guide you through what is covered in this unit. The information contained in this table is an abridged version of the content outlines with topic examples. Visit https://apstudent.collegeboard.org/apcourse/ap-psychology/ for the complete updated AP PSYCH course curriculum framework.

| AP Psychology—Unit 6: Developmental Psychology | |
|---|---|
| **Topic** | **Learning Target** |
| **The Lifespan and Physical Development in Childhood** | ■ Explain the process of conception and gestation, including factors that influence successful prenatal development (e.g., nutrition, illness, substance abuse, and teratogens).<br>■ Discuss the interaction of nature and nurture (including cultural variations), specifically physical development, in the determination of behavior.<br>■ Discuss maturation of motor skills. |
| **Social Development in Childhood** | ■ Describe the influence of temperament and other social factors on attachment and appropriate socialization.<br>■ Identify the contributions of major researchers in developmental psychology in the area of social development in childhood (Bandura, Baumrind, Lorenz, Harlow, Ainsworth, and Freud).<br>■ Discuss the interaction of nature and nurture (including cultural variations), specifically social development, in the determination of behavior.<br>■ Explain how parenting styles influence development. |
| **Cognitive Development in Childhood** | ■ Explain the maturation of cognitive abilities (Piaget's stages and information process).<br>■ Identify the contributions of major researchers in the area of cognitive development in childhood (Vygotsky and Piaget). |
| **Adolescent Development** | ■ Discuss maturational challenges in adolescence, including related family conflicts. |
| **Adulthood and Aging** | ■ Characterize the development of decisions related to intimacy as people mature.<br>■ Predict the physical and cognitive changes that emerge through the lifespan, including steps that can be taken to maximize function.<br>■ Identify the contributions of key researchers in the area of adulthood and aging (Erikson). |
| **Moral Development** | ■ Identify the contributions of major researchers in the area of moral development (Gilligan and Kohlberg).<br>■ Compare and contrast models of moral development. |
| **Gender and Sexual Orientation** | ■ Describe how sex and gender influence socialization and other aspects of development. |

## Important Terms and Concepts Checklist

This section is an overview of the important terms, concepts, language, and theories that specifically target the key topics of Unit 6. Use this list of terms as a checklist to check your personal progress. As you study the topics, place a check mark next to each and return to this list as often as necessary to refresh your understanding.

After you finish the review section, you can reinforce what you have learned by working through the practice questions at the end of the chapter. Answers and explanations provide further clarification into the perspectives of human development.

| Term/Concept | Study Page | Term/Concept | Study Page | Term/Concept | Study Page |
|---|---|---|---|---|---|
| **accommodation** | p. 183 | **Erikson's stages of psychosocial development** | pp. 169, 179–180 | **Lorenz's imprinting theory** | pp. 170, 174 |
| **adaption** | p. 183 | **fetal alcohol spectrum disorders** | p. 172 | **menopause** | p. 187 |
| **Ainsworth's attachment theory** | pp. 169, 175–176 | **fetus (fetal period)** | p. 171 | **personality** | p. 177 |
| **assimilation** | p. 183 | **Freud's stages of psychosexual development** | pp. 169, 178 | **Piaget's stages of cognitive development** | pp. 170, 182–185, 186 |
| **Bandura's social learning theory** | pp. 169, 181 | **gender orientation** | pp. 190–191 | **schema** | p. 183 |
| **Baumrind's parenting styles (permissive, authoritative, authoritarian, and uninvolved)** | pp. 169, 177 | **Gilligan's stages of moral development** | pp. 169, 190 | **secure attachment** | p. 175 |
| **conservation** | pp. 184–185 | **Harlow's monkey experiments** | pp. 169, 174 | **sexual orientation** | pp. 190–191 |
| **continuity vs. discontinuity** | pp. 177–178 | **Heinz dilemma** | p. 188 | **temperament** | p. 173 |
| **critical period** | p. 182 | **imaginary audience** | p. 187 | **teratogens** | p. 172 |
| **embryo (embryonic period)** | p. 171 | **insecure attachment styles (avoidant, resistant, and disorganized)** | p. 176 | **Vygotsky's theory on cognitive development** | pp. 170, 185–186 |
| **equilibrium** | p. 183 | **Kohlberg's stages of moral development** | pp. 170, 188–190 | **zygote (pre-embryonic period)** | p. 171 |

# Chapter Review

This chapter focuses on what contributes to the evolution of human growth by examining all aspects of development from birth to death—physical, cognitive, psychological, social, and moral development.

### Heads Up: What You Need to Know

For the AP PSYCH exam, as you work through the chapter, ask yourself this essential question: How do we perceive and understand ourselves?

## Key Contributors to Developmental Psychology

On the AP PSYCH exam, you should be able to identify the major contributors in the field of developmental research.

| Key Contributors to Developmental Psychology | | |
|---|---|---|
| **Contributor** | **Field of Study (Theory)** | **Famous For** |
| **Mary Ainsworth** (1913–1999) | Attachment theory | American-Canadian developmental psychologist Mary Ainsworth was known for her contributions to attachment theory (the bonding between a mother and child). Ainsworth devised a procedure, called *Strange Situation,* to determine how toddlers managed stress when separated from their mothers and were left alone with a stranger. The toddlers' reactions to their mothers' return were the bases for determining the patterns of attachment styles. |
| **Albert Bandura** (1925–) | Social learning theory | Canadian-American psychologist Albert Bandura is famous for his social learning theory, which suggests that children do not learn from classical conditioning, but from observing models of behavior (e.g., observing parents, teachers, or peers). Bandura demonstrated the power of observational learning with his "Bobo doll" experiment. In the experiment, well-behaved children started acting aggressively after witnessing an adult punch an inflated doll. |
| **Diana Baumrind** (1927–2018) | Parenting styles | American psychologist Diana Baumrind was well-known for developing a theory of parenting styles that influence child development: authoritarian, authoritative, and permissive. A fourth, uninvolved, was added later. |
| **Erik Erikson** (1902–1994) | Stages of psychosocial development | German-American developmental psychologist and psychoanalyst Erik Erikson was famous for his theory of psychosocial development. It is one of the best-known theories of personality development. His work was based on Freud's theory of unconscious personality development. Erikson suggested that humans progress through eight stages of development that lead toward personality formation. He theorized that in order to progress from each stage, a person had to unconsciously resolve a conflict. |
| **Sigmund Freud** (1856–1939) | Theory of psychosexual development | Freud believed that personality develops through five stages of psychosexual development: oral, anal, phallic, latency, and genital. The first three stages were the most important in shaping personality. Each stage attempted to deal with powerful urges that were psychosexual in nature. Freud theorized that how a child navigated the first three stages helped to determine personality. |
| **Carol Gilligan** (1936–) | Stages of moral development | Gilligan is an American psychologist who is famous for expanding Kohlberg's scale of moral development. Gilligan became dissatisfied with Kohlberg's scale of moral development because women consistently rated lower than men. Gilligan developed a different scale that focused on compassion, responsibility, and care, rather than abstract ideas of justice, rules, and rights. |
| **Harry Harlow** (1905–1981) | Experiments on monkeys | Harlow was famous for his experiments with baby monkeys. Harlow was one of the first psychologists to demonstrate the importance of love, affection, and mother-child attachment, but his experiments were considered unethical and cruel. He kept baby monkeys alone in a cage with two options. The monkey could choose a cage with a soft, surrogate mother doll (with no food), or the monkey could choose a surrogate mother made of wire with a scary face (with food). Even though the wire mother allowed the baby to get food, the baby monkeys preferred the cloth mother, showing that babies need comfort, love, and affection. |

*Continued*

| Contributor | Field of Study (Theory) | Famous For |
|---|---|---|
| **Lawrence Kohlberg** (1927–1987) | Stages of moral development | Kohlberg started his profession as an American developmental psychologist and then moved to the field of moral education. He was famous for developing a system to rank moral judgment. In his experiment, he would give participants a moral dilemma, known as the *Heinz dilemma*. From his experiment, he developed three levels of moral reasoning: pre-conventional, conventional, and post-conventional. |
| **Konrad Lorenz** (1903–1989) | Imprinting | Lorenz is regarded as the father of *ethology* (study of animal behavior) and studied the principle of instincts and imprinting. |
| **Jean Piaget** (1896–1980) | Theory of cognitive development | Swiss psychologist Jean Piaget was first a biologist who later became interested in the development of children. His theory of cognitive development is famous in the field of education. Piaget believed that children go through four distinct stages of thinking and mastering logical thought. The stages are determined by the child's ability to accomplish certain cognitive tasks. Piaget used naturalistic observation in his research design. The four stages of cognitive development are sensorimotor, preoperational, concrete, and formal operations. |
| **Lev Vygotsky** (1886–1934) | Sociocultural theory | Russian psychologist Lev Vygotsky was well-known for his studies of bio-social human development. He believed that children's cognitive abilities were not based on age or what tasks they could perform, and that with the help of others, children could demonstrate much greater abilities. The two concepts that Vygotsky was famous for are called *scaffolding* and the *zone of proximal development*. |

Developmental psychology, also known as child development or human development, explains the growth and changes that people face through a lifetime. Developmental psychologists originally studied infants and children, but have expanded the field of study to include adolescents, adults, and older adults. Developmental psychology covers a broad range of topics that include genetic influences, environmental factors, and other systems that interact with physical, cognitive, and social development.

## Lifespan and Physical Development

While there are many theories about development, most psychologists agree that humans do not develop randomly—there are predictable patterns of development, called *maturationism.* This is the idea that children grow according to genetic instructions, and environment plays a passive secondary role in development. Genetic instructions tell the body and brain how to grow. (For more on maturationism, see "Maturationism and Critical Period" later in this chapter.)

Let's review some of the terms that were covered in Chapter 5, "Unit 2: Biological Bases of Behavior," to refresh your memory of genetic inheritance that affects the prenatal development of an unborn infant.

**Genes and chromosomes.** Genetic instructions identify specific *genes* (encoded DNA characteristics from your parents) that make up *chromosomes* (DNA thread-like molecules in the nucleus of each cell). Genes and chromosomes determine the traits of a person.

**Genotype and phenotype.** The genetic makeup of the traits is called a *genotype.* All of the traits that can be observed are called a *phenotype.*

**Epigenetics** is the study of how environment affects gene expression, or to put it another way, just because you have a gene doesn't mean that it is active. This is important for the development of a fetus because the hormonal environment of a mother's womb can turn on and off certain genes.

## Prenatal Development

Conception begins with a *germinal stage* of development, which occurs within the first 2 weeks after a sperm cell fertilizes the ovum, forming a **zygote.** The zygote undergoes rapid cell division before it is implanted on the uterine wall. The zygote contains the genetic instructions for development.

Once the zygote is implanted, it is called an **embryo.** There are two ways to think about embryonic growth patterns. *Cephalocaudal* growth is the idea that the embryo grows from top to bottom, meaning that the brain and head form first and the body grows downward. The other way to think about embryonic growth and even early childhood growth is called *proximal distal*—not only do embryos develop from the core outward, but children develop motor skills from their core outward.

The final and longest stage of prenatal development is when the **fetus** develops, called the *fetal period.* For 7 months, the body systems grow and work toward maturity in preparation for life outside the mother's body. *Myelination,* the process of coating axons with fatty insulation, begins during this stage. Myelination allows for faster neural signals.

**Stages of Prenatal Development**

| Period | Description | Critical Period of Development |
|---|---|---|
| **Zygotic (pre-embryonic period)**<br>0 to 2 weeks | Zygote is the single cell that is formed from sperm and egg cells during conception. | Weeks 1–2: The single-cell zygote undergoes rapid cell division and replication and eventually implants itself into the uterus. |
| **Embryo (embryonic period)**<br>3 to 8 weeks | The embryo begins the process of forming organs and a human shape. | Week 3: The central nervous system begins to develop.<br>Weeks 3–4: The eyes, ears, and a primitive heartbeat begins to develop.<br>Week 5: Arms and legs begin development. |
| **Fetus (fetal period)**<br>8 weeks to delivery | The fetus continues to grow until the baby's delivery. | Week 8: The fetus is no longer an embryo and *organogenesis* is complete. The fetus can move its legs, head, and feet, but the mother will not feel the movements until the fourth month of pregnancy.<br>By the seventh month of pregnancy, the fetus is considered viable. |

### Factors That Influence Prenatal Development

Genetic (*nature*) instructions show how the fetus grows, but the environment (*nurture*)—the mother's body—is the most important factor in the development of a fetus. The mother's womb is the first environment that the baby experiences, and the unborn fetus is completely dependent on the mother.

Prenatal care and the interactions between nature and nurture actually begin before conception. It is important for both parents to recognize the possible risk factors and create a healthy and nutritious environment even before pregnancy. For example, it is important to be educated about good health habits and talk to a doctor about medical conditions, heredity factors, body weight, prescription medications, drinking, and smoking.

The *placenta* (temporary organ in the uterus that is responsible for nourishing the fetus via the umbilical cord) acts as a filter, allowing oxygen and nutrients to pass through to the fetus. The placenta is responsible for oxygen, nutrition, temperature regulation, and waste elimination, and helps to prevent toxic or harmful substances from reaching the fetus. While the placenta usually does a great job of protecting the fetus, some toxins can pass through to the fetus, such as **teratogens** (toxins that can cause malformation of the fetus), and cause harm to the unborn infant.

### Heads Up: What You Need to Know

The terms *teratogens* and *fetal alcohol spectrum disorders* frequently appear on the AP PSYCH exam. **Teratogens** are chemicals (e.g., nicotine, narcotics, and alcohol), radiation, infectious diseases, or any exposures to toxins, like pesticides or lead. Teratogens can cause birth defects and prevent normal cell division during the embryonic stage of prenatal development (2 to 8 weeks) when the embryo is forming vital organs. Teratogens can also increase the risk of congenital malformation. For example, research evidence suggests that mothers who smoke during pregnancy have a greater risk for having a premature baby with low birth weight.

**Fetal alcohol spectrum disorders** can occur when a mother drinks heavily during her pregnancy, especially in the first 12 weeks of pregnancy. They can cause brain damage, growth problems, and cognitive deficiencies. The results vary from infant to infant, but problems can emerge as abnormal appearances, short height, and a small head size. The disorders can also cause significant cognitive deficits and low intelligence.

Similarly, a fetus who is exposed to narcotics during pregnancy can be born addicted to those substances. Statistically, babies born in the United States are at greater risk of being born addicted to narcotics. The withdrawal symptoms for such babies can be fatal and can affect normal development for a lifetime.

## Social Development

Social development is based on what can be observed and learned through experiences in the environment. Early social connections are crucial in the formation of all relationships with family, friends, classmates, and partners. According to social psychologists, relationships have a lasting impact on temperament, behavior, and personality development. This is why theories of social development interface with cognitive, psychosocial, and behavioral models of psychology.

The theoretical perspectives covered in this section are organized by topics covered on the AP PSYCH exam.

- Imprinting (Konrad Lorenz)
- Attachment theory (Mary Ainsworth and Harry Harlow)
- Parenting styles (Diana Baumrind)
- Stage theories (Erik Erikson and Sigmund Freud)
- Social cognitive theory (Albert Bandura)

## Heads Up: What You Need to Know

It's important to be able to distinguish between temperament and personality on the AP PSYCH exam. Temperament and personality are interrelated, but have fundamental differences. *Temperament* is a set of innate traits that organize one's approach to the world; it is not learned through social experiences. On the other hand, *personality* is acquired through environmental and social experiences. Although temperament can influence personality, only personality adapts to social influences throughout one's lifetime. Think of temperament as the canvas that you need to create a painting, and think of personality as what you paint on the canvas to reproduce your masterpiece.

Note: Temperament is discussed below and personality will be discussed later in this chapter on p. 177.

## Temperament

**Temperament** is a set of *inborn genetic traits* that is relatively consistent throughout one's lifetime. As we discussed in Chapter 5, traits are the prevailing patterns that can influence the way people show emotional responses. If you understand temperament as a set of emotional building blocks, you will better appreciate why each person has a unique way of experiencing and emotionally reacting to the world.

Psychologists have different perspectives about temperament, but most would agree that temperament is fairly stable through the lifespan and can be seen early in life.

Why is this important to psychologists? Because psychologists, parents, and teachers can develop strategies to promote healthy development that take individual differences in temperament into account.

Of course, not all infants are born the same. It is through temperament that infants can show their individual differences. Easy babies get hungry and sleepy at regular times and will often allow a stranger to hold them. Difficult babies are irritable and have irregular feeding and sleeping schedules. Slow-to-warm-up babies are very hesitant to be held by anyone who is not in the small circle of trusted adults. Differences are not good or bad, but they help describe the three basic groups of temperament—easy, slow-to-warm-up, and difficult.

**Three Types of Childhood Temperament**

| Type | Description |
|---|---|
| **Easy** | The "easy" child is generally in a positive mood, adapts easily to new situations, is generally good natured, and does not withdraw from new situations. |
| **Slow-to-warm-up** | The "slow-to-warm-up" child has a tendency to withdraw from the first exposure to a new experience, then slowly adapts to new situations. The child slowly accepts new situations when exposed repeatedly. |
| **Difficult** | The "difficult" child has an unusually intense reaction to new situations, tends to withdraw, and is slow to adapt. The child tends to cry frequently and has a generally negative mood. |

## Heads Up: What You Need to Know

The influences of attachment are critical to the development of a child. The three theoretical views related to attachment that you should be familiar with for the AP PSYCH exam are (1) Konrad Lorenz's imprinting theory, (2) Harry Harlow's experiments with baby monkeys, and, most importantly, (3) Mary Ainsworth's attachment theory.

## Attachment

An infant's early emotional health and development is intertwined with parental relationships. Early infant-parent relationship models have emerged as important predictors of a developing child's social and emotional competence.

### Konrad Lorenz—Imprinting Theory

Konrad Lorenz studied the behavior of animals and discovered how the principle of **imprinting** relates to human development. In his experiments with geese, Lorenz discovered that attachment is innate and programmed through imprinting during the first *critical period of development* (a period when it is crucial for the infant to acquire certain skills in order for normal development to occur). Lorenz discovered that the geese followed the first large moving object they saw after hatching (even if the object was human). In psychology, imprinting is the instinctual process of bonding during the first critical stage of life. It is hypothesized that the bonding instinctually imprints onto the newborn infant to keep the infant close to the parent.

### Harry Harlow—Monkey Experiments

Harry Harlow was one of the first researchers to scientifically investigate the importance of early attachments and emotional bonds between a mother and her infant. Harlow's experiments with rhesus monkeys (1957–1963) focused on the mental effects of maternal separation and social isolation. Harlow separated infant monkeys from their mothers and provided monkeys with two options: a soft terrycloth surrogate with no food, and a wire surrogate with food. His experiments showed that while the monkeys would go to the scary wire surrogate to eat, they would spend most of their time with the soft terrycloth surrogate even though it didn't provide food. The baby monkeys became attached to the terrycloth surrogate figure that was made to resemble a mother. Harlow's observations demonstrated the essential need for infants to bond and be secure with a mother figure.

Note: Today, psychologists consider Harlow's experiments on monkeys cruel and unethical. The experiments are controversial, but the results are still considered some of the most important contributions in understanding the significance of early mother-infant attachment. The extended maternal and social deprivation experienced in infancy resulted in permanent social and emotional problems in the monkeys. Although Harlow's monkeys were eventually cared for in a proper setting, the baby monkeys showed signs of irreversible psychological deficits (e.g., fear, aggressiveness, reclusiveness, and social deficits).

## Mary Ainsworth—Attachment Theory

Psychologist Mary Ainsworth developed four types of **attachment** styles that define child-parent relationships using a paradigm called *Strange Situation* (1970). Her research was based on the groundbreaking studies of John Bowlby. Bowlby found that even during the earliest stages of life, ages 0 to 18 months, infants have an innate drive to forge a close emotional and reciprocal connection with their primary caregivers (parents). The absence or irregularity of this innate connection can cause an insecure attachment style. According to Bowlby, attachment is the key to personality development and can influence the emotional health of all future relationships.

### *Ainsworth's Experiment*

Through observations, Ainsworth was able to measure how toddlers (12–18 months old) managed stress when separated from or reunited with their parents.

The procedure consisted of simulated episodes that gradually escalated the amount of the toddler's stress. For example: (1) The toddler is comfortably playing in an observable room while the mother is nearby. (2) A stranger joins the mother and toddler. (3) The mother leaves the room, leaving the stranger to comfort the toddler. (4) The mother returns and the stranger leaves the room. Many toddlers cried when their mother left the room, but the hypothetical question at the core of Ainsworth's experiment that helped to form her theory of attachment was "What happens when the mother returns to the toddler after being absent?" Were the toddlers emotionally secure, anxious, or insecure?

The results of Ainsworth's experiment helped her to formulate a framework for patterns of attachment styles, but this framework is not considered a scientific classification of absolute values. The results of her observations were merely intended to provide general guidelines to help professionals recognize some of the early warning signs of insecure attachment. Contemporary research provides strong evidence that early intervention and treatment approaches can reduce the negative impact of insecure attachment and significantly improve the quality of a child's social and emotional responses.

The table that follows categorizes the four types of attachment styles based on the toddlers' responses.

**Framework for Patterns of Attachment Styles**

| Attachment Style | Description | Implications |
|---|---|---|
| **Secure** | **Secure attachment** describes toddlers who showed little distress when separated, or checked on the mother's whereabouts periodically. The toddlers freely separated from parent to play and calmed down shortly when the mother returned from absence. Securely attached toddlers comprised the majority of Ainsworth's sample. | Children who are securely attached are relatively comfortable with others, make appropriate eye contact, can ask for help, and can manage and express their feelings. The internalized inner message is "I am safe and secure." |

*Continued*

| Attachment Style | Description | Implications |
|---|---|---|
| **Insecure: Avoidant** | **Avoidant attachment** describes toddlers who exhibited minimal distress when separated from their mothers. Toddlers may have readily separated from the mothers, but often "snubbed" their parent upon reunion (e.g., toddler moves away, looks away, or ignores the mother upon return). | Children who are insecurely (avoidant) attached may feel "undeserving" of their parents' affection and develop defense mechanisms to compensate. The reason is that primary caretakers may have ignored, rejected, or become easily irritated with their child. Children who are avoidant may feel that others will not be able to help, may have feelings of rejection, or may act as if others don't care about them. Avoidant children may avoid playing with other children and become anxious if someone tries to get too close. |
| **Insecure: Resistant** | **Resistant attachment** describes toddlers who became very distressed by the mother's departure. These toddlers often became anxious even before the mother left and were upset during the mother's absence (e.g., could not explore or play). Toddlers became preoccupied with their parents' whereabouts and resisted comfort by crying or kicking upon the mother's return. | Children who are insecurely resistant and/or ambivalent might feel skeptical about trying new things or feel that others are unreliable. Children can become either angry or passive (hyperarousal or dissociated). These children are sometimes viewed as "contentious" or "helpless." They may become demanding, impulsive, or resort to creative distractions to seek attention. |
| **Insecure: Disorganized** | **Disorganized attachment** (sometimes called disoriented attachment) describes toddlers who showed signs of confusion (e.g., looked dazed, perplexed, or fearful) upon the mother's return. | Children who experience disorganized-disoriented attachment often feel confused, misunderstood, or become easily frustrated. Parents of disorganized-disoriented children often demonstrate an inability to manage their own emotions and behavior (e.g., depression, addictions, etc.). Therefore, children act unpredictably with others and are often fearful about new situations. These children can demonstrate a lack of self-control, can be inflexible, have behavior problems in school, and lack the ability to tolerate change. |

**Did you know?** Strong evidence suggests that attachment, whether secure or insecure, can predict how children (and adults) are able to emotionally self-regulate, cope, and tolerate frustration. Informed by the work of Bowlby and Ainsworth, modern-day neuroscientists like Allan Schore have expanded models of attachment to include important neurobiological theories of attachment. Secure attachment is not only a key for emotional and social development, but is also the primary basis for the development of the brain, limbic system, and autonomic nervous system. Specifically, secure attachment is necessary to control neurobiological regulation systems that moderate emotional responses, known as *affect regulation.*

Now that we've covered the importance of early parent-infant attachment, let's review the parenting styles that are important in identifying how the role of parents can shape child development.

## Diana Baumrind—Parenting Styles

Patterns of parenting styles are based on the research of developmental psychologist Diana Baumrind. Understanding the influence of parents on child development can help manage a child's behavior. As described by Baumrind, the two main characteristics of parenting behavior are on a spectrum between parental warmth and parental control. When parents can set standards to achieve an authoritative style of parenting, children are more likely to interact socially, have a strong self-esteem, and are able to think for themselves.

The four parenting styles that you should be familiar with for the AP PSYCH exam are *permissive, authoritative, authoritarian,* and *uninvolved.*

**The Four Parenting Styles**

| Parenting Style | Parents' Behavior | Child's Behavior |
|---|---|---|
| **Permissive** | Parents are lax; inconsistent; do not give much direction, discipline, or structure; but parents are warm and nurturing. Sometimes these parents take more of a "friend" role than a parent role, saying "kids will be kids." | The child is dependent, moody, and lacks self-control. |
| **Authoritative** | Parents are firm, fair, and consistent. Parents set reasonable goals and encourage independence. The rationale for rules is explained and the child understands why the rules change. | The child generally has good social skills, is self-reliant, and independent. |
| **Authoritarian** | Parents are rigid, punitive, and expect obedience. Rules are set without consulting the child. | The child is generally unsociable and withdrawn. |
| **Uninvolved** | Parents are emotionally detached and let the child do anything. There is little emotional warmth or communication. | The child is generally indifferent. |

## Stage Theories of Developmental Psychology

This section will cover two important models of personality development that frequently appear on the AP PSYCH exam: Sigmund Freud's psychosexual stages of development and Erik Erikson's psychosocial stages of development. Stage theories are linked to personality development. **Personality** development consists of the unique characteristics of a person—the thoughts, emotions, and behavior—that are motivated and adapted by environmental influences throughout a lifespan.

What is a stage theory of development? To answer this, let's take a look at continuity vs. discontinuity. Do you think that people change continually every day or do you think people change in spurts? If your answer is "continually," psychologists call this view a **continuity** perspective of development. This means that a person experiences gradual, cumulative, quantitative changes throughout a lifespan. For example, an infant who is crawling will gradually learn the task of pulling himself up to a standing position.

If your answer is "spurts," psychologists view this as the **discontinuity** perspective of development. This view involves a series of distinct stages in a lifespan, with specific attention to critical periods. For example, children don't all become taller or older at the same time; they are different from each other as they move through phases of their lives.

**Continuity vs. Discontinuity**

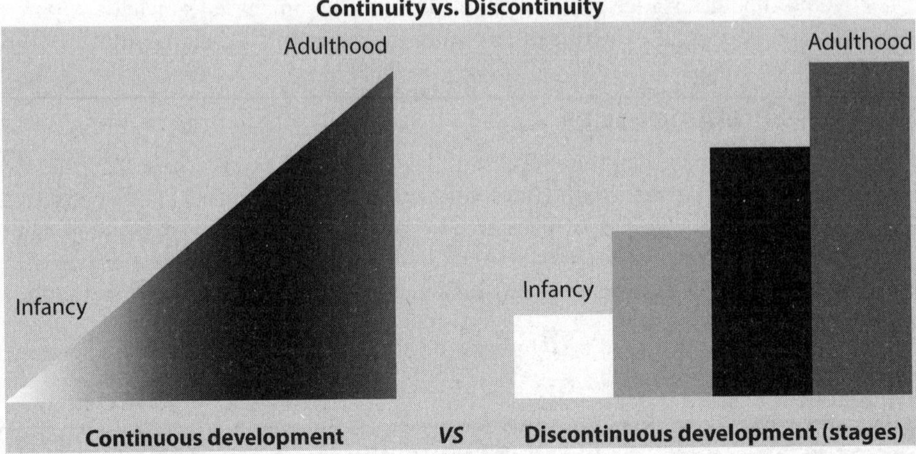


## Sigmund Freud—Stages of Psychosexual Development

Psychoanalyst Sigmund Freud was the first researcher to examine stages of development. His developmental stage theory proposed a series of fixed stages that represented sexual and aggressive drives. Each stage had a crisis that must be resolved, and if the crisis was not resolved, the person might be *fixated* (emotionally stuck) in the negative side of that particular stage.

Freud's theory of psychosexual development was based on biological and instinctual drives for personality development, but many modern-day critics agree that Freud's theory is unscientific, sexist, and focuses too much on sexual fixations. Freud's contributions, however, are invaluable to the study of consciousness and the *id* (sexual and aggressive instinctual voice), *ego* (logical decision-making voice), and *superego* (moral and ethical voice of principles) as structures of personality development.

**Freud's Stages of Psychosexual Development**

| Stage | Age | Developmental Theme | Fixation Examples |
|---|---|---|---|
| **Oral stage** | Birth to 18 months | Gains pleasure from eating and communicating verbally. | Eating disorders, drinking, or smoking. |
| **Anal stage** | 18 months to 3–4 years | Toilet training | Obsessive about neatness, or can be extremely messy. |
| **Phallic stage** | 3–4 years to 5–7 years | Sexual identity | Difficulty with intimate relationships, sexual dysfunction. |
| **Latent stage** | 5–7 years to puberty | Learning and developing social interactions. | No fixation. |
| **Genital stage** | Puberty to adulthood | Reaching intimate relationships. | If all the stages are successfully mastered, the person should reach full mental maturity. |

## Heads Up: What You Need to Know

On the AP PSYCH exam, you should know Erikson's stages of psychosocial development. It is an organized framework for the personality development and is one of the most widely accepted theories in the field of developmental psychology from birth to adulthood. Erikson's framework is useful in understanding and analyzing human development from "womb to tomb."

## Erik Erikson—Stages of Psychosocial Development

**Erik Erikson's stages of psychosocial development** focuses on unconscious themes for personality growth and development across the lifespan. Erikson was a *neo-Freudian,* which means that his theory followed in the footsteps of Sigmund Freud's psychoanalytic theory of unconscious personality development.

Erikson's famous eight-stage theory suggests that early childhood experiences help to shape personality development based on four major assumptions.

1. Each stage is associated with a specific developmental task and life crisis that must be resolved for healthy psychological development.
2. The failure to resolve each stage might result in emotional problems later in life.
3. Each person has the ability to contribute to his or her own psychological development to reverse unresolved stage tasks at any time during a lifetime.
4. Each stage takes into account cultural considerations. (Note: Stages are resolved based on cultural needs.)

**Erikson's Stages of Psychosocial Development**

| Stage | Life Crisis | Virtue | Successful Resolution | Unsuccessful Resolution |
|---|---|---|---|---|
| **Stage 1** (Birth to 1½ years) | Basic Trust vs. Mistrust | Hope | **Trust:** Infants who have their needs met develop secure attachment by feeling safe, loved, and cared for by attentive primary caregivers. | **Mistrust:** The absence of attentive primary caregivers in infancy can result in *insecure attachment* with feelings of guardedness, unpredictability, and withdrawal from future relationships. |
| **Stage 2** (1½ to 3 years) | Autonomy vs. Shame and Doubt | Will | **Autonomy:** The toddler learns to explore, experiment, make mistakes, and test limits to gain a sense of self-reliance. This is the period of "terrible (terrific) twos" (period of defiance and stubbornness). To accomplish autonomy, the toddler learns to explore within safe limits, perform tasks by himself, and say "no" to his primary caregivers without severe consequences. | **Shame and Doubt:** If the toddler is harshly punished, criticized, or overly controlled by the primary caregivers, he may be unwilling to try or inhibited from trying new activities, and may become overly dependent on others and have doubts in his abilities. |

*Continued*

| Stage | Life Crisis | Virtue | Successful Resolution | Unsuccessful Resolution |
|---|---|---|---|---|
| **Stage 3** (3 to 6 years) | Initiative vs. Guilt | Purpose | **Initiative:** The preschooler learns to take risks and "initiate" behavior that will lead to his goals. This is the period of *imaginative* (make-believe) play. | **Guilt:** If initiative is hampered, children develop a sense of guilt and inhibited creativity. The child may feel as if he is a "nuisance" to others. |
| **Stage 4** (6 to 13 years) | Industry vs. Inferiority | Competence | **Industry:** The school-aged child learns to have a strong self-image through his abilities to accomplish tasks (e.g., navigate rules, assignments, and expectations at school). Socializing with peer groups becomes important, and the child has a need to gain approval by demonstrating competencies. | **Inferiority:** If industry is not encouraged, the child begins to doubt his abilities, not feel valued, and feel inferior to others. |
| **Stage 5** (13 to 18–20 years) | Identity vs. Role Confusion | Fidelity | **Identity:** Based on previous stages, the adolescent learns to transition from childhood to adulthood by reexamining his identity and determining where he fits best in society. This is the time of experimenting with different aspects of one's life (friends, groups, music preferences, political views, and societal norms). | **Role Confusion:** This stage can be the most stressful period in one's lifetime because the teen is examining sexual and occupational identities. If the adolescent is unable to properly form an internal sense of self, it can lead to not being able to accept oneself or others, and not being sure about one's place in society. |
| **Stage 6** (20 to 40 years) | Intimacy vs. Isolation | Love | **Intimacy:** The adult learns to intimately share himself with someone else (partnerships, marriage, or friendships). Erikson stated that in order to have a successful intimate relationship, the person must first have a strong sense of self. | **Isolation:** The adult cannot be intimate until he has resolved the "Who am I?" question from the previous stage. If not successfully mastered, the adult may have difficulty developing and maintaining successful relationships with others. |
| **Stage 7** (40 to 65 years) | Generativity vs. Stagnation | Care | **Generativity:** The middle-aged adult is unconsciously driven to generate one's life work for the next generation (e.g., family, career, volunteering, or something that contributes positively to society). | **Stagnation:** If the adult does not feel productive during this period, he may develop feelings of "not leaving a meaningful mark in this world," accompanied by feelings of inactivity and worthlessness, and may not have interest in self-improvement. |
| **Stage 8** (65 and older) | Ego Integrity vs. Despair | Wisdom | **Ego Integrity:** The senior citizen reflects on life to determine if life was worth living. | **Despair:** Seniors who do not feel that they have developed a productive life may feel unsatisfied and feel that they have failed by focusing on "I should have done…" They may have feelings of regret and fall into despair, depression, or anger. |

**Did you know?** The word *psychosocial* (relating to psychological and social development) implies unconscious processing. This means that even if you are an intelligent 16-year-old who does not consciously acknowledge that you are experiencing Erikson's "identity vs. role confusion" stage of development, you are still going through this stage of development unconsciously. You probably have limited conscious awareness as to why you are choosing to gravitate toward certain philosophies, ideas, music, and friends.

## Albert Bandura—Social Cognitive Theory

Albert Bandura was recognized for his work in developmental and educational psychology, and he believed that personality development was the result of environmental influences, behavior, and psychological processes. Bandura's *social cognitive theory* is known as a bridge between behavioral and cognitive learning and provides evidence that children model behavior through observation. Bandura's theory emphasizes the value of modeling behaviors, attitudes, and emotional reactions of others to advance cognitive learning.

Bandura's experiment, called the "Bobo doll" experiment, concluded that children learn aggression by observing, modeling, and imitating adult behavior. In his experiment, well-behaved preschool children watched an adult repeatedly punching and knocking down a large blow-up doll. Children who observed this behavior later imitated the behavior and acted aggressively on the playground.

### Conditions for Modeling Behavior

According to Bandura, observational learning (social learning) requires the physical and mental developmental abilities to reproduce the behavior that is being observed. The four conditions for modeling behavior are attention, retention, reproduction, and motivation.

**Attention**
The child must pay attention and be interested in what the person is doing.

**Retention**
The child must remember by encoding what the person is doing.

**Reproduction**
The child must have the physical or cognitive developmental skills to reproduce what the person is doing.

**Motivation**
The child must have the desire to imitate (internal or external reward) what the person is doing.

## Maturationism and Critical Period

Before we discuss cognitive development, let's first review two important cognitive development concepts—maturationism and critical period.

**Maturationism** suggests that a young child's mind automatically learns over time due to biological and environmental forces determined at birth. When a child is exposed to multiple stimuli through an enriched environment, the child's mind develops passively, rather than actively. In time, the child can respond to even more sophisticated stimuli.

Why is the concept of maturationism important to cognitive development? Because research shows that socioeconomic status plays an important role in having access to an enriched cognitive environment. Children who are raised in impoverished homes are at risk for inadequate environmental exposures to cognitive stimuli. The good news is that early enrichment programs, such as a preschool head-start program, can help children catch up to their more economically privileged peers.

**Critical period** is a maturational stage when it is critical for a child to acquire certain skills in order for normal cognitive development to occur. It is a window of opportunity when the brain is especially adaptable to learning and developing new information. Research evidence shows that there are certain critical periods in bonding, visual perception, motor skills, and language acquisition. After the critical period, learning continues but is less efficient. For example, if a child doesn't learn to speak a language by the age of 5, it can be difficult for the child to become proficient at his or her primary language. Many teens are familiar with the concept of critical period when they teach a grandparent how to use an app or other technology that the grandparent didn't learn earlier in life.

Note: The concept of critical period is very similar to the concept of *sensitive period.* Although the terms are often used interchangeably, there is a slight difference in the two terms. *Sensitive period* is when a child is most able to acquire certain skills, whereas *critical period* is a time when certain skills must be learned for normal development to occur.

## Cognitive Development

Cognitive development theory is the way children think about and make meanings from the information learned through life experiences. It emphasizes how knowledge transforms mental abilities, including thought, language, and intelligence.

The main cognitive development theories that you should know for the AP PSYCH exam are Jean Piaget's stages of cognitive development, Lev Vygotsky's sociocultural theories of cognition, Lawrence Kohlberg's stages of moral development, and Carol Gilligan's moral development theory.

### Jean Piaget—Stages of Cognitive Development

Swiss psychologist Jean Piaget's contributions to cognitive development are central to understanding how children think, feel, and respond to the world. According to Piaget, a child has the innate ability to adapt to environmental influences while interfacing with the physical world in predictable, sequential stages. It is through this process that the child actively moves through new life experiences and forms new ways to modify and/or adapt to the world. The child's mind seeks to find a state of equilibrium while progressing through each stage of operation.

## Key Terms in Piaget's Theory of Cognitive Development

**TEST TIP: The AP PSYCH exam presumes that you are familiar with key concepts related to Piaget's theory. Before we discuss the stages of cognitive development, please review these key terms and concepts.**

**Schema.** Schemas are mental representations to organize experiences with the world. Schemas can be very specific or elaborate (e.g., perceptions, ideas, or actions). For example, an infant banging a rattle on the stroller may mentally organize the experience by forming a schema: "When I bang the object on the stroller, it *sounds different* from shaking the object."

**Adaption.** The process of adaptation is fundamental to Piaget's stages of development. Children continually adjust to new information about their environment in order to function more effectively. This process involves two fundamental cognitive concepts as children move from stage to stage, called *assimilation* and *accommodation.*

**Assimilation.** Assimilation refers to the way children incorporate new information with existing schemas in order to form a new cognitive structure. Children fit this new knowledge into a template of existing schemas. For example, a preschool child calls a horse "doggie" because the child only knows one type of four-legged animal.

**Accommodation.** Accommodation occurs when children take existing schemas and adjust them to fit their experience. For example, a preschool child listens to "The Wheels on the Bus" nursery rhyme song on a battery-operated toy. However, when the child tries to listen to the same song on his mother's smartphone, he quickly learns that his mother must unlock the phone and search for the song before he can hear the song. The child must accommodate this new information to fit the new experience.

**Equilibrium.** Equilibrium is an important concept to understand in Piaget's cognitive adaption process. The stages of equilibrium are as follows: (1) Equilibrium begins with a balanced state of organized motor, sensory, and cognitive schemas; (2) then information is received from the environment and thought changes; (3) adaptation emerges through assimilation and accommodation; and (4) a higher-level thought develops to form a new state of equilibrium.

**Piaget's Cognitive Learning Process**

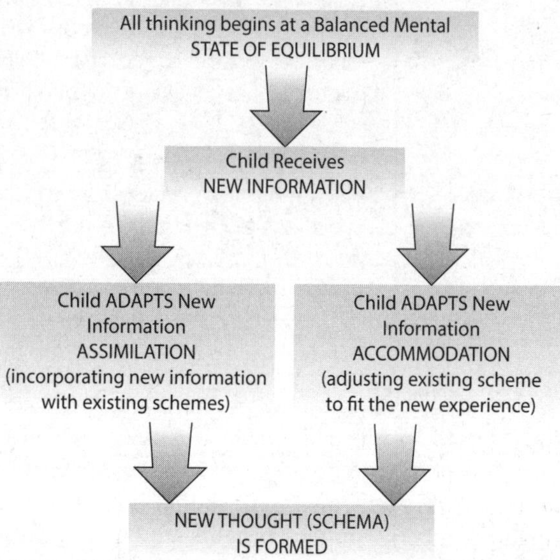

## Stages of Cognitive Development

Piaget was dedicated to observing the behavioral patterns in children and outlined four different stages of cognitive development. Piaget noted that people in advanced stages don't simply think *more* than those in earlier stages; people think *differently.*

Piaget's theory has four major assumptions.

1. Children are organically inspired to think, learn, and comprehend.
2. Children see the world differently than adults.
3. Children's knowledge is ordered into mental structures called *schemas.*
4. All learning consists of adapting new knowledge through *assimilation* and *accommodation.*

**Piaget's Stages of Cognitive Development**

| | Age | Stage | Characteristics |
|---|---|---|---|
| **Stage 1** | Infancy (Birth to 2 years) | Sensorimotor | During the sensorimotor stage, infants construct an understanding of the world through physical actions (e.g., motor skills) and their senses (e.g., what they see, touch, feel, hear, and smell). Newborns begin with instinctual reflexes and gradually progress toward developing schemas based on their immediate physical surroundings (stimuli). By 8–12 months, infants can grasp the concept of *object permanence* (recognizing that objects exist even when removed from sight). |
| **Stage 2** | Early childhood (2 to 7 years) | Preoperational | Children are the center of their universe, called *egocentrism,* until 5 years old. Preoperational children focus on symbolic thought, imitation, play, drawings, and imagination. Children use words to represent objects symbolically, and although their language sounds like adults', they cannot yet think and reason the same as adults. At about 5–6 years old, children understand the law of *conservation* (see below). |
| **Stage 3** | Middle childhood (7 to 11 years) | Concrete operations | During the concrete operations stage, children begin to think logically. Children can manipulate and classify and are capable of complex thinking. They are successful at solving problems by thinking about multiple perspectives that are real (concrete). Children have the ability to imagine the consequences of their actions. A child at this age thinks about what is tangible and real. For example, "What is fair is what is equal" because the child can count out equal portions of an item. |
| **Stage 4** | Adolescence (12 years to adulthood) | Formal operations | During the formal operations stage, adolescents and adults can think abstractly. An example is the concept of "justice." This stage is characterized by the ability to formulate a hypothesis and systematically test it to critically arrive at a conclusion. It is during this stage that the adolescent realizes the moral or ethical consequences of behavior. |

## Conservation (Concrete Operations)

Piaget's concept of **conservation** is based on Einstein's formula $E = mc^2$, which states that when changing the appearance of an object, the basic properties do not change. Mass and energy can be transformed from one to the other, but their total amount stays fixed (conserved) so that it neither increases nor decreases. Piaget used this concept when referring to numbers, volumes, weights, and matter during the concrete operations stage of development. As depicted in the image that follows, younger preoperational children fail to master this task because the way objects appear influences how the younger child thinks.

**Examples of Lack of Conservation Skills**

| Task | Manipulation | Preoperational Child's Response |
|---|---|---|
| **Concept of Numbers** | 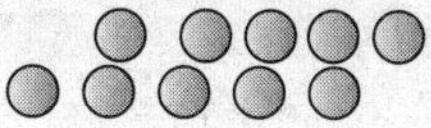 | "The row on top has more buttons." |
| **Concept of Length** |  | "The one on the bottom is longer." |
| **Concept of Liquid** | 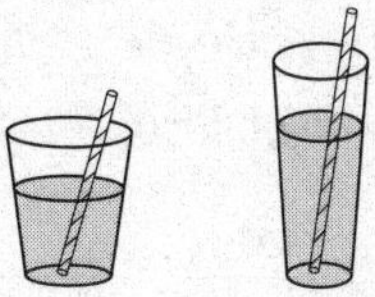 | (The same amounts of juice are poured into two different glasses.)<br><br>"The taller glass has more juice." |
| **Concept of Matter** | 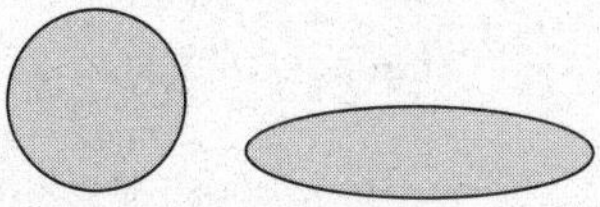 | (One ball of clay is rolled into a log.)<br><br>"The log has more clay." |

## Lev Vygotsky—Theory on Cognitive Development

**Lev Vygotsky** had a different approach to Piaget's theory. Rather than assuming that cognitive development is achieved through one's interactions within a physical environment, Vygotsky proposed that children learn socially, through their interaction with others.

When parents, older siblings, peers, or anyone who can act as a temporary "teacher" assists the child to do more than he could do by himself, it is called **scaffolding.** According to Vygotsky, effective teaching can only take place when a child is developmentally ready to learn. A 3-year-old cannot learn calculus, but when the child is ready to learn, he enters the **zone of proximal development** based on age and cognitive abilities, the "learning area" between what the child can do with guidance and what is unreachable for the child, even with guidance.

**Vygotsky's Zone of Proximal Development (ZPD)**

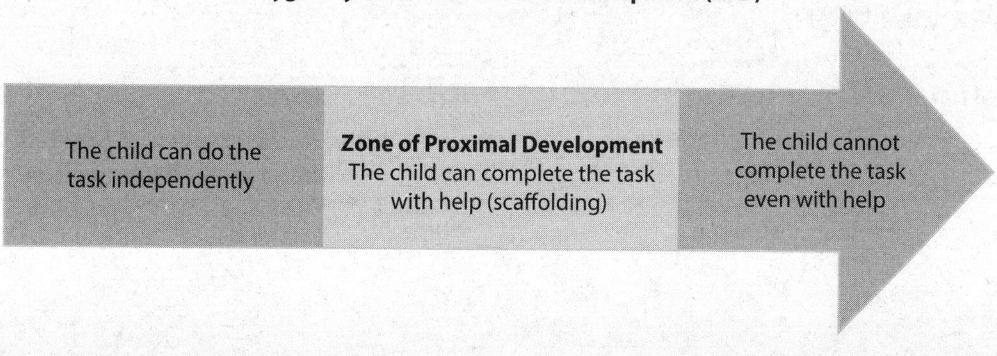

The child can do the task independently

**Zone of Proximal Development**
The child can complete the task with help (scaffolding)

The child cannot complete the task even with help

**Heads Up: What You Need to Know**

On the AP PSYCH exam, you may be asked to compare and contrast the two major cognitive development theories of Piaget and Vygotsky.

**Compare and Contrast Piaget and Vygotsky**

| Piaget | Vygotsky |
|---|---|
| **Theoretical viewpoint.** Piaget is a *cognitive constructivist* (learning occurs through experience). | **Theoretical viewpoint.** Vygotsky is a *social constructivist* (learning occurs in a social context). |
| **Stage theory.** Yes, four stages of development (discontinuity). | **Stage theory.** No stages of development suggested (continuity). |
| **Development.** Development is shaped by the innate tendency to seek equilibrium when adapting to new experiences. | **Development.** Development is shaped by the interaction with society and culture. |
| **Learning.** The child is motivated to *self-learn* by an innate curiosity of self-discovery. | **Learning.** The child learns by *guided learning* with the help of a teacher or mentor in assisted discovery. |
| **Language.** Language plays a minimal role in cognitive development. Language is the result of cognition. | **Language.** Language is the key to cognitive development and helps to shape thought. For example, competence in "thinking about" the primary language must be formed before acquisition of a second language can be learned. |
| **Mental organization.** Schemas help the child organize and understand the world to create equilibrium. | **Mental organization.** The child's mental structure is organized by *scaffolding* (building blocks of knowledge influenced by a teacher or mentor) until the child can mentally organize the knowledge. |

## Adolescent Development

Adolescent development is a transitional stage of development between the ages of 13 and 19 years old. Today, adolescent development begins earlier (possibly due to better health and diet changes) and lasts longer (possibly because it is more difficult to gain independence in today's society).

Adolescent development differs significantly from infant and child development. It is not just a time of growing, it is a time of growing differently—physically, emotionally, cognitively, and socially. Adolescence begins with the physical changes in the body during puberty and ends with social changes that move toward independence and identity.

### Physical Development during Adolescence

The physical body and nervous system are almost completely developed by the end of adolescence. Thereafter, the rate of physical change gradually declines through adulthood. Whereas some of the changes that occur are visible when the young body changes to an adult body, many of the physical changes are not visible.

If you've ever endured a health education class, you know that adolescence begins with puberty when certain hormones are released in the body. In general, girls start and end puberty earlier than boys. *Menarche* is the first instance of a girl's menstruation and *spermarche* is the first instance of a boy's ejaculation. Puberty is a time when primary and secondary sex traits develop.

- *Primary sex characteristics* are traits related to reproduction, such as the enlargement of sex organs, production of male sperm, or the release of a female egg.
- *Secondary sex characteristics* are traits that have no direct effect on physical reproduction, such as growth of body hair or deepening of voice.

Puberty is often thought of as what happens below the belt, but perhaps the most important changes in adolescent development happens between the ears. The brain is undergoing quite a few changes during adolescence. Synaptic *pruning* is occurring (the brain discards unneeded neurons and synapses), and new synapses are rapidly growing in the frontal lobe during adolescence (remember, it is the frontal lobe that acts as a brake to the gas pedal of the hypothalamus and amygdala). However, the developing brain does not fully mature until about 24–25 years old. This is why adolescents who are striving toward independence sometimes have difficulty with planning long-term goals, evaluating consequences, and making rational judgments.

## Emotional Development during Adolescence

Emotional development is the gradual ability to perceive and manage emotions and is influenced by environmental situations. Psychologist G. Stanley Hall is credited with much of the early work on adolescent development. Hall called adolescent development a time of emotional "storm and stress" that can result in rebellion, annoyance, and confusion. Hormones play a key role in heightened emotional responses as adolescents become more aware of their feelings and the challenges they face in a complex society. Many adolescents strive toward independence by driving parents away, but the need for caregiver emotional support is important to becoming mature adults. Although adolescence may appear to be a turbulent time, research shows that it is a period of great potential. Most adolescents are well-adjusted, goal oriented, think critically, and have healthy family relationships. It is during this period that both boys and girls share the idea of **imaginary audience** (when adolescents believe others are watching and evaluating them).

# Adulthood and Aging

Adulthood is a part of psychology that examines the changes that occur in biological, psychological, and interpersonal aspects of human life from the end of adolescence until the end of one's life. Adulthood spans across many decades, from 20 years old to 100 years old, or beyond. Physical changes can be gradual or rapid, and can reflect positive, negative, or no change from previous levels of functioning. The body begins to lose muscle mass, soft tissue becomes less flexible, and bones become less dense. Women go through **menopause** (the cessation of the menstrual cycle) around 50 years old. Men do not experience an equivalent to menopause, but they do experience a gradual decline in testosterone levels, sperm count, and the ability to have an erection. According to the National Council on Aging, about 40 percent of all women and men surveyed continue to show satisfaction with sex.

Evidence suggests that the stereotype of grumpy old people is not accurate. When people enter retirement age, they seem to be content, healthy, and maintain interests in a variety of pursuits. Continued exercise, social engagements, a healthy diet, and regular cognitive activity can slow and even stop these declines. In short, we don't stop being active because we get old; we get old because we stop being active.

Older people are also more susceptible to illnesses, memory decline, sensory decline, and a decline in lifestyle events. Some adults suffer from cognitive impairments like *dementia* (brain disease that causes a long-term decrease in mental functioning, particularly memory recall) and *Alzheimer's disease* (a progressive brain disorder that slowly causes memory and thinking skills to diminish). According to the National Institutes of Health (NIH), one in three senior adults dies with dementia or Alzheimer's disease.

## Moral Development

Another aspect of cognitive development focuses on how people make right and wrong decisions. *Moral development* is defined as a set of internalized rules that influence our feelings, thoughts, and behavior in deciding what is right and wrong.

The moral development theories that you should know for the AP PSYCH exam are Lawrence Kohlberg's stages of moral development and Carol Gilligan's moral development theory.

Source: © 2019 iStockphoto LP

### Lawrence Kohlberg—Stages of Moral Development

Although Piaget explored the process of moral development, it was cognitive development theorist Lawrence Kohlberg who emerged with significant contributions in the way moral dilemmas are mentally processed. Kohlberg suggested stages of moral reasoning that follow a specific sequence (i.e., you must complete stage 1 before proceeding to stage 2, etc.).

As children mature, moral reasoning changes and they begin to look internally for mature decision making based on moral standards of good and bad. Not all people reach the highest stage of moral development. The level of moral reasoning is dependent on how the person responds to challenges and experiences.

Before we introduce Kohlberg's stages of moral development, let's review one of Kohlberg's best-known experiments, the **Heinz dilemma.**

> A woman was on her deathbed. There was one drug that the doctors thought might save her. It was a form of radium that a druggist in the same town had recently discovered. The drug was expensive to make, but the druggist was charging ten times what the drug cost him to produce. He paid $200 for the radium and charged $2,000 for a small dose of the drug. The sick woman's husband, Heinz, went to everyone he knew to borrow the money, but he could only get together about $1,000, which is half of what the drug cost. He told the druggist that his wife was dying and asked him to sell it cheaper or let him pay later. But the druggist said: "No, I discovered the drug and I'm going to make money from it." So Heinz got desperate and broke into the man's laboratory to steal the drug for his wife. Should Heinz have broken into the laboratory to steal the drug for his wife?
>
> Why or why not? Remember that in a moral dilemma, sometimes there is no "right" answer.

Now let's take a look at Kohlberg's stages and apply this scenario to each level of moral development.

**TEST TIP: Kohlberg's levels of moral development are loosely tied to the chronological age of a person. One person might reach a stage on schedule, while another person might reach a stage much later. In fact, some adults never reach level 3.**

| Kohlberg's Stages of Moral Development | | | |
|---|---|---|---|
| **Stage** | **Characteristics** | **Themes** | **Examples from Kohlberg's Experiment** |
| **Level 1: Pre-conventional** | Young children (ages 4–10 years old) do what is right because adults tell them to obey. At this level, morality is judged on the basis of consequences (fear of being punished for bad actions, or self-interest by expecting to be rewarded for good actions). | Obedience or punishment<br><br>"I'm afraid of being punished." | Heinz should not steal no matter what the circumstances because he will get in trouble by breaking the law and go to prison. |
| | | Self-interest<br><br>"What's in it for me?" | Heinz's self-interest is to steal the medicine because his wife will then owe him a favor. |
| **Level 2: Conventional** | Children (ages 10–13 years old) do what is right to conform to the expectations of the majority rule. Or, children do what is right because it fulfills duties to social order and rules. | Conformity or interpersonal<br><br>"I want to show others that I am a good person." | Heinz wants to please others, so he will probably steal the medicine because he's afraid that other people might criticize him for letting his wife die. |
| | | Authority or social order<br><br>"It is my duty to do what is right." | Heinz will not steal the medicine because he thinks, "If everyone broke the rules, there would be no social order." |
| **Level 3: Post-conventional** | Teens and adults must reasonably weigh the consequences to do what is right to follow their own conscience, even if it's against the law. Or, adults do what is right because of convictions of social order, equality, and justice. | Social contract<br><br>"Laws help everyone maintain a civil society." | Heinz is conflicted. Laws exist to benefit society as a whole, so the laws can't be ignored just to benefit one person. However, Heinz must reasonably weigh the consequences, and he can't ignore his conscience to save his wife's life. Therefore, Heinz is willing to accept the legal consequences for stealing the medicine. |
| | | Universal ethical principles<br><br>"What if everyone did this?" | Heinz should steal the medicine because saving a human life is exponentially more important than the value of medicine or laws. |

**Did you know?** Kohlberg's theory may have been based on his personal moral dilemmas. At the end of World War II, Kohlberg made a moral decision to help smuggle Jewish refugees into Israel (previously Palestine). He was captured by the British and held in an internment camp, but escaped with fellow prisoners. Kohlberg then helped to establish the state of Israel, but refused to fight. Instead, he made the moral decision to practice nonviolent activism. When he returned to the United States to complete his education, he became well-known for his research in moral psychology.

## Carol Gilligan—Stages of Moral Development

Psychologist Carol Gilligan is known for expanding Kohlberg's views on reasoning to include both genders—men and women. Kohlberg interviewed only men in his studies, and Gilligan discovered that women tended to score lower on Kohlberg's scales of morality. She theorized that boys and girls have divergent views of moral reasoning due to the way that they are raised and educated in society. Boys focused morality on justice, rules, individual rights, and fairness; whereas girls focused morality on interpersonal relationships, responsibility, compassion, and empathy.

**Did you know?** According to a 1990 Yale University study, babies have an innate sense of morality. Humans are predisposed to prefer behaviors that help others. This makes sense because humans are social creatures, and without such an instinct, the human species would lose its primary advantage over other species. In the Yale study, babies as young as 6 months old and as old as 10 months old had a sense of right and wrong. Babies were observed to see if they could tell the difference between a "bad puppet" and a "good puppet." The bad puppet didn't help another puppet and slammed a box shut. The good puppet helped another puppet (prosocial behavior) by assisting to open a box. More than 80 percent of the babies picked the good puppet when selecting a puppet. The results of this study demonstrate that humans have a biological sense of morality.

# Gender and Sexual Orientation

Building new connections and establishing an identity outside of the family is an important part of healthy adolescent development. It is also a time to reflect on gender and sexual orientation.

**Gender orientation** represents a person's subjective "state of mind" as masculine, feminine, or neutral. To understand gender orientation, it is important to know that sex roles and gender roles can be the same. A person's *sex* is biologically defined as male or female, whereas gender implies the psychological, behavioral, social, and cultural aspects of being male or female. *Sex roles* are behaviors dependent on physically being a man or a woman. For example, only women can give birth to babies and breast-feed babies. *Gender roles* are the patterns of behavior that men and women exhibit that are socially expected. *Gender identity* is how a person thinks about himself or herself regardless of the sex role.

**Sexual orientation** is the unique emotional and sexual attraction toward another person—man, woman, or both. According to the American Psychological Association, sexual orientation refers to "a person's sense of identity—based on attractions, behaviors, and the membership in a community of others who share those attractions." Psychologists agree that sexual orientation is a relatively stable characteristic of a person—it is not a choice. Sexual orientation exists on a spectrum; it is not either/or. It can be patterns of emotional, romantic, or sexual attraction with someone who is heterosexual on one end of the spectrum and patterns of emotional, romantic, or sexual attraction with someone who is homosexual on the other end of the spectrum. *Heterosexual* means a person who is attracted to someone of the opposite sexual orientation, and *homosexual* means a person who is attracted to someone of the same sexual orientation. Others identify with *bisexual* (attracted to both sexual orientations) or *asexual* (not attracted to either men or women).

# Chapter Review Practice Questions

Practice questions are for instructional purposes only and may not reflect the format of the actual exam. The questions and explanations that follow focus on essential knowledge, course skills, and course content.

## Multiple-Choice Questions

1. Which of the following concepts is NOT one of Piaget's stages of cognitive development?

   **A.** Sensorimotor
   **B.** Acceptance
   **C.** Preoperational
   **D.** Concrete
   **E.** Formal

2. When a child fits new information into an existing schema, it is called __________, and when the child takes an existing schema and makes an adjustment with new information, it is called _________.

   **A.** assimilation; accommodation
   **B.** imprinting; discontinuity
   **C.** accommodation; assimilation
   **D.** adaption; equilibrium
   **E.** equilibrium; adaption

3. Which of the following stages of moral development best illustrates a political activist who is shunned by society and imprisoned for his extreme, but nonviolent, social movement activities?

   **A.** Pre-conventional
   **B.** Post-conventional
   **C.** Conventional
   **D.** Conformity
   **E.** Social order

4. Five-month-old baby Sasha loves to play "peek-a-boo" with her mother. Which of the following developmental concepts best describes Sasha's behavior?

   **A.** Egocentrism
   **B.** Abstract thinking
   **C.** Concrete operations
   **D.** Formal operations
   **E.** Object permanence

5. A preschool child is struggling to understand that two halves of a cookie are the same as one whole cookie. Which of the following cognitive development concepts has the child not yet mastered?

   **A.** Teratogens
   **B.** Pruning
   **C.** Conservation
   **D.** Critical period
   **E.** Metacognition

6. A 24-year-old pop singer routinely writes songs about lost loves and searching for the right person to love. According to Erikson's stages of cognitive development, the singer is working to resolve which of the following psychosocial conflicts?

   **A.** Industry vs. inferiority
   **B.** Intimacy vs. isolation
   **C.** Initiative vs. guilt
   **D.** Trust vs. mistrust
   **E.** Ego integrity vs. despair

7. Which of the following best describes the difference between what a child can do independently and what the child can potentially accomplish with assistance and support?

   **A.** Authoritative parenting style
   **B.** Zone of proximal development
   **C.** Authoritarian parenting style
   **D.** Scaffolding
   **E.** Permissive parenting style

## Free-Response Question

**1 question**

**25 minutes**

**Directions:** It is suggested that you take a few minutes to plan and outline your essay. Write your response on lined paper. You must demonstrate your understanding of course skills and course content. Your essay is considered a first draft and may contain some grammatical errors that will not be counted against you. However, to receive full credit, your essay must demonstrate defensible content knowledge with substantive examples where appropriate.

---

Before Ms. Schaffeld was an AP Psychology teacher, she taught preschool. As a teacher, Ms. Schaffeld likes to share the experiences she had with young children to help teach high school students about human development related to real-life experiments. Ms. Schaffeld remarked that she always knew when the preschool children had sugary cereal for breakfast because the children seemed to have a lot of energy and were squirmy during the morning reading circle. Whenever she noticed energetic children, she would ask them if they had sugary cereal for breakfast. The children would usually say, "I had a lot of cereal this morning."

In another observation, Ms. Schaffeld explained that some children became upset if a cookie was broken even if they later received both halves of the broken cookie. Other preschoolers didn't understand why a classmate received "two" halves when they only received one whole cookie. Ms. Schaffeld noted that some of the 3-year-olds grasped the idea that two halves equal a whole, but others did not understand the concept.

**Part A**

Ms. Schaffeld asked her high school students to respond to her conclusion that there is a relationship between a sugary breakfast cereal and the children's heightened activity level.

- Identify the following in Ms. Schaffeld's experimental study about the sugary breakfast cereal.
  - Research method
  - Type I error
  - A confounding variable

**Part B**

- Describe whether or not Ms. Schaffeld exhibited confirmation bias in her conclusions about the sugary breakfast cereal.
- Explain how the concept of zone of proximal development applies to Ms. Schaffeld's observations.
- Explain how the stage of initiative vs. guilt applies to Ms. Schaffeld's observations of the preschoolers with cookies.
- Explain how Piaget's idea of conservation applies to Ms. Schaffeld's observations of the preschoolers with cookies.

# Answers and Explanations

## Multiple-Choice Questions

1. **B.** *Acceptance,* choice B, is a stage in Elisabeth Kübler-Ross' stages of death and dying, and therefore, not one of Piaget's stages of cognitive development. Kübler-Ross was a well-known psychologist, but her theory will (probably) not be on the AP PSYCH exam. *Sensorimotor* (choice A) is Piaget's first stage of development, whereby an infant constructs the world through senses and movements. (Note: There is now evidence that infants can think.) The *preoperational* stage (choice C) is aligned with preschoolers using words to represent objects symbolically. The child's thoughts are not very well formed at this stage. *Concrete* operations (choice D) occur when an elementary-school-aged child begins to think logically and is successful at solving problems using multiple perspectives, but still struggles with the abstract ideas, until the stage of formal operations. The *formal* stage (choice E) is when a person can grapple with abstract thoughts, such as infinity minus 1.
2. **A.** *Assimilation* is learning new information and incorporating it with existing information. *Accommodation* is taking existing information and making adjustments to change a person's perspective. Therefore, choice A is correct. Choice B is incorrect; *imprinting* is the instinctual process of early bonding during the first critical stage of life, and *discontinuity* is the view that development occurs in stages. Choice C is incorrect because the terms are in the wrong order. Choices D and E are incorrect because although *adaption* is a possibility, it is not as specific as assimilation (adaption occurs when children adjust to new information; *equilibrium* is a balanced state of mind).
3. **B.** *Post-conventional* stage is a level in Kohlberg's theory on moral development. In this case, people who transcend what most people think of as right and wrong, or even sacrifice themselves for higher

principles, are in the post-conventional stage of moral reasoning, choice B. In the *pre-conventional* stage (choice A), people are governed by fear of punishment or by what they can get away with. The *conventional* stage (choice C) is where most people are morally; people at this stage are governed by the commonly accepted ideas of what is right or wrong. Choices D and E are incorrect because they are part of the conventional stage of moral reasoning. An example of *conformity* is "I want to show others that I am a good person," and *social order* is "It is my duty to do what is right." These concepts do not fully capture the meaning of the political activist's extreme decisions for political actions.

4. **E.** *Object permanence,* choice E, is a skill that a baby (birth to 2 years old) struggles with during Piaget's sensorimotor stage of development. Babies struggle with the idea that an object exists even though the object is hidden. *Egocentrism* (choice A) is a preoperational concept when a child (birth to 5 years old) struggles with differentiating between his or her own perspectives and those of someone else. *Abstract thinking* (choice B) is something that, according to Piaget, can only happen in the formal stage of cognitive development. *Concrete operations* (choice C) and *formal operations* (choice D) are the more advanced levels of Piaget's stages of cognitive development.
5. **C.** *Conservation,* choice C, is a cognitive concept that occurs during the later phase of Piaget's pre-conventional stage of development. It is the idea that objects can retain their properties even when similar objects appear different. *Teratogens* (choice A) are chemicals, such as alcohol, tobacco, and caffeine, that can cause birth defects in a developing fetus. *Pruning* (choice B) is a process where the brain of a young child discards unneeded neurons and synapses. *Critical period* (choice D) is the concept that a child must learn a certain skill during a specific time period or the child may have greater difficulty learning that skill in the future. *Metacognition* (choice E) is "thinking about thinking."
6. **B.** *Intimacy vs. isolation,* choice B, is the sixth stage of Erikson's psychosocial stages of development. It occurs when an adult (20–40 years old) is unconsciously driven to seek out a mate, spouse, or life partner. *Industry vs. inferiority* (choice A) is the fourth stage of development that occurs when an elementary-school-age child (6–13 years old) learns the competence to complete tasks required by school and society. *Initiative vs. guilt* (choice C) is the third stage when a preschool child (3–6 years old) learns to initiate play and develop social skills. *Trust vs. mistrust* (choice D) is the first stage of development when an infant (birth to 18 months) learns to trust that his or her basic needs and safety will be met. *Ego integrity vs. despair* (choice E) is the last stage of development when an older person (65 and older) looks back on his or her life and unconsciously decides if life was worth living.
7. **B.** This is a question about Vygotsky's theory of cognitive development, narrowing the answer down to choice B or D. The *zone of proximal development,* choice B, is a Vygotsky concept that explains the difference between what a child can do without help and what the child can do if given the necessary instructional guidance of an adult or peer with a higher skill set. *Scaffolding* (choice D) is another Vygotsky concept where a child is given a temporary support system by an adult or peer to accomplish a task. The question is not about parenting styles, eliminating choices A, C, and E. An *authoritative parenting style* (choice A) can be strict, but allows for input and compromise with the child. An *authoritarian parenting style* (choice C) is not only strict; the parents also have rigid rules and sometimes use physical punishment. *Permissive parenting* (choice E) is lax, inconsistent, and parents often do not discipline.

## Free-Response Question

To achieve the maximum score of 7, your response must address each of the bullet points in the question.

## Sample Student Response

*Research method* explains the plan for "how" to conduct the experiment. In this case, Ms. Schaffeld used the qualitative research method of observing the children in a natural setting, called *naturalistic observation.* She was watching and recording the behavior of the children in a natural preschool setting to observe the dependent variable of the energy level and an interview to confirm her suspicions of eating too much sugar. *Type I error* is known as a false alarm error (called a *false positive*). In this case, Ms. Schaffeld made a conclusion that children were energetic because they ate sugary breakfast cereal, but it is possible that the children could have been energetic for other reasons that are explained by random chance. Researchers must always take precautions to minimize Type I errors. A *confounding variable* is anything that might affect the dependent variable that is being studied. In this case, a confounding variable might have been lack of sleep the night before, if a child was excited about something at home (e.g., a birthday celebration or a relative visiting), or if a child was excited to be at school to play a new game on the playground. *Confirmation bias* is the tendency for a person to search for information that supports the preexisting conclusion. In this case, Ms. Schaffeld asked impressionable children how much sugary cereal they had for breakfast. Ms. Schaffeld presumed that the sugary cereal was the "cause" of the high energy. Researchers should always remain objective in experiments; otherwise, it can impact the results of the research study. *Zone of proximal development* is a concept by Vygotsky that states cognitive development should be measured by what a person can do without help and what the person can do with the help of others. In this case, the young children could not understand the concept of "two halves of a cookie equal one whole" without the help of Ms. Schaffeld. *Initiative vs. guilt* is the third stage of Erikson's stages of psychosocial development, when young children begin to assert their desires and tell others what they prefer. At this stage, children take the initiative to plan activities that they enjoy. In this case, children could have replied to Ms. Schaffeld that they like cookies and that they like to eat them. *Conservation* is a Piagetian concept that is based on the idea that an object's properties remain the same even if that object appears different. Conservation is not learned until about 5 years old. In this scenario, the total amount of a cookie that younger children received did not matter whether it was two halves of a whole or one whole cookie. Most children were struggling to understand the concept of conservation.

Chapter 10

# Unit 7: Motivation, Emotion, and Personality

AP Psychology Unit 7 studies the individual differences in personality, emotion, and motivation.

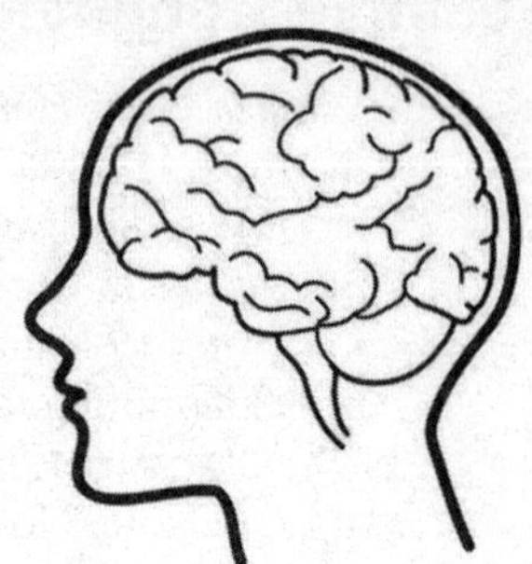

- Key Contributors to Motivation, Emotion, and Personality
- Motivation
- Emotions
- Stress and Coping
- Personality

## Overview of AP Psychology Unit 7

The overarching concepts for this chapter address personalities that are described within various domains of psychology, and the emotions and motivations that result from personality development. **The topics discussed in this unit will count toward 11–15 percent of your multiple-choice score.**

## AP Psychology Framework

Success on the exam depends on your ability to make connections to the major concepts described in the content topics of the *Course Framework for AP Psychology*. Remember that these concepts highlight the fundamental ideas that every student should take with them into the AP PSYCH exam and beyond.

Use the table below to guide you through what is covered in this unit. The information contained in this table is an abridged version of the content outlines with topic examples. Visit https://apstudent.collegeboard.org/apcourse/ap-psychology/ for the complete updated AP PSYCH course curriculum framework.

| AP Psychology—Unit 7: Motivation, Emotion, and Personality | |
|---|---|
| **Topic** | **Learning Target** |
| **Theories of Motivation** | ■ Identify and apply basic motivational concepts to understand the behavior of humans and other animals (e.g., instincts, incentives, intrinsic vs. extrinsic motivation, overjustification effect, self-efficacy, and achievement motivation).<br>■ Compare and contrast motivational theories, including the strengths and weaknesses of each (e.g., drive reduction theory; arousal theory, including the Yerkes-Dodson law; evolutionary theory of motivation; Maslow's theory; and cognitive dissonance theory).<br>■ Describe classic research findings in specific motivations (e.g., motivation systems: eating, sex, and social).<br>■ Identify contributions of key researchers in the psychological field of motivation and emotion (e.g., James, Kinsey, Maslow, Schachter, and Selye). |
| **Specific Topics in Motivation** | ■ Discuss the biological underpinnings of motivation, including needs, drives, and homeostasis. |

| Topic | Learning Target |
| --- | --- |
| **Theories of Emotion** | ■ Compare and contrast major theories of emotion (e.g., James-Lange theory, Cannon-Bard theory, Schachter two-factor theory, evolutionary theories of primary emotions, Lazarus' appraisal theory, LeDoux's theory, Ekman's research on cross-cultural displays of emotion, and facial feedback hypothesis).<br>■ Describe how cultural influences shape emotional expression, including variations in body language. |
| **Stress and Coping** | ■ Discuss theories of stress and the effects of stress on psychological and physical well-being (e.g., general adaptation theory, stress-related illnesses, Lewin's motivational conflicts theory, and unhealthy behaviors). |
| **Introduction to Personality** | ■ Describe and compare research methods that psychologists use to investigate personality (e.g., case studies, surveys, and personality inventories).<br>■ Identify the contributions of major researchers in personality theory (e.g., Adler, Bandura, Costa and McCrae, Freud, Jung, Maslow, and Rogers). |
| **Psychoanalytic Theories of Personality** | ■ Compare and contrast the psychoanalytic theories of personality with other theories of personality. |
| **Behaviorism and Social Cognitive Theories of Personality** | ■ Compare and contrast the behaviorist and social cognitive theories of personality with other theories of personality. |
| **Humanistic Theories of Personality** | ■ Compare and contrast humanistic theories of personality with other theories of personality.<br>■ Speculate how cultural context can facilitate or constrain personality development, especially as it relates to self-concept (e.g., collectivistic vs. individualistic cultures). |
| **Trait Theories of Personality** | ■ Compare and contrast trait theories of personality with other theories of personality. |
| **Measuring Personality** | ■ Identify frequently used assessment strategies, and evaluate relative test quality based on reliability and validity of the instruments (e.g., personality inventory and projective tests). |

## Important Terms and Concepts Checklist

This section is an overview of the important terms, concepts, language, and theories that specifically target the key topics of Unit 7. Use this list of terms as a checklist to check your personal progress. As you study the topics, place a check mark next to each and return to this list as often as necessary to refresh your understanding.

After you finish the review section, you can reinforce what you have learned by working through the practice questions at the end of the chapter. Answers and explanations provide further clarification into the perspectives of motivation, emotion, and personality.

| Term/Concept | Study Page | Term/Concept | Study Page | Term/Concept | Study Page |
|---|---|---|---|---|---|
| **anorexia nervosa** | p. 206 | **general adaptation syndrome** | p. 213 | **personal unconscious** | p. 217 |
| **approach-approach conflict** | p. 214 | **ghrelin** | p. 205 | **personality** | pp. 214–221 |
| **approach-avoidance conflict** | p. 214 | **homeostasis** | p. 201 | **primary motives** | p. 200 |
| **archetypes** | p. 218 | **id, ego, and superego** | p. 215 | **projective tests** | p. 220 |
| **arousal theory** | p. 202 | **incentives** | p. 200 | **push and pull factors** | p. 200 |
| **avoidance-avoidance conflict** | p. 214 | **instincts** | p. 200 | **reciprocal determinism** | p. 219 |
| **bulimia nervosa** | p. 206 | **intrinsic and extrinsic motivation** | p. 200 | **Rorschach inkblot test** | p. 220 |
| **Cannon-Bard theory of emotion** | p. 209 | **James-Lange theory of emotion** | p. 209 | **Schachter-Singer two-factor theory** | p. 209 |
| **cognitive appraisal theory** | p. 209 | **lateral hypothalamus** | p. 204 | **secondary motives** | p. 200 |
| **collective unconscious** | p. 218 | **leptin** | p. 205 | **self-actualization** | p. 203 |
| **complexes** | p. 217 | **locus of control (internal and external)** | pp. 203–204 | **self-concept** | p. 219 |
| **defense mechanisms** | p. 216 | **Maslow's hierarchy of needs** | p. 203 | **self-efficacy** | p. 200 |
| **display rules** | p. 210 | **micro-expressions** | p. 210 | **set-point theory** | p. 205 |
| **drive reduction theory** | p. 201 | **Minnesota Multiphasic Personality Inventory (MMPI)** | p. 221 | **stress** | pp. 210–214 |
| **drives** | p. 200 | **motivational conflicts theory** | pp. 213–214 | **stress reaction response** | p. 212 |
| **emotional intelligence** | p. 210 | **motives** | p. 200 | **trait theories** | pp. 219–220 |
| **eustress** | p. 211 | **needs** | p. 200 | **Type A and Type B personalities** | pp. 212–213 |
| **evolutionary theory** | pp. 201–202 | **obesity** | p. 205 | **ventromedial hypothalamus** | p. 204 |
| **factor analysis** | p. 220 | **objective tests** | p. 221 | **Yerkes-Dodson law** | p. 202 |
| **five-factor model of traits** | p. 220 | **overjustification** | p. 200 | | |

# Chapter Review

The psychological perspectives related to personality, motivation, and emotion inform us about behavior and mental health processes. This chapter will review the various perspectives among the branches of psychology to better understand the strengths and weaknesses and explain how empirical research helps to clarify the differences among psychological theories.

### Heads Up: What You Need to Know

For the AP PSYCH exam, ask yourself these three essential questions as you continue to work through the topics in this chapter and develop an understanding of motivation, emotion, and personality: What motivates us to think and act the way we do? Why do some people respond to stress in a healthier way than others? Why don't psychologists agree on theories?

## Key Contributors to Motivation, Emotion, and Personality

On the AP PSYCH exam, you should be able to identify the major contributors in the field of motivation, emotion, and personality.

| Key Contributors to Motivation, Emotion, and Personality | | |
|---|---|---|
| **Contributor** | **Field of Study (Theory)** | **Famous For** |
| **William James** (1842–1910) | Father of American psychology | James was known for writing *The Principles of Psychology* (1890), outlining his viewpoints about emotion and consciousness. James' evolutionary perspective of motivation proposed that human behavior serves a function based on survival instincts. |
| **Alfred Kinsey** (1894–1956) | Human sexuality | Alfred Kinsey is best known for the "Kinsey Reports" on human sexuality. |
| **Abraham Maslow** (1908–1970) | Maslow's hierarchy of needs | Maslow was a humanistic psychologist who studied the qualities of self-actualization and developed the hierarchy of needs. |
| **Stanley Schachter** (1922–1997) | Two-factor theory of emotion | Schachter helped to develop the two-factor theory of emotion: together, physiological arousal and cognitions result in emotional responses. |
| **Hans Selye** (1907–1982) | General adaptation syndrome of stress | Selye was the first to demonstrate the existence of biological stress on the human body and mind: alarm, resistance, and exhaustion. |
| **Julian Rotter** (1916–2014) | Locus of control theory | Rotter's theory is based on the idea that motivation is intertwined with the belief that one's actions will influence future events. |

## Motivation

Motivation has been a subject of interest in psychology since the 1930s. Although research has shown that enhancing motivation can positively impact outcomes in learning and performing, many psychologists have differing perspectives of motivation. Most psychologists agree, however, that **motivation** is the internal desire to initiate, sustain, and direct behavior to pursue a specific goal.

Motivation is controlled by internal signals monitored within the brain. Two of the three basic types of motives are discussed in this section: primary motives and secondary motives. **Primary motives** are physiological and innate based on survival, and **secondary motives** are cognitive and learned based on needs and drives that are aimed to achieve goals. The third type of motives are **personal motives;** these are based on the specific psychological temperament of the person.

Note: The terms *primary* and *secondary motives* are often used interchangeably with *primary* and *secondary needs*. **Needs** are internalized deficiencies that are used to energize behavior. **Primary needs** are basic biological needs (e.g., food, water, air to breathe); **secondary needs** are basic psychological needs (e.g., need for love, nurturing, and purpose).

The key basic concepts of motivation that you should know for the AP PSYCH exam are listed below.

## Key Concepts of Physiologically Based Primary Motives

**Drives** are internal survival forces (tension or arousal) that a person is motivated to reduce. For example, a person who is thirsty has a drive to drink a glass of water.

**Instincts** are inborn, unlearned, and genetically programmed patterns of behavior. For example, a bird building a nest.

## Key Concepts of Cognitively-Based Secondary Motives

Cognitively-based secondary motives can be intrinsic or extrinsic. **Intrinsic motivation** is based on the internalized need for achievement and reinforcement (e.g., positive feelings of accomplishment or the need for approval). **Extrinsic motivation** is when people are compelled to achieve something based on external reinforcements from the environment (e.g., good grades, money, or excelling at competition).

**Incentives** are positive and negative rewards in the environment that encourage a person to perform a certain behavior. For example, when a person is offered money to wash the dishes for a week.

**Overjustification** occurs when extrinsic rewards (e.g., money) decrease a person's intrinsic motivation. For example, if a person is suddenly paid for doing a hobby they have always loved, the compensation may reduce the joy of the hobby when it becomes a job to perform a task.

**Self-efficacy** is the confidence in the ability to control one's motivation, behavior, performance, and social environment.

### Heads Up: What You Need to Know

On the AP PSYCH exam, you should be familiar with **push and pull factors** of motivation. *Push* refers to the motives that push a person away from something unpleasant. For example, a push factor would be the fear of not doing well on an important test. *Pull* refers to the incentives that pull a person toward an activity. For example, the desire to obtain the satisfaction of receiving a grade of "A" in class (the incentive) makes one proactive to complete all assignments on time (the pull). Push and pull are powerful motivators and are often used as marketing strategies to push or pull consumers toward purchasing certain products.

## Theories of Motivation

This section will compare and contrast several theories of motivation that will be addressed on the AP PSYCH exam.

- Drive reduction theory
- Evolutionary theory
- Arousal theory
- Humanistic theory
- Locus of control theory

### Drive Reduction Theory (Clark L. Hull)

Inspired by John B. Watson, Ivan Pavlov, and Charles Darwin, Clark L. Hull's **drive reduction theory** is based on the principle that physical needs create a drive. The drive activates behavior to reduce the need and restore **homeostasis** (the process of maintaining a balanced environment).

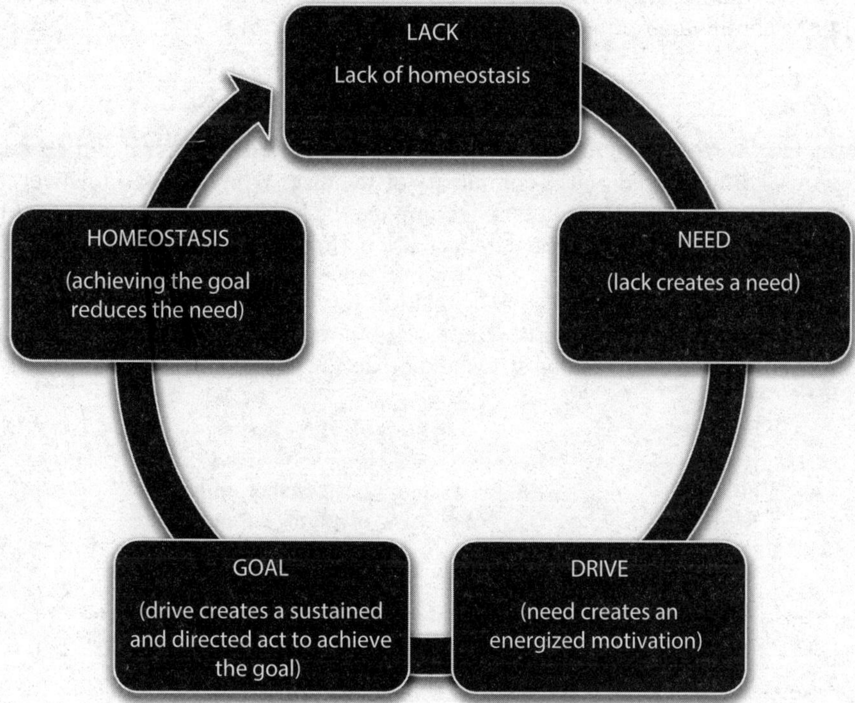


Drive reduction theory is no longer a popular theory in modern psychology, but the implications suggest that behavior is geared toward reducing internal drive conditions to satisfy physical needs (e.g., the need for food, water, and air to breathe).

### Evolutionary Theory (William James)

**Evolutionary theory** was inspired by Charles Darwin's theory of natural selection. Psychologist William James began to question the role of motivational instincts in self-survival. Chapter 4 discussed James' theory of functionalism. James' evolutionary perspective of motivation proposed that human behaviors, thoughts, and feelings must serve a certain *function* that is compelled by survival instincts. These instincts have certain goals that are driven by motivation in order to adapt. The theory proposed that people inherit certain behaviors that cause certain dispositions to generate specific behavior patterns designed to attain survival goals.

## Arousal Theory

**Arousal theory** suggests that people are motivated to engage in certain activities for the purpose of reaching an optimal level of arousal to meet psychological or physiological needs. Motivation is linked to arousal levels from environmental stimuli that activate the brain and the nervous system. For example, people are motivated to seek activities that create a level of physical stimulation and avoid activities that result in excessive stimulation. With too little arousal, a person becomes bored; with too much arousal, a person is overstimulated, anxious, and fearful. Thus, people seek *optimum arousal.*

What is a balanced level of arousal for peak performance? The right level of arousal is difficult to determine for each person at each moment in life. Imagine that there is a continuum between the **sympathetic nervous system** (stress) and the **parasympathetic nervous system** (relaxation). Where we place ourselves or want to place ourselves on the continuum frequently changes throughout our lives.

### *Yerkes-Dodson Law*

The **Yerkes-Dodson law** shows that there is a relationship between levels of arousal and performance. The optimal level of arousal differs based on the complexity of the task. When a task is relatively easy, the best performance occurs at high arousal. When a task is complex, the best performance occurs at lower levels of arousal. Too high or too low levels of arousal can decrease performance.

The inverted U-function in the image illustrates the relationship between changes in arousal and performance. As arousal increases, performance improves, but only to a certain point. When arousal levels are too high, performance decreases, causing stress and anxiety.

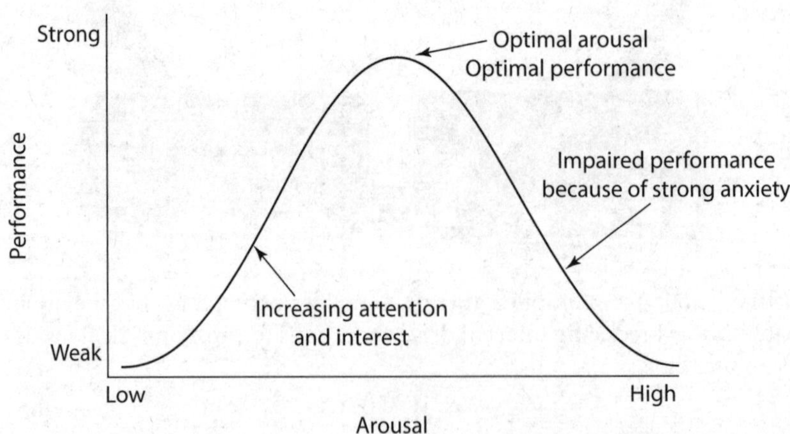

## Humanistic Theory (Abraham Maslow)

Humanistic theorists suggest that motivation is the result of the human desire for personal growth, rather than other motivation theories that are based on drive and instinct. Humanistic psychologist Abraham Maslow developed a hierarchy of human needs that centers on the potential for self-actualization, called **Maslow's hierarchy of needs. Self-actualization** compels people to become motivated to be satisfied with life.

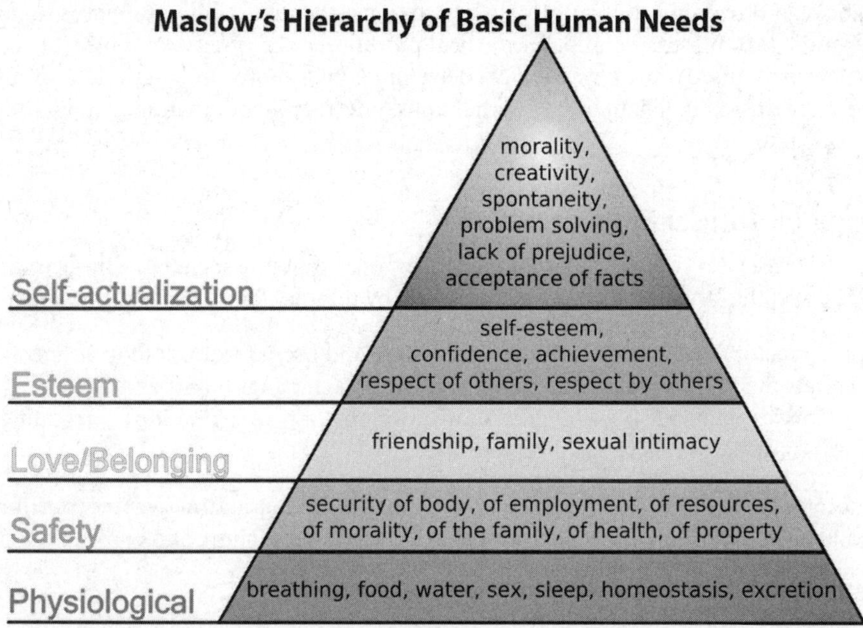


Maslow's hierarchy of needs ranges from physiological needs (e.g., hunger or thirst) to self-actualization (complete fulfillment of one's potential). Each successive level of the hierarchy is addressed only after the preceding level has been met (a concept of *prepotency*). At the lowest level there are physiological needs; once those needs are satisfied, the person becomes concerned with safety needs (e.g., having a predictable environment). Then, the person moves to the need to belong and feel accepted. Next are esteem needs (e.g., respecting and feeling good about oneself). According to Maslow, self-actualization is only possible when all of the basic needs are met. Self-actualization (e.g., transcendence) is the top of the pyramid and is rarely attained by most people. *Transcendence* is when a person seeks not just a fulfilling life, but a spiritually fulfilling life.

## Locus of Control Theory (Julian Rotter)

Rotter's theory of **locus of control** is a valid personality assessment of motivation based on internal (people believe that they can influence what will happen) and external (people believe that what happens to them is a result of outside influences) expectancies. The locus of control theory stems from a question about what control's a person's life, and whether the person receives punishment or achieves a reward. If the person believes he or she is responsible for his or her choices, that person has an *internal locus of control*. For example, students who believe good grades are achieved as a result of hard work and good study habits have an internal locus of control. On the other hand, if a person believes that external forces are responsible for life's choices, the person has an *external locus of control*. For example, students who believe that good grades are achieved as a result of a teacher's opinion. These students believe that there is not much that can be done to change the circumstances and, therefore, are exhibiting an external locus of control.

## Physiological Factors of Motivation

As mentioned above, motivation is difficult to observe and measure, but bodily responses to motivation can be scientifically studied. Brain scans and other medical procedures can observe and measure activity of the hypothalamus. Before we discuss the physiological determinants of motivation, let's first review some of the biological concepts discussed in Chapter 5: hypothalamus, pituitary gland, thyroid gland, adrenal glands, and basal metabolic rate.

### The Physiology of Hunger Motivation

The physiology of hunger is a complex internal bodily response that is associated with the brain's nervous system, hormones, and the stomach. Hunger is motivated by internal factors and external factors.

**Internal** (biological) factors of hunger are the intricate body and brain feedback loop connections. The hypothalamus signals the brain to release hormones, and stomach pangs (contractions) emerge with a desire for food. Drive theory explains the physiological motivation that a person develops when hungry or thirsty, and the need to eat or drink to relieve the discomfort.

**External** (psychological, social, and cultural) factors of hunger are food attractiveness (portion size, shape, visual cues), social cues, availability, and how people are taught to eat, shop, and cook.

#### *The Role of the Hypothalamus in Hunger*

The primary regulator of hunger is the **hypothalamus** in the brain. The hypothalamus controls basic needs and desires (the desires to eat, have sex, and fight-or-flight). Think of the hypothalamus as the gas pedal of our desires and urges, and the prefrontal cortex (logic center) as the brakes or the steering wheel. All humans have urges, but it is what we do with our natural urges and desires that can change the outcome.

Parts of the hypothalamus are involved with hunger. For example, when the **lateral hypothalamus** is stimulated, it communicates that it's time to eat. If it is damaged (see the rat on the right), it significantly decreases hunger. When the **ventromedial hypothalamus** is stimulated, it communicates the feeling of being full. When damaged (see the rat on the left), it significantly increases the desire to eat—hunger.

Experiments with rats have shown that the motivation to eat can shift dramatically when parts of the hypothalamus are stimulated or damaged.

| | Lateral Hypothalamus | Ventromedial Hypothalamus |
|---|---|---|
| If inhibited or damaged... | Reduced hunger | Increased hunger |
| If excited or stimulated... | Increased hunger | Reduced hunger |

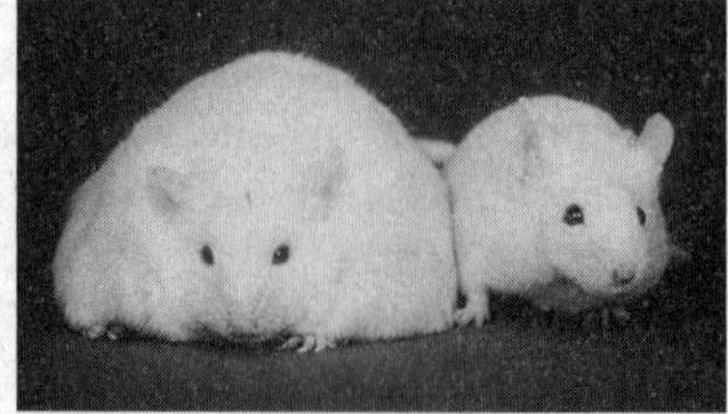

### *The Role of Hormones in Hunger*

The hypothalamus controls the *pituitary gland* (the master gland that controls hormones). The *thyroid gland* controls metabolism (how quickly the body processes energy and the need for food). *Adrenal glands* secrete adrenaline, which arouses the body (e.g., breathing rate, perspiration, and heart rate). The *basal metabolic rate* is how much energy a person is using when the body is in an inactive state.

The hypothalamus can send appetite-stimulating hormones to signal the body that it's time to eat. The primary source of the body's fuel is *glucose* (and fats) that are absorbed in the bloodstream to be used for energy or stored for later use. It is important to note that as blood sugar (glucose) goes down, insulin goes up. The hormone insulin influences hunger because it is the inverse of glucose. The hormone **leptin** reduces the motivation to eat and sends a signal to the brain: "I am full." The hormone **ghrelin** increases the motivation to eat and sends signals to the brain: "I am hungry."

**TEST TIP: Leptin acts to keep a person "lean," and ghrelin makes the stomach "growl."**

### *Eating Disorders*

Eating disorders are described as extreme eating or dieting behaviors that cause a person significant distress, a disruption in psychosocial functioning, or worsening physical health. Feeding and eating disorders (e.g., anorexia nervosa and bulimia nervosa) are discussed in Chapter 11, "Unit 8: Clinical Psychology," but it's important to acknowledge some of the concepts related to motivational overeating and undereating.

**Set-point theory** suggests humans are genetically programmed to maintain a certain body weight. It's similar to a weight thermostat that is genetically predetermined. Set point is the normal weight of a person. When the person reaches the normal weight (e.g., ratio of fat to muscles, bones, and other tissues), the brain feels satisfied to have met genetically programmed instructions. The set-point theory does not account for a modern, sedentary lifestyle that has resulted in increased body fat, and even obesity.

**Obesity,** the condition of being excessively overweight, is attributed to psychosocial, emotional, environmental, and genetic factors. Obesity overrides the motivation to eat healthy, and often results in physical and emotional health risks.

**Did you know?** It used to be thought that only certain parts of the tongue sensed certain flavors. There was even a diagram of a tongue in old psychology textbooks that showed which area of the tongue tasted different flavors. This idea is false. It is important to know for the AP Psychology exam that every flavor can be sensed throughout the whole tongue.

**Anorexia nervosa** is an intense fear of gaining weight or becoming fat. The person has a distorted view of body image that leads to extreme dieting and severe weight loss. Anorexia nervosa primarily affects adolescent girls and young women.

**Bulimia nervosa** is the recurrent episodes of *binge eating* (eating a large amount of food within a relatively short time). To avoid weight gain, the person frequently uses diuretics, medications, laxatives, excessive exercise, fasting, or self-induced vomiting.

### Physiological Factors of Sexual Motivation

Evolutionary theory provides insight into understanding the internal motivations of sexual behavior that are critical for survival. Research shows that external motivations (e.g., culture, environmental cues, and religion) also influence sexual behavior.

In the 1940s, Alfred Kinsey conducted studies in human sexuality. Human sexuality is the biological, physical, emotional, and spiritual expression of sex. Kinsey's groundbreaking studies of human sexuality were based on decades of interviews and surveys conducted by a well-trained team of interviewers who collected thousands of personal histories of men and women. Kinsey's research remains the foundation of psychological knowledge of sexual behaviors.

The hypothalamus and the pituitary gland play an important role in sexual desire. The pituitary gland is the "master gland" that controls the hormones that are involved in sexual maturity and sexual desire. Despite the fact that human sexuality is far more complex than hormonal activity, we must identify the hormones that influence sexual desire. *Androgens* and *testosterone* are a class of male hormones. Both males and females have testosterone (in differing amounts), and it is strongly linked to sexual desire. Similarly, both males and females have different levels of female hormones, *estrogen* and *progesterone*. An increase in estrogen is linked to increased female sexual desire, and an increase in progesterone seems to reduce sexual desire in women.

In the late 1950s, William Masters and Virginia Johnson studied human sexuality in a comprehensive study from the physiological viewpoint and developed a four-stage sexual response cycle.

## Emotions

**Emotions** are expressive feeling states that are interconnected with physiological, cognitive, and behavioral systems and can be either positive or negative.

### Primary Emotions

Emotions are on a spectrum based on intensity. Psychologist Robert Plutchik developed a theory of emotions (2001) that includes eight primary emotions—fear, surprise, sadness, disgust, anger, anticipation, joy, and trust. For example, in the image that follows, notice that the emotion of fear ranges from *apprehension* on one end of the spectrum to *terror* on the other end of the spectrum.

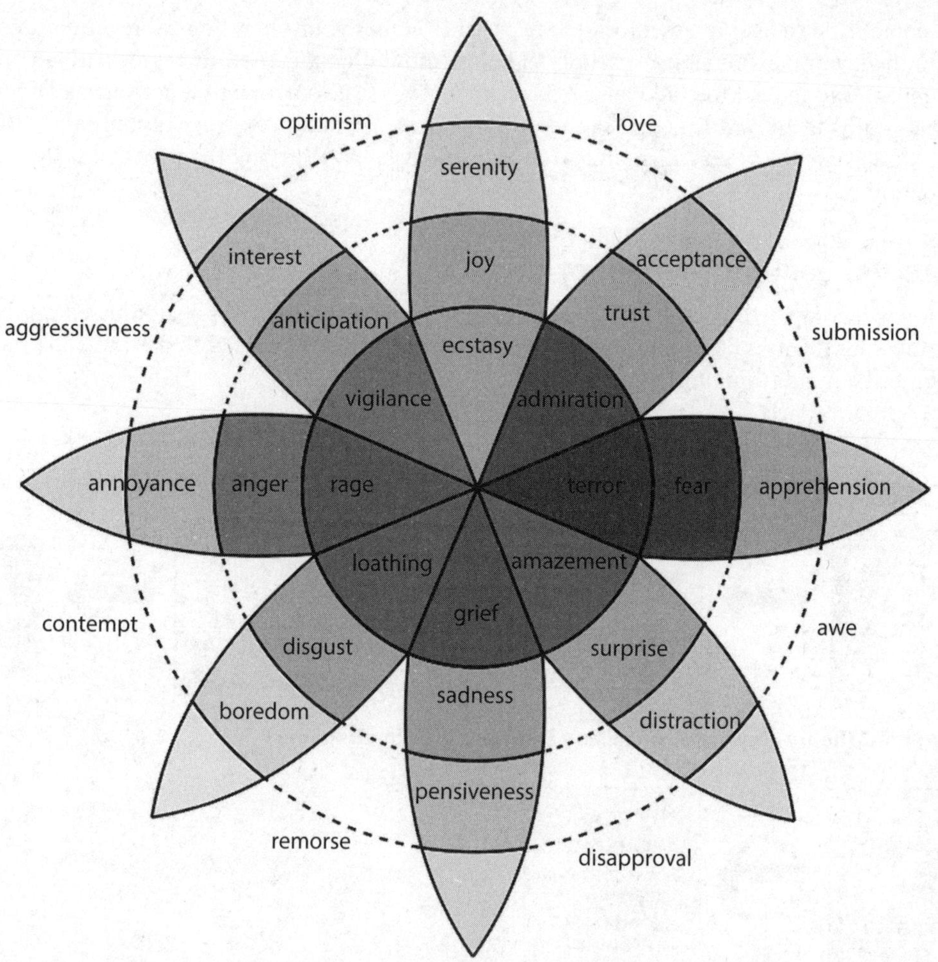


## Theories of Emotion

A useful way to think about emotions is to notice how the body reacts to the emotion, how the mind interprets the emotion, and how your behavior responds to the emotion. The greater the physiological arousal, the more intense the emotion.

**Physiological.** The brain's limbic system regulates emotions, and the brain's amygdala stores emotional experiences. The limbic system also controls the autonomic nervous system (ANS) and when under extreme stress, emotions are activated by the sympathetic nervous system, causing the body to be in a heightened state of arousal. This action causes adrenal glands to produce adrenaline in the bloodstream. The release of adrenaline can trigger rapid heart rate, high blood pressure, rapid breathing, muscle tension, and perspiration.

**Cognitive.** Emotions can arouse powerful thoughts when the person interprets the meanings of the events.

**Behavioral.** Emotions can cause people to adapt behavior to act on their emotions, particularly in self-survival.

But what comes first to lead to an emotional experience? Does your physiological reaction precede or follow cognitive or behavioral expressions? The model below shows that an emotion begins with an arousal *event* (e.g., watching a sad movie) that activates *expressive feelings* (e.g., sorrow) that activates a *bodily arousal* (e.g., crying) that results in an *emotion* (e.g., sadness). It makes sense that people cry because they are sad, but not all psychologists agree. As you will soon learn, psychologists have varying theories about the order in which emotions result.

## Compare and Contrast Theories of Emotion

This section will compare and contrast several theories of emotion that will be addressed on the AP PSYCH exam. Competing theories have different perspectives about what is aroused first—the body (heart pounding) or the mind (thinking "I'm scared").

**James-Lange Theory (Physical Arousal First)**

**Cannon-Bard Theory (Physical Arousal and Emotions are Simultaneous)**

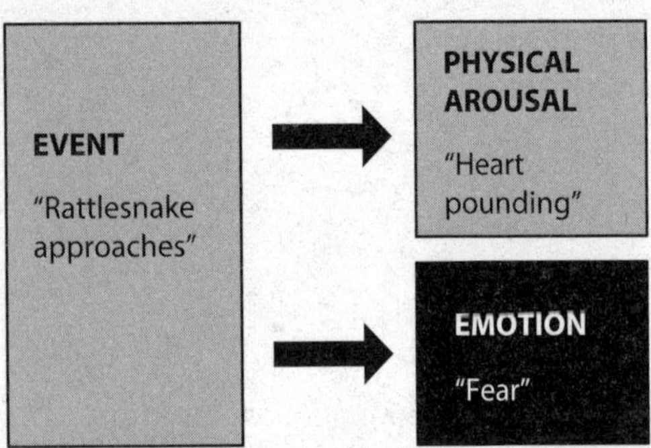


**Schachter-Singer Two-Factor Theory (Physical Arousal and based on Thinking)**

### James-Lange Theory

**Arousal event causes a physiological reaction, which then causes an emotion.**

The **James-Lange theory** of emotion was developed by William James and Carl Lange. Although many other theories suggest that an event first triggers the feelings and then the physiological reaction, the James-Lange theory turns common sense upside down. If you were to ask someone why he or she is crying, the person might say because they are sad. This theory suggests the opposite: The person is sad because he or she is crying—the physiological event (crying) precedes and *causes* emotional feelings (sadness).

### Cannon-Bard Theory

**Physical arousal and emotions occur simultaneously.**

The **Cannon-Bard theory** was developed by Walter Cannon and Philip Bard to contradict the James-Lange theory. This theory proposes that physiological arousal and emotional experiences happen simultaneously. For example, if you startle your brother unexpectedly by making a loud noise that causes him to flinch, what do you think he will say came first—the physical reaction or the feeling of fear? Chances are that the answer will be that the two arousals happened at the same time. This makes sense if you remember that the brain can unconsciously perform dual-processing actions simultaneously.

### Schachter-Singer Two-Factor Theory

**Physical arousal is interpreted as fear-inducing or exciting.**

The **Schachter-Singer two-factor theory** was developed by Stanley Schachter and Jerome Singer. The previous two theories focused mostly on the physiological responses, but Schachter and Singer realized that when an event causes an arousal, there is a need for people to interpret their feelings. Therefore, cognition (thinking about the event) is critical to understanding emotional responses. Theorists were concerned with *what* was felt and *how* people assigned labels to cognitively interpret physical arousals (called *cognitive labels*). The Schachter-Singer theory proposed that together, physiological responses and cognitions (memories, perceptions, and their interpretations) result in emotions. For example, if you startle your brother unexpectedly by making a loud noise, this event might cause him to flinch, but he might say it was funny, scary, or annoying (cognitive interpretation).

### Cognitive Appraisal Theory

**Cognitive interpretation is based on how the event will affect the person.**

The **cognitive appraisal theory** was developed by Richard Lazarus, who agreed with Schachter and Singer that cognitions play an important role in emotions, but Lazarus added that appraisal precedes cognitive labeling. The appraisal is based on how the event might affect the person. Lazarus proposed that emotions are attained from the appraisal of the event, and that people feel emotions based on these appraisals, called *cognitive appraisal*. Cognitive appraisal is how people evaluate and interpret the personal meaning of a physiological arousal.

## Cross-Cultural Displays of Emotion

Despite differences in culture and language, certain human characteristics, like emotions, are similar in people all over the world. Some cultures have strong rules about when it is appropriate to demonstrate emotion. The British, for example, are known for showing minimal emotions when aroused. Cultural guidelines of emotions are called **display rules.** Although display rules are different around the world, as members of a species, all humans exhibit similar emotions.

Charles Darwin proposed that the human face is innately programmed to show emotions. Facial expressions are universally and genetically programmed. Almost 100 years later, psychologist Paul Ekman proved Darwin's theory. Ekman suggested that emotions and expressions are hardwired in all humans. This knowledge was supported by his explanation that even blind babies smile.

Through a series of studies, Ekman found a high agreement among diverse cultures and selected emotional labels that fit universal facial expressions and named six basic emotions: anger, disgust, fear, happiness, sadness, and surprise. Ekman suggested that even tiny, but automatic, flexing of certain facial muscles occurs every time an emotion is experienced, called **micro-expressions.** Ekman also suggested that even "making faces" can cause emotional experiences.

## Emotional Intelligence

While it may seem impossible to control emotions, it is possible to work with your emotions by using emotional intelligence. **Emotional intelligence** is the ability to perceive, access, and understand emotions in order to reflectively regulate emotions. Daniel Goleman developed the concept of emotional intelligence and suggested that there are certain skills that people can employ to align emotional lives with cognitive lives. For example, *impulse control* (the ability to think through the consequences of one's actions before acting on an impulse) and *delayed gratification* (the ability to delay the reward).

According to Goleman, there are five components of emotional intelligence, as detailed in the following table.

**Components of Emotional Intelligence**

| Type | Description |
|---|---|
| **Self-awareness** | The ability to recognize and understand one's internal states, preferences, resources, and intuitions. |
| **Self-regulation** | The ability to manage one's internal states, impulses, and resources (e.g., trustworthiness, integrity, comfort with ambiguity, and an openness to change). |
| **Motivation** | The ability to be motivated to reach a goal. |
| **Empathy** | The ability to understand and be sensitive to the feelings of others. |
| **Social skills** | The proficiency in managing relationships and building networks that contribute to desirable responses from others. |

# Stress and Coping

Health psychologists study the relationship between psychological causes of physical illnesses, such as the physical symptoms of stress on the body. The body reacts physically, mentally, and emotionally. In physics, **stress** is defined as a force exerted on the physical body. Research has shown that stress is linked to the susceptibility of heart disease, lowered immunity, fatal car accidents, suicide, and even some forms of cancer.

As depicted in the graph that follows, numerous teens in the United States have developed unhealthy symptoms and lifestyle behaviors related to stress.

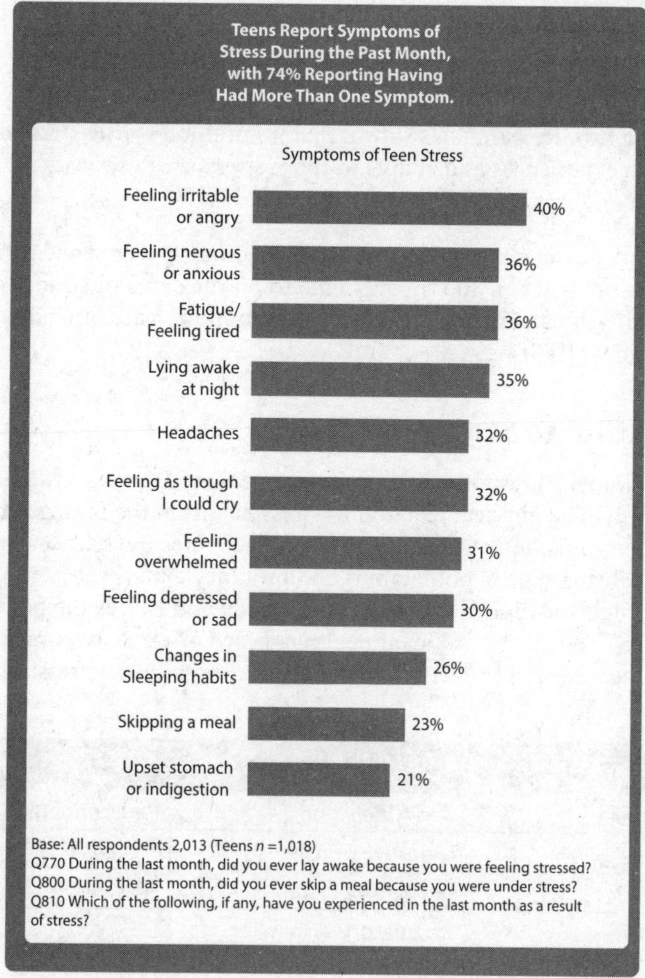


Source: American Psychological Association, "Stress in America™: Are Teens Adopting Adults' Stress Habits?"

Most people experience stress from time to time, but the stressful demands of daily challenges can cause psychological and health problems. According to research, one in five adults who live in the United States have reported experiencing chronic stress.

## Healthy vs. Unhealthy Stress

Healthy stress is short-term and is beneficial for motivation, growth, and change. Stress psychologist Hans Seyle referred to normal, healthy stress as **eustress.** For example, if you are preparing to go to the prom, it can be stressful. However, the prom is an event that is exciting, uplifting, and enjoyable.

Unhealthy stress (also called *distress*), however, is a long-term condition that is defined as a constant state of emotional tension resulting from adverse circumstances. The tension causes the person to reach an overloaded capacity to mentally adapt, cope, or adjust to the stressful circumstances.

## Stress Reaction Response

Stressors can cause a **stress reaction response.** Stress can be divided into three components: external stress (stressors produced by a change in the environment), internal stress (one's experience of the stressors), and the interaction between the two. Research has shown that it's not necessarily stressors that cause stress reactions, it's how a person experiences and adapts to those stressors. Responses are different depending on personality differences, experiences, and adaptive behaviors.

Think of stressors as an independent variable and a stress reaction as a dependent variable. Daily annoyances are small stressors that can add up over time to produce one or several stress reactions. A catastrophic event that is life-threatening can produce a severe stress reaction and possibly even result in post-traumatic stress disorder (PTSD).

## Physiological Reaction to Stress

Similar to the body's physiological response to emotions, a person responds to stress physically, emotionally, behaviorally, and cognitively. The physical reaction to stress begins in the brain's limbic system, which causes an excitation of the sympathetic nervous system and activates the release of the stress hormones epinephrine and norepinephrine. The hypothalamus and pituitary glands release cortisol from the adrenal glands, which triggers a "flight-or-flight" syndrome in the body and causes the body to experience a heightened state of arousal. The most significant health concern of excessive stress is physical exhaustion, but a heightened state of arousal can trigger a rapid heart rate, high blood pressure, rapid breathing, and muscle tension.

| Bodily Reactions to Stress | | |
|---|---|---|
| **Sympathetic** | **Bodily Reaction** | **Parasympathetic** |
| Inhibited | **Digestive processes** | Excited |
| Increased | **Circulatory system** | Slowed |
| Increased | **Respiratory system** | Slowed |
| Inhibited | **Reproductive system** | Possibly excited |
| Inhibited | **Cerebral cortex** | Active |
| Increased | **Blood pressure** | Lowered |

### Type A and Type B Personality Theory

Several different variables, such as *external factors* (e.g., social support and resources) and *internal factors* (e.g., temperament and personality), determine who is more susceptible to the effects of stress.

Type A and Type B personality traits describe two contrasting internalized personality types that relate to how people deal with stress.

- **Type A personality** describes a person who tends to be more motivated to achieve at high levels. A person with a Type A personality has a tendency to strive to be highly organized, ambitious, and competitive. The internalized drive of someone with a Type A personality can cause the vulnerability to higher levels of internalized stress. Cardiologists have theorized that people with Type A personality have a greater risk of developing coronary heart disease later in life.

- **Type B personality** describes a person who has a tendency to be relaxed, easygoing, and less motivated to achieve goals. Type B describes a person who is less vulnerable to stress-related situations.

## General Adaptation Syndrome

Hans Seyle studied reactions to stressors on animals (e.g., surgical trauma and electric shock) and discovered that the body's adaptive response to stress is generalized. Seyle developed a general adaptation syndrome that explains how the body manages stress over time. The three-phase model of stress is based on the interaction between a "force" (of stress) and the "resistance" to that force.

**Phase 1 – Alarm response.** Seyle theorized that the body recognizes a threat, arouses the sympathetic nervous system, and mobilizes a reaction by releasing adrenaline to manage the threat.

**Phase 2 – Resistance.** The second phase is when the body actively confronts and copes with the threat. The body can resist stress for a period of time, but it can't resist the stress indefinitely if the threat does not lessen.

**Phase 3 – Exhaustion.** The third phase occurs when the stressor has continued until the body becomes fatigued and the body's natural resources are depleted. Adrenaline and cortisol are short-term bursts of energy, but when released at high levels for a long period of time, health problems will result.

General Adaptation Syndrome

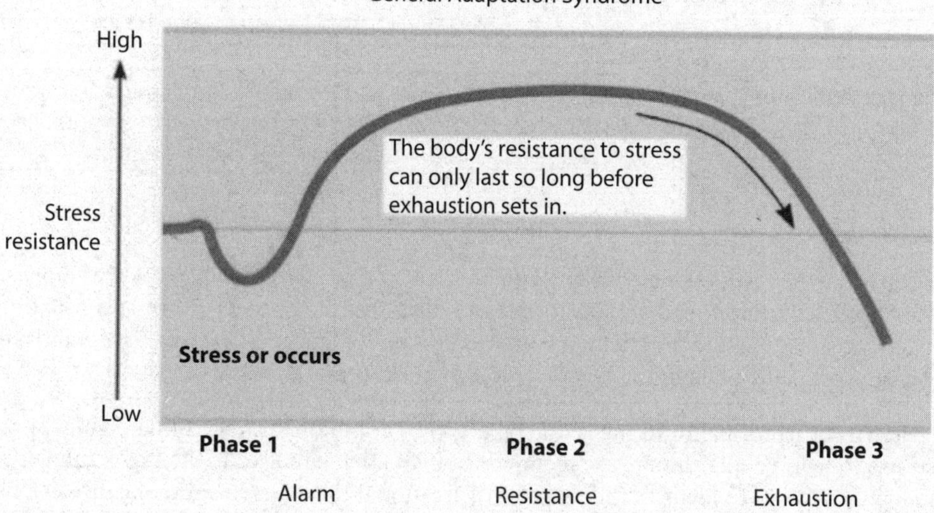


**TEST TIP: On the AP PSYCH exam, you may see Seyle's alarm stage grouped with similar concepts, such as fight-or-flight response, amygdalic response, sympathetic response, or adrenaline rush.**

## Motivational Conflicts Theory

Psychologist Kurt Lewin developed a **motivational conflicts theory** to explain how people can experience two competing forces of tension in certain situations: approach and avoidance. *Approach* is described as "moving toward something" and *avoidance* is described as "moving away from something." Conflict can occur when what you want and what you don't want are combined in the same situation. For example, clicking the "decision e-mail" from a college you would like to attend. By doing so, the emotional feelings of excitement and anxiety can occur simultaneously. Not only can you want and not want something simultaneously, but you can be forced to choose between two options you do not want and you can be torn between two competing opportunities.

According to Lewin, the factors of conflict are described in the following table.

| Motivational Conflicts Theory | |
|---|---|
| **Type** | **Description** |
| **Approach-approach conflict** | Approach-approach conflict refers to choosing between two desirable outcomes to achieve a goal. It is the least stressful type of conflict. For example, you want to go on vacation to Hawaii, but you also want to go on vacation to Costa Rica. |
| **Avoidance-avoidance conflict** | Avoidance-avoidance conflict refers to choosing between two undesirable outcomes. It is a highly stressful type of conflict and feels like no resolution is possible. For example, if you hate going to the dentist, but you also hate the way you feel because you have a painful tooth cavity. |
| **Approach-avoidance conflict** | Approach-avoidance conflict refers to when one event or goal has both desirable and undesirable outcomes. For example, you may not want to be in a relationship with someone (avoid), but you feel ambivalent because you don't like the way you feel when you are alone (approach). |
| **Multiple approach-avoidance conflicts** | Multiple approach-avoidance conflicts are complex because you must choose between two or more actions that have both desirable and undesirable elements. There are positive and negative courses of action that may move in opposite directions. |

## Coping with Stress

As you have learned, stress can take on many forms that harm a person's psychological and physiological health. Psychologists have developed coping strategies to help people cope with stressful situations. Strategies to reduce stress include practicing meditation or guided imagery, exercising regularly, developing a social support network, and challenging negative thinking (irrational thoughts).

Identifying patterns of irrational thinking is one of the most common strategies that cognitive-behavioral psychologists use to help people change exaggerated thoughts that can lead to stress and anxiety. The basic process of reducing stress is to identify the patterns of irrational thoughts, dispute the distortions, and reverse the automatic thoughts. Two common irrational thoughts that cause stress are *ruminative thinking* (the tendency to repeat and dwell on the same thoughts) and *catastrophizing* (envisioning the worst possible outcome for most situations).

# Personality

This section will review the theories of personality and the methods used to measure personality. **Personality** is a unique pattern of enduring psychological characteristics acquired through environmental influences and social experiences. Most research psychologists focus on analyzing how personality shapes behavior and how the environment influences personality development.

## Heads Up: What You Need to Know

On the AP PSYCH exam, you should be familiar with psychoanalytic, psychodynamic, humanistic, behavioral/social, and trait theories of personality.

# Theories of Personality

Theories of personality are the concepts, assumptions, and principles that explain the development of personality. The reference table that follows compares the major theories of personality that you will be expected to know for the AP PSYCH exam.

| Compare and Contrast Personality Theories | | |
|---|---|---|
| **Personality Theory** | **Theorist** | **View of Personality** |
| **Psychoanalytic** | Freud | Personality is based on unconscious dynamics, especially internal unresolved childhood or sexual conflicts. Personality depends on impulses (id, ego, and superego) and defense mechanisms that neutralize anxiety. |
| **Psychodynamic** | Jung, Adler | Personality is shaped by dynamic interplay between the conscious and the unconscious. |
| **Humanistic** | Rogers, Maslow | Personality is a private, subjective experience. |
| **Behavioral and social cognitive** | Bandura | Personality is based on learned behavior and its interaction with the physical and social environment. |
| **Trait** | Costa, McCrae | Personality is inherited at birth and is based on stable, personal characteristics (traits) that relate to behavior. Extroversion and introversion are important dimensions of personality traits, and proponents of personality include the five-factor theory of personality. |

## Psychoanalytic Theory of Personality

Psychoanalytic theory was developed by Sigmund Freud and suggests that the unconscious mind has dynamic forces of internal conflicts that shape all thoughts, behaviors, and the structures of personality. As discussed in Chapter 9, Freud developed stages of psychosexual development based on instinctual drives that influence the development of personality. Freud believed that the primary motivating force of human behavior was unconscious sexual and aggressive impulses, instincts, wishes, and desires.

### *Personality Structure*

According to Freud, three basic structures of personality regulate the conscious, preconscious, and unconscious, called the **id, ego,** and **superego.**

| Freud's Structure of Personality | |
|---|---|
| **Id** | The id is an unconscious, irrational component of personality that is governed by the *pleasure principle* (immediate satisfaction). It is a part of personality that has instinctual urges and desires. |
| **Ego** | The ego is the rational component of personality that is governed by the *reality principle* (the ability to assess the demands of the external world). |
| **Superego** | The superego is the moralistic component of personality that operates according to societal rules and the internalization of parental rules. |

### *Defense Mechanisms*

**Defense mechanisms** are automatic, unconscious mental strategies that help the mind reach a compromise with psychological conflicts and negative feelings. Freud's daughter, Anna Freud, continued her father's work and helped to develop the concepts of psychological defense mechanisms. According to Anna Freud, the ego protects itself with defenses to reduce or redirect negative feelings that arise from a situation or thought that the person perceives as threatening.

The primary defense mechanism is *repression,* but other defense mechanisms that you should know for the AP PSYCH exam are listed in the table that follows.

| Defense Mechanisms | | |
|---|---|---|
| **Defense Mechanism** | **Description** | **Example** |
| **Repression** | Involuntarily suppressing memories, thoughts, or feelings to reduce anxiety. | A person who forgets traumatic childhood events and wasn't aware that such events even existed. |
| **Denial** | Blocking unpleasant events from awareness. | A less-than-average actor who routinely ignores critical reviews and continues to pursue being rejected at auditions. |
| **Regression** | Returning to behavior that occurred at an earlier stage of development. | A teen who has a verbal temper tantrum about having to complete an excessive amount of homework. |
| **Projection** | Attributing one's undesirable behavior, thoughts, or traits to another person. Blaming others for one's own fault. | A teen who hates school believes that all of his teachers hate him. |
| **Reaction formation** | Expressing a feeling or behavior that is opposite to one's real feelings. | Declaring that certain sexual actions are immoral because you are afraid that you have those desires. |
| **Displacement** | Transferring unconscious fears, thoughts, feelings, and desires toward a person onto another person or object that is more acceptable. | A teacher who is frustrated with his first period class takes it out on his second period class. |
| **Sublimation** | Transforming unacceptable desires into socially acceptable behaviors or actions. | A person who practices martial arts to deal with aggressive desires. |
| **Rationalization** | Unconsciously creating a logical reason why objectionable behavior is acceptable. | A teen who cheats on a test rationalizes that it is okay to cheat because tests are morally unfair. It is similar to justification that occurs to reduce the unpleasantness of cognitive dissonance (see p. 269). |

**Did you know?** Freud's view of personality remains controversial in the psychological community for a few reasons: (1) Freud did not support his theory with scientifically based evidence. His claims were not testable, and he rarely collected data except for a small number of interviews. (2) Freud overemphasized sexual and aggressive impulses, drives, and instincts. (3) Freud's stages of personality are fixed, leaving people trapped by negative conflicts and struggles to deal with internal unconscious forces.

## Psychodynamic Theories of Personality

The origins of psychodynamic theories are based on the concepts of Sigmund Freud and the dynamic processes of the unconscious. Psychodynamic psychologists, sometimes called *neo-Freudians,* accepted Freud's views of the unconscious, defense mechanisms, the importance of early childhood experiences in shaping personality, and the basic structures of personality (e.g., id, ego, and superego). Neo-Freudians, however, departed from Freud's views about sexual and aggressive drives. Psychodynamic theories placed a greater value on the role of consciousness in interpreting the experience of the unconscious.

Just as some of our motivations are intrinsic, psychodynamic theories describe constructs of personality as unconscious processes. Psychodynamic theorists suggest that there is a struggle between hidden, internal messages and external messages about what society and culture suggest are acceptable. Internal conflicts are the result of early childhood experiences. While the unconscious cannot be directly observed, there are certain techniques that psychologists use to uncover hidden forces that motivate people (e.g., dream interpretation).

Two important neo-Freudians that you should know for the AP PSYCH exam are Carl Jung and Alfred Adler.

### *Carl Jung*

Carl Jung was a student of Freud who split from Freud's perspectives in the early 20th century, especially Freud's view of dream analysis. Freud believed that dreams attempted to conceal feelings, drives, and motivations. Jung believed that dreams communicate critical messages from the unconscious. Jung proposed that drives are generalized psychic energies, including creative, spiritual, and intellectual energies that offer solutions to life's problems.

Jung developed many important psychological concepts that relate to personality, including the mind's "layers" of the unconscious that hold thoughts, experiences, and perceptions. Jungian theory ascribed significance to identifying the layers as the "three-tiered structure" of the *psyche* (conscious and unconscious mind), as illustrated in the figure below.

The top floor of the psyche consists of various linked rooms that represent **consciousness** (ego and the sense of self). Immediately below is another floor that represents the **personal unconscious** (repressed parts of the self that consist of **complexes**—core patterns of emotions, wishes, and perceptions). The third level of the

**Map of the Psyche**

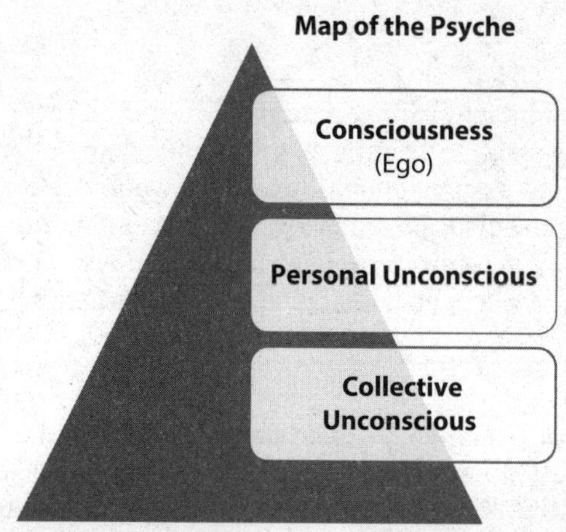

structure is the **collective unconscious** (collective human experiences embedded in all people) and **archetypes** (universal powerful energies that form the thoughts of the collective unconscious). Archetypes can take on universal mythical, divine, or spiritual context.

Jung developed types of personality to better understand characteristics of people in his 1921 study, "Psychological Types." He proposed that psychological types are not just characteristics of a person, but are "types of consciousness" that discriminate between a person's internal and external realities. Each person has a tendency toward a particular mental orientation of perceiving and functioning in the world. Over time, and through situational demands, a dominant personality preference develops.

Jung identified a person's preferences based on two distinct modes of personality attitudes (preferences): *extraversion* and *introversion*. The personality types have four orientations of functioning: thinking, sensation, intuition, and feeling. For example, a person who is extraverted has a tendency to focus attention on the outer world, and a person who is introverted has a tendency to focus attention on inner-world ideas.

### *Alfred Adler*

Psychologist Alfred Adler was another student of Freud. Adler agreed with Freud that early childhood experiences are important in the formation of personality, but he viewed social conflicts, not sexual conflicts, as a critical component in personality development. Adler emphasized the importance of the child striving for superiority as the primary motivator in forming personality. He argued that children develop either feelings of inferiority or feelings of superiority, and that children who feel inferior develop compensatory skills to overcome their weaknesses. For example, an immature personality might irrationally focus on perceived shortcomings and attempt to compensate for such shortcomings in a disproportionate way. The person might, on some level, believe they are not smart enough and dedicate an extraordinary amount of effort to acquire evidence to prove that he or she is smart. However, a mature personality seeks to find balance between inferiority and superiority.

## Humanistic Theories of Personality

Humanistic psychologists disagreed with Freud's perspectives of personality. Rather than emphasizing the negative aspects of personality formation, humanistic psychologists focused on the person's "free will" that strives toward self-realization. The humanistic (sometimes called *phenomenological*) approach to personality suggests that people are basically good and will actively seek to improve if given the right circumstances.

### *Abraham Maslow*

Abraham Maslow explained the impact of human needs in the development of personality. Maslow developed his theory by studying creative, healthy people, unlike many other psychologists whose thoughts were influenced by Freud's original work with anxious, young women. Recall Maslow's hierarchy of needs pyramid from earlier in this chapter. If basic needs are met, it plays an important role in a person achieving growth that is oriented toward self-actualization. If basic needs are not met, the person is oriented toward deficiency. A state of fulfillment is when a person achieves the highest level of satisfaction with life.

### *Carl Rogers*

Carl Rogers developed a theory of personality development that was based on a person's need to self-actualize and grow. Rogers suggested that a healthy personality develops like a tree that needs good soil, sunlight, and water to flourish. Rogers challenged Freud's view of personality formation and believed that people are basically good, and if offered a growth-promoting environment and unconditional positive regard, people will flourish and become psychologically fully functioning.

Rogers believed that a key element in personality development is the formation of **self-concept** (reflection of the beliefs about oneself). When people receive acceptance, genuineness, and empathy from others, they are free to be their ideal selves, grow in a positive direction, and perceive the world positively. For more information about Rogers' theory, see Chapter 11, "Unit 8: Clinical Psychology."

## Behavioral and Social Cognitive Theories of Personality

Behavioral and social cognitive theories of personality suggest that personality is the result of the interaction between a person and his or her environment.

### *Albert Bandura*

Psychologist Albert Bandura proposed the concept of observational learning as one of the most important influences in personality development. Bandura recognized the importance of environmental influences in the process of personality formation and provided evidence that children model behavior through observation (e.g., "Bobo doll" experiment). He called the process of interacting with the environment **reciprocal determinism.** In reciprocal determinism, three factors influence behavior: cognitive, environmental, and behavioral. For example, a child's behavior in class might change the classroom environment. The child might then negatively interpret the environment, and in turn, negatively impact the child's behavior. See chapters 9 and 11 for more information about Bandura's social cognitive theory.

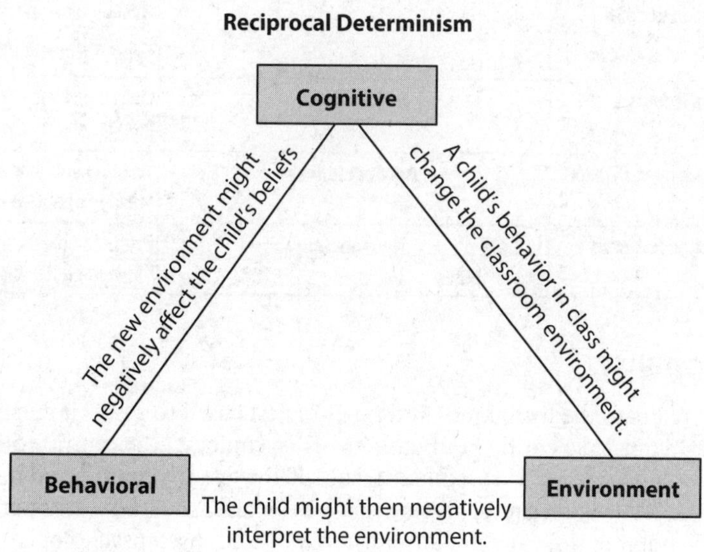


## Trait Theories of Personality

The **trait theories** of personality suggest that there are habitual patterns of behavior, thought, motive, and emotion that are consistent with personality characteristics. The main assumptions of trait theory rest on the idea that traits are stable and enduring over time, and therefore, reliable.

Although it is impossible to assess and classify the traits of distinct personality types, by using the statistical method of **factor analysis** it is possible to identify clusters of items that identify certain behaviors that correlate to basic traits (e.g., extraversion and introversion).

### *Five-Factor Model of Traits*

Modern-day psychologists Paul Costa and Robert McCrae developed and expanded trait factors related to personality, called the *five-factor model* of traits (1985). The five traits are openness, conscientiousness, extraversion, agreeableness, and neuroticism. Each of the traits is measured on a continuum from the lowest to the most extreme.

**TEST TIP: On the AP PSYCH exam, remember the acronym OCEAN to remind you of the five-factor model of traits: o̲penness, c̲onscientiousness, e̲xtraversion, a̲greeableness, and n̲euroticism.**

**Five-Factor Model of Traits**

0% ⟷ 100%

| Low Score | Trait | High Score |
|---|---|---|
| Prefers routine. Does not enjoy change, new experiences, or new ideas. | **Openness** | Curious. Wants to try new experiences and ideas. Looks at problems as opportunities. |
| Can be impulsive and careless. Does not like to have deadlines, rules, or structure. Does not finish tasks or pay attention to details.<br>**Type B Personality** | **Conscientiousness** | Hardworking, dependable, and thinks of future consequences. Plans ahead and finishes task on time.<br>**Type A Personality** |
| Can be quiet and withdrawn. Does not usually start a conversation. | **Extraversion** | Outgoing. Enjoys being social, seeks new friends, and enjoys small talk. |
| Critical of others and does not often think of the well-being of others. | **Agreeableness** | Trusting and empathetic. Thinks about the feelings of others and their well-being. |
| Even-tempered. Does not often feel sad, depressed, or worried. | **Neuroticism** | Prone to anxiety and worry. Often thinks of the worst outcome and can easily be upset. |

## Measuring Personality

Measuring personality refers to the techniques and types of tests used to assess a person's personality. As discussed in Chapter 4, "Unit 1: Scientific Foundations of Psychology," the central role of personality testing is for the test to be *reliable* (provides similar results if the test is administered multiple times) and *valid* (measures what it says it will measure). Tests are used to measure aspects of a person's psychological functioning at a specific point in time and are administered by a licensed psychologist.

Tests are used to diagnose psychological problems, establish risk assessments in court cases, screen employment candidates, and better understand human behavior in research studies. The most common types of personality tests include clinical interviews, surveys, and self-report personality inventories.

**Projective tests** are interpretative tests that help psychologists illuminate personality characteristics. The **Rorschach inkblot test,** developed by Hermann Rorschach in 1921, is the most commonly used projective test. Another commonly used projective test is the **thematic apperception test (TAT),** which reveals internal conflicts, motives, and drives. Some psychologists have argued projective tests are invalid and the results are merely subjective opinions of the psychologist.

Self-report personality tests are **objective tests** and have higher reliability and validity than projective tests. The questions are close-ended questions (e.g., true-false or multiple choice). The most commonly used objective test is the **Minnesota Multiphasic Personality Inventory (MMPI),** which contains hundreds of true-false questions that are similar, but worded differently. The MMPI is a predictive test because it is very good at identifying traits that correlate strongly with certain diseases and maladaptive behaviors.

# Chapter Review Practice Questions

Practice questions are for instructional purposes only and may not reflect the format of the actual exam. The questions and explanations that follow focus on essential knowledge, course skills, and course content.

## Multiple-Choice Questions

1. Which of the following concepts is related to a fight-or-flight reaction?

   **A.** Drive theory
   **B.** Resistance stage
   **C.** Exhaustion stage
   **D.** Sympathetic reaction
   **E.** Parasympathetic reaction

2. Brendon feels like he is starving because he hasn't eaten all day. Which of the following hormones is closely related to Brendon's feeling of hunger?

   **A.** Ghrelin
   **B.** Leptin
   **C.** Norepinephrine
   **D.** Androgen
   **E.** Cortisol

3. Which of the following refers to the stage after the peak of sexual pleasure?

   **A.** Arousal
   **B.** Set point
   **C.** Resolution
   **D.** Plateau
   **E.** Sublimation

4. Which of the following research psychologists believed that human beings are naturally motivated to improve?

   **A.** Albert Bandura
   **B.** Abraham Maslow
   **C.** Alfred Adler
   **D.** Harry Harlow
   **E.** B. F. Skinner

5. Which of the following concepts suggests that stress follows a predictable response and is divided into three stages?

   **A.** General adaptive syndrome theory
   **B.** Hedonic theory
   **C.** Humanistic theory
   **D.** Arousal theory
   **E.** Instinct theory

6. Which of the following psychological defense mechanisms best describes a 13-year-old student who throws a tantrum because she feels like it's unfair that she has too much homework?

   **A.** Reaction formation
   **B.** Repression
   **C.** Regression
   **D.** Extraversion
   **E.** Pleasure principle

7. John is a very good athlete, but dislikes competition because he dreads the possibility of losing the game. Which of the following personality traits would cause John to be reluctant to compete because of fear of losing?

   **A.** Neuroticism
   **B.** Conscientiousness
   **C.** Openness
   **D.** Agreeableness
   **E.** Empathy

## Free-Response Question

**1 question**

**25 minutes**

**Directions:** It is suggested that you take a few minutes to plan and outline your essay. Write your response on lined paper. You must demonstrate your understanding of course skills and course content. Your essay is considered a first draft and may contain some grammatical errors that will not be counted against you. However, to receive full credit, your essay must demonstrate defensible content knowledge with substantive examples where appropriate.

Katy doesn't believe her AP Psychology teacher, Mr. Collins, when he says that completing an assignment with no pressure, over a long period of time, is a good motivational strategy. Katy believes that she is more motivated when she feels the stress and pressure of completing an assignment at the last minute. Katy wants to prove her point and starts keeping track of her grades by recording when she rushes at the last minute to complete assignments vs. taking her time to complete assignments. After entering the data in a frequency distribution table, Katy created a bar graph to illustrate that students are more motivated to work under highly stressful conditions, rather than in conditions with little or no pressure.

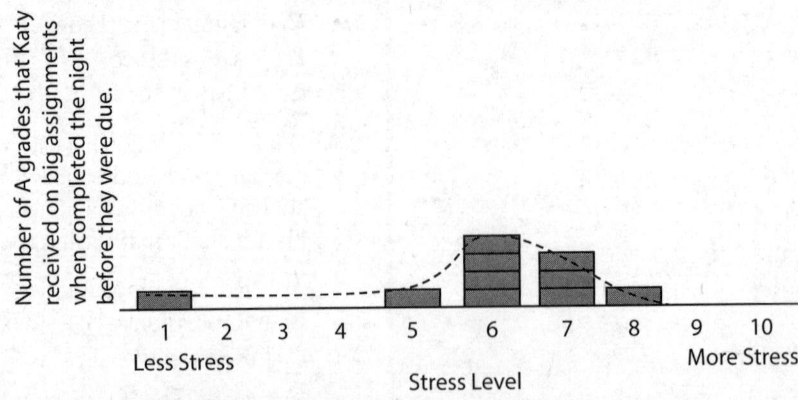

**Part A**

Identify each of the following in this study.

- Skew
- Representative sample
- Confounding variable

**Part B**

- Explain how the concept of arousal theory applies to this study.
- Explain how the concept of push factors applies to this study.
- Explain how the Schachter-Singer theory applies to this study.
- Explain how the Yerkes-Dodson law applies to this study.

# Answers and Explanations

## Multiple-Choice Questions

1. **D.** *Sympathetic reactions,* choice D, involve the body's response to stress. The brain's limbic system responds to fight-or-flight in the sympathetic nervous system (e.g., blood pressure increases, respiratory rate increases, and the digestive system shuts down). *Drive theory* (choice A) explains that when a person is hungry or thirsty, the person feels driven to eat or drink. The *resistance stage* (choice B) is phase 2 of Hans Selye's general adaptation syndrome. This three-stage theory explains how the body manages stress over time; the body can only resist stress for a short time until health problems result. The *exhaustion stage* (choice C) is the third phase of the general adaptation syndrome. The *parasympathetic reaction* (choice E) is the relaxation response to fight-or-flight when the danger has ended.

2. **A.** *Ghrelin,* choice A, is involved in hunger and sends signals to the brain, "I am hungry." *Leptin* (choice B) is involved in decreasing the appetite. *Norepinephrine* (choice C) is the neurotransmitter equivalent of the hormone epinephrine; it does not increase appetite. *Androgen* (choice D) is any natural or synthetic steroid hormone that regulates male characteristics. *Cortisol* ( choice E) is a hormone that is involved in helping the body react to stress.

3. **C.** *Resolution,* choice C, is the sexual response stage where the body recovers from the intense burst of pleasure known as orgasm. *Arousal* (choice A) is the first stage in the sexual response cycle where the body reacts to stimulation. *Set point* (choice B) is connected to a person's weight or body mass index. It is the idea that a person's BMI (body mass index) to weight is genetically predetermined. *Plateau* (choice D) is the stage of the sexual response cycle where the body is experiencing increasing pleasure. *Sublimation* (choice E) is a defense mechanism where the unconscious protects the consciousness from desires that are not socially acceptable.

4. **B.** *Abraham Maslow,* choice B, is known for his pyramid of needs (hierarchy of needs) and motivation of self-actualization. *Albert Bandura* (choice A) is known for his work with observational learning and the importance of environmental influences in personality formation. *Alfred Adler* (choice C) is known for his work with superiority and inferiority complexes. *Harry Harlow* (choice D) is known for his observations of baby monkeys and illustrated the critical need for early mother-infant bonding. *B. F. Skinner* (choice E) is known for operant conditioning, which focuses on behaviors, not motivations.

5. **A.** The *general adaptive syndrome theory,* choice A, explains the body's adaptive response to stress in three stages: alarm response, resistance, and exhaustion. *Hedonic theory* (choice B) suggests humans

are motivated by pleasure and rewards. *Humanistic theory* (choice C) is the idea that people are naturally motivated to grow and improve. *Arousal theory* (choice D) suggests that humans have an optimum level of arousal that affects motivation. The *instinct theory* of motivation (choice E) suggests that humans have innate biological tendencies to survive.

6. **C.** *Regression,* choice C, is a defense mechanism that explains when a person unconsciously reverts back to a younger developmental stage. This 13-year-old student is throwing a tantrum similar to that of a 3-year-old who is free from long-term consequences and responsibilities. *Reaction formation* (choice A) is a defense mechanism that explains when a person expresses a feeling or behavior that is opposite their real feelings. *Repression* (choice B) is a defense mechanism that explains the involuntary suppression of memories or thoughts. *Extraversion* (choice D) is a personality trait developed by Carl Jung where a person is described as being outgoing and social. The *pleasure principle* (choice E) is what defines and guides Freud's personality stage of the id.
7. **A.** All of the choices are part of the five-factor model of personality traits described by Paul Costa and Robert McCrae. All of the traits lie on a spectrum from low to high. On the high end of the spectrum, *neuroticism,* choice A, describes a person who worries frequently, imagines the worst outcomes, and becomes easily upset. *Conscientiousness* (choice B) describes a person who is organized, diligent, and methodical. *Openness* (choice C) is related to creativity and a willingness to try new things. *Agreeableness* (choice D) describes a person who exhibits kindness and humility. *Empathy* (choice E) is incorrect because John is described as having a fear of losing, not as having a fear of hurting other people.

## Free-Response Question

To achieve the maximum score of 7, your response must address each of the bullet points in the question.

### Sample Student Response

A *skewed* distribution is not a symmetrical bell curve and occurs when one extreme score affects the mean, but not the median and mode. In this scenario, most of Katy's A grades were received when she was highly stressed, but there is one A grade that she received when she took her time to complete the assignment. For that reason, the one data point (which is far below the other scores) caused the distribution to become negatively skewed (left). *Representative sample* refers to the idea that each person in a larger population has an equal chance of being included in the study. Since Katy only included herself, her sample of one is not representative of the whole high school. A *confounding variable* is anything the author did not think of, or control for, that might affect the dependent variable or results. There are many possible confounding variables in this study. One of them is experimenter bias because Katy is personally motivated to prove her hypothesis.

The *arousal theory* suggests that people need a certain level of emotional stimulation to be motivated. In this scenario, Katy might find with a low level of arousal that she is unpleasantly bored. To avoid boredom, Katy decided to take on additional work to prove her teacher wrong. *Push factors* are types of motivations that come from internal motivations, such as hunger or pride. Katy might be responding to a push motivation either to prove her point or to prove the teacher's theory wrong. The *Schachter-Singer theory* suggests that physical response to stress must be interpreted. In this scenario, Katy might think that a racing heart and butterflies in the stomach are exciting, thus allowing her to do well on assignments. The *Yerkes-Dodson law* suggests that when people experience high or low levels of arousal, they are not able to perform well on cognitive tasks. Katy's graph shows that she performs best when her stress level is only slightly elevated.

Chapter 11

# Unit 8: Clinical Psychology

AP Psychology Unit 8 explains the history, theories, and treatments of psychological disorders.

- Key Contributors in Clinical Psychology
- Introduction to Psychological Disorders
- Neurodevelopmental Disorders
- Neurocognitive Disorders
- Schizophrenia Spectrum and Other Psychotic Disorders
- Mood Disorders
- Anxiety Disorders
- Trauma- and Stressor-Related Disorders
- Somatic Disorders
- Feeding and Eating Disorders
- Personality Disorders
- Treatment of Psychological Disorders

## Overview of AP Psychology Unit 8

The overarching concepts for this chapter address psychological disorders, how to treat these disorders, and the utilization of specific theoretical perspectives. **The topics discussed in this unit will count toward 12–16 percent of your multiple-choice score.**

## AP Psychology Framework

Success on the exam depends on your ability to make connections to the major concepts described in the content topics of the *Course Framework for AP Psychology*. Remember that these concepts highlight the fundamental ideas that every student should take with them into the AP PSYCH exam and beyond.

Use the table below to guide you through what is covered in this unit. The information contained in this table is an abridged version of the content outlines with topic examples. Visit https://apstudent.collegeboard.org/apcourse/ap-psychology/ for the complete updated AP PSYCH course curriculum framework.

| AP Psychology—Unit 8: Clinical Psychology | |
|---|---|
| **Topic** | **Learning Target** |
| **Introduction to Psychological Disorders** | ■ Recognize the use of the most recent version of the *Diagnostic and Statistical Manual of Mental Disorders (DSM)* published by the American Psychiatric Association as the primary reference for making diagnostic judgments.<br>■ Describe contemporary and historical conceptions of what constitutes psychological disorders.<br>■ Discuss the intersection between psychology and the legal system (e.g., confidentiality and insanity defense). |
| **Psychological Perspectives and Etiology of Disorders** | ■ Evaluate the strengths and limitations of various approaches to explaining psychological disorders.<br>■ Identify the positive and negative consequences of diagnostic labels (e.g., the Rosenhan study). |
| **Neurodevelopmental and Schizophrenic Spectrum Disorders** | ■ Discuss the major diagnostic categories, including neurodevelopmental disorders, neurocognitive disorders, schizophrenia spectrum, and other psychotic disorders, and their corresponding symptoms. |
| **Bipolar, Depressive, Anxiety, and Obsessive-Compulsive and Related Disorders** | ■ Discuss the major diagnostic categories, including anxiety disorders, bipolar and related disorders, depressive disorders, obsessive-compulsive and related disorders, and their corresponding systems. |
| **Trauma- and Stressor-Related, Dissociative, and Somatic Symptoms and Related Disorders** | ■ Discuss the major diagnostic categories, including dissociative disorders, somatic symptom and related disorders, and trauma- and stressor-related disorders and their corresponding symptoms. |
| **Feeding and Eating, Substance and Addictive, and Personality Disorders** | ■ Discuss the major diagnostic categories, including feeding and eating disorders, personality disorders, and their corresponding symptoms. |
| **Introduction to Treatment of Psychological Disorders** | ■ Describe the central characteristics of psychotherapeutic intervention.<br>■ Identify the contributions of major figures in psychological treatment (e.g., Beck, Ellis, Freud, Cover Jones, Rogers, Skinner, and Wolpe). |
| **Psychological Perspectives and Treatment of Disorders** | ■ Describe the major treatment orientations used in therapy and how those orientations influence therapeutic planning (e.g., behavioral, cognitive, humanistic, psychodynamic, cognitive behavioral, and sociocultural).<br>■ Summarize effectiveness of specific treatments used to address specific problems.<br>■ Discuss how cultural and ethnic context influence choice and success of treatment (e.g., factors that lead to premature termination of treatment).<br>■ Describe prevention strategies that build resilience and promote competence. |
| **Treatment of Disorders from the Biological Perspective** | ■ Summarize the effectiveness of specific treatments used to address specific problems from a biological perspective. |
| **Evaluating Strengths, Weaknesses, and Empirical Support for Treatments of Disorders** | ■ Compare and contrast different treatment methods (e.g., individual, group, rational-emotive, psychoanalytic/psychodynamic, client-centered, cognitive, behavioral, sociocultural, biopsychosocial, and cognitive behavioral). |

## Important Terms and Concepts Checklist

This section is an overview of the important terms, concepts, language, and theories that specifically target the key topics of Unit 8. Use this list of terms as a checklist to check your personal progress. As you study the topics, place a check mark next to each and return to this list as often as necessary to refresh your understanding.

After you finish the review section, you can reinforce what you have learned by working through the practice questions at the end of the chapter. Answers and explanations provide further clarification into perspectives of psychological disorders and the treatment of psychological disorders.

| Term/Concept | Study Page | Term/Concept | Study Page | Term/Concept | Study Page |
|---|---|---|---|---|---|
| **active listening** | p. 250 | **electroconvulsive therapy (ECT)** | p. 257 | **person-centered therapy** | p. 250 |
| **Alzheimer's disease** | p. 236 | **empathy** | p. 250 | **phobia-related disorder** | p. 240 |
| **anorexia nervosa** | p. 244 | **exposure therapy** | p. 252 | **post-traumatic stress disorder (PTSD)** | pp. 242–243 |
| **anti-anxiety drugs** | p. 256 | **feeding and eating disorders** | pp. 244–245 | **psychoanalysis** | pp. 249–250 |
| **antidepressant drugs** | p. 256 | **flooding** | p. 252 | **psychodynamic** | p. 249 |
| **antipsychotic drugs** | pp. 256–257 | **free association** | p. 249 | **psychopathology** | p. 229 |
| **attention-deficit/ hyperactivity disorder (ADHD)** | p. 235 | **functional neurological disorder** | p. 244 | **psychopharmacology (drug therapy)** | pp. 232, 255–257 |
| **authenticity** | p. 250 | **generalized anxiety disorder** | p. 240 | **psychotherapy** | pp. 232, 249 |
| **autism spectrum disorder** | pp. 234–235 | **Gestalt therapy** | pp. 250–251 | **rational emotive behavior therapy** | p. 254 |
| **aversive conditioning** | p. 251 | **group therapy** | p. 248 | **Rosenhan study** | p. 232 |
| **behavioral therapy** | pp. 251–252 | **humanistic therapy** | pp. 250–251 | **schizophrenia spectrum disorder** | pp. 236–238 |
| **bipolar disorder** | pp. 238–239 | **illness anxiety disorder** | p. 244 | **sociocultural therapy** | p. 254 |
| **bulimia nervosa** | p. 244 | **insight therapies** | p. 249 | **somatic disorders** | p. 244 |
| **cognitive behavioral therapy** | p. 253 | **latent content** | p. 249 | **systematic desensitization** | p. 252 |
| **cognitive therapy** | pp. 253–254 | **lobotomy** | p. 247 | **token economy** | p. 252 |
| **congruence** | p. 250 | **manifest content** | p. 249 | **transference** | p. 250 |
| **counterconditioning** | p. 251 | **mindfulness** | p. 254 | **trauma- and stressor-related disorders** | pp. 242–243 |
| **deinstitutionalize** | p. 248 | **neurocognitive disorders (NCDs)** | pp. 235–236 | **traumatic brain injury** | p. 236 |
| **depressive disorders** | pp. 239–240 | **neurodevelopmental disorders** | pp. 234–235 | **trephining** | p. 247 |
| ***Diagnostic and Statistical Manual of Mental Disorders* (DSM)** | p. 232 | **obsessive-compulsive disorder (OCD)** | pp. 241–242 | **unconditional positive regard** | p. 250 |
| **dissociative disorders** | p. 243 | **panic disorder** | p. 240 | **virtual reality exposure therapy** | p. 252 |
| **dream analysis** | p. 249 | **personality disorder** | pp. 245–247 | | |

# Chapter Review

Many of the fascinating concepts in psychology, including normal mental health, can be difficult to define, but according to psychologist William James, "to study the abnormal is the best way of understanding the normal." This chapter addresses abnormal behavior and other psychological disorders as described by the American Psychological Association. An understanding of the characteristics of mental disorders enables psychologists to determine the best methods of treatment for their clients.

## Heads Up: What You Need to Know

For the AP PSYCH exam, ask yourself these two essential questions as you continue to work through the topics in this chapter and develop an understanding of psychological disorders: Why is psychological perspective necessary in the treatment of disorders? How are psychological disorders treated?

## Key Contributors in Clinical Psychology

On the AP PSYCH exam, you should be able to identify the major contributors in the field of clinical psychology.

| Key Contributors in Clinical Psychology | | |
|---|---|---|
| **Contributor** | **Field of Study (Theory)** | **Famous For** |
| **Aaron Beck** (1921–) | Cognitive therapy | Beck pioneered research in cognitive therapy to treat addiction, depression, and suicide. He developed a well-known, self-reporting measure for depression and anxiety called the Beck Depression Inventory (BDI). Beck encouraged clients to investigate and challenge their own negative, automatic thoughts so that clients could learn different, more positive, thinking patterns. |
| **Albert Ellis** (1913–2007) | Rational emotive behavior therapy (REBT) | Ellis was known for developing rational emotive behavior therapy. It is a directive therapy based on irrational expectations and judgments of life events that can cause emotional suffering. By confronting such expectations, the client can reevaluate life events and lead a happier life. |
| **Sigmund Freud** (1856–1939) | Psychoanalysis | Freud was famous for developing a clinical method for treating unconscious conflicts called psychoanalysis. He proposed that the conflicts between a person's unconscious desires and fears and what society deems acceptable can cause neurosis (anxiety and mental dysfunction). |

| Contributor | Field of Study (Theory) | Famous For |
|---|---|---|
| **Mary Cover Jones** (1897–1987) | Behavioral therapy | Jones was famous for her study of desensitization. She conducted the "Little Peter" experiment, where she eliminated a child's fear of a rabbit by desensitizing the boy. The boy received candy while pairing with and becoming gradually closer to the rabbit. |
| **Carl Rogers** (1902–1987) | Humanistic therapy | Rogers was known for a person-centered approach to therapy. He is considered one of the founders of the humanistic approach to treatment. His theory suggests that clients have a deep desire to grow toward self-actualization and that thoughts and external incongruent tendencies can prevent growth. Rogers' therapeutic treatment emphasizes a person-to-person relationship between the therapist and the client. |
| **B. F. Skinner** (1904–1990) | Behavioral therapy | Skinner applied operant conditioning principles to help people learn by consequences. By following an appropriate system of rewards and punishments, clients can relearn to achieve appropriate behavior. |
| **Joseph Wolpe** (1915–1997) | Behavioral therapy | Wolpe was known for his contributions to systematic desensitization techniques for phobias. He developed a hierarchy of anxiety-provoking procedures that helped clients learn relaxation techniques until clients began to associate anxiety with relaxation. |

## Introduction to Psychological Disorders

Psychological disorders are often referred to as *mental disorders,* and for much of recorded history, divergent behavior was considered unexplainable or a supernatural battle between good and evil. People who suffered from mental disorders were perceived to be possessed by evil spirits. The contemporary conception of mental disorders began to take form in the mid-20th century when the scientific study of mental, emotional, and behavioral disorders became known as the study of *psychopathology*. A movement toward deinstitutionalizing psychiatric patients and rethinking approaches transformed the diagnosis and treatment of psychological disorders.

**What is normal psychological health?** Let's begin by examining what is considered normal psychological health in contemporary psychology. Psychological health refers to your overall mental well-being and lies on a spectrum from mild (optimal) to severe (maladaptive) mental health. The bell-shaped graph on the next page illustrates that most people fall within the "normal" range of mental, emotional, and behavioral health. It is statistically rare to experience abnormal psychological health.

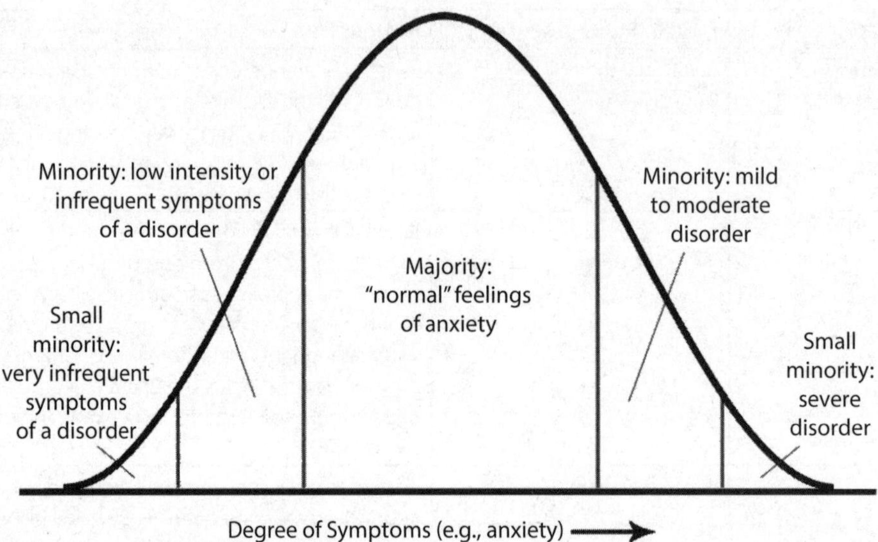


**What is abnormal psychological health?** Abnormal psychological health is defined as deviating from what is expected and typical. It is a psychological disorder that presents with chronic patterns of dysfunctional thoughts, emotions, and behaviors. Consider the following questions to determine the criteria for abnormal behavior.

1. **Is the behavior a statistical abnormality?** For example, the behavior is judged statistically strange among a particular population.
2. **Is the behavior deviating from what is typical within social or cultural norms?** For example, a woman who takes off her swimming top at a public pool is considered abnormal in the United States, but women in many other countries swim topless.
3. **Is the behavior causing ongoing personal distress?** For example, exhibiting extreme anxiety, depression, unusual despair, or losing touch with reality. It is normal to not like to see spiders around the house, but if you become obsessed with locating spiders in your home, or if you believe that spiders are "hunting" for you and it is causing extreme discomfort at home (e.g., interferes with sleeping, eating, or socializing), then it is causing ongoing personal distress.
4. **Is the behavior maladaptive (impairing daily functioning in life's tasks)?** For example, checking to make sure that you locked your car is adaptable behavior, but checking to make sure you locked the car 25 times is maladaptive behavior if it preoccupies your thoughts.
5. **Is the person a danger to self or others?** For example, acting in dangerous ways that are life threatening, like sitting on a subway platform dangling your feet over the edge.

Abnormal behavior should not be confused with unusual behavior. Just because a person's behavior is unusual does not mean it is abnormal. The ramifications of being labeled as "abnormal," "crazy," or "psycho" can unnecessarily cause people to be marginalized by society, rather than be accepted for their differences. Psychiatrist Thomas Szasz suggested that what is categorized as mental illness may simply be a different way of living.

**Legal definition of insanity.** While the discipline of psychology may sometimes have difficulties drawing a line between optimal health and mental illness, the legal profession makes a clear distinction between sanity and insanity. The legal definition of insanity is "mental illness of such a severe nature that a person cannot distinguish fantasy from reality, cannot conduct his/her affairs due to psychosis, or is subject to uncontrollable impulsive behavior." Insanity is a term used in court to distinguish guilt from innocence. It is a term that serves the legal community, not the psychology community.

**Did you know?** Someone who is an intellectual genius or an Olympic gold medal winner is considered "abnormal" (deviating from what is normal) because only about 2 percent of the population rank in these categories on a normal bell-shaped curve. In psychology, however, "abnormal" takes on a negative connotation and focuses on populations who are inadequately functioning and not psychologically thriving.

## Spectrum of Psychological Health

Although this section is called "Introduction to Psychological Disorders," a person's mental health is not determined by one single disorder; there are progressive indicators presented as *symptoms.* Note: Psychological health is not categorized as three distinct sectors, as depicted in the table that follows; rather, imagine a person's mental health on a continuum of observable criteria (e.g., symptoms) linking conditions that affect emotions, feelings, thinking, and behaviors.

**Spectrum of Psychological Health**

Maladaptive Mental Health → Normal Mental Health → Optimal Mental Health

| Maladaptive | Normal | Optimal |
|---|---|---|
| Poor judgment or thinking<br><br>Inability to have meaningful relationships<br><br>Mood fluctuations (e.g., depressed, easily agitated, defiant)<br><br>Unable to work or go to school<br><br>Inappropriate or illogical behavior<br><br>Impairment in reality testing<br><br>Frequently incoherent; behavior influenced by delusions or hallucinations<br><br>Danger of harm to self or others | Generally satisfied with life<br><br>Good daily functioning in social, occupational, or school setting, but occasionally has issues (e.g., temporarily falling behind at school)<br><br>Ability to maintain meaningful interpersonal relationships<br><br>Has mild symptoms (e.g., depressed mood or insomnia)<br><br>If symptoms are present, they are temporary due to psychosocial stressors (e.g., argument with a family member or friend). | Good functioning in all areas of life (e.g., emotional, relational, social, occupational, and school)<br><br>Life's problems never seem to get out of control, no more than everyday problems or concerns.<br><br>Interested and involved in a wide range of activities<br><br>Minimal symptoms (e.g., anxiety before giving a speech) |

**Source:** DSM-5, "The Global Assessment of Functioning" (GAF)

## Diagnostic Reference Guide for Classifying Disorders

The ***Diagnostic and Statistical Manual of Mental Disorders*** **(DSM)** is the standard reference used by psychology and psychiatry professionals to classify a wide range of mental disorders. It is the encyclopedia of mental disorders. The first diagnostic manual was published in 1952, with only 60 categories based on theories of psychopathology. Since that time, many different classification systems have been added, deleted, revised, or renamed, and the DSM-5 now contains nearly 300 categories.

Note: The criteria for diagnosing mental disorders are categorized in the DSM-5, but keep in mind that only trained and licensed professionals can diagnose mental disorders. Even with professional training, psychologists must spend time with their clients before they give a diagnosis. The *Goldwater Rule* is an ethical guideline that states psychologists should not diagnose a person without a therapeutic relationship and consent. On the AP PSYCH exam, you will not be expected to conduct a psychological assessment, but you are expected to be familiar with some of the categories of psychological disorders. The next section will introduce the categories that you may encounter on the exam.

### Heads Up: What You Need to Know

On the AP PSYCH exam, you should be familiar with the drawbacks associated with labeling mental disorders. Although the DSM-5 is a valid and comprehensive tool for understanding and diagnosing psychological disorders, an experiment was conducted to determine the validity of psychiatric diagnosis. In 1975, David Rosenhan conducted a study "on being sane in insane places" called the **Rosenhan study** (also called the Thud experiment). Rosenhan asked participants to fake (called *feign*) symptoms of psychosis in order to enter a psychiatric hospital. Once admitted to the psychiatric hospital, participants were told to tell the staff that their "voices" had disappeared and that they wanted to be discharged, but it took 7 to 52 days before the participants were released. When they were released, they had a diagnosis of schizophrenia in their medical records. Rosenhan concluded that it is easy to be misdiagnosed as mentally ill, but it is even more difficult to detach from diagnostic labels. Rosenhan determined that psychiatric labels have a negative impact on a person's future mental state.

## Psychological Perspectives of Mental Disorders

As you might remember from Chapter 4, "Unit 1: Scientific Foundations of Psychology," there are different approaches used to understand mental disorders such as psychoanalytic, humanistic, cognitive, behavioral, sociocultural, and biological. These approaches help to form the basis of therapeutic treatments. We will discuss many approaches to treat mental disorders later in this chapter, but for now it might be helpful to divide treatments into two main categories: psychotherapy and biologically based treatments. **Psychotherapy** treatment is primarily based on talk therapy, and **biologically based** treatment is primarily based on drug therapy (also known as *psychopharmacology*).

Few psychologists attribute their perspective to only one approach. An integrative approach that includes psychological, biological, and sociocultural influences is the preferred model in the treatment of mental disorders. When psychologists integrate multiple approaches to explain and treat disorders, it is called *eclectic psychology*. Below is a basic description of six major perspectives of mental disorders that appear on the AP PSYCH exam.

| Approaches to Explain Psychological Disorders | | |
|---|---|---|
| **Perspective** | **Cause of the Mental Disorder** | **Treatment** |
| **Psychoanalytic approach** | Suggests that psychological disorders are caused by unconscious mental conflicts. The psychoanalytic approach was the leading approach for the first half of the 20th century. | Psychoanalytic therapy |
| **Humanistic approach** | Suggests that mental disorders are the result of the person's failure to fully accept and understand oneself. | Person-centered therapy that offers unconditional positive regard |
| **Behavioral approach** | Suggests that mental disorders are the result of maladaptive reinforcement, punishment, and the environment. | Behavioral therapies (e.g., counterconditioning, dialectical behavior therapy, exposure therapy, flooding, systematic desensitization, aversion therapy, behavior modification, and token economies) |
| **Cognitive approach** | Suggests that mental disorders are caused by irrational thinking. | Cognitive behavioral therapy (e.g., modeling, cognitive distortions, homework, cognitive rehearsal, and journaling thoughts) |
| **Sociocultural approach** | Suggests that mental disorders are caused by the dysfunction of society. | Family systems therapy or group therapy |
| **Biological approach** | Suggests that mental disorders are caused by biochemical imbalances, genetic predispositions, and abnormalities in the nervous system. | Biomedical drug therapy |

## Major Diagnostic Categories

Mental health practitioners use the DSM-5 as a tool to diagnose clients. It is based on a medical model of mental disorders and is similar to how physicians use a desk reference guide for medical illnesses. The DSM-5 is an organized system of diagnostic criteria that highlights *clusters of related symptoms*. It does not focus on the causes of symptoms (called *etiology*) or treatment plans. The symptoms of mental disorders can be complex, and some clients present with more than one disorder, called *comorbidity*.

## Heads Up: What You Need to Know

The AP PSYCH exam frequently addresses the major diagnostic categories of psychological disorders. Descriptions of each category are described in this section.

- Neurodevelopmental disorders
- Neurocognitive disorders
- Psychotic disorders
- Bipolar and related disorders
- Depressive disorders
- Anxiety disorders
- Obsessive-compulsive and related disorders
- Trauma- and stressor-related disorders
- Dissociative disorders
- Somatic disorders
- Feeding and eating disorders

Note: The DSM-5 is a comprehensive tool for licensed professionals only. For that reason, this section focuses on an overview of material covered in an introductory psychology course, including a summary of treatment methods that address specific disorders.

# Neurodevelopmental Disorders

**Neurodevelopmental disorders** are infant, childhood, and adolescent disorders that can affect intellectual development, other forms of development, and delayed communication. For the AP PSYCH exam, you should be able to identify two neurodevelopmental disorders.

## Autism Spectrum Disorder

**Autism spectrum disorder (ASD)** is an umbrella for developmental disorders, with symptoms usually starting at birth to 2 years old. The symptoms may limit or impair daily functioning. Note: ASD is classified by the range of severity and a wide variation in the type of symptoms.

### Key Facts about the Symptoms of Autism Spectrum Disorder

**Communication and social-emotional deficits.** Exhibits patterns of difficulty with communication that is reciprocal. Has difficulty in developing and maintaining relationships, and has reduced social and emotional "connectedness" with others. For example, may not look at or listen to people.

**Restricted or repetitive behaviors.** Exhibits patterns of behavior such as repetitive speech or motor movements, ritualized behavior, or fixated interests, or may be sensitive to sensory input (e.g., sounds, sights, and textures).

**Daily functioning deficits.** Exhibits difficulty in functioning properly in school and other areas of life.

### Treatment of Autism Spectrum Disorder

Treatment for ASD should begin as soon as possible after diagnosis. Therapies have differing results that depend on the level of functioning and the goal of the therapy. Even though symptoms can last a lifetime, treatment can greatly improve daily functioning. Some treatments include behavioral therapy to learn skills, psychological therapy to reduce challenging behaviors, and educational therapy to learn communication and language skills.

## Attention-Deficit/Hyperactivity Disorder

**Attention-deficit/hyperactivity disorder (ADHD)** is a brain disorder in which the person is described as having an ongoing pattern of inattention and/or hyperactivity/impulsivity that interferes with daily functioning or development. It is the most common neurodevelopmental disorder and has a varying number of symptoms and degrees.

### Key Facts about the Symptoms of Attention-Deficit/Hyperactivity Disorder

**Inattention.** Exhibits significant inattention across many areas with no signs of hyperactivity or impulsivity. For example, does not seem to listen, has trouble holding attention, loses focus, has trouble organizing tasks, or loses things. Note: Used to be called attention deficit disorder (ADD).

**Hyperactivity/impulsivity.** Exhibits adequate attention and control, but has significant difficulties with activity-level and impulse control. For example, restlessness, fidgets/squirms, unable to remain quiet, has trouble waiting his or her turn, interrupts, or talks excessively.

**Combination.** Exhibits a combination of inattentiveness and hyperactivity. This is the most common form of ADHD.

### Treatment of Attention-Deficit/Hyperactivity Disorder

If you think of behavioral and cognitive characteristics that make it difficult for a student to succeed, those traits would probably be included in the list of ADHD symptoms (e.g., being distracted, impulsive, forgetful, and unable to think about the consequences of an action). School is structured in a way that causes many students with attention issues to struggle with schoolwork.

Medication (e.g., stimulants) and behavioral/cognitive therapies are effective in treating ADHD. It might seem odd to prescribe stimulants for symptoms of ADHD because the person already has excessive energy, but the part of the brain that organizes attention is actually inhibited, so the stimulant will help to unblock this part of the brain. Research shows that behavioral and cognitive therapies help the person learn to strengthen positive behaviors, provide skills and strategies, and manage symptoms of ADHD. In school and at home, teachers and parents can help by making changes to the environment. For example, classrooms and home environments can be adjusted to prevent distractions.

## Neurocognitive Disorders

**Neurocognitive disorder (NCD)** is a general term that explains decreased mental function due to a medical condition. Disorders can be major (significant cognitive decline that impacts a person's independence) or minor (mild cognitive decline that does not impact a person's independence). NCDs are a decline in brain function. It is not a psychological illness, and it is not a developmental disorder; rather, it represents a person's declining mental abilities due to a medical condition. It is sometimes incorrectly referred to as *dementia* (a degenerative disorder that impairs thinking, remembering, and reasoning in the elderly).

Neurocognitive disorders can result from delirium, Alzheimer's disease, vascular disease, traumatic brain injury, Lewy body dementia, and several others. **Alzheimer's disease** and **traumatic brain injury** are the neurocognitive disorders that may appear on the AP PSYCH exam.

### Key Facts about the Symptoms of Neurocognitive Disorders

**Alzheimer's disease.** Symptoms can begin as early as mid-adulthood. The symptoms begin with a gradual decline of cognitive functioning, but can go far beyond memory loss. Other symptoms include a decline in judgment, learning, or language; shortened attention span; difficulty coping with new situations; and mood swings. As the disease progresses, the sufferer loses nearly every cognitive ability.

**Traumatic brain injury.** At the onset of the injury, the person can lose consciousness, be confused or disoriented, or have amnesia. In the weeks and months following the injury, the symptoms can influence learning, memory, perceptual-motor skills, executive function, attention, and social cognition.

### Treatment of Neurocognitive Disorders

Treatment for NCDs varies, depending on the underlying cause. While researchers are working to find a cure for Alzheimer's disease, currently there are no medications to reverse or even stop the degeneration of the brain and related cognitive impairments. Treatments for traumatic brain injury include medication therapy, occupational therapy, physical therapy, and behavioral therapy. The damaged neural tissue might not repair itself, but because of plasticity, other neural tissue can reach out and relearn the tasks in the damaged areas of the brain.

## Schizophrenia Spectrum and Other Psychotic Disorders

**Schizophrenia** is translated as "split mind," but it is important to know that it has nothing to do with dissociative identity disorder, which is often called a split personality. According to the APA, psychotic disorders are fairly uncommon (affecting 1 percent of the population), but people who experience psychosis can experience lifelong struggles because it is the most severe of the psychological disorders. It develops gradually in late adolescence to early adulthood.

On the AP PSYCH exam, you should be familiar with schizophrenia because it's the most severe of the spectrum disorders, but for your reference, some of the classifications within schizophrenia spectrum disorders include delusional disorder, brief psychotic disorder, schizophreniform disorder, schizophrenia, schizoaffective disorder, substance/medication-induced psychotic disorder, and psychotic disorder due to another medical condition and catatonia.

### Key Facts about the Symptoms of Schizophrenia Spectrum Disorder

Like any disorder, the symptoms may develop gradually, making it difficult to identify at the onset of the disorder. This reminds us that a person should never be defined by his or her symptoms. People who suffer from schizophrenia can be symptom-free for a long time. However, schizophrenia typically begins with irrational thinking.

Schizophrenia has both positive and negative symptoms. **Positive symptoms** include *hallucinations* and *delusions*. A common positive symptom is a thought disorder that presents as irrational, bizarre, nonsensical, or distorted thinking that appears as disorganized speech or language. Sometimes the person might make up words, called *neologisms*, or might rhyme words together, called *clang associations*. It is important to note that a positive symptom is not necessarily good or pleasant; it is the addition of something that shouldn't exist. **Negative symptoms** are lack of social interests, lack of motivation, flat affect, poor speech, loss of energy, and lack of pleasure. Negative symptoms can distort internal emotional states.

Two physical symptoms are catatonia and waxy flexibility. *Catatonia* is a motor problem when the person may remain in the same, fixed position for hours, disconnected from the rest of the world. *Waxy flexibility* refers to the way a person will move into a position and remain in that position for an extended period of time.

**TEST TIP: On the AP PSYCH exam, you should be familiar with the terms "hallucinations" and "delusions." *Hallucinations* can be hearing or seeing things that are not real, but can also be tasting, smelling, or feeling things that are not real. For example, a tactile (feeling) hallucination means that the person may "feel" a severe burning or itching bodily sensation causing the person to feel like he/she is "coming out of his/her skin," but the person has no medical explanation for the feeling. *Delusions* are false beliefs that are not based in reality. For example, a delusion of paranoia or persecution means the person thinks "they are out to get me." The term "they" commonly refers to a large organization, government agency, or supernatural entity. Another form of delusion is a *delusion of grandeur*. The person with schizophrenia believes that he or she is someone important, famous, a historical person, or chosen by a higher power.**

On the AP PSYCH exam, you should know the difference between schizophrenia and dissociative identity disorder (dissociative identity disorder is described on p. 243). Both are serious and chronic mental health disorders, but only affect 1–2 percent of the population. Many people have trouble distinguishing between the two disorders. Schizophrenia often presents with hallucinations and/or delusions and the sufferer has trouble with reality testing.

**Compare and Contrast Schizophrenia and Dissociative Identity Disorder**

| Schizophrenia | Dissociative Identity Disorder |
|---|---|
| Schizophrenia is a psychotic disorder that frequently presents with symptoms of hallucinations and/or delusions. | Dissociative identity disorder is *not* a psychotic disorder. |
| Evidence suggests that schizophrenia is a neurobiological abnormality and may have a genetic inheritance component. | Evidence suggests that dissociative identity disorder may be caused by extreme traumatic experiences in early childhood. |
| The person has a loss of contact with reality, or "splits from reality." | The person has a loss of contact with the core self, and the person *does not* split from reality. The person has periods of amnesia. |
| The goal of treatment is to acknowledge that the voices are not real and are "outside" of the self. | The goal of treatment is to integrate the real personalities (voices) "within" the self. |
| Antipsychotic medication is the first line of treatment. | Treatment *does not* include antipsychotic medication. |

## Treatment of Schizophrenia Spectrum Disorder

Treatment of schizophrenia should begin as soon as possible after diagnosis to manage the psychotic symptoms. Medications, such as antipsychotic drugs, help to treat hallucinations, delusions, and disordered thinking. Even though symptoms can last a lifetime, treatment can greatly improve daily functioning.

Psychotherapy, and psychosocial and psychoeducational therapies in conjunction with supportive services, help the person recognize the illness, set goals, reduce stress, and manage daily problems. Family therapy can also help family members deal more effectively with their loved one. Once the symptoms are managed, cognitive behavioral therapy is an effective treatment for assisting clients to change attitudes about the illness and comply with medications.

**Did you know?** The **dopamine hypothesis** is a model that suggests symptoms of schizophrenia (like psychotic behavior) are associated with excessive dopamine signaling—back-and-forth activity between neurons. This means that neurochemical imbalances in the brain help to explain the reasons for psychotic behavior. Treatment for schizophrenia frequently involves prescribing antipsychotic medications (dopamine antagonists that help to lower the dopamine levels) to decrease the symptoms. As an example, think of running down a hill. If you run too fast, you will probably have difficulty stopping yourself (like the excessive dopamine activity). Antipsychotic medications help to slow down the brain enough to get its feet under it so that the brain becomes more balanced.

## Bipolar and Related Disorders

**Bipolar and related disorders** are brain disorders that can have lifelong symptoms including dramatic mood and energy swings in a person, sometimes alternating between extremes of excessive euphoria and depression. The idea of having flexible moods is often good, but when a person has extreme moods, it can disrupt daily functioning.

There are three main types of bipolar and related disorders: bipolar I, bipolar, II and cyclothymic. For the purpose of the AP PSYCH exam, we will focus on bipolar I disorder.

### Key Facts about the Symptoms of Bipolar I Disorder

**Bipolar I disorder** is sometimes called a "manic-depressive disorder" because mood swings can fluctuate between increased energy to depressed mood. The symptoms include mania, hypomania, and depression.

Mania and hypomania have similar symptoms, except that *mania* is much more intense and can interfere with social, work, and school functioning. Mania can also trigger an episode of *psychosis* (a break from reality). *Hypomania* is a mild form of mania and does not usually interfere with daily functioning. *Depression* has many of the symptoms described in the "Depressive Disorders" section (e.g., sadness, loss of interest, and fatigue).

A person with bipolar I sometimes starts off with a pleasant energy boost and sense of optimism, but as time progresses, normal inhibitions that keep us from reckless impulses seem to fade away. Manic and hypomanic symptoms include extreme confidence, sleeplessness, talkativeness, racing thoughts, distractibility, impulsivity, recklessness, and sometimes odd or eccentric thinking. For example, the person may go on a spending spree, binge eat, or have extreme irritability.

### Treatment of Bipolar and Related Disorders

Bipolar disorders require long-term treatment because the disorders have a high tendency to relapse. Medications like lithium carbonate have been effective in reducing extreme mood swings. The most effective treatment is a combination of medication, cognitive behavioral therapy, family therapy, and social support. Effective therapeutic interventions help the person to gain insights, learn coping strategies, and make lifestyle changes.

## Depressive Disorders

Depressive disorders broadly describe all types of depression and explain the lowering of a person's affective mood. Depression is an internalized emotional state that is usually brief, but in some cases it can last for an extended period of time. When depression lasts for a prolonged period of time it can present psychological problems leading to **major depressive disorder** (called *clinical depression*). It is so common that it is known as the "common cold of mental illness." As with many diagnoses, the symptoms follow a pattern, but vary from person to person.

### Key Facts about the Symptoms of Depressive Disorders

**Disruptive mood dysregulation disorder (DMDD)** is a childhood condition. The signs and symptoms are extreme and persistent irritability, anger, and temper outbursts that are present at least three times per week.

**Major depressive disorder (MDD)** is one of the most common mental disorders. Common symptoms can disrupt a person's daily functioning, including a depressed mood (sadness most of the day), loss of interest or pleasure, feelings of emptiness, appetite changes, insomnia or hypersomnia, reduced energy, changes in psychomotor function, fatigue, feelings of worthlessness or hopelessness, and an inability to concentrate. In extreme cases, the person has recurrent thoughts of death. It is important to note that sometimes all of us have some of these symptoms, but to be diagnosed with major depression, the person must have at least five of these symptoms for at least 2 weeks or longer.

**Persistent depressive disorder** is a type of depression where the symptoms are less intense and rarely reach the level of a crisis. However, symptoms can be persistent and last at least 2 years. Symptoms can be misinterpreted as an aspect of someone's personality rather than as part of a disorder, or symptoms can go undiagnosed because the person copes and muddles through life.

**Premenstrual dysphoric disorder** often accompanies PMS (premenstrual syndrome). It is a real medical condition that can cause disabling symptoms such mood swings, sadness, anger, appetite changes, body aches, and irritability.

### Treatment of Depressive Disorders

Treatment of depressive disorders includes cognitive behavioral therapies, psychotherapy, and drug therapy. New electroconvulsive therapies have been extremely effective in reducing the symptoms of depression.

In cognitive behavioral therapy (CBT), the therapist works to change cognitions. In depressive disorders, cognitive thoughts are trapped in a vicious circle that is self-defeating. The sufferer tends to *ruminate* (dwell on negative thoughts), which often leads to *catastrophizing* (consistently imagining the worst possible results).

Physically, the sufferer may have altered sleep patterns, altered digestive patterns, and loss of appetite. Therefore, the therapist may recommend increased exercise. Depression leads to hormonal changes and neurological changes, especially a reduction of serotonin in the synapses. Therefore, antidepressant drugs are effective to block the reuptake of serotonin into the presynaptic cell so that more of the molecules are left in the synapse.

## Anxiety Disorders

For the AP PSYCH exam, you should be able to identify four anxiety disorders: generalized anxiety, panic disorder, specific phobia-related anxiety, and agoraphobia.

**Anxiety disorders** are fairly common and are accompanied by chronic feelings of fear, worry, and nervousness without an appropriate or identifiable cause. A certain amount of anxiety is a necessary part of life and normal for optimal mental functioning. For example, it is normal to experience some anxiety if you are preparing for a test. The anxiety, while unpleasant, is a good motivator. It signals that something must be done. But what if the anxiety becomes overwhelming and continually signals a false alarm? Then it becomes an anxiety disorder.

### Key Facts about the Types and Symptoms of Anxiety Disorders

**Generalized anxiety disorder** can be described as chronic worry or nervousness about almost everything and does not have an identifiable or justifiable cause. While the anxiety might not rise to the level of panic, the sufferer has trouble relaxing and letting go of the tension.

A **panic disorder** is heightened anxiety accompanied by feelings of intense terror. It suddenly and unexpectedly escalates into a terrifying *panic attack*. The physical symptoms include a racing heart, dizziness, numbness, sweating, trembling, heart palpitations, and shortness of breath. Panic attacks cannot kill a person, but the person has a fear of dying, losing control, or going crazy. If you've ever experienced a panic attack, you were probably physically, mentally, and emotionally terrified and exhausted. The frequency and duration can vary, but most panic attacks last about 10–15 minutes and are always unpleasant. Panic attacks frequently occur in the context of another condition (e.g., post-traumatic stress, substance abuse, medical condition, or depressive disorder).

A **phobia-related disorder** is directed toward a specific object, activity, or situation. A specific phobia is a condition where irrational fear or panic can occur in response to a certain stimulus. As the graph on the next page depicts, spiders, public speaking, confined spaces, heights, or nearly anything can become the subject of a phobia. **Agoraphobia** is an anxiety that describes the fear of being in open, public, or crowded places; using public transportation; standing in line or in a crowd; or being outside of the home.

### Treatment of Anxiety Disorders

Anti-anxiety medications can help with short-term feelings of fear and panic, but for consistent results, it's important for the person to undergo cognitive behavioral therapy to learn about the cause of the anxiety and the anxiety-related behavior. Mindfulness-based therapies have been very effective in preventing the symptoms of anxiety-based disorders. Mindfulness-based therapies are cognitive-behavioral therapies that incorporate techniques like deep-breathing exercises and meditation in therapy to help the person break away from negative thoughts.

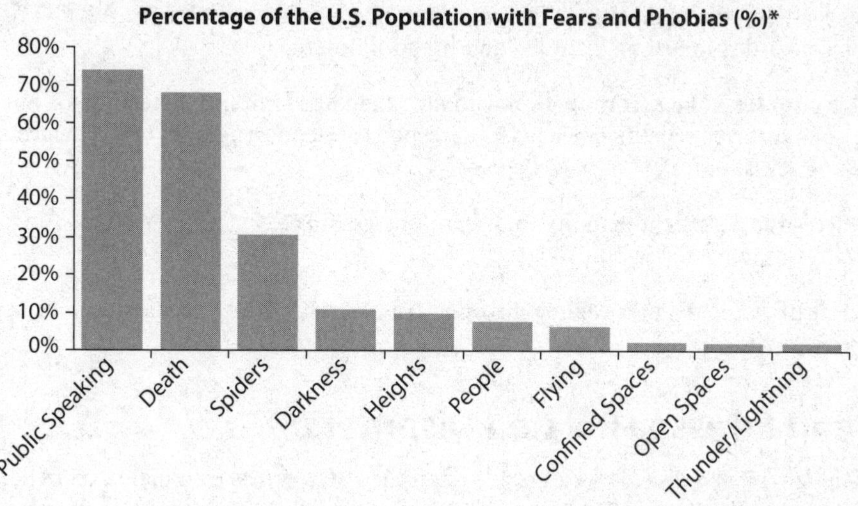


Similar to anxiety-based disorders, obsessive-compulsive disorders can be treated effectively with behavioral therapies and cognitive behavioral therapies for long-term changes, while medication can be effective for suppressing the chemical interactions within the brain that can trigger OCD and disrupt daily functioning.

## Obsessive-Compulsive and Related Disorders

**Obsessive compulsive disorder (OCD)** follows a pattern of heightened anxiety and intrusive thoughts that can affect daily living. All of us can be obsessed with certain thoughts, but the person who is experiencing OCD may have unreasonable thoughts and engage in compulsive and ritualistic behaviors in an attempt to make the thoughts go away.

Two important OCD concepts are obsession and compulsion. An *obsession* is having a nagging, almost irresistible, thought or idea. A *compulsion* is a behavior that is repetitive that the person thinks will make the thoughts go away, even if only temporarily. People frequently joke about a person with OCD behaviors, but the reality is that OCD can cause the sufferer a great deal of mental distress; it can take over a person's life, impact interpersonal relationships, and limit involvement in work and/or school.

| Symptoms of Obsessive-Compulsive and Related Disorders | |
|---|---|
| **Symptom** | **Example** |
| **Checking** | The need to unreasonably recheck things (e.g., doors, windows, or receipts). |
| **Ordering** | The need to meticulously bring order into the environment (e.g., lining up the fork, spoon, and knife in a restaurant). |
| **Cleaning** | Washing your hands once is normal; but washing your hands 10 consecutive times to avoid germs is not normal. |
| **Fearing contamination** | The fear of germs, viruses, dirty surfaces, and even contact with others (e.g., frequent body or hand washing to the point of picking at one's skin, called *excoriation*). |
| **Intrusive thinking** | The inability to stop unwanted thoughts about "what if" scenarios (e.g., a person may ruminate, "What if someone breaks into my home?"). |

The three obsessive-compulsive disorders that you should be familiar with for the AP PSYCH exam are: body dysmorphic disorder, hoarding disorder, and trichotillomania.

**Body dysmorphic disorder** is the preoccupation with an "imagined" physical defect that is not observable to others. The person performs repetitive behaviors in response to concerns (e.g., excessive grooming, skin picking, or seeking reassurance).

**Hoarding disorder** is the persistent inability to discard possessions (e.g., overly accumulating unused, unsafe, damaged, or worn-out items or trash).

**Trichotillomania** is also called a hair-pulling disorder. It is irresistible urge to pull out hair (e.g., from the scalp and eyebrows).

## Trauma- and Stressor-Related Disorders

Trauma- and stressor-related disorders can result when the stress of the traumatic experience overwhelms the person's ability to mentally cope or process the emotions involved with the stressful experience. Complex anxiety disorders can develop after exposure to a traumatic or stressful event that the person directly experienced, indirectly experienced, or witnessed. For example, exposure to physical or emotional violence, abuse, or neglect can cause traumatic disorders. For the AP PSYCH exam, you should be able to identify two trauma- and stressor-related disorders: post-traumatic stress disorder (PTSD) and dissociative identity disorder (DID).

### Key Facts about the Types and Symptoms of Trauma- and Stressor-Related Disorders

**Adjustment disorders.** Adjustment disorders are characterized by emotional or behavioral problems in reaction to an "identifiable" stressor (e.g., school, work, divorce, move, or birth of a sibling). Symptoms include nervousness, misconduct, depressed mood, and behavioral problems. Symptoms occur within 3 months of the stressful event, but don't last for more than 6 months.

**Reactive attachment disorder (RAD).** RAD is a serious emotional attachment disorder that begins in early childhood when there is emotional neglect and limited caregiving. Children with RAD may appear to want emotional comfort, but have difficulty seeking comfort when distressed. Children with RAD often lack remorse after bad behavior or do not show a response to emotional triggers.

**Post-traumatic stress disorder (PTSD).** PTSD occurs when a person experiences or witnesses a life-threatening event. Symptoms can be *acute* (starting as early as weeks and lasting up to 3 months after the event), *chronic* (lasting longer than 3 months), or *delayed onset* (developing 6 months after the event). Symptoms include the following: intrusion of distressing memories, thoughts, flashbacks, or dreams; negative alterations in mood (e.g., fear, guilt, depression, shame) and difficulty remembering aspects of the event; avoidance of trauma-related feelings; irritable behavior or angry outbursts; hyperarousal that causes being easily startled or jumpy; and reckless self-destructive behavior.

As illustrated in the graph on the next page, PTSD is prevalent among emergency personnel and military veterans who are repeatedly exposed to traumatic events, but the greatest prevalence is among children and those abused or assaulted.

**Acute stress disorder.** Acute stress disorder is similar to PTSD, but occurs and ends within 4 weeks of the traumatic event. Symptoms last for at least 2 days but less than a month.

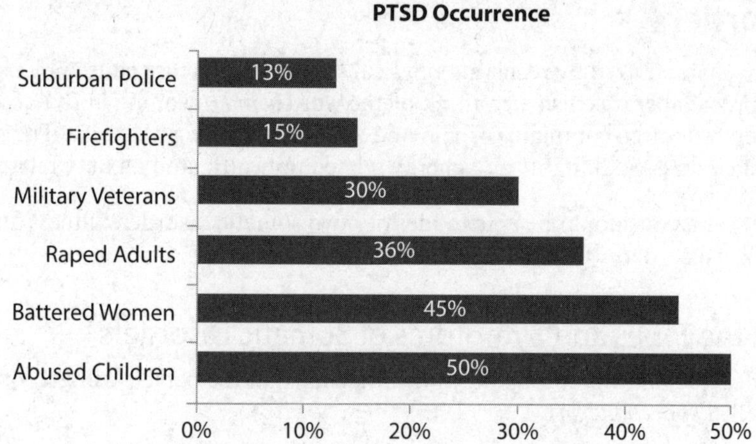


## Treatment of Trauma- and Stressor-Related Disorders

A number of treatments are effective for trauma- and stressor-related disorders, but treatment should begin with psychotherapy or cognitive behavioral therapy. The main purpose of therapy is to create a safe environment, stabilize and reduce the symptoms, and work through and integrate the memories and the emotions caused by the traumatic event.

Cognitive behavioral therapy treats both anxiety and trauma-related disorders and is effective in providing an understanding of the symptoms accompanied by the event. Research has shown that eye-movement desensitization and reprocessing (EMDR) has been effective once the therapist has established therapeutic alliance and trust with the client. Antidepressants, such as selective serotonin reuptake inhibitors (SSRIs), are effective in treating the depression caused by the traumatic event.

# Dissociative Disorders

**Dissociative disorders** are a disruption in consciousness, memory, identity, or the perception of the environment. **Dissociative identity disorder (DID),** formerly called multiple personality disorder, is a dissociative disorder. The main symptoms are as follows: the person has two or more distinct identities (personality states) that cause the person to experience a disconnection between memories, thoughts, and identity; and the person experiences amnesia. DID is as if the mind divides itself, like pieces of a pie. Personalities can be different ages, genders, or races. One part of the personality can hide certain information from the other parts of the mind, so the person has gaps in recall about everyday events, personal information, and the traumatic event that caused DID. DID occurs when one part of the mind separates from other parts in an effort to protect itself from psychological or emotional trauma. The symptoms of DID can cause significant distress or impairment in social or occupational functioning. Note: The treatment goal for dissociative identity disorder is to sufficiently integrate and cooperate alternate identities that promote optimal mental health functioning.

**Dissociative amnesia** occurs when a person cannot remember important personal information. **Dissociative amnesia with fugue** describes a person who temporarily loses his/her identity and wanders away from home. Note: Dissociative amnesia is often related to a traumatic event, but may not be limited to the traumatic or stressful event.

## Somatic Disorders

**Somatic disorders** are characterized by recurring physical symptoms that are caused by psychological distress. To help you remember this disorder, think of the word *soma* (meaning body) of a neuron discussed in Chapter 5. Sufferers will often complain of pain and the fear of having a disease. The symptoms include disruption in daily life, excessive thoughts and energy related to health, and anxiety related to health.

For the AP PSYCH exam, you should be able to identify two somatic disorders: illness anxiety and functional neurological disorder.

### Key Facts about the Types and Symptoms of Somatic Disorders

**Illness anxiety disorders** include a preoccupation with the idea that the person will get (or have) a serious illness (previously called *hypochondria*).

**Functional neurological disorder** is also called **conversion disorder.** It is when mental stress from an internal conflict turns into physical symptoms. It has its roots in Sigmund Freud's psychoanalytic theory of the unconscious. Freud's female clients complained of negative symptoms (e.g., numbness in a body part). (Remember that negative symptoms are the lack of something that a person should have, such as feeling in one hand.) Freud, who was a medical doctor, found no underlying physical cause for the symptoms. Therefore, Freud hypothesized that some physical symptoms could be associated with psychological or emotional crises. Some of the common symptoms include difficulty swallowing, difficulty hearing, paralysis, speech problems, vision problems, numbness, memory problems, fatigue, tremors, and general weakness.

### Treatment of Somatic Disorders

Symptoms can be resolved without treatment, particularly if the person is assured that the symptoms are not related to a more serious illness. However, cognitive behavioral therapy is known as the best treatment for somatic disorders to help the clients recognize that there is no biological reason for their complaints. For people who have experienced a traumatic event, psychotherapy is effective, as well as anti-anxiety medications to treat the stress or anxiety.

## Feeding and Eating Disorders

Feeding and eating disorders include avoiding, restricting, or indulging in food intake. The disorder causes clinically significant distress, impairs daily psychosocial functioning, and significantly affects physical health. For the AP PSYCH exam, you should be able to identify two feeding and eating disorders: anorexia nervosa and bulimia nervosa.

### Key Facts about the Types and Symptoms of Feeding and Eating Disorders

**Anorexia nervosa** is an intense fear of gaining weight or becoming fat. The person has a distorted view of body image that leads to extreme dieting and severe weight loss. Anorexia nervosa primarily affects adolescent girls and young women.

**Bulimia nervosa** is exhibited by recurrent episodes of *binge eating*—eating a large amount of food within a distinct period of time (e.g., a 2-hour period). To avoid weight gain, the person frequently uses diuretics, medications, laxatives, excessive exercise, fasting, or self-induced vomiting.

### Treatment of Feeding and Eating Disorders

Treating anorexia should include medical treatment, including hospitalization to ensure that the sufferer's nutritional and physiological needs are being met. Psychotherapy treatment and family therapy are recommended for help with the related emotional issues. In addition, clients should receive education regarding nutrition. Medications are often prescribed in the treatment of anorexia.

The treatment for bulimia involves a multidimensional approach. The primary concern is the stabilization of the person's physical health by a medical professional. Behavioral therapies or cognitive therapies are important to assist in lifestyle changes and family support.

## Personality Disorders

A **personality disorder** can affect how a person thinks and behaves throughout a lifetime. Personality disorders usually begin in adolescence or early adulthood. The DSM-5 classifies personality disorders into three clusters:

- Cluster A – Odd or eccentric behaviors (e.g., paranoid or schizoid).
- Cluster B – Dramatic, emotional, or erratic behaviors (e.g., borderline, narcissistic, or histrionic).
- Cluster C – Anxious or fearful behaviors (e.g., dependent, avoidant, or obsessive-compulsive).

### Key Facts about the Types and Symptoms of Personality Disorders

What if many of your behaviors, thoughts, and feelings frequently put you into conflict with others, society, and sometimes the law? Would you assume you were the problem, or someone else? Social functioning impairments are not always the result of anxiety, depression, or psychosis. Sometimes maladaptive social behavior can be the result of a personality disorder.

Personality disorders can lead to unhealthy patterns of behaving, relational problems, and emotional distress because people with personality disorders will often believe that others are the cause of their problems. Personality disorders are enduring, uncompromising patterns of behavior that affect social functioning.

The DSM-5 describes personality disorders by clusters. This section will walk you through each of the types of personality disorders that are presented in clusters based on their characteristics and symptoms. You are not required to memorize the details of these disorders for the AP PSYCH exam, but you should have a broad familiarity with personality disorders.

| Personality Disorders | |
|---|---|
| **Personality Disorder** | **Description** |
| **Cluster A: Odd or Eccentric** | |
| **Paranoid** | Paranoid personality disorder is characterized by being suspicious and mistrustful of the behavior of others. A person with paranoid personality disorder frequently questions the loyalty of peers, believes that there are hidden meanings in conversations, and is easily insulted. |
| **Schizoid** | Schizoid personality disorder is defined by a flat emotional response that is indifferent. While this shares the same prefix as schizophrenia, it is an unrelated condition. Adjectives that describe this type of personality disorder are cold, secretive, and having limited interest in social activities. |

*Continued*

| Personality Disorder | Description |
|---|---|
| **Schizotypal** | Schizotypal personality disorder manifests as social anxiety and social withdrawal. Although it has some of the similar symptoms of schizophrenia disorders (e.g., peculiar thoughts and behaviors, eccentric beliefs, suspiciousness, odd usage of words, and inappropriate dress), a person with schizotypal personality can lead a relatively normal life. A person with schizotypal personality disorder can have short-term delusions and hallucinations. Symptoms are less severe, and people with this disorder can often think rationally about their delusions, whereas someone with a schizophrenia disorder believes the delusions are real. |
| **Cluster B: Dramatic, Emotional, or Erratic** | |
| **Antisocial** | Antisocial personality disorder (formerly called *sociopathy* or *psychopathy*) is a disorder that is disturbing to most people. The person has a consistent pattern of disregard for the rights of others and lacks a conscience. There is little sense of shame or guilt and little fear of anticipated punishment. Someone with an antisocial personality may exhibit amoral behavior and disregard others' feelings before the age of 15 years old. Despite the behavior, most criminals do not fit the profile of antisocial personality. Most people who are diagnosed with antisocial personality lead normal lives and are not considered "evil." In fact, personality traits allow the person to do highly stressful jobs without emotional distractions or regret. |
| **Borderline** | Borderline personality disorder (BPD) is defined by a consistent pattern of emotional instability, instability in relationships, impulsivity, extreme fear of abandonment, and chronic feelings of emptiness. This can be mistaken for bipolar disorder, but the key with this pattern of symptoms is relationship instability. Often the person will "test" the relationship by saying things like "if you love me you would . . . " |
| **Histrionic** | Histrionic personality disorder is similar to borderline personality disorder, but people are more positive and outgoing. Self-esteem depends on the approval of others. The person with histrionic personality disorder uses social skills to get attention and has an overwhelming desire to be noticed. The person is often flirtatious and engages in sex-seeking behavior even though the goal is not to engage in sex. |
| **Narcissistic** | Narcissistic personality disorder is characterized as a preoccupation with a grandiose sense of self-importance, extreme self-love, and the belief that one is special. A person with narcissistic personality disorder usually neglects, exploits, or is envious of others. The person requires excessive admiration and often has a sense of entitlement. |
| **Cluster C: Anxious or Fearful** | |
| **Avoidant** | Avoidant personality disorder is characteristic of a person who avoids situations that might lead to disapproval, humiliation, or rejection. The person might avoid school activities for fear of rejection. The person is easily hurt by criticism and is reluctant to form close relationships. Ironically, the person has a strong desire to belong, but is socially withdrawn. |
| **Dependent** | Dependent personality disorder is characteristic of someone who has a strong need to be taken care of and has a fear of being abandoned. The person often avoids being alone and can become easily hurt by criticism or disapproval. |
| **Obsessive-compulsive personality** | Obsessive-compulsive personality disorder (OCPD) is not the same as obsessive-compulsive disorder (OCD), but there are similarities that overlap. A person with OCPD has an excessive need for perfection and a firm adherence to orderliness and a control over one's environment. The person also has a preference for details, rigid schedules, and rules. |

### Treatment of Personality Disorders

Depending on the personality disorder, the treatment of most personality disorders involves psychotherapy to reduce the symptoms associated with the disorder. Personality disorders have deep-rooted patterns of maladaptive behavior, and therefore, months or even years of treatment are needed before symptoms are well-controlled. Psychosocial treatment that includes social skills training or cognitive behavioral therapy is recommended for changing unwanted behavior. Specifically, *dialectical behavior therapy* (DBT) is a cognitive behavioral treatment that has been successful in reducing intense emotions. Its focus is a combination of mindfulness, interpersonal skills, tolerance, and emotional regulations. Medication is a possible treatment for anxiety, depression, mood fluctuations, or psychosis that accompanies some of the disorders, but most disorders do not necessitate medication.

## Treatment of Psychological Disorders

This section will examine selected therapeutic approaches appearing on the AP PSYCH exam. The effectiveness of treatment methods for psychological disorders helps people to overcome upsetting thoughts, feelings, and behaviors.

When you first started learning about AP PSYCH, your teacher probably introduced the course by saying that there are numerous points of view and theories in psychology. Because there are many ways to look at psychology, we will be discussing a variety of theoretical perspectives aimed at the treatment of mental disorders.

It is important to understand that this section provides an overview of the systematic techniques and methods used to overcome disorders. It is not intended to be a comprehensive guide to treatment approaches. As you review the various treatment approaches, keep in mind that the best predictor of effective therapy is not the method of therapy; it is the relationship between the therapist and client. Research shows that the human dimension of relationship is the most powerful determinant in the treatment of psychological disorders.

Before we discuss the treatment approaches, let's take a look at the history of psychological treatment and the format of psychological treatment.

### History of Psychological Treatment

Across every continent, in every time period, culture, and age group, there has been treatment for those suffering from mental illnesses. It wasn't until the second half of the 20th century that treatment shifted from doctrine-inspired theories of treating "madness" to research-based scientific treatments.

Prior to the 20th century, many cultures around the world believed that mental illness was the result of evil spirts, known as a *spirit possession theory.* Unfortunately, this perspective caused the sufferer to be tormented instead of being treated with compassion and humanity. For example, a method of drilling holes into the head and skull, called **trephining,** was an attempt to release evil spirits from the person. This method was practiced before anesthesia was invented and caused the person tremendous mental and physical pain. As primitive as this method appears, from the 1930s to the 1950s the radical surgical treatment for mental disorders was called a **lobotomy.** Physicians would sever the connection in the brain between the frontal lobe and the limbic system. In most cases, patients had negative effects on personality, initiative, and the ability to function. Lobotomies are now illegal worldwide.

In the United States, mental hospitals were not founded until the early 1960s. Prior to that time, mental hospitals were considered *asylums* for the mentally insane. However, such hospitals were considered *warehouses,* not treatment hospitals, to separate those suffering from the rest of society. Patients were neglected in overcrowded, noisy, and unsanitary conditions. Dorothea Dix fought to reform the treatment of the mentally ill. She was influential in passing a bill for government funding to support mental asylums, but for much of the 1900s, perhaps due to our culture's fear of mental illness, stigma, and lack of effective treatments, mental asylums were filled with people who were not improving.

Governmental resources for treating mental disorders paved the way to reform mental health hospitals. By the mid-1950s, over a million patients resided in state, county, or private mental hospitals. As western society progressed, humanitarian reform in the 1960s–1980s caused many lawsuits against the extreme abuses in the hospitals and caused a movement to **deinstitutionalize** patients. Many mental hospitals were closed, and psychiatric treatment began moving to community services because it became more cost-efficient. Although it was a positive move for some people because they were now free, it has led to a rise in homelessness and jail detention because those afflicted by serious mental illnesses tend not to comply with treatment and have few options for housing.

## Format of Psychological Treatment

Therapeutic experiences are available in several different formats: individual, couples, family, and group therapy, as detailed in the following table.

**Psychological Treatment Formats**

| Format | Description |
|---|---|
| **Individual therapy** | Individual therapy occurs when at least one therapist works with a single person in the same session to form a therapeutic alliance that leads to the resolution of the problems. Note: *Interpersonal therapy* is a brief psychotherapy that focuses on resolving personal relationships to improve mental disorders. It is a brief form of therapy that addresses a person's attachment to people, feelings, and relationships. |
| **Couples therapy** | Couples therapy occurs when at least one therapist delivers therapy to assist couples in resolving the problems in their relationship. In couples therapy, partners make a commitment to work together, learn communication techniques (e.g., reflecting, clarifying, and developing a shared frame of reference), learn boundary techniques, and discover differentiation and interdependence. |
| **Family therapy** | Family therapy occurs between parents/caretakers and children. The most common form of family therapy is called *family systems therapy*. The focus is on how family members emotionally relate to one another. It emphasizes the importance of changing the interaction among family members to achieve psychological health within the family unit. Family systems therapy holds that an individual's mental symptoms are inextricably part of a system. When the dynamics of the family system change, individual members within the system change. |
| **Group therapy** | Group therapy occurs between at least one therapist and members of a group (7 to 10 members) to accomplish specific goals. Group therapy can be a powerful treatment experience for members. Members meet regularly to give and receive emotional support. It can recreate meaningful relationship experiences, offer support and feedback, and an opportunity to self-disclose. The therapeutic factors of the experience provide an instillation of hope, make members feel that their problems are universal, impart information, improve socializing skills, and improve interpersonal skills. Sometimes group therapy is based on a self-help model. The most common of these is Alcoholics Anonymous' (AA) 12-step program. |

## Treatment Approaches

Two main approaches that we will be examining are psychological and biological perspectives of treating mental disorders.

### Heads Up: What You Need to Know

The section that follows discusses the psychological perspectives of treatment covered on the AP PSYCH exam. Collectively, psychological approaches to treatment are called **insight therapies.** Insight therapy is a broad term that refers to psychoanalysis and psychodynamic therapies (e.g., humanistic therapy and Gestalt therapy). As the name implies, the goal of treatment is to have clients gain insight into themselves and the source of their problems. Psychological health is shaped by the clients' understanding of their thoughts, feelings, emotions, coping mechanisms, and behaviors.

Note: Many students ask about the difference between psychoanalytic treatment and psychodynamic treatment. Both terms are used to describe **psychotherapy** and are based on Sigmund Freud's psychoanalytic principles, but **psychoanalysis** is intensive psychotherapy that takes place several times a week with a certified Freudian psychoanalyst. **Psychodynamic** therapies are guided by Freud's theory, but the techniques are radically different, and psychotherapy takes place once per week by a trained psychologist (not a certified psychoanalyst).

### Psychoanalytic Therapy

The purpose of psychoanalytic therapy is to help the client become conscious of unconscious mental conflicts. Psychoanalytic approaches to treating mental disorders are one of the oldest forms of treatment and have roots in the theory of Sigmund Freud's "talking cure." The main objective of therapy is to uncover the childhood unconscious experiences that cause emotional, cognitive, or behavioral conflicts. Resolving conflicts involves psychoanalysis to change the elements of unconscious psychic energy to consciousness. Psychoanalysis techniques are used in psychodynamic therapy (e.g., free association, dream analysis, transference, and hypnosis).

**Free association.** Free association is the most commonly used technique in psychoanalysis. The therapist (called an *analyst* in psychoanalysis) asks the client to reveal whatever thoughts, feelings, or images come to mind. For example, the therapist says a word, and the client replies without hesitation to say the first word that comes to mind. The client is encouraged to make free associations to make connections between patterns of thoughts and patterns of behaviors. This projective technique is used to uncover the client's unconscious processes.

**Dream analysis.** According to Freud, dreams are the "royal road" to unconscious knowledge. In therapy, clients are instructed to write in a dream journal and share the contents with the therapist. Dream analysis is a classic Freudian technique in which the therapist interprets a client's dreams to bring insight into the content of the dreams. The two types of dream content are **manifest content** (the dream content that is perceived by the client) and **latent content** (the underlying meaning of the dream revealed in therapy). The therapist attempts to interpret the hidden meanings of latent content expressed in images, symbols, and emotions. The hidden themes of the dream can bring insight, diagnose, and facilitate treatment of unresolved conflicts.

**Transference.** Transference is a client's emotional reaction to the therapist. Clients will often experience feelings and attitudes toward the therapist that are similar to experiences in previous significant relationships. Many psychoanalysts believe that transference is essential in therapy so that the client has an opportunity to resolve relational conflicts in a nonjudgmental therapeutic setting.

**Hypnosis.** Hypnosis (called *hypnotherapy*) is when the therapist uses verbal suggestions to induce a trancelike state of mind. Hypnosis is used to provide a deep state of relaxation to explore unconscious conflicts.

## Humanistic Therapy

The purpose of **humanistic therapy** is to help the client focus on the uniqueness of his or her strengths and perspectives. Unlike psychodynamic therapies that focus on personal unconscious conflicts, humanistic psychology focuses on the positive, subjective experiences of a person. The theory of humanism is guided by the principle that humans have the capability to express free will, self-determination, and self-actualization. The approach rejects the idea that the therapist knows better than the client. The therapist's role is to help the client communicate feelings and thoughts to improve behaviors. This section will cover two types of humanistic treatments: person-centered (client-centered) therapy and Gestalt therapy.

### *Person-Centered Therapy*

**Person-centered therapy** was founded by Carl Rogers in the 1930s. Carl Rogers earned recognition around the world for originating and developing the humanistic movement in psychotherapy. Rogers challenged Freud's deterministic view and psychodynamic treatment that dominated psychology in the United States. Rogers suggested that many mental disorders were the result of incongruence between a person's self-concept and psychosocial experiences that originally caused ego defenses to emerge (e.g., denial or distortion).

The primary approach in treatment is for the therapist to offer a therapeutic environment of **unconditional positive regard** (respect for the client as a human being) and **empathy** (recognize the client's feelings through the client's worldview) so that the client might feel valued and supported. According to Rogers, using genuine empathy while responding to the client's needs penetrates layers of the ego toward the genuine self. In person-centered treatment, it is critical for the therapist to understand the client's worldview by using the therapeutic techniques of congruence, authenticity, and active listening. **Congruence** is a genuine feeling of empathy and positive regard, rather than playing the part of a neutral, disengaged therapist. **Authenticity** is therapeutic genuineness. **Active listening** is rephrasing what the client said so that the client feels validated and heard.

One of the broad dimensions of Rogers' theory was his emphasis on the role of *becoming*. Rogers reflected on the process of change and asked himself, "Can I meet this person who is in the process of becoming, or will I be bound by his past and by my past?"

### *Gestalt Therapy*

**Gestalt therapy** (pronounced "geshtalt") was developed by Fritz Perls in the 1940s. The assumption in Gestalt therapy is that people disown parts of themselves and pretend to be something that they are not. The main purpose of treatment, therefore, is to help people accept and integrate the conflicting parts of the self.

Similar to person-centered therapy, it focuses on the context of "here and now" experiences and personal responsibility. Unlike person-centered therapy, Gestalt therapy is highly directive. The therapist leads the client through experiential techniques (e.g., dialogues in role playing) as the client develops an awareness of a whole self. For example, the therapist following the Gestalt approach might challenge clients to examine the relationship between their choices and their life circumstances.

The client is directed not to daydream about the future or reminisce about the past, but to live a fully present life. The client is encouraged to effectively integrate and take responsibility for actions and behaviors. Through treatment, the person learns to live in the present and develop self-awareness, acceptance, and balance. Gestalt therapy emphasizes a whole view of a person; the mind and body are seen as one, not separate. But it is more active than person-centered therapy.

## Behavioral Therapy

Behavioral approaches to treating psychological disorders are unlike the psychoanalytic or psychodynamic approaches to treatment that were developed and practiced in a clinical setting. As you may recall from Chapter 7, "Unit 4: Learning," behavioral approaches to treatment were developed in a laboratory setting. Behavioral theorists suggest that behavior, thoughts, and emotions are learned. The learning outcomes are based on observable, measurable, and specific criteria. Therefore, in behavioral treatment, maladaptive behavior can be "unlearned" by using techniques that are based on conditioning. Behavioral therapists do not need to delve into the unconscious reasons for behavior; they help clients learn new behaviors to replace the old behaviors.

The underlying assumptions of behavioral treatment are as follows: All behavior is caused by stimuli (environment); all behavior is shaped by the response to the stimuli (consequences); behavior is determined by immediate experiences, not previous experiences; and behavior must be reinforced or it can be extinguished.

Although there are several behavioral treatment approaches, for the purpose of the AP PSYCH exam, we will examine classical and operant conditioning treatment approaches.

### *Classical Conditioning*

Therapies based on classical conditioning are very effective for treating various disorders, especially anxiety and phobia disorders. Recall that psychologist John Watson taught Little Albert to fear a white rat, which then led to Little Albert's fear of similar stimuli. Mary Cover Jones demonstrated that through counterconditioning, clients were able to replace a conditioned response of fear with a conditioned response of relaxation. **Counterconditioning** pairs the trigger stimulus with a new response that is incompatible with fear. For example, a person who fears rats is shown a picture of a rat when presenting another stimulus, such as a hug or lollipop. The outcome will not only result in the extinction of fear, but a new association of happiness is learned.

Two specific counterconditioning techniques are *aversive conditioning* and *exposure therapy.*

**Aversive conditioning,** discussed in Chapter 7, "Unit 4: Learning," is a type of avoidance learning. It involves training a person to respond negatively to a stimulus. Recall that psychologist John Garcia conditioned coyotes with food poisoning to learn to be "bait shy" and stay away from herds of sheep. Similarly, behavioral therapists use aversive conditioning to help clients stop smoking. Imagine if the smell of tobacco was paired with something noxious. Such a pairing might help to reverse the association between addiction cues and automatic responses.

**Exposure therapy** is a slightly different attempt to reduce fear or unpleasant reactions. As clients are exposed to anxiety-provoking stimuli, they habituate to the stimuli and become less fearful.

- **Systematic desensitization** is a widely used exposure therapy. Psychologist Joseph Wolpe suggested that it is impossible to be anxious and relaxed at the same time. Therefore, if the therapist repeatedly presents relaxing stimuli when the client is feeling anxiety, the anxiety will gradually be desensitized and eliminated.

  For example, if the client has a fear of flying, the therapist begins by teaching the client a series of relaxation techniques. Next, the client rates the anxiety level when imagining to fly on an airplane on a scale of 1 (extremely relaxed) to 10 (extreme terror). The therapist continues to expose the client to relaxation (e.g., breathing or muscle relaxation) each time the client is slowly exposed, step by step, to the fearful stimuli of flying. The level of anxiety is rated at each exposure. The client imagines each step of flying on an airplane (e.g., entering the airport, walking to the terminal, entering the airplane, finding the seat) simultaneously with relaxation techniques until the anxiety level decreases. If the client's anxiety increases, the therapist returns to the previous stage until it is resolved.
- **Virtual reality exposure therapy** is effective in treating anxieties, phobias, and post-traumatic stress disorder. Exposures are presented *in vivo,* meaning that the stimulus is presented in real life. Clients wear head-mounted gear so that they can view a lifelike series of scenarios. As the client turns, motion sensors adjust the real-life scenes. Research suggests that virtual reality therapy has been highly successful in treatment. Some behavioral therapists use virtual reality exposure therapy because it is difficult to replicate live phobias like spiders, rats, snakes, oceans, or closed spaces.
- **Flooding** is another form of exposure therapy. The client is repeatedly exposed to anxiety-producing images for a prolonged period of time until the images no longer cause fear and anxiety. When that happens, the association between the stimulus and the response of fear becomes weakened. While it might sound extreme, it can be quite effective in treating phobias. Remember the concept of plasticity and the phrase "neurons that fire together, wire together." That means that with repeated exposure, the brain will eventually "rewire" itself.

### *Operant Conditioning*

Operant conditioning uses *behavior modification* techniques to strongly influence the consequences of a client's behavior. Behavior modification is used to positively reinforce desired behaviors and to deny positive reinforcement for objectionable behaviors. Therapies based on operant conditioning are very effective in reinforcing the extinction of undesirable behavior. In operant conditioning, it is not only valuable to understand the importance of changing undesirable behaviors, but it is also important to understand what desired behaviors the client is not doing. For example, if a student has a school phobia, the student might have developed a pattern of fearing school and retreating into the bedroom to avoid going to school. By not going to school, the fearful student learns negative reinforcement because the fear of school is removed as a result of not going to school. The interaction of avoiding school results in a short-term pleasant outcome of reducing fear. This can be changed by applying a new system of consequences to behaviors. The new system can offer positive or negative reinforcement for the desired behavior. Using the *shaping techniques* discussed in Chapter 7, behaviors can be successfully modified to reduce suffering and maladaptive behaviors.

**Token economy** is a type of operant conditioning that may appear on the AP PSYCH exam. Token economies reward positive behavior. Token economies have been successful in schools, homes, and juvenile detention centers in modifying negative behavior. For example, positive reinforcements might be given to students (e.g., a sticker for packing a school bag, getting ready on time, or walking halfway to the bus stop). Eventually the stickers might be exchanged for a toy or something of value to the student. Most importantly, the desired behaviors will eventually replace the maladaptive behaviors.

## Cognitive Therapy

**Cognitive therapies** help teach clients how to think about their problems and use problem-solving techniques to change unwanted emotions and self-defeating behaviors. Cognitive therapists suggest that maladaptive behavior is triggered by irrational thinking patterns. Cognitive therapy is instructive and directive and guides clients toward new constructive ways of thinking in order to change emotions. Cognitive therapy is a powerful way to improve a person's life because it helps clients actively think, instead of letting thoughts become overwhelming.

Cognitive psychologist Aaron Beck developed cognitive therapy based on the premise that a person's problems originate from erroneous thoughts. Beck was originally a Freudian therapist. When he analyzed clients' dreams, he realized that there were recurring patterns of negative themes that were realized in their lives. Beck sought to reverse the clients' distorted, but highly personal, thoughts and beliefs. Beck was especially successful in treating depression using cognitive therapy. He used the concept of a cognitive triad to explain depression. For example, a depressed person has a negative mindset, believes himself to be inadequate or worthless, and the result is depression.

**Cognitive behavioral therapy (CBT).** Cognitive therapists now use an integrated therapy to reverse automatic thoughts, called cognitive behavioral therapy or CBT. The basic processes used to restructure the thoughts are identifying the cognitive distortions and disputing the thoughts using rational thinking. Common cognitive errors include all-or-nothing thinking, overgeneralizing, discounting the positives, jumping to conclusions, magnifying or minimizing events, catastrophizing, and making "should" statements. In treatment, clients learn to use a journal to record daily dysfunctional thoughts of situations, moods, behaviors, or emotions. Homework is essential to treatment so that clients can learn to identify negative behavior and *reattribute* thoughts (use new information to change behavior or events). According to Beck, many people attribute their problems in life to the wrong source. Thoughts must be restructured to stop maladaptive cognitive elements.

The diagram that follows depicts the cycle of cognitions—thoughts create feelings, feelings create behavior, and behavior creates thoughts.

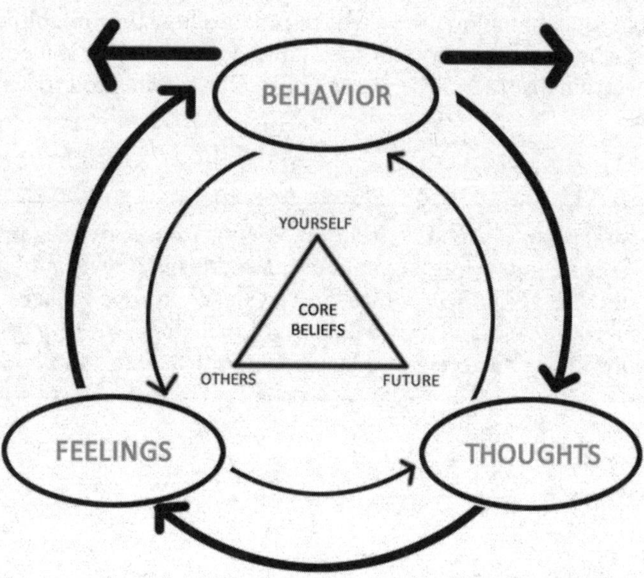

**Rational emotive behavioral therapy (REBT).** Psychologist Albert Ellis developed REBT in the mid-1950s as another approach that blends cognitive therapy and behavioral therapy. Similar to Aaron Beck, Ellis believed that thoughts and emotions are intertwined, and faulty, irrational thinking must be restructured. Both REBT and CBT attempt to change erroneous thoughts, but REBT explores the problem in depth.

The main premise is that certain thoughts precede negative feelings and behaviors. If the client can pay attention to and control his thoughts, he can reduce the unpleasant consequences of those thoughts. For example, consider the automatic thought of a student who thinks he will never get accepted into college. CBT addresses that illogical thought process by challenging the client's ideas of the admissions criteria. REBT addresses the erroneous thought process, but also attempts to uncover the source of the original thought process. Ellis introduced an *A-B-C theory*. A is activating, B is the belief system, and C is the consequences. A is the activating experience that the client wrongly believes causes C (the consequences). B (the client's belief system) is what needs to be restructured.

## Sociocultural Therapy

**Sociocultural theory** is an emerging therapeutic model of treatment based on unique social or cultural perspectives. Treatment focuses on the importance of the social and cultural aspects that influence a person's behaviors and emotions. According to social psychologists, all therapies consider modalities of psychosocial influences in therapy. Clients are impacted by individual cultural norms, beliefs, attitudes, and values. What is unique to one culture may not be unique to another culture. In order to make positive shifts in therapy, therapists must account for social and cultural patterns of behavior in individual, couples, family, or group therapies.

Psychologist Albert Bandura's observational learning techniques have been applied to therapeutic treatment in *social learning therapy.* Therapists treat a multitude of psychological disorders by clients watching the therapist model how to appropriately respond to situations and events in a safe environment. This demonstration might allow the client to observe appropriate behaviors. Elements of treatment include modeling and verbal instruction to reach desired goals. For example, *role playing* (acting out a part of a particular person) is a technique that allows the client to practice how they might behave in a stressful situation. Imagine a client who has difficulty with social interaction, such as someone who might have been diagnosed with autism spectrum disorder. Role playing is an effective method to learn new social skills to practice desired behaviors.

**Did you know? Mindfulness** is a cognitive technique that is frequently used in treatment. It is a state of being actively engaged in observing one's thoughts and feelings, without judgment. Research shows that it promotes well-being, acceptance, and awareness of one's inner processes and emotions. Mindfulness is a technique used in Marsha Linehan's *dialectical behavior therapy.* It helps to improve the person's ability to accept and be present in the "here and now."

## Biological Therapy

Psychological treatments are methods to treat mental disorders, but remember that everything psychological is also biological. Biological, medical-based, or physiological-based therapies (sometimes called *biomedical*) physically change the person with pharmacological (drug) therapy, electroconvulsive therapy (ECT), or psychosurgery.

**TEST TIP: Research shows that biologically based treatments work best when drug therapy is used in conjunction with psychological treatment to significantly reduce the symptoms of mental disorders.**

### *Drug Therapy*

**Drug therapy** (also called *psychopharmacology*) is the foundation of the biological approach to treatment and is used in conjunction with psychological treatment. Drug therapy has helped millions of people around the world and can be applied to many types of psychological disorders. While medicines do not work the same on every person, they have been proven to be effective for most people. The number of patients residing in state and county mental hospitals has decreased significantly since the introduction of drug therapy and deinstitutionalization in the mid-1950s.

**Impact of Drug Therapy on Psychiatric Hospitalizations**

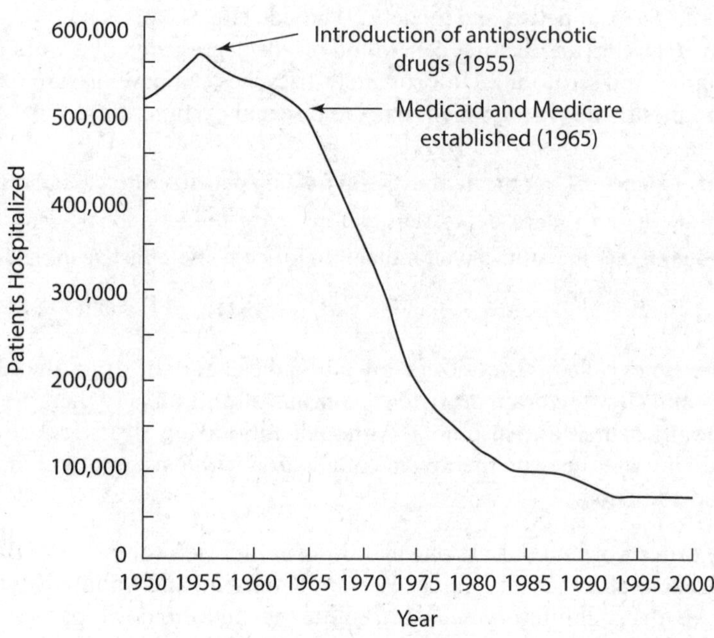


In drug therapy, an *acute dose* of medication is prescribed when symptoms are extreme or the client is in crisis and a *maintenance dose* is prescribed regularly to prevent symptoms. Drug therapy is effective in treating disorders, but it can be expensive, take time to have an effect, and can sometimes develop unpleasant side effects. Drug therapies generally work on the idea that there is too little or too much of a certain hormone or neurotransmitter. As such, many psychological medications are either agonists or antagonists. In addition, drug therapy works best when paired with psychological therapy. For example, anti-anxiety medicines might reduce the biological aspects of panic, but they do not teach a person how to deal with fearful situations.

The three types of drug therapies that may appear on the AP PSYCH exam are antidepressants, anti-anxiety drugs, and antipsychotic drugs.

**Antidepressants** are used to elevate the mood of a person who is severely depressed. Antidepressants work on at least one neurotransmitter—serotonin, norepinephrine, or dopamine—and can help people with other conditions. For example, antidepressants work to increase serotonin levels and are prescribed to people who suffer from disorders related to trauma, anxiety, panic, social anxiety, and obsessive-compulsive disorders. Recall from Chapter 5, "Unit 2: Biological Bases of Behavior," that serotonin is important for a person to have the feeling of well-being and contentment.

Antidepressants are a broad class of drugs that increase serotonin levels by using different mechanisms. Psychiatrists match symptoms based on neurotransmitters and side effects. Any given person may respond to one drug and not to another. In addition, side effects may vary from one person to another. The three classes of antidepressants that may appear on the AP PSYCH exam are SSRIs, MAOIs, and tricyclics.

The most common class of antidepressants is **selective serotonin reuptake inhibitors (SSRIs).** Recall that reuptake is the process of the presynaptic cell reabsorbing the neurotransmitter molecules that it just released. If reuptake is blocked or inhibited, then there is more serotonin left in the synapse. The side effects can include nausea, tremors, weight gain, apathy, and sexual dysfunction. **Monoamine oxidase inhibitors (MAOIs)** are another type of antidepressant. They slow down the natural breakdown of serotonin in the body so that there is more of it available in the synapses. MAOIs are especially useful in treating atypical depression (e.g., increased sleep, appetite, and anxiety). The side effects can include weight gain, insomnia, and sexual dysfunction. **Tricyclics** are the first generation of antidepressants that work by blocking the reuptake of norepinephrine and serotonin. Unfortunately, tricyclics can have disagreeable side effects (e.g., increased heart rate, dry mouth, dizziness, weight gain, and sexual dysfunction).

**TEST TIP: Lithium is a natural mineral salt that is effective in treating patients with bipolar disorder. By maintaining regular doses of the drug, it can reduce depression and minimize the emotional swings between mania and depression. Note: Research shows that anticonvulsant medications are also effective in reducing the symptoms of bipolar disorder.**

**Anti-anxiety drugs** (sometimes called tranquilizers) are a broad category of drugs that depress central nervous system activity and slow the brain down. Mechanisms of anti-anxiety therapy work on anxiety, panic, alcohol withdrawal, seizures, and insomnia. Although anti-anxiety drugs reduce the symptoms of anxiety, many people do not use the drug therapy in conjunction with psychological therapy. This can lead to drug dependence and addiction.

Nearly all anti-anxiety drugs work on at least one neurotransmitter: serotonin or GABA. The two most common types are **benzodiazepines** such as Xanax, Ativan, Klonopin, and Valium, which increase the levels of GABA. Because GABA is an inhibitory neurotransmitter, it can calm down parts of the limbic system and reticular activating system that may become too excited. **Barbiturates** such as Prozac and Zoloft are another type of anti-anxiety medication. Barbiturates are tranquilizers that act to calm the brain and produce a feeling of relaxation.

**Antipsychotic drugs** are a broad category of drugs that suppress psychosis. Antipsychotic drugs have been revolutionary in the treatment of the positive symptoms of severe mental illnesses such as hallucinations and delusions. These drugs work on at least one neurotransmitter: dopamine or serotonin. Until the 1990s, antipsychotic therapy consisted of typical, first-generation drugs such as Haldol, Thorazine, and Prolixin to slow down the brain when a person is in a psychotic state. After 1990, many atypical, second-generation drugs were introduced such as Clozaril, Risperdal, Zyprexa, Seroquel, and Abilify to prevent psychotic symptoms. Side effects depend on which drug the person is prescribed and can include dry mouth, constipation, sedation, weight gain, sexual dysfunction, and restless leg syndrome.

Many antipsychotic drugs work on the *dopamine hypothesis,* which holds that too much dopamine makes the brain become overactive and then develop psychosis. By giving clients dopamine antagonists that block the receptor sites on postsynaptic neurons, antipsychotic drugs can calm down the brain. However, because dopamine is also involved in smooth muscle movement, blocking it can cause *tardive dyskinesia* (an involuntary twitching of facial muscles and limbs).

**TEST TIP: Too much dopamine can cause psychosis. Too little dopamine is related to Parkinson's disease. Dopamine agonists like L-Dopa are used to treat Parkinson's disease, and dopamine antagonists are used to treat and prevent psychosis. The side effects of blocking dopamine for psychosis can cause Parkinson's-like symptoms like tardive dyskinesia.**

### *Electroconvulsive therapy (ECT)*

**Electroconvulsive therapy (ECT)** is a medical procedure that administers small electric currents through the right hemisphere of the brain while the patient is under anesthesia. It induces a brief seizure to treat psychiatric conditions. Research shows that it has been highly effective in treating major depression that is resistant to drugs. ECT is painless, but some patients have had some memory loss.

An alternative to ECT is **transcranial magnetic stimulation (TMS).** The prefix "trans" means *across* and the suffix "cranial" refers to the *skull.* TMS is a noninvasive brain stimulation procedure that involves exciting or inhibiting neurons in different areas of the brain. TMS does not require surgery. It is performed for 20 to 30 minutes while the patient is awake (over a period of 2 to 4 weeks) and sends magnetic waves that affect the electrical function of neurons of the brain that play a role in mood regulation.

**Biofeedback** is a noninvasive form of therapy that involves using an electroencephalograph (EEG) to measure the electrical activity on the surface of the brain (cerebral cortex). It measures bodily processes that are involuntary (e.g., blood pressure, muscle tension, and heart rate). Clients develop an awareness for how the mind interacts with the body and can adjust arousal states. Biofeedback works well for people who need to slow down their thoughts, such as those who struggle with attention issues or sleep issues.

# Chapter Review Practice Questions

Practice questions are for instructional purposes only and may not reflect the format of the actual exam. The questions and explanations that follow focus on essential knowledge, course skills, and course content.

## Multiple-Choice Questions

1. Gabrielle told her therapist that she has felt lethargic and has been unable to get out of bed in the morning for a month. She has no interest in participating in social activities because she feels worthless and alone. Which of the following psychological diagnoses best describes Gabrielle's symptoms?

   **A.** Major depressive disorder
   **B.** Antisocial personality disorder
   **C.** Paranoid schizophrenia
   **D.** Post-traumatic stress disorder
   **E.** Bipolar disorder

2. Jason frequently misses work and social engagements because he is extremely uncomfortable in overcrowded places or wide-open spaces. Which of the following diagnoses best describes Jason's symptoms?

   **A.** Panic disorder
   **B.** Generalized anxiety disorder
   **C.** Agoraphobia
   **D.** Obsessive-compulsive disorder
   **E.** Borderline personality disorder

3. Dr. Snyder is an emergency room physician who cannot feel empathy for patients who are in pain. She disregards the patient's feelings, and most people consider her an "uncaring" doctor. Dr. Snyder sees patients as medical problems, not as human beings. Which of the following diagnoses best describes Dr. Snyder's symptoms?

   **A.** Neurocognitive disorder
   **B.** Dissociative disorder
   **C.** Paraphilic disorder
   **D.** Impulse control disorder
   **E.** Antisocial personality disorder

4. Which of the following concepts best explains the consistent worrying about one's personal problems?

   **A.** Flight of ideas
   **B.** Seasonal affective disorder
   **C.** Catatonia
   **D.** Obsessive thinking
   **E.** Ruminative thinking

5. Humanistic therapists use which of the following therapeutic techniques?

   **A.** Active listening
   **B.** Transference
   **C.** Exposure
   **D.** Systematic desensitization
   **E.** Aversive conditioning

6. Which of the following choices best matches the procedure that affects brain functioning without performing surgery?

   **A.** Lobotomy
   **B.** Transcranial magnetic stimulation
   **C.** Deep brain stimulation
   **D.** Severing the corpus callosum
   **E.** Trepanning

7. Jimmy is a 5-year-old who is afraid of the dark. His grandfather suggests that the best way to overcome this fear is to put Jimmy in a dark room until the boy realizes there is nothing to fear. Which of the following psychodynamic techniques best matches the grandfather's approach to overcoming a phobia?

   **A.** Restructuring
   **B.** Flooding
   **C.** Modeling
   **D.** Unconditional positive regard
   **E.** Rational emotive behavioral therapy

## Free-Response Question

**1 question**

**25 minutes**

**Directions:** It is suggested that you take a few minutes to plan and outline your essay. Write your response on lined paper. You must demonstrate your understanding of course skills and course content. Your essay is considered a first draft and may contain some grammatical errors that will not be counted against you. However, to receive full credit, your essay must demonstrate defensible content knowledge with substantive examples where appropriate.

A group of AP Psychology students are attempting to prove that mental illness is quite common and is not shameful. The students designed a website with a link to a survey with a set of questions regarding the participants' symptoms of anxiety and depression. The questions included students' attitudes, beliefs, personal experiences, and family experiences about their symptoms of mental illness. The questionnaire asked students to answer 10 questions and score each question using a scale from 1 to 5, with 1 being the lowest and 5 being the highest. The website link was e-mailed to all of the 11th graders at the high school. The high school researchers received 240 responses from a population of 300 students. Students were told that responses would be anonymous, but the findings would be available to the entire student body. The data was analyzed, organized, and presented in a bar graph that was published in the school newspaper.

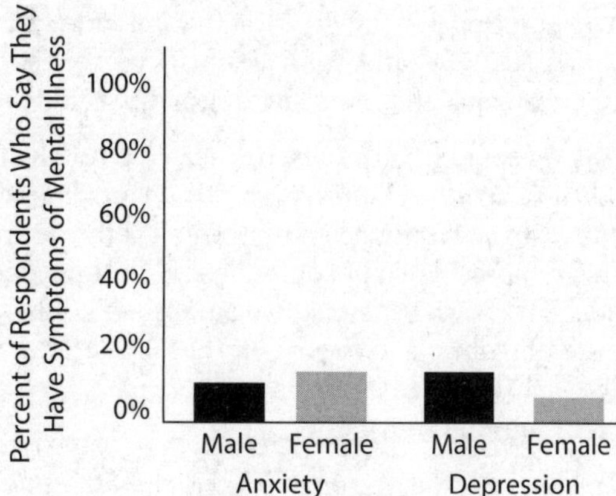


**Part A**

Identify and explain each of the following in this study.

- Categorical variable in the graph
- Operationalization
- Random sampling
- Self-report bias

**Part B**

- Explain the difference between a bar chart and histogram.
- Describe the research method that was used in this scenario.
- Estimate the percentage of the lowest-occurring diagnosis for either sex from the information in the graph.

# Answers and Explanations

## Multiple-Choice Questions

1. **A.** *Major depressive disorder,* choice A, is the clinical term for depression. The symptoms described in the question—bedridden, lack of social interaction, and feelings of worthlessness—are common symptoms of major depressive disorder. *Antisocial personality disorder* (choice B) is characterized by a lack of empathy for others. *Paranoid schizophrenia* (choice C) is a type of schizophrenia where a person has delusions, hallucinations, and irrational thought processes, but the person also believes that someone or groups are watching the person. *Post-traumatic stress disorder* (choice D) has many different symptoms, including the symptoms in the question, but because the question did not mention trauma, choice D is not the correct answer. *Bipolar disorder* (choice E) has some overlapping symptoms with major depressive disorder, but the question did not mention symptoms of mania cycling through the different stages of bipolar disorder; therefore, choice E is incorrect.
2. **C.** *Agoraphobia* is the irrational fear of leaving one's home or fear of open spaces, choice C. *Panic disorder* (choice A) is characterized by a sudden and strong fear that disrupts one's ability to participate in life's activities. *Generalized anxiety disorder* (choice B) is a common condition where a person often feels nervous for reasons that don't match the intensity level of the situation. *Obsessive-compulsive disorder* (choice D) is characterized by chronic thoughts, obsessions, compulsions, and urges to perform routines that will make the fearful thoughts go away. *Borderline personality disorder* (choice E) is characterized by emotional instability, fluctuating moods, and fear of abandonment. Borderline personality disorder (BPD) would not necessarily prevent someone from going to a party, but can result in relationship problems and impulsive actions.
3. **E.** *Antisocial personality disorder*'s main symptoms are lack of empathy for others and disregard for the rights of others, choice E. *Neurocognitive disorders* (choice A) are characterized by decreased mental function due to a medical disease, including dementia, which is the decline of cognitive functioning. *Dissociative disorder* (choice B) has as its main component a disconnection from something. That something could be one's identity, as with dissociative amnesia. People with *paraphilic disorder* (choice C) are sexually aroused by objects to the extent that it interferes with intimate relationships. *Impulse control disorder* (choice D) is when a person has an urge to do something illegal or immoral (e.g., stealing [kleptomania] or lighting fires).
4. **E.** The verb "to ruminate" means to dwell on something. *Ruminative thinking* is persistent thinking about one's problems and thinking about the expected outcome pessimistically, choice E. *Flight of ideas* (choice A) is when the mind is generating many unrelated thoughts at a rapid speed. *Seasonal affective disorder* (choice B) is a temporary but very real depression that arises due to lack of sunlight; it is correlated with the winter months. *Catatonia* (choice C) is a symptom of schizophrenia when the person does not respond to stimuli and is in a state of immobility. *Obsessive thinking* (choice D) is a symptom of obsessive-compulsive disorder, in which a person has frequent thoughts of a particular event.
5. **A.** *Active listening* is a therapeutic technique in which the therapist is fully present and rephrases what the client says to affirm that the therapist understands what is being said, choice A. *Transference* (choice B) is the unconscious tendency to assign significant emotional meaning to another person (therapist). *Exposure* (choice C) is a therapeutic technique in which the client is gradually presented with the object of his or her anxiety. *Systematic desensitization* (choice D) is a therapeutic technique used to encourage relaxation by pairing the anxiety-inducing object with relaxation. *Aversive*

*conditioning* (choice E) is a therapeutic technique that is used by the therapist to pair an enjoyable stimulus with an unpleasant stimulus in order to cease behavior (e.g., smoking cigarettes).

6. **B.** The definition of the prefix *trans* is "across." Therefore, *transcranial* means across the skull, not through the skull. *Transcranial magnetic stimulation* is a medical technique that is used to excite or inhibit brain regions without brain surgery, choice B. A *lobotomy* (choice A) is a surgical procedure performed on the frontal lobe. *Deep brain stimulation* (choice C) involves performing surgery to insert an electronic device inside the brain to regulate electrical signals in certain areas. *Severing the corpus callosum* (choice D) is a rare surgery that is performed when other methods to control seizures have not worked. *Trepanning* (choice E) is an ancient technique that was often misused by multiple civilizations. The modern use of trepanning is to temporarily surgically remove part of the skull to allow the brain to swell in order to heal itself after an injury.
7. **B.** *Flooding* is a type of exposure therapy that the phobic person experiences in therapy. The therapist floods the client with fearful images until the client realizes that the fear is irrational, choice B. *Restructuring* (choice A) is a cognitive therapy technique that is used to encourage the client to focus on troubling thoughts in order to modify the thoughts. *Modeling* (choice C) is a behavioral therapy approach in which the therapist (or other group members) demonstrates appropriate behavior; the client then attempts to imitate, practice, and learn from the appropriate responses. *Unconditional positive regard* (choice D) is a humanistic therapy technique in which the therapist does not judge or give advice, but rather offers support and respect for the client. *Rational emotive behavioral therapy* (choice E) is a directive therapeutic approach that helps clients identify and change underlying causes of irrational beliefs.

## Free-Response Question

To achieve the maximum score of 7, your response must address each of bullet points in the question.

## Sample Student Response

A *categorical variable* is a non-number-based variable such as preference for chocolate or vanilla ice cream. In this case, a categorical variable would be the sex (male or female) of the respondent or the type of illness in which their symptoms might occur. *Operationalization* is the process of taking an abstract (or difficult to define) concept and changing it so it can be measured. In this case, having the respondents describe their experiences on a scale of 1 to 5 operationalizes the symptoms. *Random sampling* occurs when every member of a population has an equal chance of being asked to be in the study. In this case, it might not be random because some students may not have access to the Internet to answer the survey questionnaire. *Self-report bias* is a confounding variable in which respondents might give inaccurate information about themselves because they might be seeking a certain outcome. In this case, students might think they have symptoms of clinical depression, but may not have been professionally diagnosed. A *bar chart* is typically used to show categorical or nominal variables such as ice cream flavor preference, type of disorder, or sex of respondent. A *histogram* is used to show variables that are numerical such as GPA, height, or age. A *survey* method is the design method used in this study. From the graphic representation of the data, the *lowest occurrence* of mental illness is females with depression. It is estimated that 5 to 10 percent of the females surveyed struggle with depression.

Chapter 12

# Unit 9: Social Psychology

AP Psychology Unit 9 explores the overarching philosophy that humans are social beings. How we interact with others and how others interact with us influences our attitudes, thoughts, beliefs, and behaviors.

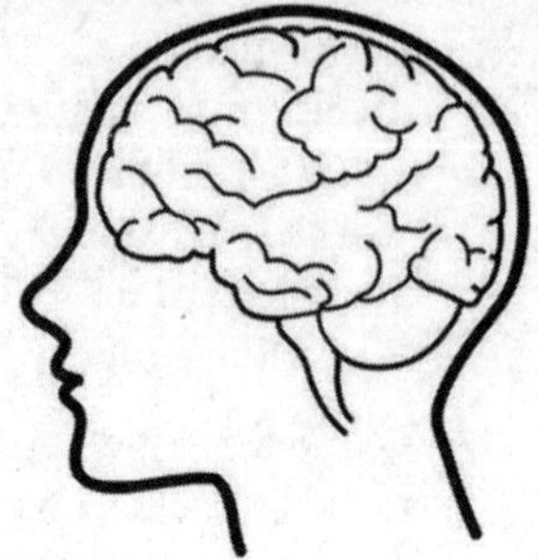

- Key Contributors in Social Psychology
- Attribution Theory
- Attitude Formation
- Attitude Change
- Prosocial Behavior
- Group Influences on Behavior
- Prejudice, Discrimination, and Bias
- Aggression
- Resolving Conflict

## Overview of AP Psychology Unit 9

Chapter 12 covers a range of topics related to social and group influences on behavior and mental processes including attitude, conformity, compliance, obedience, bias, prejudice, discrimination, and aggression. **The topics discussed in this unit will count toward 8–10 percent of your multiple-choice score.**

## AP Psychology Framework

Success on the exam depends on your ability to make connections to the major concepts described in the content topics of the *Course Framework for AP Psychology*. Remember that these concepts highlight the fundamental ideas that every student should take with them into the AP PSYCH exam and beyond.

Use the table below to guide you through what is covered in this unit. The information contained in this table is an abridged version of the content outlines with topic examples. Visit https://apstudent.collegeboard.org/apcourse/ap-psychology/ for the complete updated AP PSYCH course curriculum framework.

| AP Psychology—Unit 9: Social Psychology | |
|---|---|
| **Topic** | **Learning Target** |
| **Attribution Theory and Person Perception** | ■ Apply attribution theory to explain motives (e.g., fundamental attribution error, self-serving bias, false consensus effect, confirmation bias, just-world hypothesis, and halo effect).<br>■ Articulate the impact of social and cultural categories on self-concept and relations with others (e.g., gender, race, and ethnicity).<br>■ Anticipate the impact of self-fulfilling prophecy on behavior. |
| **Attitude Formation and Attitude Change** | ■ Identify important figures and research in the areas of attitude formation and change (e.g., Festinger).<br>■ Discuss attitude formation and change, including persuasion strategies and cognitive dissonance (e.g., central route to persuasion, peripheral route to persuasion, cognitive dissonance, and elaboration likelihood model). |
| **Conformity, Compliance, and Obedience** | ■ Identify the contributions of key researchers in the areas of conformity, compliance, and obedience (e.g., Asch, Milgram, and Zimbardo).<br>■ Explain how individuals respond to expectations of others, including groupthink, conformity, and obedience to authority. |
| **Group Influences on Behavior and Mental Processes** | ■ Describe the structure and function of different kinds of group behavior.<br>■ Predict the impact of the presence of others on individual behavior (e.g., bystander effect, social facilitation, social inhibition, group polarization, deindividuation, diffusion of responsibility, in-group/out-group bias, reciprocity norms, social norms, social traps, prisoner's dilemma, conflict resolution, and superordinate goals). |
| **Bias, Prejudice, and Discrimination** | ■ Describe processes that contribute to differential treatment of group members (e.g., in-group/out-group dynamics, ethnocentrism, prejudice, bias, discrimination, scapegoat theory, stereotype, out-group homogeneity bias, and mere-exposure effect). |
| **Altruism and Aggression** | ■ Describe the variables that contribute to altruism and aggression. |
| **Interpersonal Attraction** | ■ Describe the variables that contribute to attraction. |

# Important Terms and Concepts Checklist

This section is an overview of the important terms, concepts, language, and theories that specifically target the key topics of Unit 9. Use this list of terms as a checklist to check your personal progress. As you study the topics, place a check mark next to each and return to this list as often as necessary to refresh your understanding.

After you finish the review section, you can reinforce what you have learned by working through the practice questions at the end of the chapter. Answers and explanations provide further clarification into the perspectives of social psychology.

| Term/Concept | Study Page | Term/Concept | Study Page | Term/Concept | Study Page |
|---|---|---|---|---|---|
| actor-observer discrepancy | p. 266 | elaboration likelihood model | pp. 268–269 | norm of reciprocity technique | p. 272 |
| aggression | p. 277 | foot-in-the-door technique | p. 272 | normative conformity | p. 270 |
| altruism | p. 273 | frustration-aggression hypothesis | p. 277 | obedience | pp. 272–273 |
| Asch's conformity experiments | pp. 270–271 | fundamental attribution error | p. 266 | out-group bias | p. 276 |
| attitude | pp. 267–273 | game theory | p. 275 | peripheral route to persuasion | pp. 268–269 |
| attribution theory | pp. 266–267 | group polarization | p. 274 | persuasion | p. 268 |
| bystander effect | p. 274 | groupthink | p. 274 | prejudice | p. 276 |
| central route to persuasion | pp. 268–269 | halo effect | p. 267 | prisoner's dilemma | p. 275 |
| cognitive dissonance | p. 269 | identification conformity | p. 270 | prosocial behavior | p. 273 |
| compliance | pp. 271–272 | implicit bias (implicit attitude) | p. 276 | self-fulfilling prophecy | p. 267 |
| conformity | pp. 269–271 | informational conformity | p. 270 | self-serving bias | p. 266 |
| consensus effect | p. 266 | in-group bias | p. 276 | social facilitation | p. 274 |
| deindividuation | p. 274 | internalization conformity | p. 270 | social loafing | p. 274 |
| diffusion of responsibility | p. 273 | just-world hypothesis | p. 267 | social trap | p. 274 |
| discrimination | p. 276 | low-ball technique | p. 271 | Stanford Prison Experiment | p. 270 |
| door-in-the-face technique | p. 271 | Milgram obedience experiments | pp. 272–273 | zero-sum game | p. 275 |

## Heads Up: What You Need to Know

For the AP PSYCH exam, ask yourself one essential question as you work through the topics in this chapter: How does bias affect the researchers' conclusions about social psychology?

# Chapter Review

Social psychology is different from other disciplines in psychology because it focuses on the understanding that "all humans are fundamentally social beings" (Aristotle). It should, therefore, be studied within the social context of other people. Social psychologists take into account how individuals influence and are influenced by others in the formation of attitudes, beliefs, and values. It is the idea that social interaction is essential to the psychological development of all individuals, and that in most situations, most people will behave like most other people.

## Key Contributors in Social Psychology

Let's begin by identifying some of the leading figures in social psychology. These scientific theories will be discussed in the review section that follows and are some of the most important contributions in the field of social psychology. For the AP PSYCH exam, be sure to know at least the last name and why each psychologist is famous.

| Key Contributors in Clinical Psychology | | |
|---|---|---|
| **Contributor** | **Field of Study (Theory)** | **Famous For** |
| **Fritz Heider** (1896–1988) | Attribution theory | Heider famously wrote *The Psychology of Interpersonal Relations* (1958) and was a pioneer in human behavior in attribution theory. Attribution theory describes how human beings explain (make attributions about) the behavior of themselves or others. Human behavior is credited to either the *situation* (peer pressure, social norms, etc.) or the individual's *disposition* (personality, motives, etc.). |
| **Leon Festinger** (1919–1989) | Cognitive dissonance theory and<br><br>Social comparison theory | Festinger was known for his theory of cognitive dissonance (suggesting that inconsistency in people's beliefs or behaviors causes uncomfortable psychological tension). Festinger's theories discredited Pavlov's leading theory of "stimulus-response conditioning" of human behavior (a theory in which a specific stimulus conditions a particular response). |
| **Solomon Asch** (1907–1996) | Conformity | Asch was known for his conformity experiments, the Asch paradigm. Asch studied to see "if and how people yielded to, or defied, the group majority." Important factors of conformity include the task, age, gender, and culture. |
| **Stanley Milgram** (1933–1984) | Obedience | Milgram was interested in understanding why people were willing to inflict harm on others during the Holocaust. People followed the orders of their authority figures to commit atrocities against helpless victims. In the 1960s, Milgram conducted controversial electric shock experiments on humans to determine "how far people will go to justify their acts" of obedience. |
| **Philip Zimbardo** (1933–) | Stanford Prison Experiment | Zimbardo conducted the Stanford Prison Experiment in 1971 to examine "what makes a good person do bad things." His study of blind obedience to authority demonstrated how social influences can have a negative impact on one's life. |

## Attribution Theory

What causes certain behavior in people? Social psychologist Fritz Heider attempted to answer this question by suggesting that there are reasons why people act a certain way in social situations based on **attribution.** According to Heider's attribution theory, most people assign a *cause* to explain their own behavior and the behavior of others. Some people tend to use attribution theory to explain their own failures or shortcomings because external factors will often influence the outcome of situations. Attributions are credited to either a *situation* or the person's *disposition*.

- **Situational (external).** In situational attribution, behavior is due to an *external* cause from a situation or event. That is, one's behavior is due to peer pressure, social norms, or accidental or random acts. For example, if a sports fan of a rival team chants loudly, an observer might attribute this to the entire school's excitement of the game because the team hasn't yet won a game in the season.
- **Dispositional (internal).** In dispositional attribution, one's behavior is due to *internal* personal motives, beliefs, and personality characteristics. For example, if a sports fan of a rival team chants loudly, an observer might negatively attribute the chants to the internal personalities of the rival fans, thinking "Those fans are trying to annoy us by screaming loudly; they think their team is the best in the league."

## Attributional Biases

Situational and dispositional attributions can be explained by the following types of biases.

| Attributional Biases | | |
|---|---|---|
| **Attribution** | **Description** | **Examples** |
| **Fundamental attribution error** | Fundamental attribution error is when people judge another person negatively based on the person's internal personality, rather than considering the external circumstances. Sometimes people see the negative internal qualities of others as permanent flaws. | You accidentally trip over someone's backpack and assume that the person is inconsiderate and lazy instead of thinking that the person was in a rush and didn't have time to put the backpack away. |
| **Actor-observer discrepancy** | Actor-observer discrepancy is the tendency for a person (as an actor) to blame personal behavior on external situational causes and (as the observer of others) blame others' behaviors on internal causes. | When you are late for class, you reason, "There was a traffic jam in the parking lot." But when a classmate is late for class, you reason, "That person is inconsiderate because he is disturbing the class." |
| **Self-serving bias** | Self-serving bias is the tendency to view oneself positively and attribute success to internal causes. Failures are attributed to external, situational causes. | A student who earns an "A" in an English class considers himself intelligent, but if the student receives a "D" in the class, he blames the teacher for giving an unfair test. |
| **Consensus effect** | Consensus effect (also known as false consensus effect) is the tendency to overestimate the degree to which people agree with your values, ideas, and beliefs. That is, you see your own values as normal and believe that others agree with these values. | A person enjoys the taste of walnuts in chocolate chip cookies and tends to think that most people will also like walnuts, so the person makes cookies with walnuts for a party. The reality is that many people may not like walnuts in their cookies. |

| Attribution | Description | Examples |
|---|---|---|
| **Just-world hypothesis** | The just-world hypothesis is the tendency to believe that what happens in the world is fair and that others are justly rewarded or punished. Members of one group might not help the members of another group because they believe the world is *fair* and *just*—people get what they deserve. The just-world hypothesis frames a person's thoughts, which promotes victim blaming. | If a woman is walking to the store late at night and suffers the misfortune of being robbed and beaten by an attacker, other people might assume that she deserved it because she was out late at night. This assumption allows these people to continue to think that the world is fair and just because bad things will not happen to "good people" who follow the rules. |
| **Halo effect** | Halo effect refers to a baseless presumption of the positive or negative characteristics of a person just because your initial impressions of that person were positive or negative. | A person believes that someone who is attractive will also be kind and honest, and someone who is unattractive will likely have other undesirable characteristics. |
| **Self-fulfilling prophecy** | Self-fulfilling prophecy refers to an expectation (positive or negative) that prompts a person to act in a certain manner to make the expectation come true. | Many people in society expect boys to perform better than girls in some abilities (e.g., math and sports). Thus, boys are steered into certain activities, may practice more, and become better as a result. |

**TEST TIP: On the AP PSYCH exam, you should know that fundamental attribution error is similar to actor-observer discrepancy, self-serving bias, and correspondence bias.**

# Attitude Formation

An **attitude** is a way to process likes and dislikes and can either be positive or negative. Attitudes help people process social information and influence decision-making practices. The formation of an attitude is based on internal schemas, values, beliefs, and life experiences that people perceive to be true for themselves.

Psychologists view attitudes as a combination of affective, behavioral, and cognitive factors that are shown in personal, social, and circumstantial situations. For the AP PSYCH exam, remember the following ABC components of an attitude.

**The ABC Components of Attitude**

| Affective | Behavioral | Cognitive |
|---|---|---|
| • Definiton: A person's emotions (feelings) about something.<br>• Example: "I strongly dislike my coach." | • Definition: A person's disposition to act a certain way.<br>• Example: "I will complain until someone listens to me about the terrible soccer coach." | • Definition: A person's thoughts, beliefs, and values can create an attitude.<br>• Example: "I think that I will never work hard again for my coach because he doesn't deserve to get credit for my performance." |

# Attitude Change

Social psychologists attempt to explain the reasons that people change their attitudes and behavior by describing the social influences that prompt change. For the AP PSYCH exam, you should be able to compare and contrast the following direct and indirect social influences of attitude change.

- **Persuasion.** The ability to influence the attitude or behavior of another person.
- **Cognitive dissonance.** A mental state of conflict that occurs when a person's thoughts and feelings are contrary to his or her behavior.
- **Conformity.** A social influence that changes a person's attitude, values, and behavior.
- **Compliance.** A change in behavior that is *requested* or *forced* by another person (or group).
- **Obedience.** A change in behavior that is *demanded* by another person (or group).

## Persuasion

**Persuasion** is a process of communication. It is the conscious attempt to directly influence the attitude or behavior of another person to achieve a desired goal. Persuasion has often been associated with people who scam others to get what they want. However, persuasion can be positive or negative.

Researchers have identified that persuasion is dependent on the *interaction* of several factors.

1. **Source**—Who is communicating and attempting to persuade? The person who is persuading must be credible and likeable. For example, a salesperson appears unselfish and attempts to sacrifice his own monetary commission for the good of a customer.
2. **Audience**—Whom is being persuaded? The person who is being persuaded is the audience. Variables (called *demographics*) like age, race, gender, education, and income are considered when evaluating a person's persuasive ability. For example, an audience of women may be more easily persuaded by a well-spoken female speaker than by a male speaker when talking about equal pay for women.
3. **Message**—How is the message being communicated? The message presented must be logical and reasonable. The two types of messages are: (1) **central route** to persuade someone by using FACTS, and (2) **peripheral route** to persuade someone by using EMOTION.
4. **Medium**—What is the means by which the message is communicated? The person who is being persuaded tends to be influenced by how the information is presented. For example, advertisers will repeatedly expose consumers to their products using television commercials.

**TEST TIP: The AP PSYCH exam frequently contains a question related to the way people respond to messages using the *central route* and the *peripheral route* described in the elaboration likelihood model.**

### Elaboration Likelihood Model (ELM)

The **elaboration likelihood model** is a dual theory that explains how attitudes are changed by persuasive arguments. In other words, why does a person change his or her mind, and to what extent does a person scrutinize the relevant information in the argument? The two paths of persuasion that can change a person's attitude are the *central route* and the *peripheral route*. Elaboration levels (the extent to which a person scrutinizes the information) can be *high* using the central route or *low* using the peripheral route.

- **Central route** involves a high level of elaboration and persuades using *facts*. It occurs when the content of the message strongly motivates the target audience because there is time to investigate the message's content, critically think about the message, and focus on its strengths.
- **Peripheral route** involves a low level of elaboration and persuades using *emotion*. It occurs when other factors influence the audience to make quick decisions. For example, if there is a distraction, if the decision is not important, or if the argument is weak. This route uses heuristics and cues to form simple and quick decisions.

## Cognitive Dissonance

Psychologist Leon Festinger's theory of cognitive dissonance refers to social influences that cause an internal mental conflict. If people realize that their behavior is not consistent with their core beliefs, values, and attitudes, it could lead to two contradictory states of mind, called **cognitive dissonance.** They will then act to explain or justify why their behavior was acceptable by changing their beliefs, attitudes, or values.

**Stages of Cognitive Dissonance**

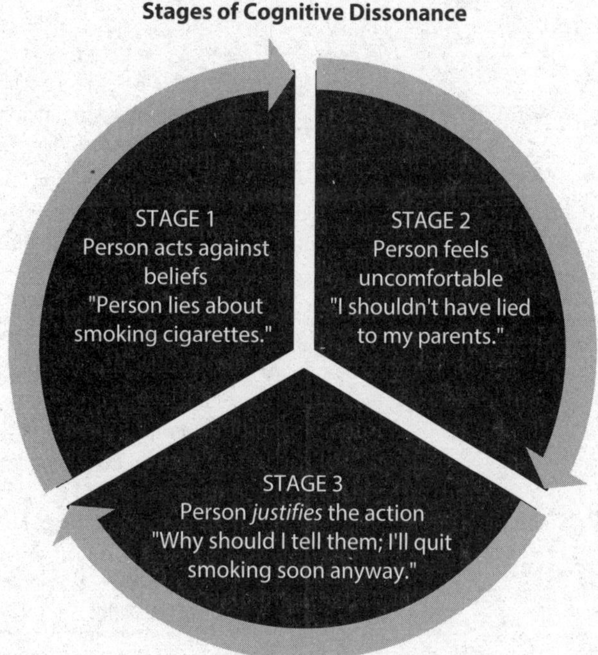


## Conformity

Social influence causes a person to change beliefs, attitudes, and/or behaviors in order to *fit into a group*. This type of social influence that changes behavior is conformity. **Conformity** is when a person adjusts his or her attitudes and beliefs to match the social norm standards.

An important question to ask when thinking about conformity is "Why do people conform?" Group influences, whether real or imagined, cause people to conform to the pressures of the majority of the group or the minority of the group, called *majority influence* and *minority influence,* respectively. For example, behaving according to a perceived social situation in order to fit in with the majority group of people at a class party.

## Types of Conformity

| Types of Conformity | | |
|---|---|---|
| **Type** | **Description** | **Example** |
| **Normative conformity** | Normative conformity (also known as *compliance*) is when a person yields to group pressure to fit in, but does not necessarily agree with the group. It is often a person's *temporary* emotional desire to be liked and belong to the group. | When listening to rap music at a party, a person privately does not like rap music, but will publicly accept the group's music selections in order to feel accepted by the group. |
| **Informational conformity** | Informational conformity is when a person believes that others have greater knowledge and information, so the person yields to the group for direction, rather than trusting his or her own knowledge. | The power of informational conformity was demonstrated by the **Solomon Asch conformity experiments** (1951) that showed the power of group pressures. Asch asked a group of seven participants to view three straight lines and select the line that matched the "standard" line. It seems like a simple task, but Asch secretly asked six actors to deceive one person by selecting the wrong line. When Asch asked the group which line was most similar to line "X," each actor deliberately gave an incorrect answer. As more actors answered incorrectly, the participant began to feel the social influence (informational conformity) and also gave the wrong answer in order to match the rest of the group. If the participant felt like the group was watching him, he became anxious because he felt like he was alone in the spotlight, called *spotlight effect*. |
| **Identification conformity** | Identification conformity is when a person changes an attitude to identify himself with a particular group or role. | A person wants to define and identify himself with a specific social role (e.g., police officer, firefighter, IT specialist, writer, or doctor). In the **Stanford Prison Experiment** (1971), psychologist Philip Zimbardo assigned specific roles to participants in a "mock prison." Participants were to act as prison guards or prisoners. The result was that prison guards began to over-identify and conform to the role, and the psychological effects of the perceived power caused them to treat the prisoners with extreme hostility, aggression, and psychological abuse. |
| **Internalization conformity** | Internalization conformity is when a person changes his or her beliefs, values, and behavior to *permanently* conform with a group because the person may share a similar point of view with the group, both publicly and privately. It is the deepest level of conformity. The person may accept the influence of the group because the behavior of the group is similar to his or her perceived internal value system. | A person is born and raised in a Jewish household, but attends a private Catholic school from kindergarten to high school. The person internalizes the religious messages, marries a Catholic person later in life, and converts to Catholicism. |

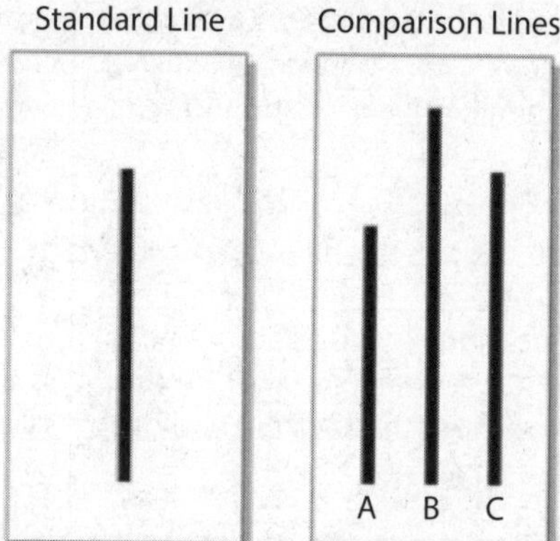


One of the pairs of cards used in the experiment. The card on the left has the reference line and the one on the right shows the three comparison lines.

## Compliance

**Compliance** is a type of social influence that refers to changing one's behavior due to someone's request or suggestion. Compliance and conformity are very similar, but the underlying functions are different. Compliance is changing a *behavior* at the direction of another person and conformity is a person changing an *attitude* to fit into a group.

Several techniques that are used by persuaders to get people to comply with their goals are listed in the table that follows.

| Compliance Techniques | | |
|---|---|---|
| **Type** | **Description** | **Example** |
| **Door-in-the-face technique** | The door-in-the-face technique describes a negotiation process in which the persuader first makes an extremely unreachable demand that the person will likely reject. However, the persuader continues to offer lower requests until the person complies with the demand. In part, the person agrees because he believes that the deal was a successful bargain. | Car dealers set auto sticker prices ridiculously high so that even when customers feel like they have negotiated the price down, the dealerships still make a huge profits on auto sales. |
| **Low-ball technique** | The low-ball technique is used to persuade a person to sell something for a price that is very low by offering them a low price and convincing them it is fair. It is similar to door-in-the-face, but is usually applied to buying something. | You want to buy a house and you know that the sellers need to sell the house quickly. You offer a very low price and buy the house below what it is actually worth. |

*Continued*

| Type | Description | Example |
|---|---|---|
| **Foot-in-the-door technique** | The foot-in-the-door technique is used when the persuader starts with a small request, and then once the person agrees, the persuader increases the demands. | A car salesperson quotes you a sales price that you mutually agreed on, but when you get ready to sign the auto loan documents, you notice additional fees. The salesperson then convinces you to pay for other customary dealer fees. |
| **Norm of reciprocity technique** | Norm of reciprocity is "rewarding kind for kind." It is when the persuader gives a small gift, gesture, or favor to the person so that the person will feel obligated to return the favor. | For example, if you receive a gift from someone in class on your birthday, you may feel obligated to reciprocate by giving a gift to that person on his or her birthday. |

## Obedience

**Obedience** is a form of social influence that involves doing what you are told to do regardless of how you feel. For the AP PSYCH exam, you should be familiar with the **Stanley Milgram obedience experiments** (1960).

Stanley Milgram's experiments on obedience to authority are some of the most important research studies conducted in social psychology. Milgram's experiments were motivated by the horrendous actions of German Nazis during World War II. He questioned the extent to which people were willing to blindly follow the instructions of authority figures.

Do you think you could commit an act of violence simply because an authority figure asked you to obey? Well, Milgram's experiments showed that the average male had the tendency to obey the orders of an authority figure either out of fear or the desire to cooperate. A person who might normally detest the act of performing violent acts that were contrary to his/her moral principles obeyed instructions demanded by an authority figure with relative ease. Participants would obey instructions by giving what they believed were increasingly high-voltage electric shocks to others (even to the point of death) when carried out under strict orders. Those who questioned the authority were in the minority. While no one was actually harmed by the electric shocks because the person being shocked was an actor, the participants reported emotional distress as a result of believing they had caused suffering to another human being.

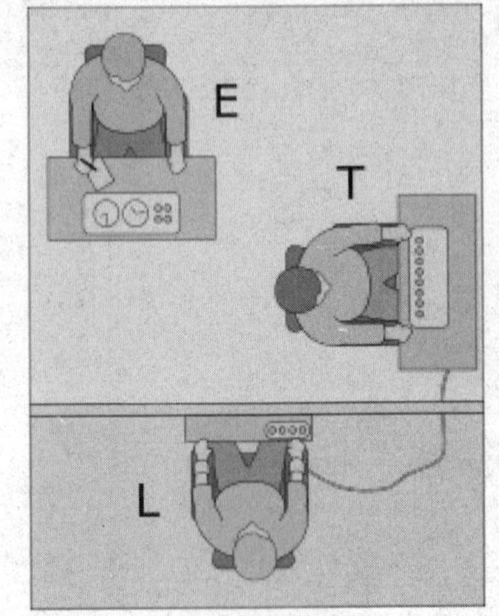


In the diagram at right, the experimenter (E) orders the teacher (T) (who is the subject of the experiment) to give what the teacher believes are painful electric shocks to a learner (L) (who is actually an actor). The teacher was led to believe that for each wrong answer, the learner was receiving actual electric shocks, though in reality there were no such punishments.

## Heads Up: What You Need to Know

The AP PSYCH free-response questions frequently focus on research ethics. Milgram's experiments were controversial and the findings were alarming. In the 1960s, Milgram did not provide the participants with enough information about the experiments for them to be aware of the consequences of their volunteer experiences. The lack of informed consent is a serious ethical concern in psychological research experiments. Use Milgram's experiments as an example of an unethical psychological research study.

# Prosocial Behavior

Before we discuss some of the key concepts of group influences on behavior, let's compare and contrast a couple of closely related terms that frequently appear on the AP PSYCH exam: prosocial behavior and altruism. The main difference between prosocial behavior and altruism is that prosocial behavior is a broad term for helping others, and altruism is a subcategory of prosocial behavior.

| Prosocial Behavior | Altruism |
|---|---|
| Prosocial behavior is volunteering to benefit other people or a society as a whole. The prefix *pro* means "supporting," and *social* means "a relationship with another person or a group of people." Therefore, *prosocial* means cooperating or helping other people. | Altruism is a type of prosocial behavior in which someone helps another person without expecting repayment or benefits in return. |

# Group Influences on Behavior

Research has identified common impacts of group influences on a person's behavior. Social roles, interactions, group structure, and group norms can have an impact on a person's decision-making behavior. For example, how are individual members of the school band, football team, drama club, chess club, or science club impacted by being part of the group? Social psychologists have studied the straightforward-to-complex interactions among an individual and a group and have found that people are influenced even by the mere presence of one other person in a group.

For the AP PSYCH exam, you should be familiar with the social influences that operate in groups, as defined in the table that follows.

| The Impact of Group Interaction on Individual Behavior | | |
|---|---|---|
| **Concept** | **Description** | **Example** |
| **Diffusion of responsibility** | Diffusion of responsibility is a category of social psychology that occurs when people feel less of a responsibility to take the right action when other people are present. | Consider driving on a busy highway and you notice a small fire on the side of the road. Because there are dozens of other vehicles passing by the fire, you might think that someone else will call 911 to report the fire. Other terms that explain diffusion of responsibility are *social loafing, bystander effect, social trap,* and *groupthink.* |

*Continued*

| Concept | Description | Example |
| --- | --- | --- |
| **Social facilitation** | Social facilitation is the tendency for a person to demonstrate a stronger performance on a well-practiced task in the presence of a group. | When you do well, you are likely to do even better in front of a friendly audience. |
| **Social loafing** | Social loafing is the phenomenon that occurs when members of a group don't work as hard to achieve a goal when working in a group. | When a teacher assigns a group project in class, many students don't work as hard as they would when working alone. |
| **Deindividuation** | Deindividuation is a temporary loss of self-awareness due to the immersion in a group. It can increase and diminish a person's sense of personal responsibility. The loss of self can cause people to feel less restrained and less self-conscious and do things they might not do when alone. | Think of how badly some fans behave when they attend a baseball playoff game. When part of an emotional crowd, some people yell "boo" when players make mistakes, but they might not yell under normal circumstances. |
| **Social trap** | Social trap occurs when members of a group focus too heavily on short-term individual gains and lose sight of long-term goals for the group as a whole. | If all members of a basketball team competed to score goals, each person's individual stats might look good, but the team might lose because of a weak defense. |
| **Bystander effect** | Bystander effect is a type of diffusion of responsibility in which people are less likely to offer help to a victim when other people are present. Each person in a large crowd is less likely to intervene than if alone. | The story of Kitty Genovese is the most cited example of bystander effect. She was a young woman who was brutally killed in New York City in 1964. The initial report was that many witnesses heard her cries for help, but no one acted to help her (bystander effect). In 2007, however, it was discovered that there were many inaccuracies in the initial report. Several people *did* call the police. Despite this revelation, Genovese's name is still used as the tragic example of the bystander effect. |
| **Groupthink** | Groupthink occurs when well-intentioned members of a group have a desire for harmony that overrides each group member's creativity and logical decision-making process. To avoid groupthink, each group member must be willing to contribute a realistic appraisal of each situation and not conform to the consensus of the group. As each member proves how far he or she is willing to go to avoid conflict, the group becomes in danger of irrational decision-making outcomes. | Consider Republicans and Democrats who agree with their political party even when they do not agree with their party's policy-making decisions. This causes each party to move further from center and become more extreme about issues because the members do not voice opposition. |
| **Group polarization** | Group polarization is when the group members' decisions and opinions become more extreme than originally. | It can be beneficial to become more extreme when the group is helping others (e.g., volunteering for Habitat for Humanity to help to build homes for the less fortunate). However, people who are prejudiced and join a radical political group tend to become more extreme and prejudiced once they belong to the radical group. |

## Prisoner's Dilemma

On the AP PSYCH exam, you may be asked about prisoner's dilemma. **Prisoner's dilemma** is based on an experiment from **game theory** in which two people must make simultaneous critical decisions. The dilemma is that neither person knows what the other person has decided. Should each person make the decision to protect him- or herself (self-interest), or should each person make the decision based on what he or she perceives the other person will decide to achieve a favorable outcome for both parties (collective interest)? For example, let's say that two friends are caught stealing mixing blenders because they both have a smoothie addiction. The police don't have all of the facts, but try to separately convince each person to privately make a deal for a lighter sentence in exchange for a confession. The police escort each person to a separate room so neither is aware what the other person might reveal. Which friend will confess to the crime and serve jail time: Friend A or Friend B?

Although the decision of both parties remaining silent results in the best outcome, it is not rational because most people demonstrate self-interest. This natural selfishness often leads to a **zero-sum game**—mathematically, one winner (+1) and one loser (−1) equals zero (0) and no one wins. Zero-sum game is related to the concept of social trap where intense competition for short-sighted goals can result in hurting all participants in the long run. **Nonzero-sum game** is a type of compromise where each competitor gains because the competitors do not only focus on their own personal gains.

**The Prisoner's Dilemma**

| | **Friend B confesses and betrays Friend A** | **Friend B stays silent and doesn't confess** |
|---|---|---|
| **Friend A confesses and betrays Friend B** | Both serve 2 years in jail | Friend A goes free and Friend B serves 5 years in jail |
| **Friend A stays silent and doesn't confess** | Friend A serves 5 years in jail and Friend B goes free | Both serve 2 years in jail |

**Did you know?** John Nash was a math genius who suffered from schizophrenia. Nash developed a game theory that earned him a Nobel Peace Prize. His game theory focused on whether it was better to compete or cooperate with others. Nash attempted to find a point at which a person or group should compete or cooperate. As illustrated in the classic prisoner's dilemma, Nash's theory suggests that when resources are scarce, each participant does not need to see the conflict as a *zero-sum game* (total wins minus total losses equals zero); that is, when there is one loser and one winner.

Nash was the subject of the Oscar-winning movie *A Beautiful Mind.* Many AP Psychology teachers show this film in class to shed light on the development of schizophrenia.

# Prejudice, Discrimination, and Bias

Today's American society is a cultural *melting pot* (different people, beliefs, values, and styles are blended together into a whole society). Social psychologists support policies of human diversity and equality, and yet prejudice, discrimination, and bias contribute to conflicting attitudes, behaviors, and social influences that divide some groups.

## Key Concepts about Prejudice, Discrimination, and Bias

**Prejudice** is an unjustifiable negative *attitude* or *stereotype* of a group member or whole group without having sufficient information to support such ideas. Subtle and overt prejudice could be toward a particular cultural, ethnic, racial, or gender group and influences how a person interprets actions toward the group. **Stereotypes** are generalized beliefs based on the characteristics of a few members of a group. The judging of other cultures according to the preconceptions based on their own culture is called **ethnocentrism.**

**Discrimination** is a negative behavior based on prejudices. Discrimination involves irrational decision making and restricts members of a group from opportunities that are available to others. For example, it wasn't until 1964 that the United States enacted laws to protect minorities from discrimination based on race, religion, and nationality. The Civil Rights Act of 1964 ensured equal employment and prohibited discrimination in public places. Although most Americans now object to discriminatory practices, discrimination continues to be a problem in the United States.

**Bias** is the predisposition of being for or against someone (or a group) that is typically considered unfair. The terms and concepts in this section do not suggest that most people are actively prejudicial, discriminatory, or biased. In fact, some people are unaware of their negative biases. The lack of awareness of negative attitudes is called *implicit bias* (also called *implicit attitude*). Implicit bias is unintentional and occurs automatically.

The dynamics of prejudices divide people in the world into two groups of thinking—*us* (in-group) vs. *them* (out-group). **In-group bias** is when group members favor their own group and have a strong sense of togetherness with their group. The members of an in-group discriminate against the out-group, distinguish in-group friends from out-group enemies based on incompatible goals, and criticize those outside the in-group. In-group members don't often take the time to learn about out-group members as individual people. Instead, they use a cognitive bias called *out-group homogeneity,* which refers to how in-group members think out-group members are all the same.

**Out-group bias** is when people are inclined to favor in-group members and are less favorable to those outside of the group. For example, people from other cultures around the world who are suffering deserve to suffer (a similar concept to the just-world hypothesis). Out-group bias is dependent on the idea that "other" people are somehow different from people in the in-group.

## Aggression

**Aggression** is hostile behavior toward another person. It can destroy social relationships. Psychologists study aggression from several different perspectives—evolutionary, biochemical, and psychodynamic.

The **evolutionary** perspective suggests that aggression is part of a natural evolutionary process.

The **biochemical** influences related to aggression show a genetic link to high testosterone levels, low levels of serotonin, and, in certain instances, traumatic brain injuries that can lead to violent behavior.

The **psychodynamic** perspective from Sigmund Freud suggested that aggressive impulses may be linked to frustration. Over the years, a **frustration-aggression hypothesis** was developed. The hypothesis states that when a person blocks the internal feelings of frustration, it can lead to emotional tension. This tension leads to aggression. Often, the person *displaces* anger onto another person. When displacement occurs, aggressive or violent acts are perpetrated against a blameless person (or group) because the aggressor is unable to confront the true cause of his or her angst.

Two types of aggression include instrumental and hostile aggression. *Instrumental aggression* is when aggression is a secondary concern or a tool used to acquire what the aggressor desires. *Hostile aggression* is when causing physical or emotional harm is the goal. It usually occurs when a person or a group acts violently toward others because of a strong negative emotion.

Another type of aggression is scapegoating. *Scapegoating* is blaming an innocent person (or group) for the faults of others. The projection of blame by scapegoating is a form of anger and fear.

## Resolving Conflict

Conflict is inevitable and can trigger deep emotional responses. It is a psychological state of mind when contrasting motives cannot be resolved. Conflict can emerge when frustration, opposition, or disagreement occurs due to differences in beliefs, values, or actions. Resolving conflict can lessen tension and frustration. Psychologists have developed conflict resolution practices to facilitate peaceful solutions and opportunities for change depending on the type of conflict. For example, see the case study of psychologist Muzafer Sherif below.

### Heads Up: What You Need to Know

Use the following example on the AP PSYCH exam when asked about techniques to use to decrease group divisions. Social psychologists propose many theories to explain prejudice, discrimination, and bias, but in 1954 Muzafer Sherif demonstrated an effective way to reduce the negative effects of group differences. In the Robbers Cave Study, Sherif divided boys into groups for a summer camp experience. After group rivalries reached a peak, he then engineered their experiences so that the groups had to work together to achieve a superordinate goal. The act of *interdependence* (a mutual dependence) not only forced the boys to work together, but it also actually changed their attitudes about each other.

# Chapter Review Practice Questions

Practice questions are for instructional purposes only and may not reflect the format of the actual exam. The questions and explanations that follow focus on essential knowledge, course skills, and course content.

## Multiple-Choice Questions

1. Which of the following best represents the view that people are not consciously aware of their prejudices?

   **A.** Ethnocentrism
   **B.** Cultural relativism
   **C.** Out-group homogeneity
   **D.** Halo effect
   **E.** Implicit attitude

2. Which of the following group influences on behavior occurs when an individual's performance improves because they are part of a group?

   **A.** Social facilitation
   **B.** Social loafing
   **C.** Foot-in-the-door technique
   **D.** Scapegoating
   **E.** Social trap

3. Which of the following best describes an individual's temporary loss of self-awareness and self-restraint that occurs in a group that fosters arousal and anonymity?

   **A.** Door-in-the-face technique
   **B.** Fundamental attribution error
   **C.** Just-world hypothesis
   **D.** Deindividuation
   **E.** Zero-sum game

4. Based on the outcome of the Stanley Milgram obedience experiments, which of the following best represents an important conclusion?

   **A.** Most people will yield to electric shocks when given by an authority figure.
   **B.** Most people will harm a stranger to obey the instructions of an authority figure.
   **C.** Men have a tendency to obey in order to give an electric shock to women.
   **D.** Rich men have a tendency to obey in order to give an electric shock to poor men.
   **E.** Most people did not obey authority figures when participants were being harmed.

5. Which of the following research psychologists provided evidence that a person will conform to the group's majority, even if the person clearly disagrees with the group's consensus?

   **A.** Leon Festinger
   **B.** Norman Triplett
   **C.** Philip Zimbardo
   **D.** Muzafer Sherif
   **E.** Solomon Asch

6. After studying social psychology experiments, many students exclaim that they would never conform if they were participants in a prison or obedience research study. Which of the following cognitive biases best represents the students' response?

   **A.** Imaginary audience
   **B.** Cognitive dissonance
   **C.** Fundamental attribution error
   **D.** Bystander effect
   **E.** Correspondence bias

7. When like-minded members of a club are afraid to speak out against ideas, it is called

   **A.** normative conformity
   **B.** groupthink
   **C.** informational conformity
   **D.** diffusion of responsibility
   **E.** low-ball technique

## Free-Response Question

**1 question**

**25 minutes**

**Directions:** It is suggested that you take a few minutes to plan and outline your essay. Write your response on lined paper. You must demonstrate your understanding of course skills and course content. Your essay is considered a first draft and may contain some grammatical errors that will not be counted against you. However, to receive full credit, your essay must demonstrate defensible content knowledge with substantive examples where appropriate.

Jasmine transferred to her current high school 3 weeks ago. At first, she hated school. She refused to change her style of clothing just to fit in with the other students, but eventually she tried to fit in and make the best of the situation. Other students wouldn't help her find her classes, but somehow she managed on her own to figure out the new school system. Now, Jasmine knows the names of a few other students and has received some smiles from students while walking down the hallway. The situation has improved and she feels better, but it still seems strange to attend the new school compared to her old school.

Explain how the following terms will affect Jasmine's efforts to flourish at the new school.

- Cognitive dissonance
- Informational conformity
- Foot-in-the-door
- Social facilitation
- Compliance
- Situational attribution
- Just-world hypothesis

# Answers and Explanations

## Multiple-Choice Questions

1. **E.** *Implicit attitude,* choice E, is the only choice that describes something underlying in the unconscious that is not in your awareness. It is similar to implicit memories covered in Chapter 8. Implicit attitudes are the negative thoughts, feelings, and beliefs about specific groups that are not in our conscious awareness. *Ethnocentrism* (choice A) is thinking from the point of view of your own culture and judging others from that point of view. *Cultural relativism* (choice B) means that good and bad actions are judged based on the person's own culture. For example, if a mother spanks a child, but was raised in a culture where spanking is a normal discipline, then it is permitted. *Out-group homogeneity* (choice C) is a complex name for the misguided idea that some people believe that all the people of an out-group are the same. The *halo effect* (choice D) is the idea that physically good-looking people are thought to be more honest, kind, and intelligent.
2. **A.** Think of the word *facilitate;* it means to help or to make better. Thus, having other people around helps to improve a person's performance, *social facilitation,* choice A. *Social loafing* (choice B) is the opposite of social facilitation. In a group task, some people exert less effort because they believe the group, not the individual, will accomplish the task. *Foot-in-the-door technique* (choice C) is a persuasive technique where a person asks another person for a small favor, and then each favor become increasingly greater. *Scapegoating* (choice D) is when a person or group blames its failure on another person or group. *Social trap* (choice E) is the unfortunate result of focusing on short-term gains and losing sight of the big picture.
3. **D.** *Deindividuation,* choice D, is a temporary loss of one's self-awareness when part of a group. For example, a person losing self-awareness and acting badly at a concert. *Door-in-the-face technique* (choice A) is a persuasive technique where a person asks for a huge favor. Once the favor is rejected, the person then asks for a reasonable favor, which then has a better chance of being granted. *Fundamental attribution error* (choice B) is when people attribute other people's behavior to a relatively permanent characteristic (e.g., age, race, or gender). *Just-world hypothesis* (choice C) is the false idea that the world is fair and just. *Zero-sum game* (choice E) is the idea that in competition, there can be only one winner (+1) and one loser (–1).
4. **B.** Stanley Milgram's obedience experiments showed that the average person will obey orders from an authority figure to harm a stranger, choice B. Choice A is incorrect because the experiments tested the person administering the shocks; actors were pretending to be in pain when electric shocks were administered. Men did not shock women more easily (choice C). Rich and poor people were not compared in the study (choice D). The conclusions regarding authority figures were not determined (choice E).
5. **E.** *Solomon Asch,* choice E, studied conformity. In his classic "line experiment," he showed that most people will communicate the wrong answer if others in the group are unified in communicating an incorrect response. *Leon Festinger* (choice A) studied cognitive dissonance. *Norman Triplett* (choice B) is known for his ideas on social facilitation. *Philip Zimbardo* (choice C) is known for his research of conformity and the Stanford Prison Experiment. *Muzafer Sherif* (choice D) is known for his work on the Robbers Cave Study.
6. **C.** The *fundamental attribution error,* choice C, suggests that people view others negatively based on internal qualities, rather than external circumstances. *Imaginary audience* (choice A) is the idea that

people sometimes think that they are being observed, and thus change their behavior to react to the fictitious social pressure. *Cognitive dissonance* (choice B) is the uncomfortable feeling of experiencing conflicting thoughts, or when thoughts and behavior are not consistent. *Bystander effect* (choice D) is the social phenomenon that people are unwilling to help a stranger because they assume someone else will help. *Correspondence bias* (choice E) is the tendency to draw inferences about a person's negative behavior based on the person's personality, even though the behavior might be explained by something else.

7. **B.** *Groupthink,* choice B, is not just when people agree; it occurs when people in a group "over agree." In order for a person to show that she is 100 percent loyal to a group, she might push the group's objective one step further. *Normative conformity* (choice A) is when a person complies with group pressure to fit in and feel part of the group. *Informational conformity* (choice C) is when a person believes that others have greater knowledge and information. *Diffusion of responsibility* (choice D) occurs when someone feels less responsible to do what is right when others are present. The person may say, "Someone should do something." *Low-ball technique* (choice E) is a persuasive technique that is used to persuade a person to comply by offering an extremely low price. When the first offer is rejected, the second offer will sound more reasonable and has a better chance of being accepted.

# Free-Response Question

To achieve the maximum score of 7, your response must address each of the bullet points in the question.

## Sample Student Response

*Cognitive dissonance* is an uncomfortable mental state where a person feels torn between two conflicting thoughts, or the person feels conflicted between her thoughts and her actions. Jasmine might feel cognitive dissonance if she feels torn between wearing what she feels comfortable wearing and the style of clothes that will help her fit in with students at her new school. *Informational conformity* is when a person perceives that others know more about how to act in a social situation. Since Jasmine assumes the students at her new school know more about style than she does, she is most likely imitating their style and their behaviors. *Foot-in-the-door* is a persuasive technique in which a person asks for a small favor and then once the person agrees to the small favor, the request become increasingly more demanding. Jasmine might ask a student to do her a favor by telling her the time, then she could ask to borrow a pen. Eventually, she could request other favors, like asking the student to save her a seat in class. This technique might help Jasmine form a relationship with the new student. However, it might hinder her ability to flourish in her new school because her repeated requests for favors might make other students avoid her. *Social facilitation* is when a person does better on a task when being watched by other people. If Jasmine is being watched by students in her new physical education class, she might perform better during warmups. *Compliance* is changing behavior, but not attitude. Jasmine might comply with some of the expectations of a new friend group, even though she doesn't agree, because they have social resources that she does not. *Situational attribution* is mentally ascribing the cause of behavior to an external situation, and not because of a relatively permanent characteristic (e.g., religion, ethnicity, socioeconomic status, or physical characteristics). This might affect Jasmine if the students at her new school think that her quiet, reserved behavior is the result of being at a new school and not because she transferred from an economically privileged community. *Just-world hypothesis* is the false belief that the world is fair and just. Therefore, when bad things happen to someone, the person somehow deserved the consequences. Jasmine would be affected by this phenomenon because the students who have this belief might interpret her struggles as being justly deserved. These students might not make an effort to help Jasmine feel part of the school community.

Chapter 13

# Full-Length Practice Exam

This chapter contains a full-length practice exam that will give you valuable insight into the mastery of content questions. It is for assessment purposes only. As you take this practice exam, try to simulate testing conditions and time limits for each of the sections:

| Section | Questions | Time |
|---|---|---|
| Section I: Multiple-Choice Questions | 100 questions | 70 minutes |
| Section II: Free-Response Question: Concept Application | 1 question* | 25 minutes |
| Section II: Free-Response Question: Research Design | 1 question* | 25 minutes |

*Note: The total testing time for two essays is 50 minutes. It is common for students to spend too much time on the first essay and not leave enough time for the second essay. Remember to leave 25 minutes to write the second essay and check your work.

## Section I: Multiple-Choice Questions

**Directions:** Choose the best answer for each question.

**100 questions**
**70 minutes**

1. Which of the following best identifies the scientific field that studies environmental effects on gene expression?
   **A.** Epigenetics
   **B.** Plasticity
   **C.** Gestalt
   **D.** Long-term potentiation
   **E.** Contralateral

2. Which of the following statements best explains when children learn language according to the nativist theory?
   **A.** Children learn language through scaffolding.
   **B.** Children's brains are innately hard-wired to learn language naturally.
   **C.** Children's social experiences develop language skills.
   **D.** Children learn language when they can master the complex system of grammar rules.
   **E.** Children learn language by completing specific psychosocial developmental stages.

3. Which of the following choices would a cognitive psychologist most likely report regarding the results of intelligence tests?
   **A.** The results are not valid and not reliable.
   **B.** The results depend on genetic factors.
   **C.** Mental age does not change when chronological age changes.
   **D.** Twins raised in different environments always have the same result.
   **E.** Test results must be reliable over time.

4. Mei has the ability to draw a different picture with each hand simultaneously. Which of the following phenomena has she most likely experienced?
   **A.** Severed corpus callosum
   **B.** Frontal lobotomy
   **C.** Lesioning of her parietal lobe
   **D.** Broca's aphasia
   **E.** Synaptic pruning

5. Sigmund Freud's research of the unconscious in the early 1900s mainly consisted of interviews with a small number of young, rich women. Which of the following statements would contemporary psychologists most agree with about Freud's research?
   **A.** Freud should have used surveys.
   **B.** Freud's sample did not represent the population.
   **C.** Freud's research was not valid because it did not include brain scans.
   **D.** Freud's interviews were not a valid method for gathering psychological information.
   **E.** Freud's theory of the unconscious was a measured scientific study.

6. Hakim is attending a new school. In order to fit in, he is following the advice of the first student he meets. Which of the following best describes Hakim's strategy to observe other students to help him fit in?
   **A.** Normative social influence
   **B.** Informational conformity
   **C.** Compliance
   **D.** Spotlight effect
   **E.** Personal fable

7. Which of the following demonstrates that what the brain perceives is not completely dependent on what the body senses?
   **A.** Blind spot
   **B.** Visual area of the thalamus
   **C.** Frequency of sound waves
   **D.** Olfactory bulb
   **E.** Ossicles

8. Which of the following identifies the stage of sleep when the brain is least active?
   **A.** NREM 1
   **B.** NREM 2
   **C.** NREM 3
   **D.** REM sleep
   **E.** Saccadic sleep

9. Which of the following scenarios best describes diffusion of responsibility?
   **A.** One person administers CPR and another person calls 9-1-1 when an elderly woman stops breathing.
   **B.** A student refuses to contribute to a group project.
   **C.** A man falls while walking in the airport and no one stops to help him.
   **D.** A student plays her violin the best when in a large crowd.
   **E.** A man helps a stranger cross the street.

10. A speck of dirt in your eye will naturally cause a blinking reflex. The speck of dirt is a(n)
    **A.** conditioned stimulus
    **B.** unconditioned stimulus
    **C.** neutral stimulus
    **D.** second-order stimulus
    **E.** token stimulus

11. Which of the following symptoms are associated with a conversion disorder?
    **A.** Enlarged ventricles
    **B.** Panic attacks
    **C.** Withdrawal
    **D.** Flat affect
    **E.** Inability to feel sensations with the left hand

12. According to psychologist Paul Ekman, human emotional expressions are
    **A.** dependent on one's culture
    **B.** dependent on one's gender
    **C.** dependent on interracial groupings
    **D.** the same for all cultures
    **E.** always different for people

13. The parietal lobes are responsible for helping which of the following brain structures?
    - **A.** Sensory strip
    - **B.** Motor strip
    - **C.** Broca's area
    - **D.** Wernicke's area
    - **E.** fusiform gyrus

14. Which of the following is the best example of out-group bias?
    - **A.** Just-world hypothesis
    - **B.** Peripheral route of persuasion
    - **C.** Obedience
    - **D.** Social facilitation
    - **E.** Social loafing

*Question 15 refers to the following graph.*

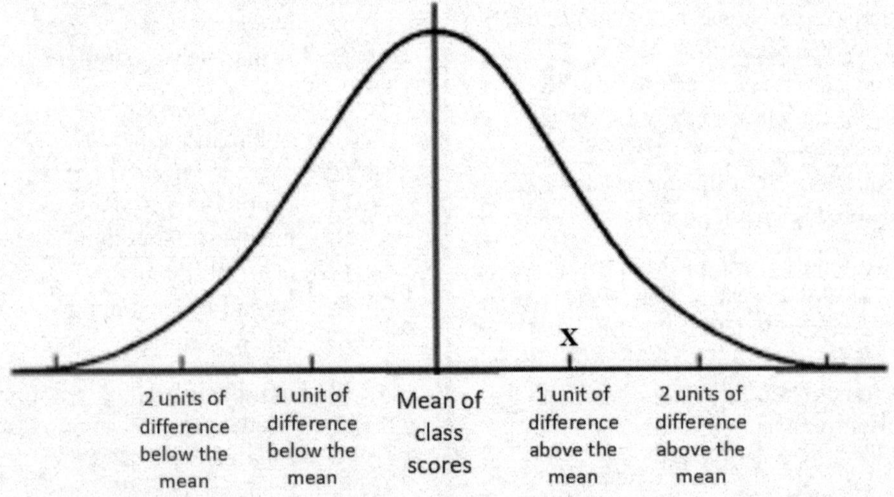


15. Gerald's AP Psychology teacher, Mrs. Fenton, didn't tell him his score on a test. Instead, she showed him a graphic representation of where his score is relative to the class mean. Given that the *X* on the graph is Gerald's score, what can be said about Gerald's grade?
    - **A.** Gerald has a *z*-score of –2.
    - **B.** Gerald's score is statistically significant.
    - **C.** Gerald's score is the mode.
    - **D.** Gerald's score is skewed.
    - **E.** Gerald's score is one standard deviation above the mean.

16. Which of the following best describes mental structures that a person uses to organize experiences of the world?
    - **A.** Retrieval
    - **B.** Working memory
    - **C.** Schema
    - **D.** Episodic memory
    - **E.** Implicit memory

17. Professor Howard wants to avoid the Hawthorne effect and experimenter bias in her study. Which of the following research design methods should Professor Howard use in her study?
    - **A.** Double-blind study
    - **B.** Naturalistic observation
    - **C.** Cross-sectional study
    - **D.** Longitudinal study
    - **E.** Single-blind study

18. When Marissa left the movie theater at 2:30 p.m., she was surprised by the brightness of the sun on her eyes, but after only a few minutes she didn't even notice the brightness. Which of the following concepts best describes this phenomenon?
    - **A.** Sensory habituation
    - **B.** Temporal coding
    - **C.** Sensory adaptation
    - **D.** Differential threshold
    - **E.** Sensory transduction

19. Which of the following is responsible for the transmission of vibrations to the cochlea?
    - **A.** Basilar membrane
    - **B.** Auditory nerve
    - **C.** Semicircular canals
    - **D.** Stapes
    - **E.** Tympanic membrane

20. Steven memorizes a list of 20 vocabulary words. Which of the following neurological processes best describes Steven's biological learning experience?
    - **A.** Reuptake
    - **B.** Polarization
    - **C.** Lateral inhibition
    - **D.** Myelination
    - **E.** Long-term potentiation

21. Sarah is in therapy to end her habit of smoking. Her therapist suggests that Sarah should reward herself with a bowl of ice cream or a latte if she makes it through the whole day without smoking a cigarette. Which of the following best describes this type of therapy?
    - **A.** Pharmacological therapy
    - **B.** Humanistic therapy
    - **C.** Cognitive therapy
    - **D.** Psychodynamic therapy
    - **E.** Behavioral therapy

22. Which of the following neurological structures releases neurotransmitters?
    - **A.** Myelin sheath
    - **B.** Dendrite
    - **C.** Vesicles
    - **D.** Sodium gates
    - **E.** Receptor sites

23. Which of the following early psychologists believed that introspection was a scientific method to study the mind?
    - **A.** G. Stanley Hall
    - **B.** Wilhelm Wundt
    - **C.** Franz Joseph Gall
    - **D.** Sigmund Freud
    - **E.** William James

24. Which of the following brain structures is NOT associated with the limbic system?
    - **A.** Amygdala
    - **B.** Hippocampus
    - **C.** Thalamus
    - **D.** Pons
    - **E.** Hypothalamus

25. Which of the following symptoms is NOT associated with a bipolar disorder?
    - **A.** Flight of ideas
    - **B.** Major depression
    - **C.** Memory loss
    - **D.** Mania
    - **E.** Flat affect

26. Which of the following psychologists proved that training an animal's reflexes is possible?
    - **A.** Ivan Pavlov
    - **B.** Edward Thorndike
    - **C.** B. F. Skinner
    - **D.** Wilhelm Wundt
    - **E.** Hermann von Helmholtz

27. Grace realizes whenever she hugs her mom, her mom offers to do something nice for her. This is an example of which of the following concepts?
    **A.** Association
    **B.** Internalization
    **C.** Fixed action pattern
    **D.** Neutral stimulus
    **E.** Entrainment

28. Which of the following is NOT a Piagetian concept?
    **A.** Formal stage
    **B.** Schema
    **C.** Accommodation
    **D.** Assimilation
    **E.** Anxious-avoidant attachment

29. Which of the following processes might have the effect of speeding up an action potential?
    **A.** Long-term potentiation
    **B.** Myelination
    **C.** Reuptake
    **D.** Perceptual set
    **E.** Transduction

30. Ms. Lindenberg hypothesizes that playing music while students are taking tests reduces the stress level. Because there are 91 students in her combined classes with a wide range of musical preferences, she conducts a survey about the students' preference for classical music. The data results suggest that nearly twice as many female students prefer classical music than male students.

    Which of the following graphic illustrations best represents the results of the survey?

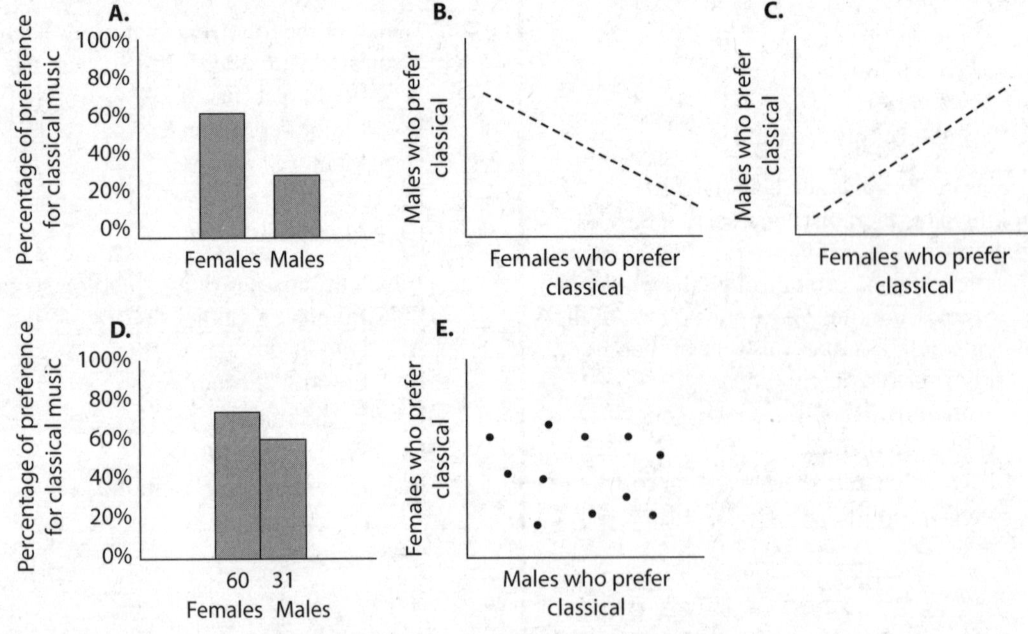

31. Sebastian is pleasantly surprised that his grandmother has a broad knowledge of facts that she learned throughout her lifetime. Which of the following best represents his grandmother's form of intelligence?
   **A.** Flynn effect
   **B.** Fluid intelligence
   **C.** Crystalized intelligence
   **D.** Mental age
   **E.** Deviation IQ

32. According to social psychologist Albert Bandura, which of the following concepts describes a person who has the confidence to successfully execute specific tasks that have never been attempted?
   **A.** Locus of control
   **B.** Introversion
   **C.** Archetypes
   **D.** Self-efficacy
   **E.** Self-actualization

33. Lesioning in this part of a rat's brain can block new memories from forming.
   **A.** Hippocampus
   **B.** Cerebellum
   **C.** Frontal lobe
   **D.** Occipital lobe
   **E.** Medulla

34. An intelligence test must have which of the following constructs to be considered an accurate measure of human intelligence?
   **A.** Reliability
   **B.** Fluid intelligence
   **C.** Validity
   **D.** Psychometrics
   **E.** Factor analysis

35. The transduction of light waves takes place in which of the following visual structures?
   **A.** Blind spot
   **B.** Fovea
   **C.** Lens
   **D.** Pupil
   **E.** Cornea

36. Cognitive appraisal is an outcome of which of the following theories of emotion?
   **A.** Yerkes-Dodson theory
   **B.** Schachter-Singer two-factor theory
   **C.** Cannon-Bard theory
   **D.** James-Lange theory
   **E.** Zajonc-LeDoux theory

37. Which of the following *best* describes Carl Jung's theory of the collective unconscious?
   **A.** Humans in certain cultures are more likely to share thoughts.
   **B.** Humans in certain cultures have the same urges and drives.
   **C.** Humans all share common dreams and nightmares.
   **D.** The human psyche shares common human experiences.
   **E.** Humans share genetically inherited unconscious memories based on instincts.

38. Which of the following best explains a null hypothesis in statistical research?
   **A.** The correlation coefficient is equal to zero.
   **B.** The mean is the same value as the median.
   **C.** The research findings result in a Type II error.
   **D.** The prediction that there is not a significant effect or relationship
   **E.** The prediction that one variable causes another variable to change

39. Which of the following shows the correct order to explain cognition in the information processing model series?
   **A.** Working memory, sensory memory, long-term memory
   **B.** Short-term memory, medium-term memory, long-term memory
   **C.** Sensory memory, short-term memory, long-term memory
   **D.** Echoic memory, iconic memory, working memory
   **E.** Sensory memory, cognitive memory, working memory

40. The lowest frequency of sound that humans can detect is
    A. 4–7 Hz
    B. 20,000 Hz
    C. Humans cannot detect low frequency, only low amplitude.
    D. Humans cannot perceive low frequencies, but can sense low frequencies.
    E. 30 Hz

41. Color vision genes are located in which of the following chromosomes?
    A. X chromosome
    B. Y chromosome
    C. 14th chromosome
    D. 5th chromosome
    E. Color vision is randomized across the human species.

42. Dr. Mazzola is a psychologist who has the primary responsibility of responding to the needs of employees at a large corporation. Which of the following best describes this type of psychologist?
    A. Industrial/organizational psychologist
    B. Behavioral psychologist
    C. Clinical psychologist
    D. Developmental psychologist
    E. Research psychologist

43. In statistical testing, which of the following provides strong evidence that the results are not due to chance?
    A. When 68% of the results fall within one standard deviation of the mean
    B. When $p > 90\%$
    C. When the results are positively skewed
    D. When the median, mode, and mean are all the same value
    E. When $p < 0.05$

44. Darrell feels anxious whenever he hears the sound of a dentist's drill because of a painful encounter at the dental office 2 years ago. Which of the following best describes the high-pitched squeal of the dentist's drill?
    A. Conditioned stimulus
    B. Unconditioned stimulus
    C. Neutral stimulus
    D. Unconditioned response
    E. Conditioned response

45. Which of the following is the most sensitive to changes in stimulus intensity?
    A. Brightness
    B. Weight
    C. Saltiness
    D. Pitch
    E. Loudness

46. The following traits are dimensions of the five-factor model of personality EXCEPT
    A. neuroticism
    B. agreeableness
    C. openness
    D. conscientiousness
    E. insightfulness

47. Mrs. Rice rewards students for writing a thesis statement and supporting evidence in their essay assignment. She then gives them an additional reward when they provide a second supporting idea. Which one of the following is NOT related to Mrs. Rice's reward strategy?
    A. Differential reinforcement
    B. Successive approximation
    C. Shaping
    D. Fixed-interval reinforcement
    E. Chaining

48. Which of the following graphs best represents the serial position effect?

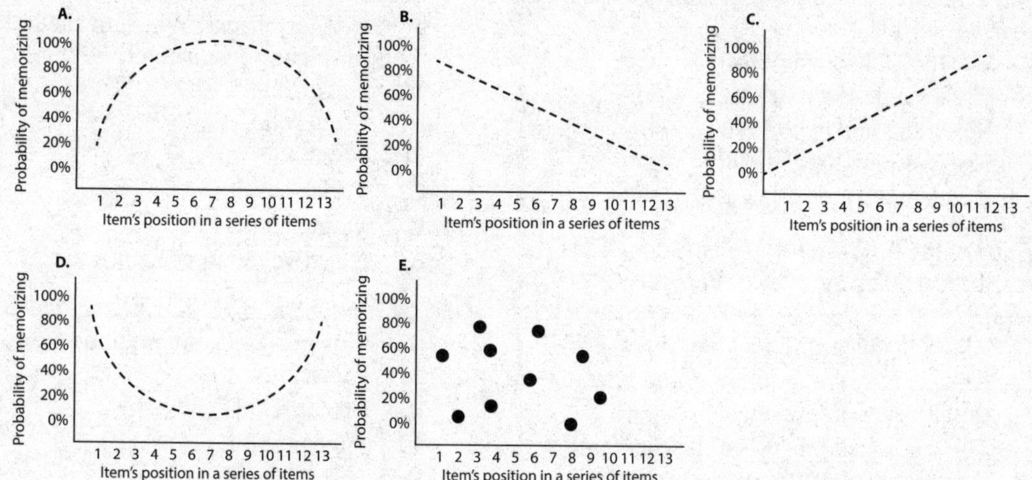


49. Which of the following early research psychologists believed that the best way to study the mind was to examine the functions instead of the structures of the mind?
   A. Max Wertheimer
   B. Edward Thorndike
   C. William James
   D. Wilhelm Wundt
   E. Edward Titchener

50. Which of the following neurotransmitters, when blocked, creates symptoms of Alzheimer's disease?
   A. Serotonin
   B. Norepinephrine
   C. Acetylcholine
   D. Dopamine
   E. GABA

51. Fred has deep-seated racist feelings for members of a certain ethnic group. However, he goes out of his way to be polite to members of that group. According to Freud, Fred is unconsciously exhibiting which of the following defense mechanisms?
   A. Denial
   B. Displacement
   C. Reaction formation
   D. Projection
   E. Regression

52. Which one of the following is the type of therapy that specifically borrows techniques from multiple types of therapies?
   A. Individual therapy
   B. Group therapy
   C. Eclectic therapy
   D. Family therapy
   E. Behavioral therapy

53. Which of the following is the best method for a researcher to reduce the possibility of experimenter bias?
   **A.** Use the Hawthorne effect.
   **B.** Use a single-blind design.
   **C.** Reject the null hypothesis.
   **D.** Use a double-blind design.
   **E.** Use demand characteristics.

54. Which of the following statements does NOT describe Carl Rogers' view of humanistic therapy?
   **A.** All clients have different worldviews.
   **B.** All clients desire to improve and have the ability to improve.
   **C.** The relationship between the client and therapist relies on empathy, acceptance, and genuineness.
   **D.** The client controls the content of the dialogue.
   **E.** The therapist controls the content of the dialogue.

55. Eighteen-month-old Angela is crying in her crib because her pacifier fell out of her mouth. She knows the pacifier is in her crib, but she can't find it. Which of the following Piagetian concepts best describes Angela's experience?
   **A.** Formal operations
   **B.** Concrete operations
   **C.** Accommodation
   **D.** Object permanence
   **E.** Assimilation

56. James wants his curfew extended on weekends because most of his friends have a curfew of 11:30 p.m. Which of the following best explains the strategy of James sitting down with his mom to suggest that a curfew of 2:30 a.m. is fair and reasonable?
   **A.** Cognitive dissonance
   **B.** Foot-in-the-door technique
   **C.** Door-in-the-face technique
   **D.** Out-group homogeneity
   **E.** Just-world hypothesis

57. Desmond does not enjoy his part-time job, but he always looks forward to receiving bi-weekly paychecks. Which of the following reinforcement phenomena is Desmond experiencing?
   **A.** Fixed ratio
   **B.** Fixed interval
   **C.** Variable ratio
   **D.** Variable interval
   **E.** Negative reinforcement

58. Your phone number is stored in which one of the following levels of consciousness?
   **A.** Conscious
   **B.** Preconscious
   **C.** Subconscious
   **D.** Unconscious
   **E.** Nonconscious

59. The unconscious desire for the opposite sex parent occurs during which of the following psychodynamic stages of development?
   **A.** Oral
   **B.** Phallic
   **C.** Latent
   **D.** Genital
   **E.** Anal

60. In a scientific experiment, a rat presses a lever and receives a small injection of cocaine. The rat learns to associate the lever with the injection, and presses the lever more and more frequently, proving that cocaine is a
   **A.** neutral stimulus
   **B.** negative reinforcer
   **C.** conditioned stimulus
   **D.** variable interval
   **E.** positive reinforcer

61. Maria wants to join the varsity cross-country team, so she begins training with other teammates. Maria notices that she runs faster when she trains with her teammates. Which of the following best describes the influence that Maria's teammates have on her ability to run faster?
   **A.** Social loafing
   **B.** Social facilitation
   **C.** Bystander effect
   **D.** Diffusion of responsibility
   **E.** Deindividuation

62. Alyah passed her driver's license test and is excited to run errands for her family. When Alyah's mom sent her to the grocery store, she continuously repeated the list of groceries to herself to try to remember everything that she needed to buy. Which of the following memory techniques is Alyah using to remember the list of groceries?
   **A.** Working memory
   **B.** Elaborative rehearsal
   **C.** Effortful processing
   **D.** Maintenance rehearsal
   **E.** Peripheral route processing

63. Which of the following is NOT true about the normal distribution of intelligence scores?
   **A.** The mean, median, and mode are all the same value.
   **B.** The approximate number of scores above and below the mean are the same.
   **C.** The value of the mean is noticeably different from the other measures of central tendency.
   **D.** A small number of scores are far away from the mean.
   **E.** A normal curve is not skewed by extreme scores.

64. Pharmacological therapy includes which of the following treatments?
   **A.** MAO inhibitors
   **B.** Dichotomous thinking
   **C.** Insight therapy
   **D.** Counterconditioning
   **E.** Flooding

65. Jason's parents told him that he was grounded until his grades improved. When his grades improved, his parents were happy to end the grounding. Jason changed his behavior by learning which of the following conditions?
   **A.** Negative punishment
   **B.** Positive punishment
   **C.** Negative reinforcement
   **D.** Positive reinforcement
   **E.** Variable interval

66. The symptoms of major depressive disorder include all of the following EXCEPT
   **A.** appetite changes
   **B.** loss of interest
   **C.** reduced social interactions
   **D.** mania
   **E.** fatigue

67. Kayla is a 4-year-old who is proud of herself because she ate all of her vegetables. She exclaims, "Look I eated it all up." Which of the following stages of language acquisition best describes Kayla's speech?
   **A.** Babbling
   **B.** Holophrase
   **C.** Telegraphic speech
   **D.** Fast mapping
   **E.** Overgeneralization

68. All the following drugs are classified as depressants EXCEPT
   **A.** alcohol
   **B.** benzodiazepines
   **C.** barbiturates
   **D.** MDMA (ecstasy)
   **E.** Xanax

69. A major neurological task of a young child's brain is to reduce the number of unnecessary brain synapses. Which of the following physical development changes best describes this process?
    **A.** Maturationism
    **B.** Pruning
    **C.** Adaptation
    **D.** Accommodation
    **E.** Myelination

70. Frederica is frustrated that her classmate seems to receive good grades with little or no effort. She is convinced that her classmate is a genius and wants to figure out what causes some people to have high intelligence. Which of the following types of research methods should Frederica design to study this phenomenon?
    **A.** Experimental
    **B.** Naturalistic observation
    **C.** Longitudinal study
    **D.** Cross-sectional study
    **E.** Case study

71. Which of the following acts to increase serotonin in the synapses?
    **A.** SSRIs
    **B.** ECT
    **C.** Anti-anxiety medication
    **D.** Anti-psychotic medication
    **E.** L-Dopa

72. Wayne's therapist suggests a therapeutic technique that requires him to use an electronic monitor to help him learn to relax. Which of the following best describes this technique?
    **A.** Transcranial magnetic stimulation
    **B.** Token economy
    **C.** Tricyclics
    **D.** Biofeedback
    **E.** Cognitive behavior therapy

73. Rachel has enthusiastic school spirit that is always good natured. However, during a school game when she was cheering for her team, a few rival students shouted offensive insults. As a result, Rachel believes that all of the students from the rival school are rude. Which of the following best describes Rachel's belief?
    **A.** In-group bias
    **B.** Groupthink
    **C.** Prisoner's dilemma
    **D.** Out-group homogeneity
    **E.** Social trap

74. Vera learns that a woman was evicted from her home right before the holiday season. Vera thinks that the woman was evicted because she did not manage her money well and was lazy. Vera did not consider that the woman had unexpected medical expenses and lost income because her roommate unexpectedly moved out. Which of the following best describes Vera's rationalization for her bias?
    **A.** Social loafing
    **B.** Deindividuation
    **C.** Fundamental attribution error
    **D.** Compliance
    **E.** Bystander effect

75. The Cannon-Bard theory suggests that
    **A.** physical reactions and emotions occur simultaneously
    **B.** physical reactions cause emotional interpretations
    **C.** the cognitive appraisal of one's physical state determines the emotional interpretation
    **D.** emotional interpretations dictate which physical response occurs in the body
    **E.** emotional interpretations cannot prevent the physical reaction

76. Which of the following is a symptom of Wernicke's aphasia?
   - **A.** Difficulty forming spoken words
   - **B.** Difficulty understanding spoken language
   - **C.** Difficulty knowing when not to apply the rules of grammar
   - **D.** Difficulty reading simple graphs or charts
   - **E.** Difficulty recognizing sight words (e.g., "the" and "and")

77. Which of the following types of research methods is advantageous to reducing the influence of a demand characteristic?
   - **A.** Survey
   - **B.** Interview
   - **C.** Laboratory experiment
   - **D.** Naturalistic observation
   - **E.** Any study requiring informed consent

78. The hypothesis of the Harlow's monkey experiments focused on whether surrogate mothers would be able to take the place of the biological mothers' love, but Harlow's findings suggested that
   - **A.** love is a chemical reaction
   - **B.** love is a limbic system response
   - **C.** monkeys do not need love and mother-child bonding for survival
   - **D.** monkeys need to cuddle, touch, and love
   - **E.** monkeys need food and water for survival, but not love

79. Which of the following is NOT considered a psychological symptom of schizophrenia?
   - **A.** Disorganized thinking
   - **B.** Distorted perceptions
   - **C.** Psychosis
   - **D.** Word salad
   - **E.** Extreme concern with physical appearance

80. Which of the following terms best matches the concept of a neuron firing?
   - **A.** plasticity
   - **B.** polarization
   - **C.** long-term potentiation
   - **D.** depolarization
   - **E.** reuptake

81. Which of the following best defines the *Diagnostic and Statistical Manual of Mental Disorders* (DSM-5)?
   - **A.** It is based on the medical model of understanding mental disorders.
   - **B.** It provides treatment plans for mental disorders.
   - **C.** It was written using everyday language for nonprofessionals to understand mental disorders.
   - **D.** It is used by research psychologists only.
   - **E.** It focuses on the causes of mental disorders, but not the symptoms.

82. In an experiment, a chimpanzee learned that he could receive a plastic poker chip for doing certain behaviors, and then the chimpanzee could trade three poker chips for a banana. Which of the following concepts best describes this scenario?
   - **A.** Variable interval
   - **B.** Token economy
   - **C.** Law of effect
   - **D.** Counterconditioning
   - **E.** Aversive conditioning

83. According to genetic heritability, which of the following best describes the idea that traits are inherited by multiple genes?
   - **A.** Phenotype
   - **B.** Epigenetics
   - **C.** Genotype
   - **D.** Polygenic
   - **E.** Teratogens

84. According to Hermann Ebbinghaus and his "forgetting curve," people forget about 80 percent of newly learned meaningless material, such as nonsense syllables, within
   **A.** 1 hour
   **B.** 1 day
   **C.** 3 days
   **D.** 3 weeks
   **E.** 3 years

85. Which of the following best explains that the average IQ improves with each successive generation?
   **A.** Criterion validity
   **B.** Crystallized intelligence
   **C.** Fluid intelligence
   **D.** Stereotype threat
   **E.** Flynn effect

86. Arden flinches and ducks her head whenever she hears a buzzing sound because she believes that a bee is nearby. Which of the following best describes Arden's reaction to the buzzing sound?
   **A.** Generalization
   **B.** Spontaneous recovery
   **C.** Aversive conditioning
   **D.** Escape conditioning
   **E.** Discrimination

87. Which of the following approaches to therapy is highly interactive and focuses on "here-and-now" client-centered experiences?
   **A.** Behavioral therapy
   **B.** Pharmacological therapy
   **C.** Psychoanalytic therapy
   **D.** Humanistic therapy
   **E.** Electroconvulsive therapy

88. Mr. Honma is frustrated with his class because the students will not settle down and listen to his instruction. He believes that students today are disrespectful. Which of the following concepts best matches Mr. Honma's attitude?
   **A.** Situational attribution
   **B.** Ethnocentrism
   **C.** Dispositional attribution
   **D.** Cognitive dissonance
   **E.** Spotlight effect

89. Which of the following neurotransmitters is known to play a role in regulating the body's sleep-wake cycle and contributing to a general sense of well-being?
   **A.** Dopamine
   **B.** Noradrenaline
   **C.** Endorphins
   **D.** Histamines
   **E.** Serotonin

90. The higher levels of Maslow's hierarchy are most closely associated with which of the following concepts?
   **A.** Extrinsic rewards
   **B.** Secondary reinforcers
   **C.** Continuous reinforcement
   **D.** Instincts
   **E.** Intrinsic rewards

91. Benito was told by his teacher, Mrs. Fitter, that the best way to store information in the long-term memory so that it can be retrieved later is to use
   **A.** schema
   **B.** sensory memory
   **C.** primacy effect
   **D.** recency effect
   **E.** elaborative rehearsal

92. A researcher does not inform the participants about some of the details of a study in order to protect the integrity of her study. To prevent unethical violations after the volunteers have participated, the researcher should
   **A.** contact the Institutional Review Board of the university
   **B.** debrief the participants
   **C.** ask the participants to sign an informed consent document
   **D.** use a double-blind design
   **E.** keep the results confidential

93. Which of the following best describes someone who has a neurocognitive disorder?
   A. Bipolar disorder
   B. Dysthymia
   C. Anterograde amnesia
   D. Alzheimer's disease
   E. Anorexia nervosa

94. Jamie's parents were pleasantly surprised when she demonstrated good manners at an exclusive restaurant. Although her parents had instructed her on the importance of good manners, Jamie never had an opportunity to show that she understood the lessons. Which of the following best describes Jamie's good behavior?
   A. Latent learning
   B. Association
   C. Discrimination
   D. Acquisition
   E. Extinction

95. A researcher looks at the results of her study and concludes that there is not a significant relationship between two variables. Later, she analyzes the results again and finds that there is a significant effect between the two variables. Which of the following concepts best describes this scenario?
   A. Type II error
   B. Type I error
   C. Hindsight bias
   D. Confirmation bias
   E. Fundamental attribution error

96. Which of the following demonstrates the correct order of the primary components that a neural signal goes through in the process of neurotransmission?
   A. axon terminal, dendrite, soma, axon
   B. dendrite, soma, axon, axon terminal
   C. terminal buttons, axon, soma, dendrite
   D. receptor sites, end bulbs, axon, soma
   E. soma, axon, end bulbs, terminal buttons

97. Which of the following describes the part of the brain that is most active when a person is happy?
   A. Pons
   B. Optic chiasm
   C. Thalamus
   D. Nucleus accumbens
   E. Superchiasmatic nucleus

98. Which of the following is responsible for perceiving binocular depth cues?
   A. Motion parallax
   B. Retinal disparity
   C. Linear perspective
   D. Interposition
   E. Relative size

99. Which of the following correlational coefficients represents the strongest relationship?
   A. −0.8
   B. 0.2
   C. 0.05
   D. 0.5
   E. −0.34

100. Which of the following hormones is most closely related to experiencing hunger?
   A. Leptin
   B. Ghrelin
   C. Androgen
   D. Cortisol
   E. Norepinephrine

IF YOU FINISH BEFORE TIME IS CALLED, CHECK YOUR WORK ON THIS SECTION ONLY. DO NOT WORK ON ANY OTHER SECTION IN THE TEST.

# Section II: Free-Response Questions

**2 questions**

**50 minutes**

**Directions:** It is suggested that you take a few minutes to plan and outline your essay. Write your response on lined paper. You must demonstrate your understanding of course skills and course content. Your essay is considered a first draft and may contain some grammatical errors that will not be counted against you. However, to receive full credit, your essay must demonstrate defensible content knowledge with substantive examples where appropriate.

## Question 1

*Read the scenario and answer the question that follows.*

> Mr. Reed is widely recognized as a successful basketball coach. Coaches from other districts have asked him how he influences his players to perform at their highest levels.

Explain how each of the concepts might contribute to the players' success in the scenario.

- Collectivism
- Social facilitation
- Elaborative rehearsal
- Selective attention
- Observational learning
- Depth perception
- Locus of control

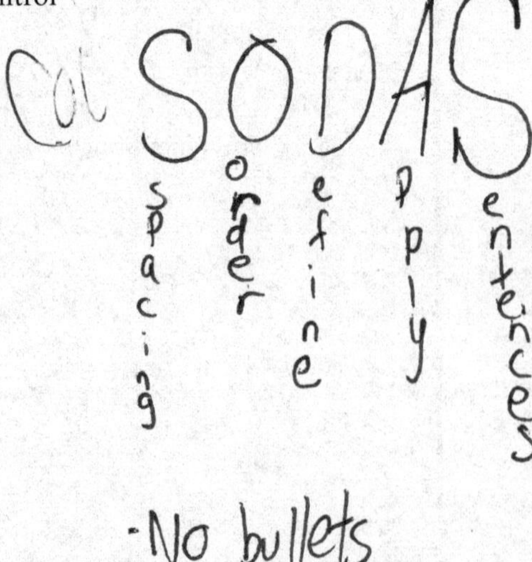

## Question 2

*Read the scenario and answer the question that follows.*

The students in Ms. Vita's AP Psychology class were interested in investigating whether starting school at a later time would improve students' academic performance. The students conduct the experiment by first obtaining permission from the school principal and Mrs. Vita so that the AP Psychology class could be held after school instead of during its usual first-period time slot. The students also obtained permission to distribute coffee to the students in the after-school class.

**Part A**

Identify each of the following in relation to this study.

- The independent variable
- The dependent variable
- The null hypothesis

**Part B**

- Operationally define one variable in this study.
- Identify one confounding variable in this study.
- Describe one ethical issue in this study.
- Explain how the *y*-axis would be labeled if the students presented their results in graphic form.

IF YOU FINISH BEFORE TIME IS CALLED, CHECK YOUR WORK ON THIS SECTION ONLY. DO NOT WORK ON ANY OTHER SECTION IN THE TEST.

# Answer Key for Multiple-Choice Questions

1. A
2. B
3. E
4. A
5. B
6. B
7. A
8. C
9. C
10. B
11. E
12. D
13. A
14. A
15. E
16. C
17. A
18. C
19. D
20. E
21. E
22. C
23. B
24. D
25. C
26. A
27. A
28. E
29. B
30. A
31. C
32. D
33. A
34. C
35. B
36. B
37. E
38. D
39. C
40. E
41. B
42. A
43. E
44. A
45. D
46. E
47. D
48. D
49. C
50. C
51. C
52. C
53. D
54. E
55. D
56. C
57. B
58. B
59. B
60. E
61. B
62. D
63. C
64. A
65. C
66. D
67. E
68. D
69. B
70. A
71. A
72. D
73. D
74. C
75. A
76. B
77. D
78. D
79. E
80. D
81. A
82. B
83. D
84. B
85. E
86. A
87. D
88. C
89. E
90. E
91. E
92. B
93. D
94. A
95. A
96. B
97. D
98. B
99. A
100. B

# Answer Explanations

## Section I: Multiple-Choice Questions

1. **A.** *Epigenetics,* choice A, is a science that seeks to understand how environmental factors modify (turn on or off) certain genes. An example of this is how a mother's hormonal state creates an environment that can "switch on" or "switch off" some of the fetus' genes at different times during the pregnancy. *Plasticity* (choice B; also called neuroplasticity) refers to how the brain can change throughout a person's life due to environmental factors. *Gestalt* (choice C) refers to the concept of seeing or thinking of the whole, rather than the individual parts. *Long-term potentiation* (choice D) is a process that strengthens neurons. In the process, neurons grow closer together, which causes the synapse to become smaller and produce an increase in signal transmission between two neurons. *Contralateral* (choice E) corresponds to the opposite side of the body. The hemispheres of the brain control the contralateral sides of the body. For example, the left side of the brain controls the right side of the body, and the right side of the brain controls the left side of the body. *(Chapter 5)*
2. **B.** According to nativist theory, children learn language *naturally,* choice B, even if not taught. Noam Chomsky suggested that infants have an instinctive ability to learn language. *Scaffolding* (choice A) refers to Lev Vygotsky's theory that children can learn when they are assisted by older peers or adults. According to Albert Bandura, *social learning* (choice C) takes place when children observe or model others. According to Chomsky, infants and children intuitively know how to combine linguistic and grammatical patterns of words. For example, children do not need to *master grammar rules* to learn spoken language, eliminating choice D. *Psychosocial* refers to Erik Erikson's stages of child development, eliminating choice E. *(Chapter 8)*
3. **E.** Test results must be *reliable* and stable over time, choice E. For an intelligence test to be reliable, it must have the same consistent results if taken twice. *Validity* means that the test measures what it is supposed to measure. A test can be reliable but not valid. For a test to be beneficial, it must measure what it says it measures (validity), and it must provide consistent results (reliability); therefore, choice A is incorrect. Choice B is incorrect because psychologists believe that the environment, as well as *genetic factors,* plays an important role in the development of intelligence. Choice C is incorrect because *mental age* may increase throughout childhood. Although twins raised in different environments (choice D) may have the same test results, it is not absolute. Note: When you see an answer choice on the AP PSYCH exam that has the word *always, only,* or *never,* it is probably incorrect. *(Chapter 8)*
4. **A.** The *corpus callosum* is the part of the brain that connects the two hemispheres. In rare surgeries to improve epileptic seizures, the corpus callosum is sometimes severed. Severing the hemispheres helps Mei to draw different shapes at the same time, choice A. A *frontal lobotomy* (choice B; think about *frontal lobe*) is an outdated and misused surgery that was used to treat many types of psychological disorders. *Lesioning* (choice C) is a surgical procedure to purposely damage a part of the brain in order to assess behaviors; lesioning would not allow Mei to perform two different tasks at the same time. *Broca's aphasia* (choice D) is the loss of ability to communicate that is caused by brain neural damage. *Synaptic pruning* (choice E) is the process by which the brain removes unneeded connections. *(Chapter 5)*
5. **B.** Freud is known for working with a limited population (e.g., young, upper-class women). Because he did not expand his sample base to different ages, genders, or socioeconomic groups, Freud's theory is not representative of a general population, choice B. Based on Freud's theory, there is no indication that surveys would have been better than interviews (choice A). Many psychological research efforts are valid without the use of modern scanning technologies (choice C). Interviews are a valid tool for

collecting information from participants (choice D). Freud's theory was not based on a measured scientific study (choice E). *(Chapter 4)*

6. **B.** *Informational conformity,* choice B, is when a person believes that someone else has greater information and yields to a person (or group) for direction. In this case, Hakim wants information so that he will know how to behave in order to fit in with other students. *Normative social influence* (choice A) relates to changing thoughts, values, or behavior for the sake of wanting to be liked and accepted by others (i.e., peer pressure). In normative social influence, the person conforms on the outside, but not on the inside. *Compliance* (choice C) is yielding to cooperate or become obedient. The *spotlight effect* (choice D) is the tendency for some people to believe that others are focusing their attention on them; some people feel that there is a spotlight on them at all times. *Personal fable* (choice E) is similar to Piaget's *imaginary audience* and the spotlight effect that are common in adolescence. It is the self-perception that one is "special," similar to delusions of grandeur. *(Chapter 12)*
7. **A.** *Blind spots,* choice A, are certain areas in a person's visual field that he or she cannot sense. Because there are no rods or cones in the area where the optic nerve joins the retina, when light from an object touches that area of the retina, the eye can't sense it. The *visual area of the thalamus* (choice B) works to send incoming information from the optic nerve all over the brain. The *frequency of sound waves* (choice C) is sensed by the cochlea and can be measured by machines independent of human perception. The *olfactory bulb* (choice D) is the part of the nasal mechanism that transduces chemical molecules into scents we can sense. The *ossicles* (choice E) are the three bones that help carry vibrations from the tympanic membrane to the cochlea. *(Chapter 6)*
8. **C.** *NREM 3,* choice C, is the stage of sleep when the person is in a deep sleep and does not dream, hence the abbreviation of "Non-REM" sleep. In *NREM 1* (choice A), the person is relaxed, daydreaming, or meditating—the person is somewhat asleep and somewhat awake. In *NREM 2* (choice B), the person is asleep, but not deeply. *REM sleep* (choice D) is when the person experiences rapid eye movement (REM); during this stage, the person is difficult to wake and is able to dream. *Saccadic sleep* (choice E) is another word for REM sleep. *(Chapter 5)*
9. **C.** *Diffusion of responsibility* is a social psychology concept in which people feel no responsibility to help others because the person assumes someone else will help, as in the scenario in choice C. When two people choose to help an elderly person (choice A), it is the opposite of *diffusion* (spreading out) of responsibility. If a group member chooses not to help with a group project (choice B), it would be *social loafing*. If someone performs better when others are watching (choice D), it is called *social facilitation.* If someone helps a stranger (choice E), it is called *altruism. (Chapter 12)*
10. **B.** Because a person does not learn that a speck of dirt in the eye is irritating, it is an *unconditioned stimulus,* choice B. A *conditioned stimulus* (choice A) is something that must be learned. A *neutral stimulus* (choice C) is sensory input that has no value and can easily be ignored. A *second-order stimulus* (choice D) is something that is learned after first learning a stimulus response association. For example, if you learned that the school bell means class is over and then learn that students close their notebooks 1 minute before the bell, the sight and sound of notebooks closing would be a second-order stimulus that is connected to the relief of class being over. A *token stimulus* (choice E) is a false prompt. It is a play on the concept of token economy in which a child, animal, or student learns that if they earn enough of something meaningless (e.g., tickets), those things can be traded for something that is meaningful such as a piece of candy. *(Chapter 7)*
11. **E.** A *conversion disorder* is when someone is suffering from a physical symptom, but has no medical explanation (such as a person who has no feeling in the left hand), choice E. *Ventricles* (choice A) are hollow cavities in the middle of each hemisphere of the brain, and enlarged ventricles are associated with schizophrenia. *Panic attacks* (choice B) are one of the symptoms of a panic disorder, but panic

attacks can also be a symptom of other disorders like post-traumatic stress disorder and obsessive-compulsive disorder. *Withdrawal* (choice C) happens when a person discontinues drug use. *Flat affect* (choice D) is when a person does not show appropriate emotional expressions. It is a symptom of many disorders, such as major depressive disorder, schizophrenia, and autism spectrum disorder. *(Chapter 11)*

12. **D.** Paul Ekman was influenced by Darwin's theory of evolution, which suggested that a species' characteristics, such as facial expressions, are universal within the species. Facial expressions are biological in nature and are the same for all humans, choice D. While certain cultures, genders, and races might have rules about showing certain emotions, choices A, B, C, and E are incorrect because Paul Ekman did not propose these assumptions. *(Chapter 10)*

13. **A.** The parietal lobes (remember you have two, one for each hemisphere) are the parts of the brain that interpret sensations from the skin. The *sensory strip,* choice A, is on the surface of the parietal lobes. The *motor strip* (choice B) is similar to the sensory strip and is parallel to the sensory strip; it is a map on the surface of the frontal lobe that connects with different muscles throughout the body. *Broca's area* (choice C) is on the surface of the left frontal lobe (remember: left, language, logic) and generates speech. *Wernicke's area* (choice D) is on the surface of the left temporal lobe and helps us to understand spoken speech. *Fusiform gyrus* (choice E) extends to both of the temporal lobes and the occipital lobes, and plays an important part in recognizing faces and other familiar objects. *(Chapter 5)*

14. **A.** Out-group bias is another way of saying "them vs. us." The *just-world hypothesis,* choice A, suggests that if something bad happens to someone, the person probably deserved it and the person is to blame for his or her own suffering. *Peripheral route of persuasion* (choice B) is a technique of convincing someone to do something by using an emotional appeal. Television commercials frequently use this technique to appeal to audiences. *Obedience* (choice C) is not related to out-group bias. *Social facilitation* (choice D) is the idea that people perform better at well-practiced tasks when they are being observed. *Social loafing* (choice E) is the idea that some people will not work as hard on a task when others will do the work. *(Chapter 12)*

15. **E.** *Standard deviation* is a way to measure how far a score deviates from the mean. It can be thought of as constant units. Because the *X* is directly over the first unit of difference to the right of the mean, Gerald's score is one standard deviation above mean, choice E. *Z-scores* (choice A) are labels for standard deviations. The *X* is not over the second unit to the left of the mean; therefore, Gerald's score does not have a *z*-score of –2. *Statistically significant* (choice B) is the result of a study that is highly likely due to the researcher's purposeful efforts and not due to accidental efforts, mistakes, or other confounding variables. The *mode* (choice C) is a measure of central tendency that is derived from the score. It appears most often in a set of scores. *Skewed* (choice D) is when an outlier or extreme score affects the mean. *(Chapter 4)*

16. **C.** *Schema,* choice C, is a concept that describes a pattern of thought or behavior that organizes mental structures. *Retrieval* (choice A) is getting something out of your memory. *Working memory* (choice B; also known as short-term memory) is immediate memory. It has a limited capacity and holds information temporarily (e.g., about seven entries for about 30 seconds). *Episodic memory* (choice D) is a conscious memory of a previous experience (e.g., who was there, what happened, when it happened). *Implicit memory* (choice E; also known as nondeclarative memory) consists of automatic, day-to-day memories that influence thoughts and behaviors without conscious awareness. *(Chapter 8)*

17. **A.** The Hawthorne effect suggests that participants change their behavior simply because they are being watched. A *double-blind study,* choice A, is when neither the researchers nor the participants know who is receiving the treatment. Because participants do not know important aspects of the study, it limits their ability to match behavior with characteristics of the study. A double-blind study also

prevents the researcher from knowing which participants received the independent variable, thus, limiting the researcher's ability to influence the results. *Naturalistic observation* (choice B) observes humans or animals in a real-world environment. A *cross-sectional study* (choice C) compares two groups at the same time. A *longitudinal study* (choice D) is any type of study that follows the participants over a period of time. A *single-blind study* (choice E) is when the participants do not know an important aspect of the study, thereby limiting their ability to match their behavior with the demand characteristics of the study. *(Chapter 4)*

18. **C.** *Sensory adaptation,* choice C, is the answer because Marissa's sense organs (i.e., eyes) adapted to the level of stimulus using diminishing sensitivity to the environment. *Sensory habituation* (choice A) is similar, but is a reduced response to something that previously prompted a stronger response (like a habit). *Temporal coding* (choice B) is an auditory concept that explains the number of times a neuron fires and recharges in a second. *Differential threshold* (choice D) is the smallest change in a stimulus you can notice. *Sensory transduction* (choice E) is the process that converts sensory stimulations into perceptions. *(Chapter 6)*
19. **D.** The eardrum vibrates from the incoming sound waves and sends these vibrations to three small connected bones in the middle ear called the ossicles: malleus (hammer), incus (anvil), and stapes (stirrup). The last bone, the *stapes*, choice D, pounds on the oval window of the cochlea. The movement sends a signal to the cochlea in the inner ear and causes fluid to move in the inner ear. The *basilar membrane* (choice A) is inside the cochlea and is important in turning vibrations into what people perceive as sound. The *auditory nerve* (choice B) is the bundle of neurons that sends information from the cochlea to the brain. The *semicircular canals* (choice C) are half-loops that contain fluid. Since fluid will always maintain a parallel state with the ground and since the three half-loops correspond with the three dimensions of space, the three semicircular canals signal the brain which direction the head is moving. The *tympanic membrane* (choice E) is the eardrum and is that place where vibrating air is changed into vibrations within the inner ear. *(Chapter 6)*
20. **E.** *Long-term potentiation,* choice E, is the process of neurons communicating with each other by narrowing the space between them (synapses). As the synapses get narrower, the neurons communicate more efficiently. This needs to happen for the brain to make the changes that are required to learn. *Reuptake* (choice A) is the process by which the presynaptic neuron reabsorbs the neurotransmitter molecules it just released. *Polarization* (choice B) means separation. In this case, it is the neuron separating the sodium ions from the potassium ions. It recharges the neuron so it can create another action potential. *Lateral* means sideways and *inhibit* means to prevent. Therefore, *lateral inhibition* (choice C) means the capacity of an excited neuron to prevent the surrounding neurons from firing. *Myelination* (choice D) is the process by which glial cells create fat-based insulation that surrounds the tube-like neuron. This protects the electrical charge known as the action potential just like rubber insulation surrounds copper wires on a charging cord. *(Chapter 5)*
21. **E.** *Behavioral therapy,* choice E, is the correct answer because Sarah is being rewarded for doing a positive behavior (e.g., not smoking). *Pharmacological therapy* (choice A; think pharmacy) is incorrect because Sarah's therapist did not suggest prescribing a medicine for treatment. *Humanistic therapy* (choice B) is incorrect because the therapist is taking a direct approach in changing Sarah's behavior instead of helping Sarah reach her own conclusions about what is right for her. *Cognitive therapy* (choice C) is incorrect because Sarah's therapist is not asking Sarah to examine or change her thoughts regarding smoking. *Psychodynamic therapy* (choice D) is incorrect because Sarah's therapist isn't concerned with the "real" unconscious reason that Sarah smokes. *(Chapter 11)*
22. **C.** *Vesicles,* choice C, are molecule-filled bubbles in the axon terminal that burst open to release the neurotransmitters to the neuron on the other side of the synapse (postsynaptic cell). *Myelin sheath*

(choice A) is a fatty coating that acts as a rubber insulation that surrounds the tube-like axon. *Dendrites* (choice B) are the antennas of the neuron that receive messages from other cells. *Sodium gates* (choice D) are the passages that help sodium ions cross the axon's membrane and mix with potassium to create an action potential. *Receptor sites* (choice E) are proteins on the dendrite that allow the neurotransmitter molecules to stimulate or inhibit the postsynaptic neuron. (*Chapter 5*)

23. **B.** *Wilhelm Wundt,* choice B, used introspection as a way to examine consciousness. Psychologists now know that the mind cannot focus on two things at once (e.g., a person cannot observe oneself think and do the thinking at that same time). *G. Stanley Hall* (choice A) was a psychologist who established the first experimental laboratory in America. He formed the modern concept of adolescence. *Franz Joseph Gall* (choice C) is known for his theory of *phrenology* (a connection between the shape of the skull and mental and personality characteristics). While we can respect his desire to simplify the complexities of the body-mind problem, Gall's theory is considered a pseudoscience (not based on the scientific method). *Sigmund Freud* (choice D) founded psychoanalysis. *William James* (choice E) was an intellectual rival of Wilhelm Wundt, but he did not value introspection in his theory of emotion. (*Chapter 4*)

24. **D.** The limbic system is at the center of emotions. All of the terms listed are part of the limbic system except the *pons,* choice D. The pons is located in the hindbrain (lower brain) and integrates brain functions (e.g., sensory messages, sleeping, digestion, and eye movement). The *amygdala* (choice A) is known for storing emotional experiences in your memory (e.g., fear, disgust, and unpleasantness). The *hippocampus* (choice B; remember, everyone has two, just like the amygdala, hippocampi, thalami, and hypothalami) regulates emotions and forms (not stores) long-term memories. The *thalamus* (choice C) is the router system that flows to and from the forebrain (including all senses). The *hypothalamus* (choice E) is responsible for your motivation and primitive urges. (*Chapter 5*)

25. **C.** *Memory loss,* choice C, is not a typical symptom of bipolar disorder. *Flight of ideas* (choice A) is a symptom mania in bipolar disorder. It is a rapid succession of thoughts. *Major depression* (choice B) and *mania* (choice D) are both symptoms of bipolar disorder. *Flat affect* (choice E) is a symptom of many disorders, including when a person is experiencing a depressive episode of bipolar disorder. (*Chapter 11*)

26. **A.** *Ivan Pavlov,* choice A, is known for his theory of classical conditioning (also known as reflexive conditioning). Pavlov trained dogs to respond with a salivation reflex at the sound of a chime. *Edward Thorndike* (choice B) is known for his "law of effect" that suggests that the consequences of a previous behavior will influence and even predict future behaviors. *B. F. Skinner* (choice C) is known for expanding Thorndike's theory of behaviorism and suggested that people learn from the consequences of their behavior, called operant conditioning. *Wilhelm Wundt* (choice D) is known as the founder of modern psychology and for establishing psychology as a science. *Hermann von Helmholtz* (choice E) is known for his work in sensation and perception (i.e., trichromatic theory). (*Chapter 7*)

27. **A.** *Association,* choice A, is a mental connection of learning between stimuli and responses. The hug is the unconditioned stimulus, and the mother's desire to do something nice for her daughter is the unconditioned response. *Internalization* (choice B) is when the rules and values of a person become a deep-rooted part of the person. *Fixed action pattern* (choice C) is another name for a reflex. *Neutral stimulus* (choice D) is a sound or sight that has no meaning; it is a concept of Pavlov's classical conditioning theory. *Entrainment* (choice E) is the synchronization of behavior. For example, the process in which a baby learns to sleep and eat according to her parents' schedule. (*Chapter 7*)

28. **E.** *Anxious-avoidant attachment,* choice E, is an attachment style in Mary Ainsworth's theory of attachment; it is not Piagetian. As the name implies, a child with this attachment style is both stressed and avoids contact. *Formal stage* (choice A) is Jean Piaget's formal operations stage of cognitive

development. *Schema* (choice B) is the framework with which a person experiences the world. *Accommodation* (choice C) and *assimilation* (choice D) are both Piagetian concepts. *Accommodation* occurs when the person takes existing schemas and adjusts them to fit the new experience. *Assimilation* is when new information is incorporated into an existing schema. *(Chapter 9)*

29. **B.** *Myelination,* choice B, is the process that describes a neuron's axon covered by a fatty insulation (myelin sheath). Myelination allows for a faster transmission of the electrical charge. *Long-term potentiation* (choice A) is when neurons communicate more efficiently with each other by narrowing the space between them (synapses). *Reuptake* (choice C) is the process by which the presynaptic neuron reabsorbs the neurotransmitter molecules it just released. *Perceptual set* (choice D) is the idea that the brain perceives something based on the environment and our expectations. *Transduction* (choice E) is your brain's sensory process of turning light, pressure on the skin, or sound into a perception. *(Chapter 5)*
30. **A.** The graph shown in choice A is a bar chart. It shows categorical data of males vs. females. Because men and women cannot be quantified into a numeric value, a bar chart (not a histogram) is the correct answer. Choice B is incorrect because the graph depicts a positive correlation between males who prefer classical music and females who prefer classical music. Choice C is incorrect because the graph depicts a negative correlation between males who prefer classical music and females who prefer classical music. Choice D is a histogram (note that the columns are touching). Choice E is incorrect because it is a scatterplot that shows no relationship. *(Chapter 4)*
31. **C.** *Crystallized intelligence,* choice C, is accumulated knowledge throughout a lifetime. The *Flynn effect* (choice A) is a phenomenon that shows how each generation of Americans has performed increasingly better on intelligence tests than the generation before. *Fluid intelligence* (choice B) is biologically based intelligence (e.g., ability to reason and problem solve). *Mental age* (choice D) was developed by Alfred Binet, but has since been outdated. It defines the measure of a person's psychological abilities in comparison to the number of years it takes an average person to reach the same level. *Deviation IQ* (choice E) refers to comparing a person's score on an intelligence test to those of other people of the same age. *(Chapter 8)*
32. **D.** *Self-efficacy,* choice D, is a person's belief in his or her competence. *Locus of control* (choice A) is the degree to which a person believes that he or she has control over the results of a situation. *Introversion* (choice B) is a personality trait associated with being shy or having a preference for being alone. *Archetypes* (choice C) is a concept developed by Carl Jung. Archetypes are universal ideas, patterns, themes, and symbols that many people and cultures around the world intuitively share. *Self-actualization* (choice E) is the highest level of Abraham Maslow's hierarchy of needs. *(Chapter 10)*
33. **A.** Lesioning through an electrical current destroys brain cells. The *hippocampus,* choice A, is responsible for memory in the brain; therefore, lesioning that part of the brain causes memory problems. The *cerebellum* (choice B; called the little brain) is responsible for many functions (balance, muscle coordination, motor movements, etc.), but it is not directly involved in storing explicit memories. The *frontal lobe* (choice C) is responsible for many higher-order mental processes including memory formation, but it is not as directly associated with memory formation as the hippocampus. The *occipital lobe* (choice D) is primarily responsible for receiving and interpreting visual stimuli from the eye. The *medulla* (choice E) is the part of the brain that automatically regulates vital life functions (e.g., heartbeat, breathing, and circulation) to keep a person alive. *(Chapter 5)*
34. **C.** *Validity,* choice C, means that the test measures what it was intended to measure. It is the most important part of developing and administering a psychological test. *Reliability* (choice A) is the idea that a test will consistently yield the same results. For example, if a bathroom scale is broken and shows a different weight each time you step on it, the scale is not reliable; therefore, the results are not

valid. *Fluid intelligence* (choice B) is the innate ability to process information quickly. *Psychometrics* (choice D) is a general term to identify measuring mental abilities. *Factor analysis* (choice E) is a statistical technique that expresses significant statistical relationships between a different number of possible variables to find which have the strongest relationship. *(Chapter 8)*

35. **B.** The transduction of light waves takes place in the *fovea,* choice B, which is at the center of the retina and contains millions of cone cells. The *blind spot* (choice A) is in the back of the eye and is where the optic nerve enters the eye. At that point, there are no rods and cones. The *lens* (choice C) is in the front of the eye. It bends light, but does not convert it into a neural signal. The *pupil* (choice D) is the hole in the front of the eye that lets in light. The *cornea* (choice E) is the clear outer covering in the front of the eye. *(Chapter 6)*

36. **B.** The *Schachter-Singer two-factor theory,* choice B, suggests that raw physical arousal (e.g., increased heart rate) is not enough to control emotion. Emotional states have two components: physical arousal and cognitive interpretation. The *Yerkes-Dodson theory* (choice A) suggests that people cannot think very well when they are highly emotional. The *Cannon-Bard theory* (choice C) suggests that physical reactions (e.g., flinching) and emotions (e.g., fear) occur simultaneously. The *James-Lange theory* (choice D) suggests that physical reactions (e.g., flinching) cause emotions (e.g., fear). The *Zajonc-LeDoux theory* (choice E) is a blend of ideas from two theorists and suggests that emotions are automatic and without a cognitive component. *(Chapter 10)*

37. **E.** The *collective unconscious* refers to the universal idea that humankind shares unconsciously inherited patterns of memories, instincts, and experiences, choice E. Although choices A, B, and D may be true statements, these choices are limited to "certain cultures" and "experiences," and the collective unconscious is a broader, universal term for all humanity. Remember, you are looking for the "best" answer among the choices. While Jung suggested that many people share the same unconscious raw material in dreams (choice C), this is not the best description of the collective unconscious among the choices listed. *(Chapter 10)*

38. **D.** *Null hypothesis* is a prediction that there is no *significant* observed change in the dependent variable, choice D. The null hypothesis is a prediction; the *correlational coefficient* (choice A) is a statement of the relationship between variables. For example, a correlational coefficient of zero states that there is no relationship between eye color and favorite ice cream. Choice B is incorrect because the null hypothesis does not predict a relationship between the *mean and median*. Choice C is incorrect because a *Type II error* is when a person does not notice that something significant *did* happen. A *prediction* that one variable causes another variable to change (choice E) is called an alternate hypothesis. *(Chapter 4)*

39. **C.** The information processing model starts with a temporary memory storage (*sensory memory,* also called sensory register) before it is processed into the working memory (*short-term memory*). Then, if the memory is stored for a prolonged period of time, it is stored in the *long-term memory*. Thus, choice C is correct. Choices A, B, D, and E are incorrect because they do not correspond with the flow of information to the memory. *(Chapter 8)*

40. **E.** The lowest frequency that humans can perceive is *30 Hz,* choice E. Remember the basilar membrane is like a curlicue spectrum of hair cells. At one end, hair cells are stimulated by tiny waves of cochlear fluid that send signals to the brain to interpret signals as a high-pitched sound. When the hair cells at the other end of the basilar membrane are stimulated, the brain interprets them as low-pitched sounds. Since we have a certain range of hair cells on the basilar membrane that can respond to a specific type of wave, humans cannot perceive sound below 30 Hz. Therefore, choices A, B, C, and D are all incorrect. *(Chapter 6)*

41. **B.** Genes for color vision are located on the Y chromosome, choice B. Scientists suggest color blindness is encoded in the Y chromosome for men and that color blindness occurs when one or more of the color cone cells is absent. This contributes to the theory of why only men are color blind. Choices A, C, D, and E are all incorrect. *(Chapter 6)*

42. **A.** An *industrial/organizational psychologist,* choice A, is also known as a human factors psychologist. Psychologists who work in this profession require in-depth knowledge of organizational development, decision-making theories, human performance and attitudes, consumer behavior, and career development. Industrial/organizational psychologists help employees in a workplace work more efficiently, enjoy work, and be more productive. *Behavioral psychologists* (choice B) are similar to industrial/organizational psychologists, but generally focus on changing the behavior of employees, not necessarily changing the work environment. *Clinical psychologists* (choice C) are generally concerned with the assessment and treatment of mental disorders. *Developmental psychologists* (choice D) focus on understanding how people change as they age and help to correct disorders caused by developmental deficits. *Research psychologists* (choice E) is a broad term that implies that the psychologist is working for a university or experimental lab to study phenomena. *(Chapter 4)*

43. **E.** The abbreviation $p$ represents probability (chance, accident, or randomness). If $p < 0.05$ (or 5%), that means that there is less than a 5% chance that the results are by accident and a 95% chance that the results are due to the independent variable. If the researcher finds that the $p$-value is less than 5%, then the researcher can conclude that the results are significant and not due to chance, choice E. Choice A refers to the distribution of scores in a large data set—specifically the scores between one standard deviation above the mean and one standard deviation below the mean. When $p > 90\%$, it means that there is only a 10% certainty that the results are not an accident, choice B. *Positively skewed* results (choice C) mean that most of the scores are grouped together, but a few scores are very high. When all of the measures of central tendency (mean, median, and mode) have the same value (choice D), it means the bell-shaped curve is symmetrical. *(Chapter 4)*

44. **A.** The sound of a dentist's drill is a stimulus and is associated with pain; therefore, it is a *conditioned stimulus,* choice A. The sound of a dentist's drill is not something to fear, so it would not be an *unconditioned stimulus* (choice B). A *neutral stimulus* (choice C) does not elicit a response. Because the dentist's drill elicits a response, choice C is incorrect. The sound of the dentist's drill is a stimulus, not a response; Darrell's reaction is the response. Therefore, choices D and E (responses) are incorrect. The difference between an *unconditioned response* (choice D) and a *conditioned response* (choice E) is the condition that the stimulus causes. For example, Pavlov's dogs drooled at the smell of meat, so the drooling is an unconditioned response. Then, the dogs drooled at the sound of a chime without the accompanying meat. Notice that the drooling was the same—a conditioned response occurred under a different condition. *(Chapter 7)*

45. **D.** People are most sensitive to changes in *pitch,* choice D. Scientists suggest that humans evolved to notice tiny changes in pitch to distinguish tones of voices (e.g., the sound of a baby crying and the ability to pick out a mother's voice are traits that helped the human species survive). Choices A, B, and C are incorrect because while some people might notice changes in *brightness, weight,* or *saltiness* (taste), most people are not sensitive to these changes. The same is true for loudness (choice E). For example, if you are listening to your music really loudly and your parents tell you to turn down the volume, if you only turn down the music a slight amount, your parents probably won't detect the lower volume, and will ask you again to turn it down. *(Chapter 6)*

46. **E.** The five-factor model of personality (known as the big five) is a model used to describe personality traits. While *insightfulness,* choice E, is a valuable character trait, it is NOT a trait listed in the five-factor model. The five traits are openness, conscientiousness, extraversion, agreeableness, and

neuroticism. *Neuroticism* (choice A), like all of the five-factor traits, occurs on a spectrum. Neuroticism is the tendency toward unstable emotions. *Agreeableness* (choice B) is how friendly, cooperative, and good natured a person might be. *Openness* (choice C) is how curious, imaginative, and open with feelings a person might be. *Conscientiousness* (choice D) is how prepared, competent, and goal-driven a person might be. *(Chapter 10)*

47. **D.** *Fixed-interval reinforcement,* choice D, is reinforcing after a specific set time. Mrs. Rice's reward system is NOT time-based. *Differential reinforcement* (choice A) is when something pleasant is given for behavior that is close to the desired behavior. *Successive approximation* (choice B) is similar to differential reinforcement; it is rewarding a behavior that is approximately the same as the targeted behavior. *Shaping* (choice C) is used to guide behavior toward a specific result. Both differential reinforcement and successive approximation are described within the domain of shaping behavior. *Chaining* (choice E) is linking a simple behavior with other simple behaviors so that they are combined to form a complex behavior. *(Chapter 7)*
48. **D.** Choice D shows that the item at the beginning and at the end of the series is recalled nearly 100 percent of the time. Notice that items in the middle of the list have a lower probability of being recalled. Choice A is incorrect because it shows that there is a higher likelihood of remembering items that are in the middle positions. Choice B is incorrect because it shows that there is a good chance of only recalling an item at the beginning of the list, but not at the end of the list. Choice C is incorrect because it shows that there is high likelihood of recalling items at the end of a series, but not at the beginning of a series. Choice E is incorrect because it does not show a relationship between where something is in a series and one's ability to recall the item. *(Chapter 4)*
49. **C.** *William James,* choice C, was influenced by Darwin's theory; James' theory of functionalism suggested that all things evolved for a specific function, including the human mind, and that it is not by random chance. *Max Wertheimer* (choice A; pronounced Verthimer) is known as one of the founders of Gestalt psychology. He studied how the mind perceives the whole, rather than the sum of its parts. *Edward Thorndike* (choice B) is known for the "law of effect," which states that the consequences of any action will influence and predict future actions. *Wilhelm Wundt* (choice D) is known as the father of psychology and founded the first psychology laboratory. *Edward Titchener* (choice E) studied under Wilhelm Wundt and focused on the structures of the mind, called structuralism. *(Chapter 4)*
50. **C.** In experiments with rodents, when *acetylcholine,* choice C, was blocked from certain receptor sites of the rodents, it caused Alzheimer's-like symptoms. *Serotonin* (choice A) is known for its positive effect on mood. *Norepinephrine* (choice B) is both a hormone and a neurotransmitter; it does not directly affect memory, but it is involved with a sympathetic reaction (e.g., fight-or-flight syndrome). *Dopamine* (choice D) is involved in pleasure, reward, and movement. GABA (choice E) is involved in making sure neurons are turned off when they need to be. *(Chapter 5)*
51. **C.** All of the answer choices are Freudian unconscious defense mechanisms. Fred is unconsciously exhibiting *reaction formation*, choice C, replacing an unacceptable emotion with a completely opposite emotion or behavior. *Denial* (choice A) is blocking unpleasant events from awareness. *Displacement* (choice B) is when a person transfers emotions (e.g., frustrations) onto something or someone else (e.g., fear of needles may actually mean fear of death). *Projection* (choice D) is when a person doesn't face their painful thoughts and feelings, blaming others for these feelings in order to avoid confronting them. *Regression* (choice E) is a temporary reversion to an earlier stage of development as a child. *(Chapter 10)*
52. **C.** The word *eclectic* means deriving from a wide range of sources. Although most therapies use techniques from other therapies, only *eclectic therapy,* choice C, is specificallly based on using multiple

therapeutic techniques. *Individual therapy* (choice A) is not based on techniques, but is a form of therapy that consists of one client and one therapist. *Group therapy* (choice B) is not based on techniques, but is a form of therapy that consists of one or more therapists working with several people at the same time. *Family therapy* (choice D) is a form of therapy that helps family members reduce conflict and improve the entire family system. *Behavioral therapy* (choice E) is an approach to therapy that uses behavioral techniques. *(Chapter 11)*

53. **D.** A *double-blind design,* choice D, reduces the possibility of experimenter bias because some aspect of the study is unknown to the researcher and the participants. This means that the researcher may not know who is in the control group and who is in the experimental group (e.g., who is receiving the placebo and who is receiving the real treatment). The *Hawthorne effect* (choice A) is the result of the participant acting differently, knowing that he or she is being observed. In a *single-blind design* (choice B), only the participants don't know all aspects of the study; the researchers do know. A null hypothesis predicts that the independent variable will not influence the dependent variable. Thus, *rejecting the null hypothesis* (choice C) means the results of the experiment were significant. *Demand characteristics* (choice E) are subtle behaviors that a participant might engage in because the participant may anticipate what the experimenter expects in the study. *(Chapter 4)*
54. **E.** Carl Rogers was a humanistic psychologist who developed person-centered therapy, in which the therapist does NOT control what topics a client might discuss in therapy, making choice E correct. Humanistic psychologists believe that each person *views the world differently* (choice A) and that such views are valuable and respected in the therapeutic setting. According to the humanistic perspective, *all people are good and have a desire to improve* (choice B). In person-centered therapy, *the relationship between the client and the therapist relies on empathy, acceptance, and genuineness* (choice C), and the therapist respects the client. Humanistic psychologists believe that *the client should control the topics discussed* in the therapeutic setting (choice D). *(Chapter 11)*
55. **D.** All of the terms listed in the answer choices are part of Jean Piaget's theory of cognitive development. *Object permanence,* choice D, is understanding that an object exists even when the object cannot be seen. Object permanence occurs in the first of Jean Piaget's four stages of development. *Formal operations* (choice A) is the fourth stage of development, in which adolescents and adults are able to think abstractly. *Concrete operations* (choice B) is the third stage of development, in which children begin to think logically. *Accommodation* (choice C) happens when new concepts are introduced into an existing schema (mindset) and are adjusted to fit the experience. *Assimilation* (choice E) is when new information is acquired and incorporated into an existing schema. *(Chapter 9)*
56. **C.** By starting with an extreme opening offer, James is negotiating by using the *door-in-the-face technique,* choice C, a persuasive strategy to change behavior. Eventually James' mom might comply or compromise by extending the curfew a little bit (e.g., 12:30 p.m.). *Cognitive dissonance* (choice A) is not a persuasive strategy. It is an unpleasant feeling that a person gets when his or her thoughts and actions are not congruent. *Foot-in-the-door technique* (choice B) is when someone starts with a small request, such as James asking if he can stay out until 10 p.m., and then gradually asking for small increases. *Out-group homogeneity* (choice D) is the mistaken, stereotypical bias that describes in-group people who are biased against people who are not part of their group. *Just-world hypothesis* (choice E) is the tendency for people to believe that what happens to others in the world is fair and that others are rewarded (or punished) justly. *(Chapter 12)*
57. **B.** *Bi-weekly* means every 2 weeks. *Fixed interval,* choice B, is a schedule of reinforcement that is rewarded after a specific time, such as a bi-weekly paycheck. *Fixed ratio* (choice A) is a schedule of

reinforcement where a reinforcement is given after a certain number of behaviors (e.g., after you buy five items, you will get a free coffee). *Variable ratio* (choice C) is when reinforcement happens after a varying number of responses. *Variable interval* (choice D) is when reinforcement happens after varying lengths of time. *Negative reinforcement* (choice E) is when something unpleasant is removed by doing a correct behavior. *(Chapter 7)*

58. **B.** The *preconscious* level, choice B, holds information that is stored in your memory and can be brought into conscious awareness at any time. Preconscious is information that you are *not* currently thinking about, but can easily recall, such as your phone number. The *conscious* level (choice A) is what you are thinking about right now, like reading this sentence. The *subconscious* level (choice C) handles information below your level of awareness, such as implicit memories. The *unconscious* level (choice D) has deep human drives, such as feelings and emotions. The *nonconscious* level (choice E) is what is necessary for human survival. For example, your body organs that function automatically without your conscious awareness (e.g., respiration). *(Chapter 5)*

59. **B.** All of the choices are Freudian stages of psychosexual development. The *phallic stage,* choice B, is when sexual identity occurs. This is when children try to figure out what being male or female means (ages 3–7 years old). The *oral stage* (choice A) is when a baby is concerned with learning about the world through gaining pleasure from eating (ages birth to 18 months). In the *latent stage* (choice C), children learn to develop social interactions (ages 5–7 years old). The *genital stage* (choice D) starts at puberty and is the stage when adolescents and young adults become interested in intimate relationships. The *anal stage* of development (choice E) is when toilet training occurs (18 months to 4 years old). *(Chapter 9)*

60. **E.** A *positive reinforcer,* choice E, is a reward that will increase the likelihood of the response. Cocaine activates the dopamine circuits and dopamine is a neurotransmitter related to pleasures and rewards. A *neutral stimulus* (choice A) is a sound, sight, smell, touch, or taste that has no emotional or cognitive value. With a *negative reinforcer* (choice B) an unpleasant stimulus is removed once the desired outcome is achieved. A *conditioned stimulus* (choice C) is any sight, sound, smell, taste, or touch that triggers a response from a previous neutral response. A *variable interval* (choice D) is a random time that a reinforcement or punishment occurs. *(Chapter 7)*

61. **B.** *Social facilitation,* choice B, is the phenomenon that describes when people perform better with well-practiced tasks when they know they are being watched. *Social loafing* (choice A) is the phenomenon in which people do not work as hard on a team task when others will do their work. *Bystander effect* (choice C) is the phenomenon that people are less likely to help a victim when others are present. *Diffusion of responsibility* (choice D) is similar to bystander effect. People are less likely to take action to help in the presence of a large group. *Deindividuation* (choice E) relates to a person losing self-awareness in a large crowd. *(Chapter 12)*

62. **D.** *Maintenance rehearsal,* choice D, is a method of memorization in which a person attempts to keep the information in his or her long-term memory by repeating the information over and over. *Working memory* (choice A; also called short-term memory) has a limited capacity and is concerned with immediate conscious information (not memorizing or encoding). *Elaborative rehearsal* (choice B) is a method of attaching meaning or associations to a concept so that it can be stored and later retrieved in the long-term memory. *Effortful processing* (choice C) is a method of encoding and is similar to elaborative rehearsal; it requires attention and effort to encode the information. *Peripheral route processing* (choice E) is a persuasion technique in which the person uses emotion, rather than facts from an argument, to change someone's mind. *(Chapter 8)*

63. **C.** Normal distribution is symmetrical. It has the same number of above-average scores as it does below-average scores. Therefore, a normal distribution would NOT have a *mean that is noticeably*

*different from the other measures of central tendency* (median and mode), choice C. The other answer choices are all true statements and are, therefore, incorrect. Choice A is incorrect because *the mean, median, and mode ARE the same* in a normal distribution. Choice B is incorrect because in a normal distribution, *the approximate number of scores above and below the mean are the same*. Choice D is incorrect because in a normal distribution, there are *a small number of scores that are far away from the mean* and many scores near the mean. Choice E is incorrect because *a normal curve is not skewed by extreme scores*. *(Chapters 4 and 8)*

64. **A.** *MAO inhibitors,* choice A, are antidepressant medications that prevent an enzyme, called monoamine oxidase, from breaking down neurotransmitters like serotonin and dopamine. *Dichotomous thinking* (choice B) is not a treatment; it is considered "black and white thinking." It is a symptom of many mental disorder diagnoses. *Insight therapy* (choice C) is a broad category of therapy that helps clients express feelings, reflect, talk, and come to an awareness about how past experiences can negatively influence current thoughts and emotions. *Counterconditioning* (choice D) is a type of therapy that attempts to replace unpleasant emotional responses with more pleasant responses. *Flooding* (choice E) is a therapeutic technique that is a form of desensitization to reduce anxieties and phobias. The client is exposed to fearful objects and learns to confront fears. *(Chapter 11)*
65. **C.** *Negative reinforcement,* choice C, helps to change behavior when a response is strengthened by removing a negative outcome (or aversive stimulus). *Negative punishment* (choice A) is the removal of something pleasurable. *Positive punishment* (choice B) is the addition of unpleasant consequences. *Positive reinforcement* (choice D) is the addition of something pleasurable. *Variable interval* (choice E) means that punishments or rewards are given at random times that are unrelated to a behavior. *(Chapter 7)*
66. **D.** *Mania,* choice D, is a heightened state of mental (and physical) arousal; it is not a symptom of a major depressive disorder (MDD). Symptoms of mania can include inflated self-esteem, elevated mood, racing thoughts, and decreased need for sleep. All of the other answer choices are symptoms of a major depressive disorder and are, therefore, incorrect. *Appetite changes* (choice A), either increased or decreased appetite, is a common symptom of MDD. *Loss of interest* (choice B) is when a person has lost interest in previously rewarding or enjoyable activities. *Reduced social interactions* (choice C), such as not wanting to contact friends and family, is another common symptom of MDD. *Fatigue* (choice E) is also a common symptom of major depressive disorder. *(Chapter 11)*
67. **E.** *Overgeneralization,* choice E, is when children (ages 4–5 years old) misapply grammar rules, which is what Kayla is doing in this scenario. *Babbling* (choice A) is sounds a baby (ages 3–12 months old) makes as it practices the necessary mouth movements to make consonant-vowel sounds. *Holophrases* (choice B) are the first words spoken (ages 8–24 months). For example, familiar nouns like objects or persons that express a complete and meaningful thought such as "juice" or "mama." *Telegraphic speech* (choice C) is an early form of speech and can be observed when a toddler (ages 18–24 months) selectively omits or simplifies words in a phrase to communicate his or her message. For example, "juice spill." *Fast mapping* (choice D) is a mental process that describes when young children (ages 2–5 years old) are able to use the "context" of a word or phrase and accurately arrive at the word's meaning. *(Chapter 8)*.
68. **D.** *MDMA* or ecstasy, choice D, is not a depressant; it is stimulant. All of the other answer choices are depressants: *alcohol* (choice A), *benzodiazepines* (choice B), *barbiturates* (choice C), and *Xanax* (choice E). *(Chapter 5)*
69. **B.** *Pruning,* choice B, is the trimming of unneeded neurons and synapses. *Maturationism* (choice A) is a biological process that occurs automatically in predictable, sequential stages over time. For example, a baby will eventually learn to walk because it is a biological imperative. *Adaptation* (choice C) is a biological process in which humans adapt to the environment through assimilating and

accommodating new information into an existing schema. *Accommodation* (choice D) occurs when a person takes existing schemas and adjusts them to fit the new experience. *Myelination* (choice E) is the process of glial cells creating myelin to insulate the axon. *(Chapter 9)*

70. **A.** The important word in this question is *causes*. An *experimental* research design method, choice A, is the only way to prove causation because it allows for experimental control. In experimental research, all variables are removed that might cause a result other than the one variable that the researcher is interested in studying (independent variable). *Naturalistic observation* (choice B) describes when a researcher observes humans in their real-world environment; simply watching someone do something will not result in a cause. In a *longitudinal study* (choice C), the participants are studied over a long period of time. A longitudinal study might result in a cause if it is an experimental research design, but since a longitudinal study can be any type of research design, it is not the best answer among the choices. A *cross-sectional study* (choice D) is when the researcher compares different groups at a specific point in time. Just like a longitudinal study, a cross-sectional study could be any type of research method; therefore, it is not the best answer. A *case study* (choice E) is a detailed investigation of a participant; because it does not have experimental control, determining cause is not possible. *(Chapter 4)*

71. **A.** *SSRIs,* choice A, is an abbreviation for *selective serotonin reuptake inhibitors*. The important word is *reuptake*. Reuptake occurs when a cell reabsorbs the neurotransmitters it released, and it occurs on the presynaptic cell. The postsynaptic cell receives the neurotransmitters on the receptor sites of its dendrites. *ECT* (choice B) is an abbreviation for *electroconvulsive therapy;* it is not a pharmacological treatment. *Anti-anxiety medications* (choice C) are usually agonists that imitate the neurotransmitter GABA and thus stimulate neurons that are involved in relaxation. *Anti-psychotic medications* (choice D) are often antagonists for dopamine and work on postsynaptic cells. *L-Dopa* (choice E) is a medication that imitates dopamine, fits into dopamine receptor sites, and stimulates neurons involved in movement (e.g., Parkinson's disease). Hence, L-Dopa is a medication that works on postsynaptic cells, not presynaptic cells. *(Chapter 11)*

72. **D.** *Biofeedback,* choice D, is a technique that uses electronic sensors attached to the body to measure body functions, such as muscle relaxation and pulse. *Transcranial magnetic stimulation* (choice A) is a technique used by medical doctors to direct magnetic waves to certain parts of the brain to reduce the symptoms of depression. *Token economy* (choice B) is not an electronic monitor. It is a positive reinforcement technique to help a person (usually a child) learn a task for good behavior. For example, tickets or points can later be exchanged for an actual reward. *Tricyclics* (choice C) are antidepressants. *Cognitive behavior therapy* (choice E) is not a technique; it is an approach to therapy to help people change patterns of thinking and behavior. Note: On the AP PSYCH exam, it is important to know the difference between an *approach* to therapy (e.g., behavioral therapy, humanistic therapy, psychoanalytic therapy, etc.) and a *technique* that is used as a strategy with a specific outcome in mind (e.g., biofeedback, systematic desensitization, etc.). *(Chapter 11)*

73. **D.** *Out-group homogeneity,* choice D, is a person's tendency to believe that members of another group are "all alike" *In-group bias* (choice A) is the tendency for people to see members of their own group more favorably (e.g., family, friends, and others). *Groupthink* (choice B) is both a process and a state of mind. It is when the consensus of the group holds more importance than critical reasoning. *Prisoner's dilemma* (choice C) is based on simultaneous decision making by two people. It exemplifies the nature of trust between two people and possible outcomes that might arise from trust or betrayal. *Social trap* (choice E) is a short-term solution to a problem that leads to a long-term loss. For example, when competitors focus on short-term winning and forget to look at the overall effects of competition. *(Chapter 12)*

74. **C.** *Fundamental attribution error,* choice C, is the tendency for a person to negatively judge another person based on the person's internal personality, rather than considering the external circumstances. *Social loafing* (choice A) is when a person does not put forth as much effort on a team project due to the belief that others will complete the project. *Deindividuation* (choice B) refers to the diminished sense of one's individuality that occurs in a group because the person may feel protected by anonymity. *Compliance* (choice D) refers to changing one's behavior, or submitting, due to another person's request. *Bystander effect* (choice E) is a phenomenon that occurs when the presence of others discourages people from intervening to help those in distress. Bystanders believe that someone else will intervene when others are present.*(Chapter 12)*

75. **A.** The *Cannon-Bard theory* of emotions suggests that the physical response (e.g., laughing) happens at the same time as the emotional feeling (e.g., humor), choice A. Choice B is incorrect because it refers to the *James-Lange Theory*. Choice C is incorrect because it refers to the *Schachter-Singer theory* of emotion. Choice D is incorrect because the Cannon-Bard theory does not suggest that one's emotional interpretation dictates which physical response occurs. Choice E is incorrect because the Cannon-Bard theory does not suggest that emotional interpretations cannot prevent the physical reaction. *(Chapter 10)*

76. **B.** Wernicke's area is on the surface of the left hemisphere's temporal lobe. Damage to Wernicke's area would result in *difficulty recalling spoken language,* choice B, known as Wernicke's aphasia. *Difficulty forming spoken words* (choice A) is related to damage in Broca's area on the left side of the frontal lobe. Wernicke's aphasia is not directly related to *grammar rules* (choice C), *reading simple graphs and charts* (choice D), or *recognizing sight words* (choice E). *(Chapter 5)*

77. **D.** *Naturalistic observation,* choice D, refers to a research study that occurs in a real-world setting without the participant knowing. Demand characteristic is when a participant acts in accordance with how he or she believes the experimenter expects. Therefore, choice D is the correct answer because the participant does not know that he or she is being observed. *Survey* research (choice A) expects that the participant will answer questionnaires truthfully, but participants might be subject to demand characteristics or biases. The participant comes face-to-face with the researcher in an *interview* (choice B); therefore, the participant might answer or act in a way that he or she thinks that the researcher desires. People who participate in a *laboratory experiment* (choice C) know they are the participants in an experiment; therefore, there is a chance that the participants will not act naturally and may act according to demand characteristics. If a study requires *informed consent* (choice E), then the participant knows about the study and may change his or her behavior to match the demand characteristics. *(Chapter 4)*

78. **D.** In Harlow's experiments, he separated baby monkeys from their mothers and discovered that the babies spent more time with the a soft surrogate mother doll to cuddle with no food, rather than the cold surrogate mother doll with food. Because the monkeys preferred the soft surrogate mother doll, they demonstrated the importance of the need to cuddle, touch, and love exhibited in early mother-child bonding, choice D. Harry Harlow did not prove that love was a chemical reaction (choice A). While love is most likely rooted in the limbic system (choice B), Harlow did not discuss the limbic system in his research. Harlow did not operationalize love as cuddling, but his experiments confirmed the importance of John Bowlby's theory of attachment (mother-child bonding) when Harlow discovered that maternal deprivation seriously affected the baby monkeys' mental health; therefore, choice C is incorrect. Harlow discovered that food and water were not enough for mental health survival. The baby monkeys needed some type of physical, emotional, or social reassurance (i.e., love) even if it was with a stuffed animal, making choice E incorrect. *(Chapter 9)*

79. **E.** While schizophrenia has a variety of symptoms, *extreme concern with physical appearance,* choice E, is generally NOT a symptom of schizophrenia. *Disorganized thinking* (choice A) is perhaps the most

common symptom of schizophrenia. *Distorted perceptions* (choice B), such as hearing voices, are a common symptom of schizophrenia. *Psychosis* (choice C) is when a person has a mental break from reality and may see, hear, or believe things that aren't real. *Word salad* (choice D) is disorganized speech that presents as incoherent jumbled words that have no apparent connection to one another. *(Chapter 11)*

80. **D.** *Depolarization,* choice D, means not being separated. It refers to the sodium and potassium ions crossing the membrane of the axon and mixing. The mixing of charged ions creates an electrical charge called "neuron firing." *Plasticity* (choice A) is when the brain changes itself to adapt to circumstances. Long-term potentiation at a cellular level enhances the possibility of plasticity. *Polarization* (choice B) is the process of a neuron separating from charged ions that, when together, create an action potential. *Long-term potentiation* (choice C) is the process in which neurons reach out to one another to communicate. This causes the synapse to become smaller and produce an increased signal transmission between neurons, strengthening the neurons. *Reuptake* (choice E) is the process in which the presynaptic neuron reabsorbs the neurotransmitter molecules that were just released. *(Chapter 5)*

81. **A.** The *Diagnostic and Statistical Manual of Mental Disorders* (DSM-5) is based on a medical model of disease symptoms, choice A. The advantage of a medical model is that by understanding the symptoms, it makes it easier to diagnose mental disorders. However, the disadvantages of the medical model are that the complexities of human behavior have a tendency to become oversimplified, and diagnostic labels can be stigmatizing. The DSM-5 is considered a living document and is expected to change periodically as newly developed psychological research becomes known. The DSM-5 does not provide treatment plans (choice B). The DSM-5 was written for licensed clinicians, not nonprofessionals (choice C). The DSM-5 is the product of decades of accumulated psychological research, but is used in all domains of psychology, not just research psychology (choice D). Much like a physician might not consider "why" a person contracted the flu, the DSM-5 does not focus on the causes of mental disorders (choice E); it focuses on symptoms. *(Chapter 11)*

82. **B.** Think of a token that is used for a video game. The token itself is not valuable, but it is valuable when it can be traded for something (e.g., a banana). *Token economy,* choice B, is a behavior modification motivation technique that is used to reinforce positive behavior. *Variable interval* (choice A) refers to randomly receiving a reward (or punishment) after a random number of behaviors. Edward Thorndike's *law of effect* (choice C) suggests that the consequences of a preceding action will influence future actions. *Counterconditioning* (choice D) is a therapeutic technique that reconditions a person's or animal's current reaction to a stimulus. *Aversive conditioning* (choice E) is a type of avoidance learning in which an unpleasant stimulus is paired with a pleasant stimulus. *(Chapter 7)*

83. **D.** *Polygenic,* choice D, refers to DNA traits that are influenced by multiple genes (e.g., eye color). *Phenotypes* (choice A) are the physically observable characteristics of a person's genotype. *Epigenetics* (choice B) is the scientific study of how the environment and life experiences can change genes. *Genotype* (choice C) is a person's genetic makeup that is passed down from his or her parents. *Teratogens* (choice E) are chemicals (e.g., alcohol, caffeine, nicotine) that, when ingested during pregnancy, can cause birth defects in the unborn baby. *(Chapter 5)*

84. **B.** Hermann Ebbinghaus (1885) was interested in the rate in which information is forgotten after it is initially learned. Ebbinghaus developed a mathematical formula in his famous experiment, the Ebbinghaus forgetting curve, which demonstrated that the stronger the memory, the longer the period of time a person is able to recall the memory. In general, people forget 80 percent of newly learned material within 1 day, choice B. Therefore, choices A, C, D, and E are incorrect. *(Chapter 8)*

85. **E.** The *Flynn effect,* choice E, is a phenomenon that implies that each generation shows a rise in the average fluid and crystallized intelligence. People taking IQ tests attain slightly higher IQ scores than the previous generation. *Criterion validity* (choice A) shows how well one measure predicts the outcome of another measure. *Crystallized intelligence* (choice B) is lifelong accumulation of facts, strategies, and knowledge. *Fluid intelligence* (choice C) is general intelligence, the ability to reason and solve problems. *Stereotype threat* (choice D) is a situational predicament that explains when people who are exposed to a negative stereotype are at risk of conforming to the stereotype of their social group. *(Chapter 8)*

86. **A.** *Generalization,* choice A, refers to a person who groups similar stimuli in the same category and reacts the same to similar circumstances, such as the sound of buzzing. *Spontaneous recovery* (choice B) refers to the reappearance of learned behavior or associations that are believed to be extinguished. *Aversive conditioning* (choice C) is when an unpleasant stimulus is paired with a harmful but pleasant stimulus. *Escape conditioning* (choice D) is a form of aversive conditioning; the person learns to leave in order to stop experiencing the unpleasant stimulus. *Discrimination* (choice E) is the ability to perceive and discern the differences between stimuli. *(Chapter 7)*

87. **D.** *Humanistic therapy,* choice D, is a client-centered approach to therapy. The client decides the what, when, and how that will be discussed in the therapeutic setting. *Behavioral therapy* (choice A) focuses on attending to disagreeable behaviors or associations, not necessarily the causes of behavior. *Pharmacological therapy* (choice B) is drug therapy. *Psychoanalytic therapy* (choice C) focuses on the unconscious forces that interfere with daily functioning. *Electroconvulsive therapy* (choice E) is a surgical procedure that uses small electrical impulses that pass through the brain to change brain chemistry and reverse the symptoms of mental disorders, such as major depressive disorder. *(Chapter 11)*

88. **C.** *Dispositional attribution,* choice C, is the assumption that a person's attributing behavior is linked to a relatively permanent characteristic (e.g., personality, attitude, or beliefs). *Situational attribution* (choice A) is the assumption that a person's behavior is influenced by a temporary external environmental influence (e.g., a student who will not settle down because it is the day before spring break). *Ethnocentrism* (choice B) is seeing the world through one's own "cultural lens," and the belief that one's own culture is superior to all others. *Cognitive dissonance* (choice D) is the unpleasant mental state of having conflicting beliefs, ideas, or thoughts. *Spotlight effect* (choice E) is the tendency to think that other people are watching, even though others are not noticing. *(Chapter 12)*

89. **E.** Like all neurotransmitters, *serotonin,* choice E, has many functions, but it is known for providing a sense of well-being and promoting sleep. *Dopamine* (choice A) is associated with the brain's rewards and pleasure system. It facilitates communications between nerve cells in the nervous system. While dopamine provides a sense of well-being, it is not the best answer among the choices listed. *Noradrenaline* (choice B) is the neurological equivalent of the hormone adrenaline, which is known for increased heart rate and respiration. *Endorphins* (choice C) decrease the feeling of pain and generally make the body feel better. *Histamines* (choice D) are hormones that help a body repel an attack from invading chemicals, like allergens. *(Chapter 5)*

90. **E.** *Intrinsic rewards,* choice E, are nonphysical, higher levels of motivation (e.g., a sense of achievement, pride, altruism, and contentment). Intrinsic rewards are necessary for self-actualization, described in Maslow's hierarchy of basic human needs. *Extrinsic rewards* (choice A) are physical rewards that come from an external source (e.g., paycheck, good grades, or prizes). *Secondary reinforcers* (choice B) are conditioned reinforcers that are associated with primary reinforcers. *Continuous reinforcement* (choice C) means a reward or punishment is given every time a behavior occurs. *Instincts* (choice D) are the inborn patterns of human behavior, not part of Maslow's hierarchy. *(Chapter 10)*

91. **E.** *Elaborative rehearsal,* choice E, refers to the memory encoding process of attaching meaning to the information (e.g., emotions or associated ideas) that you are trying to learn or encode. *Schema* (choice A) is a pattern of thoughts or behavior that organizes information in the brain; it helps with memory consolidation. *Sensory memory* (choice B) is the brief, short-term memory described in the Atkinson-Shiffrin information processing model that allows a person to retain sensory information. It contains iconic and echoic memories. *Primacy effect* (choice C) is the tendency to remember more items at the beginning of a list better than items in the middle or end of the list. *Recency effect* (choice D) is the tendency to remember things at the end of a series rather than at the beginning or middle of the series. *(Chapter 8)*

92. **B.** *Debriefing,* choice B, is a critical part of an experiment. It is when the experimenter provides a full explanation of the research study, details about the study, and most importantly, encourages participants to ask questions so they are not mentally impacted by the research study. *Contacting the Institutional Review Board* (choice A) must be completed before any research study can begin. *Consent paperwork* (choice C) should be completed after the participants are provided information about the study and given an informed consent form to make an educated decision about participating in the study. A *double-blind design* (choice D) is a method of conducting research in which certain aspects of the study are not known to the researcher or participants to prevent bias. *Keep the results confidential* (choice E) is a necessary and important part of a research study; however, this answer is not the best choice because it does not address the problem of withholding information from the participants. *(Chapter 4)*

93. **D.** *Alzheimer's disease,* choice D, is the slow deterioration of brain tissue. As the neural tissue becomes damaged, so does the cognitive functioning. *Bipolar disorder* (choice A) is a mood disorder and is not a cognitive decline. *Dysthymia* (choice B) is a type of depression in which the symptoms are less intense than a major depressive episode, but can last longer. *Anterograde amnesia* (choice C) is usually the result of trauma or a disease and is not considered a neurocognitive disorder. Both Alzheimer's and anterograde amnesia have symptoms of forgetfulness, but Alzheimer's is a gradual progression that more closely resembles retrograde amnesia. *Anorexia nervosa* (choice E) is a potentially life-threatening eating disorder that is a pattern of self-starvation because of the intense fear of being overweight. *(Chapter 11)*

94. **A.** *Latent* means hidden. *Latent learning,* choice A, is the unconscious retention of information. The information becomes clear when the person has a motivation to show it. *Association* (choice B) refers to a classical conditioning strategy in which two stimuli, an unlearned unconditioned stimulus and a conditioned stimulus (one that is learned), are linked together so the person (or animal) will respond to the learned stimulus in the same way as he or she responds to the unlearned stimulus. *Discrimination* (choice C) refers to the ability to recognize the differences between stimuli. *Acquisition* (choice D) refers to acquiring or learning a new association between stimuli. *Extinction* (choice E) refers to the gradual disappearing of a conditioned response. *(Chapter 7)*

95. **A.** *Type II errors,* choice A, occur when the researcher doesn't notice that the study could disprove the null hypothesis. *Type I errors* (choice B) are known as "false alarms" and occur when the researcher thinks the results are significant and that null hypothesis can be rejected. However, the results are not significant. *Hindsight bias* (choice C) is known as the "I knew it all along" phenomenon. This means that people have a tendency to perceive the results as being more predictable than before the study took place. *Confirmation bias* (choice D) refers to the tendency to interpret new evidence as support for one's existing theory. The *fundamental attribution error* (choice E) is the tendency to blame a person's permanent characteristics for his or her behavior. *(Chapter 4)*

96. **B.** The correct order in neurotransmission is shown in choice B: Neurotransmitters send signals to *dendrites,* then the *soma* (cell body) decides if there are enough (or the correct type of) neurotransmitters. Then the soma communicates to the *axon* to let in the sodium ions. Sodium ions intermingle with potassium ions to create an action potential. The electric action potential transmits down the axon and stops at the *axon terminal,* choice B. Choices, A, C, D, and E are incorrect. *(Chapter 5)*

97. **D.** The *nucleus accumbens,* choice D, is a region in the brain's pleasure center that is linked to addiction and depression. The *pons* (choice A) is in a region of the lower brain and is known for helping the medulla regulate life functions and sleep. The *optic chiasm* (choice B) is where the two optic nerves cross. The images that are on the left side of both retinas travel to the right hemisphere, and images that are on the right side of both retinas travel to the left hemisphere. The *thalamus* (choice C) is the router of the brain. It receives incoming, afferent signals from the senses and directs them to the correct region of the brain. The *superchiasmatic nucleus* (choice E) sits above the optic chiasm and is known as the sleep switch. *(Chapter 5)*

98. **B.** *Retinal disparity,* choice B, refers to the difference between the retinas, which is responsible for perceiving binocular depth cues. The brain receives different images from each retina. For example, close one eye and then the other eye. You will notice that there is a greater disparity the closer an object is to your eyes. *Motion parallax* (choice A) is a depth cue; when objects are far away, like an airplane, they appear to be moving slowly. *Linear perspective* (choice C) refers to objects appearing farther away as they converge at a distance to give the illusion of depth. *Interposition* (choice D) is a visual depth cue whereby objects appear closer because they are in front of other objects. *Relative size* (choice E) is a perceptual cue; when objects are smaller, they appear farther away. *(Chapter 7)*

99. **A.** The farther away a correlational coefficient is from zero in any direction, the stronger the relationship. Of the choices given, −0.8, choice A, represents the strongest relationship because it is the farthest away from zero. Choices B, C, D, and E are incorrect because they are not as far from zero as −0.8. *(Chapter 4)*

100. **B.** *Ghrelin,* choice B, is a hormone that increases the motivation to eat and sends signals to the brain: "I am hungry." *Leptin* (choice A) is a hormone that is related to lack of hunger. *Androgens* (choice C) are a group of hormones that play a role in male traits and reproductive activity. *Cortisol* (choice D) is a stress hormone that is activated during stressful situations and helps a person manage short-term stress, but it can be harmful if it is present for long periods of time. *Norepinephrine* (choice E) is both a hormone and a neurotransmitter and is involved in the activation of the sympathetic nervous system which "turns off" hunger. *(Chapter 10)*

## Section II: Free-Response Questions

### Question 1

To achieve the maximum score of 7, your response must address each of the bullet points in the question.

#### Sample Student Response

*Collectivism* is a social psychology explanation that relates to the priorities of a group; individual needs become secondary. Mr. Reed explains that the team has a collectivist culture viewpoint and that students recognize that scholarships and personal success will only occur if the team is successful as a whole. *Social facilitation* occurs when the performance on a well-practiced skill improves in the presence